BOOK 1 • SERVANT OF THE VINEYARD TRILOGY

# The TRUE GRAFT

## That it May Bring Forth Good Fruit

## A Witness of the Restoration

### What Joseph Smith Learned and Taught

MICHAEL CLARIDGE

Publishing works that prepare the vineyard for the Lord's return.

**The True Graft**


Published by **Graft of Zion Publishing**
*"Publishing works that prepare the vineyard for the Lord's return."*

ISBN: 979-8-9933078-0-0

Book One of the *Servant of the Vineyard Trilogy*

The True Graft: *That it May Bring Forth Good Fruit—A Witness of the Restoration: What Joseph Smith Learned and Taught*

Cover and title page design: Graft of Zion Publishing Design
Printed in the United States of America

First Edition

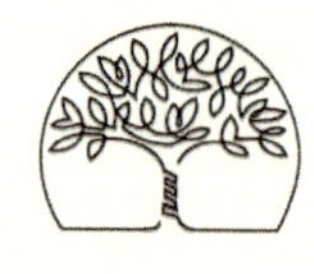

10 9 8 7 6 5 4 3 2 1

# Dedication

To all who have walked beside me on this path of restoration—
to ***Daddy's Girls,*** who believed with me when the world could not:
***Sharon, Michelle, and Joanna,*** still carrying the flame;
and ***Robin*** and ***Carol,*** who now carry it from the other side.

To ***Mike,*** who opened my eyes to the vast possibilities of eternity—whose vision of divine potential and eternal offering has blessed my life beyond measure. His example has been priceless, and I shall always love and cherish him for it.

To ***Kristen,*** who helped steady the ark even against the storms.

To my ***FHE family***—those who have gone on: ***Peggy, Theresa, Tom, and Dan***; and those who remain: ***Catherine, Billy, and Cathy***—thank you for your faith, your laughter, and your prayers.

To my many ***friends in the Church,*** too numerous to name, whose steady faith and quiet examples of love have blessed my journey.

To ***Conrad*** and ***Dolores,*** to measure how much you have positively impacted me is almost impossible. I love you and am eternally grateful to you for being part of this journey.

***To Todd and Carolyn, and to Linda and Jim***—your friendship has been a steady light through many seasons. My prayer is that you may come to feel what I have felt, to know what I know, and to love what I love.

To my ***parents,*** whose faith and foundation gave me the will to be true, no matter the cost.
To my dear sister, who has stood with me through thick and thin.
To my ***sons and daughters-in-law***, each courageously finding their own path.
To the son who walked through the refiner's fire and emerged with faith intact—
I honor you and the man you have become. You have my eternal devotion.
And to my grandchildren, may you grow up knowing
that your grandfather sought truth without fear,
and that the Lord met him there.

This book is for you all.
Every page, every wrestle, every flame of revelation—
was written with your names upon my heart.

# Table of Contents

# Preface

## Why This Book Exists

On July 4th, 2023, I was in a devastating car accident that took my mother's life. My body was broken, but my spirit was not. I died—at least briefly. While my body lay in that demolished vehicle, I found myself in conversation with Deity. I don't remember what I saw, but I remember what I felt—and most of all, I know I was taught by the Master.

It may sound strange to say, but lying lifeless in the rubble of that accident was a sacred moment. I spoke with the Lord. He gave me a commission: to open my eyes and see the truth, and to have the courage to bear solemn witness of that truth.

That commission has become a trilogy—The Servant of the Vineyard—three volumes, each with its own witness and purpose.

Book One, The True Graft, is about the Lord working anew in His olive tree vineyard to restore it, and about the servant He chose to lead that restoration—Joseph Smith. It is about how the Lord mentored and tutored him, how He grafted a new branch into His ancient tree, and how Joseph was tasked to nurture and care for it so that it might bring forth good fruit.

This book has one clear and singular purpose: to share the truths that Joseph Smith learned directly from the Lord through revelation, and to carefully explore and examine the doctrines he taught based on those sacred revelations.

Joseph Smith didn't have a manual. He didn't have a tutor. He had no formal education. He was raw, unpolished—and that was exactly what the Lord wanted: a young man willing to obey. And so, the Lord taught him directly, revealing amazing things about Himself, His gospel, and eternity. Joseph learned how to walk with God, how to grow in light, and that joy follows obedience to His voice.

The truths he received were not for him alone. He turned and taught the people the very things the Lord had taught him. And it is for this very reason that this book exists—to share those same truths Joseph Smith learned from the Lord, and to explore how they apply to us today.

And so, there are several reasons why this book exists.

### 1. Because the Lord asked me to.

I am not seeking the spotlight. I don't want a platform or a following. I am not trying to build a cause. I am simply obeying the Lord, because He asked me to. For years He has taught me to search deeply, patiently, and prayerfully until I could understand His mysteries clearly and share them with confidence in His truth.

But when the Lord asks something of you, it rarely comes with a manual. Instead, He prepares you for the work—patiently, persistently. And when He finally said, "*It's time*," I knew I had to move.

That is the first reason I am writing this: not to convince, not to critique, but to respond. Because when the Lord says, "*Write*," you don't argue. You write.

But obedience is not without cost. Writing this trilogy has required me to risk misunderstanding, judgment, even rejection from those I love. It has meant standing in a lonely place—bearing witness to truths that challenge deeply held beliefs, including my own.

It has cost me cherished friendships, the ease of family harmony, thousands of hours in tireless searching, and the comfort of silence. Yet every sacrifice pales in comparison to the weight of disobedience.

I cannot unsee what the Lord has shown me. I cannot unhear what He has spoken to my heart. And so, I write—not because it is easy, but because it is required.

### 2. Because people are hurting and don't know why.

I have met too many disciples who go through all the motions of faith and yet feel spiritually exhausted. They pray, they attend, they serve—but their wells have run dry. Many blame themselves. Some even blame God. And some, heartbreakingly, stop believing altogether.

This book is for them. Not to condemn, but to point them again to the source Joseph Smith found: the living water of Christ, flowing with plain and precious truth, teaching who He is—the same loving God Joseph came to know.

### 3. Because Joseph Smith wasn't the end of the story.

Joseph himself testified that he was only laying a foundation. He was a servant, not the destination. His mission was to point people to Christ and to prepare the way for Zion, where Christ will rule and reign for a thousand years.

This book bears witness that the Restoration did not end in 1844—it continues. And Zion cannot be established until a people are prepared to live as citizens of that glorious society. Therefore, the Restoration must continue.

### 4. Because truth sets people free.

Through years of searching, I have learned that some truths are hard to face. Yet the Spirit of Truth never shames. It clears the signal and points unfailingly to Christ. Always.

This book is not an attack. It is a witness—for those who feel the dissonance and long for harmony within their hearts. Its purpose is to tune the soul to the truths of Jesus Christ, cutting through the static of Babylon so His voice may be heard, and His peace felt.

### 5. Because Zion is yet to be built.

The Lord is still working to build Zion. And not just a metaphorical one, but a literal, powerful, radiant city of holiness. He is preparing a people who are ready to inhabit it—people educated in the school of trial and refined in the furnace of affliction.

People who have walked narrow paths, heard His voice, and chosen to obey. People who love much because they have been forgiven much. Above all, a people of one heart and one mind—ready to establish Zion in all her glory.

If you have ever felt that tug in your soul—that sense that something is coming, and you long to be part of it—this book is my handshake across the miles. We are not alone. The Lord is gathering His people. And He is not gathering the polished. He is gathering the grafted.

This is the beginning of a larger testimony.

Book Two of this trilogy, *The Watersprout*, will examine what sprang up after Joseph Smith's death—a growth that struggled at first, but then became quite prolific and bore much fruit.

Book Three, *The Graft Returns*, will bear witness of the Lord's promise to restore His vineyard to its strength—when the wild growth will give way, and a true branch will be grafted in once more. It will speak of the Endtime Servant, the preserved remnant, and the Lord's great labor to raise Zion, the New Jerusalem, in preparation for His glorious return.

This book exists because the Restoration isn't finished.

And this first book must come first. It is about the root, the graft, the foundation. It is a witness of Jesus Christ, telling what Joseph Smith actually learned from Him, and what he taught us about Him.

The Savior warned:

> *"And at that day, when I shall come in my glory... then shall the parable be fulfilled which I spake concerning the ten virgins. For they that are wise, and have received the truth, and have taken the Holy Spirit for their guide, and have not been deceived—verily I say unto you, they shall not be hewn down and cast into the fire, but shall abide the day."* (D&C 45:56–57)

This trilogy is written for the wise virgins, because the burning is coming.

The Lord Himself warned through Malachi:

> *"For behold, the day cometh that shall burn as an oven; and all the proud, yea, and all that do wickedly, shall be stubble; and the day that cometh shall burn them up, saith the Lord of Hosts, that it shall leave them neither root nor branch."* (3 Nephi 25:1)

Neither root nor branch. That is the fate of those who refuse the graft—who reject the gospel of Jesus Christ and remain wild, bitter, disconnected from the Lord's olive tree.

But for those who accept the graft—for those who receive the restored gospel and draw their nourishment from Christ, the true root—the fire does not destroy. It purifies. It sanctifies. It makes them burn as He burns.

The difference is not in the fire. The fire comes for all. The difference is in whether you have accepted the graft and draw life from the true root, and whether you bear His fruit.

Each of us will either be consumed by the fire of His presence—or burn as He burns, with glorious light. These books are for those who choose to be like Him—those who accept the true graft, draw strength from the root, and burn with that same holy flame.

# Introduction

The Lord of the vineyard looked upon His vineyard, and it was in peril. The branches were withering, the roots at risk. He had nourished it, set watchmen to guard it, and provided every protection. Yet, like a neglected tree, it was slowly losing its strength.

In the world of horticulture, there is an art to grafting—particularly with trees like citrus and olives, which are most commonly grafted by farmers.

The process is delicate and deliberate: a shoot from a healthy older tree is carefully joined to the rootstock of a younger tree. The goal is to preserve the strength of the root while introducing a new branch that will bear fruit. If done correctly, the graft takes hold, and the tree produces sweet fruit again.

But grafting is not simple. It requires a patient and careful hand. Without the right care, the graft can fail, and the tree will not return to its intended purpose. It takes diligence to nurture, prune, and care for the graft so it can grow strong and bear fruit.

This is the backdrop of the Restoration. It is the story of a vineyard that had been laid waste by apostasy long before Joseph Smith, and the Lord—the Master of the vineyard—who refused to let it die.

Joseph Smith was a man—imperfect, mortal, and learning line upon line just as we all must. His life was filled with difficulty, and his ministry sparked deep questions. Much has been said about Joseph Smith, and for many, his story has brought confusion or even pain.

This book will not shy away from acknowledging that reality. But it will also not dwell on it. The purpose here is not to defend Joseph Smith as a man, nor to dissect every difficult moment of his life. The purpose is to invite you to see him as he truly was—to know what he actually learned from the Lord, and what he taught. That is where the power of his mission lies, and that is what this book will explore.

When we encounter something in Joseph's life that is hard to understand, we must remember: the Lord does not call perfect men. He calls willing ones. And He teaches them. What matters most is not the man's weakness, but what the Lord revealed through him.

This book is about that revelation. It is about the graft—the restored gospel of Jesus Christ that the Lord revealed through Joseph Smith. It is not a biography. It is not an apologetic. It is a testimony of what Joseph learned from the Lord, and what he passed on to us before his death.

If you are looking for a defense of every action Joseph took, or an explanation of every controversy, you will not find it here. But if you are looking for the doctrine he received—the foundation he laid—you will find it in abundance.

I will not pretend that writing this has been easy. It has cost me. There are relationships I have strained. There are communities where I will no longer be welcome. There are people who will read this and assume I have been deceived, or that I have turned away from the faith.

I have not turned away. I have turned toward.

But that distinction will not matter to some. And I have had to make peace with that. I have had to count the cost—and then pay it anyway.

Because the Lord asked me to write this. And when He asks, the cost becomes irrelevant. What matters is obedience. What matters is truth.

I do not write this lightly. I write it knowing what it may cost me. But I also write it knowing what it has already given me—a clearer vision of the Lord's work, a deeper understanding of His servant Joseph, and a testimony that burns brighter than any fear I might carry.

So I write. Not because it is safe. But because it is true.

Because that foundation was not Joseph's invention. It was revelation—taught to him directly by the Lord, in a time when the vineyard had been laid waste and was in peril.

Into that moment, He sent a servant—a prophet named Joseph Smith.

Joseph was called by Christ to restore the vineyard. His call? To plant a graft that would bring forth good fruit again—to restore the fullness of His gospel to the earth.

Joseph Smith learned from the Lord what the fullness of the priesthood was, and how it could bless and sanctify a people—and that the Church of Christ was to grow like a living tree, drawing life directly from the root—Christ Himself.

This book is about that graft—the restored gospel of Jesus Christ that the Lord revealed through Joseph Smith. It will not attempt to explain the many changes or conflicts that followed Joseph's death. It is only about what Joseph Smith learned from the Lord, and what he taught us. It is about the foundation Joseph laid for the Lord's vineyard.

This book will speak with great discipline about one thing only: what Joseph Smith learned from the Lord, and what he taught the people. Nothing else.

That discipline is not easy. The pull to speculate about what came later, or to interject doctrinal ideologies that followed Joseph's death, is strong. But I'll resist that temptation, and I challenge you to do the same. For this book to work, we need to stay focused on the basics—on what Joseph actually received and taught—though the impulse to explore later developments will be ever-present.

To stay true to this discipline, it is necessary to recognize that some of what you read in this book may sound different from what you have been taught about Joseph Smith.

That is because Joseph never taught some of the things that later became associated with him. For example, many doctrinal changes after his death were introduced in ways that did not fully align with what he originally taught.

As you read, I invite you to carefully distinguish between what Joseph actually said and what was introduced later. If something in this book feels unfamiliar or at odds with the narrative you've been taught, it is most likely because Joseph never taught it—it was introduced after his death.

What you will find here is simply a return to the true graft—the original teachings Joseph Smith received from the Lord.

If you have ever wondered whether the story you were taught is the whole story—and if you desire to know Joseph Smith as he truly was, not just as tradition has described him—this book is for you.

Here's how I invite you to approach this journey:

Come with prayer. Ask the Lord to open your eyes to see what He wants you to see. This book is not meant to replace revelation—it's meant to point you toward it. The truths contained here were received through the Spirit, and they can only be fully understood by the same Spirit.

Come with an open mind and heart. Some of what you read may challenge what you've been taught, or what you've always believed. That's okay. Don't reject it outright, but don't accept it blindly either. Test everything against the word of God and the witness of the Holy Ghost.

Come as a researcher, not just a reader. If something I've written seems wrong to you, please double-check my work. Look up the references. Find out for yourself. Don't just take my word for it—but don't just accept the known narrative either. This book will challenge what has long been taught as settled truth. I don't shy away from that. But I'm not asking you to trade one blind faith for another. I'm asking you to seek, to study, and to let the Lord show you what is true.

Come with patience. This is not a book to rush through. Take your time. Pause when something strikes you. Let the doctrine settle into your soul. Read it in conjunction with your scripture study—especially the words of Joseph Smith himself, found in the Doctrine and Covenants, the Lectures on Faith, and his recorded teachings.

And come humbly, as a learner. The Lord delights in teaching those who seek Him with real intent. If your desire is to know Him better, to understand His gospel more fully, and to prepare yourself for Zion—He will meet you in these pages.

Now, come back to the vineyard, and learn of the true graft.

*In all ages the Savior's chosen have been educated and disciplined in the school of trial. They walked in narrow paths on earth; they were purified in the furnace of affliction. For Jesus' sake they endured opposition, hatred, calumny. They followed Him through conflicts sore; they endured self-denial and experienced bitter disappointments. By their own painful experience they learned the evil of sin, its power, its guilt, its woe; and they look upon it with abhorrence. A sense of the infinite sacrifice made for its cure humbles them in their own sight and fills their hearts with gratitude and praise which those who have never fallen cannot appreciate. They love much because they have been forgiven much. Having been partakers of Christ's sufferings, they are fitted to be partakers with Him of His glory.*

*(Ellen G. White, The Great Controvery)*

# The Song of the Vineyard

"You were in the dress rehearsal," He said.

The paramedics had just removed my mother's broken body from the passenger seat. One knelt over me, trying to free my leg from where it was jammed under the gas pedal. Another leaned in behind him and asked my birth date.

*"July 6th"* I answered.

*"That's in two days. Happy birthday!"* he said. And right there in the wreck, they began to sing: *"Happy birthday to you..."*

Then one of them announced, *"We're never going to get him out the door. We'll have to take him out the back."*

The paramedic at my left tried to lower the seat back, but it was stuck. A moment later another crawled in behind me with a crowbar. With a loud snap the seat gave way, and I fell back as if hit by a jackhammer. Before I could catch my breath, a stretcher board was jammed beneath me. Four sets of hands lifted me out, strapped me in, and fastened a brace around my neck.

And the strangest thing? Every one of those moments had already happened—I knew them seconds before they came. A déjà vu so strong it shook me. In confusion I asked the voice I had been talking with, *"How could I know these things?"*

And the voice answered, gentle and sure: *"You were in the dress rehearsal."*

Does God care? Does He care about us—about me, about you—or are we merely pawns in some vast cosmic game?

David asked this very thing: *"Stir up thyself, and awake to my judgment"* (Psalm 35:23). Fearing he had been cast off, he cried, *"Awake, why sleepest thou, O Lord?"* (Psalm 44:23). Though he knew God never slumbers (Psalm 121:4), he felt forgotten.

Habakkuk raised the same cry: *"O Lord, how long shall I cry, and thou wilt not hear!"* (Habakkuk 1:2)

In the New Testament, in a moment of desperation, the disciples cried out to Jesus, *"Master, carest thou not that we perish?"* (Mark 4:38)

We have all asked it: If God is love, why doesn't He love me?

I tell you the story of my accident because it is my witness that He does. God speaks. God answers. God cares.

Look around you, the evidences abound.

In the heavens. The moon is set at just the right distance from the earth—far enough to keep us steady, close enough to govern the tides. If it shifted even a fraction, the earth would wobble and life would unravel. The heavens declare His perfect balance.

In the earth beneath. The soil beneath our feet teems with life. Millions of unseen organisms turn waste into nourishment, cycling death into life again and again. What we throw away, He renews.

In the body. Your stomach holds a living world within it—a microbiome of countless tiny creatures working together so you can digest food. Without them you would bloat and die. Even at the smallest scale, God provides helpers so you can live.

In the sky above. Every sunrise testifies of order. The earth spins with such precision that clocks are set by its rhythm. Morning follows night because His hand sustains the turning.

In the womb. A child forms from a single cell, multiplying, differentiating, and weaving bones, skin, nerves, and a beating heart in silence. *"Thou hast covered me in my mother's womb"* (Psalm 139:13). Each birth is a reminder that God's work continues.

In the storms. Even lightning, terrifying as it is, splits nitrogen in the sky and returns it to the earth in rain, fertilizing the ground for crops to grow. What looks like chaos is provision.

In the stillness. A whisper of peace in the heart when we pray. A scripture verse that meets us at just the right moment. A thought or prompting that saves us from harm. These are not coincidences. They are the voice of a God who cares.

David said it best:

> *"When I consider thy heavens, the work of thy fingers, the moon and the stars, which thou hast ordained; What is man, that thou art mindful of him? and the son of man, that thou visitest him? For thou hast made him a little lower than the angels, and hast crowned him with glory and honour."* (Psalm 8:3–5)

Great and small, the evidences surround us. The heavens, the earth, the body, the storm, the whisper—all testify that God is not silent. He speaks. He answers. He cares.

The pattern continues.

Just as He spoke through the creation, through prophets of old, and through His quiet voice in our lives, He is always involved in our lives.

One of my favorite evidences that God is mindful of us is that He called a servant—Joseph Smith—and spoke to him too. He gave him tools, teachings, parables, and visions to strengthen him for the labor he would be called to do. Among them was the allegory of the vineyard.

## The Allegory of the Vineyard

The allegory of a vineyard is one of the Lord's oldest and most consistent ways of teaching about His work and His glory. *"For behold, this is my work and my glory—to bring to pass the immortality and eternal life of man."* (Moses 1:39)

The Lord of the Vineyard is Jesus Christ. The tree is His work among men. And the servant He directed to labor in these last days was Joseph Smith.

Isaiah described in Isaiah chapter 5 what is called his song of the vineyard: the Lord planted a grape vineyard on a fruitful hill, cleared the stones, built a tower, and made every provision for it to flourish. Yet when He looked for grapes, He found only wild ones (Isaiah 5:1–2).

Zenos, whose words Jacob preserved, gave a long allegory of the master's persistence: the olive vineyard decayed, but he dug, pruned, nourished, and grafted again and again, laboring that it might bring forth good fruit (Jacob 5).

And in modern times, the Lord spoke to Joseph Smith using the same allegory. In his parable, the servants planted trees and built a hedge, but neglected the tower He commanded. While they delayed, the enemy came by night and spoiled the vineyard (D&C 101:43–52).

Three witnesses—Isaiah, Jacob, and Joseph Smith—each in harmony with the same vineyard song. Together they testify of a God who plants, nourishes, and labors, never abandoning His vineyard.

## The Pattern of the Vineyard

Have you ever planted a fruit tree, or a garden?

> *You tuck the seed into the soil, water it, and watch for the first tender green to break the surface.*
> *You wait through the weeks and months, watering, pulling weeds, and fertilizing.*
> *You pray the sun and rain will be what is needed; not too much, not too little.*
> *You feel joy in seeing a plant you nurtured stretch upward and finally blossom.*
> *You wait with great anticipation for the day when fruit begins to swell—when you can taste the harvest.*

But, alas, sometimes there is also heartbreak. Sometimes the fruit withers before it ripens. Sometimes the sun scorches. Sometimes pests destroy what you had hoped for.

Sometimes it grows, but the fruit is not what you expected—hard, sour, tasteless, or worse—bitter.

Every grower knows this grief. All the work, all the hope, all the care—and still the harvest fails.

This is the grief Isaiah described in his song. The Lord Himself had done everything for His Vineyard to thrive. Yet when the fruit came, it was wild and sour.

The Lord's question in that song is the same question every gardener has asked in frustration:

*"What more could have been done?"* (Isaiah 5:4)

Isaiah helps us feel the heart of God—not as a distant judge, but as a patient caretaker whose hopes were dashed by a failed harvest. His grievance was not cold anger. It was the sorrow of a gardener who had loved, and labored, and looked for sweetness, only to taste bitterness instead.

If Isaiah helps us feel the sorrow of a failed harvest,[1] Zenos helps us see the stubborn love of the gardener who refuses to quit.[2] His allegory, preserved in Jacob's record, stretches across ages.

The master of the vineyard walks again and again among his trees.

> *He sees decay.*
> *He sees branches withering.*
> *He sees wild shoots spreading where he had hoped for fruit.*

But instead of cutting it all down, he goes to work. He digs around the roots. He prunes away what he can. He nourishes with dung. He grafts in new branches and transplants others to different soil.

When the corruption worsens, he pleads:

*"What could I have done more for my vineyard?"* (Jacob 5:41)

The image is not of a farmer who plants once and then gives up. It is of a master who labors tirelessly, season after season, doing everything in his power to preserve life in His vineyard.

Zenos' story is long because love is long. It's unrelenting. It refuses to abandon what it has cared for.

Where Isaiah shows us the Lord's grief, Zenos shows us His persistence. The God of Israel is not only a planter—He is a keeper. His hands stay in the soil, His eyes stay on the branches, His heart stays with the tree.

In Joseph's day, the parable came again.[3]

The Lord compared His church to a vineyard and His Saints to the servants who tend it. He gave simple, clear instructions: plant the trees, set a hedge around them for protection, and build a tower and place a watchman in it to alert others so the enemy could not come by stealth.

It was not busywork. Anyone who has cared for a field knows the value of these important steps.

> *A hedge keeps out the wandering animals.*
> *A tower lets you see what's coming before it arrives.*
> *A watchman can warn the workers below.*

These are the safeguards every good grower builds if he expects to keep his vineyard safe, and enjoy his harvest.

But the servants in Joseph's parable delayed. They reasoned with one another, and said the tower was not needed. They neglected the very commandment that would have secured the vineyard. And while they lingered, the enemy came at night, broke down the hedge, and spoiled the vineyard (D&C 101).

The grief of Isaiah shows us the harvest gone wrong. The persistence of Zenos shows us the gardener who keeps laboring anyway. But the parable given through Joseph shows us something more immediate: love requires vigilance.

The Lord does not only plant and nourish—He commands His servants to watch. If they delay, if they grow complacent, the loss is real.

Yet the loss is never final.

Each story, in its own way, bears witness that the Master of the vineyard does not abandon what He has planted.

His labor continues. His hands remain in the soil. His eye is on the fruit He still desires to see.

## Joseph's Role: The Servant of the Vineyard

The vineyard imagery now comes to life in Joseph Smith. Isaiah sang of failed fruit. Zenos told of a master's relentless labor. Joseph did more than echo their words—he lived the allegory.

Through him the graft—the Gospel of Jesus Christ—was tended in flesh and blood: questions asked, prayers offered, answers received, actions taken, and the word written.

When Joseph entered the field, he did not bring tools of his own. He brought only a question.

As a young boy he searched the scriptures and found a promise: *"If any of you lack wisdom, let him ask of God"* (James 1:5). He believed it. He acted on it. He went into the grove and prayed.

That first question set the course for all that followed.

## Prayer–Joseph's Lifelong Orientation

Joseph learned early that prayer was the soul's lifeline to heaven. At times, he paired it with fasting, for fasting magnifies prayer. It clears distraction, sharpens faith, and opens the heart with greater power—

bringing spiritual clarity, stronger faith, steadier hope, and deeper charity.

Joseph did not discover prayer for the first time when he entered the grove. The habit had been planted much earlier in his home.

His mother, Lucy, poured out vocal prayers and taught her children to look heavenward for answers.[4] His father, Joseph Sr., was a man of vision and knew scripture, whose nightly dreams and biblical language created an atmosphere where heaven felt near.

In their home, prayer was not a formality but the breath of daily life—a family kneeling together, reading aloud from the Bible, and seeking heaven's help in want and in sickness.

This culture of prayer was Joseph's soil.

By the time he walked into the woods as a boy of fourteen, he already knew prayer was real. The grove did not plant faith in him; it revealed the fruit of faith already growing.

The spring morning in the grove was not Joseph's first prayer. It was the living proof of a boy who had already learned to bend his heart and voice toward heaven.

> *He prayed because he believed God would answer.*
> *He entered the trees not to test prayer but to rely on it.*

The grove prayer was a living example of a young man who had faith enough to ask what his heart yearned to know. And when he asked, heaven replied.

His prayer shows us the way: if we follow his example—faith that speaks, heart that bends, body that turns heavenward—we too may receive answers.

In the Book of Mormon, Amulek's words make prayer tangible:

*"Cry unto him in your houses, both morning, mid-day, and evening"* (Alma 34:17–27). In the house, prayer orders the day. The family kneels together, voices joining, children learning that the first and last word in a home belongs to God. This was Joseph's upbringing, where scripture was read aloud and his mother's voice rose heavenward in prayer over her children.

*"Cry unto him in your fields."* Prayer belongs to labor. The plow in the soil or the sweat of the brow is not too common for heaven's ear. A whispered voice while binding sheaves or felling timber turns work into worship. Joseph's life as a farm boy, swinging an axe or sowing

seed, was threaded with such cries—petitions for strength, for relief, for understanding.

*"Cry unto him against the power of your enemies."* Prayer arms the soul when no earthly weapon will suffice. It is the cry of protection, the yielding of fear to One who delivers. Joseph prayed in the face of mobs, lawsuits, and betrayal, not merely for safety but for courage and forgiveness.

*"Cry unto him over the crops of your fields, that ye may prosper in them. Cry over the flocks of your fields, that they may increase."* Prayer lays even the most ordinary needs before God. Grain and flocks were not beneath His notice. In Joseph's day, survival itself rested on such petitions—asking the Lord to preserve harvests, to prosper herds, to feed the family through winter.

*"Pour out your souls in your closets, and your secret places."* Prayer belongs in solitude, where no eye sees but God's. Joseph sought such places often—the grove being only the most remembered. There he could speak freely, with no one to overhear but heaven. Closet prayer is where the soul lays itself bare.

*"Yea, in your wilderness."* Prayer belongs even in exile and desolation. For Alma's people it meant barren lands and wandering; for Joseph it meant prison cells, lonely flights, and nights under the open sky. Wilderness prayers are cries from the margins, where nothing seems certain but God's nearness.

*"When ye do not cry unto the Lord, let your hearts be full, drawn out in prayer unto him continually"* (Alma 34:27). Even when lips fall silent, the heart may still bend heavenward. Prayer becomes orientation—walking, speaking, eating, laboring, all with a heart turned toward God.

This sweep of scripture leaves no space untouched: house and field, closet and wilderness, bread and flock, enemy and friend. In every circumstance the soul must cry out.

The cry itself is not chiefly about words, nor about tears, though both may come. It is about posture, intent, humility, and faith. To cry unto God is to bring Him into every place and every condition of life—despair and joy alike, and all the ordinary moments in between.

This is why Joseph prayed.

Prayer was not a duty to be checked, nor a pious display. It was the means by which he bent himself toward heaven and invited heaven's power into every circumstance.

It was how he conquered temptation, how he gained light, and how he heard the Lord.

Joseph's practice of prayer bore the same character as the scriptures he translated.

In private he prayed vocally and particularly, not because God needed words, but because speaking shaped faith and invited heaven's reply. A thought may wander, but a spoken prayer fixes intent. His journals and revelations show him retreating to fields, attics, or woods to pour out his heart, because he knew God not only heard but would answer.

The "why" of his private prayer was orientation—he could not carry the weight of visions, persecution, and responsibility without bending himself daily toward the Lord.

And in his household he taught the same.

His family knelt together, not as a ritual, but because a kneeling family learns to be governed by heaven. A home where children hear their parents speak aloud to heaven becomes a house where heaven abides.

The reason was never form—it was that a family cannot be knit together without the Lord's Spirit.

Joseph taught his people to pray in their houses morning, noon, and night because he knew that no household would prosper if it did not rise and fall on its knees.

Among the Saints he prayed communally.

In congregations he joined his voice with theirs in extemporaneous petitions. He showed that public prayer was not the privilege of leaders alone, but the lifeblood of the whole assembly.

On certain occasions the Lord revealed the very words to be spoken—most notably the dedicatory prayer of the Kirtland Temple (D&C 109), where Joseph's voice became a mouthpiece for heaven.

Apart from a few revealed occasions, Joseph prayed without prepared words, trusting the Spirit to give utterance. The "why" of communal prayer was unity—hearts and voices rising together, creating a channel through which revelation could descend upon the body of Saints.

For Joseph, prayer was not confined to the mind, nor reserved for the pulpit. It was a spoken orientation of heart and household, a communal yielding of hearts joined together, and a daily act of dependence upon God.

Joseph's prayers were not only words; they were embodied.

Posture mattered because posture proclaimed what words alone could not. A bowed knee shows humility before God. To fall prostrate portrays utter surrender. To lift hands displays openness, a readiness to receive. In Joseph's day the Saints often combined these gestures—kneeling with uplifted hands—so that body and soul bore the same witness.

And it was more than symbolism.

Posture is testimony. Just as the direction of a person's feet will eventually carry them to that place their feet are pointed, so the posture of the body demonstrates where the heart is turned.

> *A bowed knee shows the will yielding.*
>
> *Uplifted hands display the soul reaching.*
>
> *A circle kneeling together demonstrates unity before God.*

In this way the body becomes part of prayer, giving visible evidence to heaven of what the soul intends.

The circles Joseph formed in Kirtland and later in Nauvoo embodied this truth.

Men and women, sometimes clasping hands, sometimes with arms raised, faced inward toward a shared center. In those moments posture became theology: all equal before God, all oriented toward Christ. The Lord answered with visions, manifestations, and knowledge, confirming that prayer was not mental habit alone but embodied communion.

When posture is reduced to folded arms or silent formality, the channel weakens—because of what it displays to God. It portrays closure rather than openness, containment rather than surrender. Joseph's practice reminds us that heaven desires the whole being: heart, voice, body, and will, all turned toward Him.

When prayer is lived in this way—spoken with faith, embodied with intent—it bears fruit.

> ***Forgiveness flows,*** *because confession spoken with a bowed heart invites mercy.*
> ***Revelation comes,*** *because questions uttered aloud with real desire bring heaven's reply.*
> ***Healing follows,*** *because hands laid in prayer display reliance on God's power rather than human strength.*

> ***Deliverance is granted,*** *because cries against enemies show trust in the Lord of Hosts.*
> *And* ***unity grows,*** *because families and congregations that kneel together demonstrate before heaven that they will be governed by one Spirit.*

These were the fruits of Joseph's life. When he prayed, answers followed: visions opened, comfort descended, direction came.

The Saints who joined him found the same. Their meetings often closed with prayer that filled the room with power; their homes were strengthened by prayer that knit them together in love.

Prayer was never ornamental. It was the instrument by which heaven blessed, guided, and sanctified.

To "pray always" is not to multiply words; it is to let every word come from real desire and from the Spirit who gives it.

> *"They did not multiply many words, for it was given unto them what they should pray, and they were filled with desire." (3 Nephi 19:24)*

The power wasn't in length but in the source of the words.

The Lord taught the early Saints the same principle:

> *"If ye are purified and cleansed from all sin, ye shall ask whatsoever you will in the name of Jesus and it shall be done... But know this, it shall be given you what ye shall ask."* (D&C 50:29–30)

True prayer is born when heaven supplies both the yearning and the request; the soul simply bends and speaks them. Prayer, then, is not about saying more; it is about yielding more—seeking words and desires that God Himself gives.

Prayer becomes orientation—the daily habit of bending, speaking, and listening until it reshapes how a person stands in the world.

> *A house that begins and ends the day on its knees becomes a dwelling of light.*
> *A family that lifts its voice together becomes a household knit by heaven.*
> *A congregation that joins in prayer becomes a body that can hear revelation.*

Joseph's life showed this plainly: prayer was not an interruption to his work; it was the way his work was governed.

The prayer he spoke in the grove was not the first but the fullest expression of a habit already alive within him.

His whole life testified that heaven responds to those who cry with faith, speak with intent, and yield their will. When prayer was lived vocally, bodily, and continually, the people were oriented heavenward—and heaven inclined its voice to them, guiding, delivering, and blessing.

This is the hinge on which Joseph's story turns: every revelation he received and every ordinance he set in motion arose from this living orientation of prayer.

The same posture that bent his soul in prayer also ordered the work the Lord gave him to do.

## How Prayer and Fasting Governed His Ministry

Again and again, Joseph lived the same sequence:

> *He had a question.*
> *He prayed—often with fasting.*
> *He asked God.*
> *God answered.*
> *He took action.*
> *It was preserved as scripture—the law of the kingdom.*

The Lord also named Joseph's stewardship: prophet, seer, and revelator.

**As a prophet**, he taught from truth he received from the Lord, bringing the Bible and the Book of Mormon into clearer light.

**As a seer**, he uncovered hidden truth through the gift of translation ancient records—the Book of Mormon, the inspired Bible translation.

**As a revelator**, he opened the heavens, receiving commandments and mysteries directly from the Lord for the Saints.

Each role flowed from the same living pattern.

Consider these examples:

> **The Vision of the Degrees of Glory (D&C 76).**[5]
> Joseph and Sidney Rigdon were pondering John 5:29 about the resurrection of the just and the unjust. Their question

became a vision, not creating new law, but revealing the mystery and giving greater understanding of what God had already spoken—and then it was preserved as new scripture, bringing that truth into greater clarity.

**The Law of the Church (D&C 42).**[6]
The Saints in 1831 already knew they must live by the Lord's word. Joseph's prayer was how to order a people striving to be Zion. The revelation did not invent new morality; it gathered and clarified the Lord's requirements, then was preserved as scripture to govern consecration, teaching, healing, and community life.

**The Call to Emma and the Women of the Church (D&C 25).**
Joseph asked concerning his wife Emma. The Lord's answer disclosed the calling already known to Him: *"Thou art an elect lady, whom I have called"* (v. 3). The revelation confirmed and recorded it, becoming a pattern for women's formal labor later realized in the Relief Society.

**The Word of Wisdom (D&C 89).**
The Saints already believed their bodies should be holy. Joseph sought guidance for a school clouded with smoke and excess. The revelation clarified principles and attached promises of hidden treasures of knowledge[7] to obedience. Preserved as scripture, it witnesses that God cares for body and spirit.

**The Olive Leaf (D&C 88).**[8]
Seeking how the Saints should prepare for Zion and the Lord's return, Joseph prayed. The answer unfolded light and law, resurrection and sanctification, and the order of a House of Learning (School of the Prophets). Recorded and preserved, it remains among the richest revelations, giving cosmic scope and practical commandment.

Many examples stand as a witness. Joseph may have begun as a boy searching for light, and the method he used to do so worked.

It was simple: he prayed, he fasted, he asked, the Lord answered, and the word was written.

In every case, the heavens responded to humble questions, and those answers became the Lord's word for His people.

The bottom line: it worked so well Joseph continued in it the rest of his life—and he taught it to us. His ministry was proof that the Lord had planted a graft anew, and that it could yet bear fruit.

### The Fruit of the Graft

The grafting process succeeded. The Gospel of Jesus Christ was alive again, scripture was flowing, and the Saints were beginning to taste the fruit.

Joseph's own ministry bore fruit in his communion with heaven. Across thirty-eight years of his life, he met with more than fifty heavenly messengers.[9] Moroni appeared again and again, instructing him for years.[10] And the Savior Himself appeared more than once.[11] For Joseph, the veil was thin. These were not distant legends but living visitations, each confirming that the graft was real and that heaven was near.

Each visitation added strength to the graft, binding ancient roots with living branches.

The work also bore fruit among the Saints themselves:

> **Scripture multiplied.** The Book of Mormon was published.[12] The Doctrine and Covenants grew,[13] line upon line, revelation upon revelation. The Pearl of Great Price gathered prophetic visions into one place.[14] Joseph's inspired revision of the Bible (JST)[15] opened passages with new light and clarity. What had been a silence of centuries broke open into a flood of scripture.
>
> **A Temple arose.** In Kirtland, a house of the Lord was built and dedicated.[16] Angels were seen. Visions were given. In Doctrine and Covenants 88, the Lord declared that nine men had their calling and election made sure.[17] It was a glorious time.
>
> **Cities flourished.** Kirtland became a thriving community of Saints. And later, a swamp on the Mississippi became Nauvoo,[18] a beautiful city[19] with schools, shops, farms, and commerce. The Saints built not just structures, but society—working together, consecrating their labor, and lifting one another.

> **The gifts of the Spirit operated.**[20] Healings, tongues, prophecy, visions, discernment—signs that God was among His people were not only claimed, they were experienced.
>
> **The gospel went abroad.**[21] Missionaries left family and home to carry the message across the United States, into Canada, to Great Britain, and even to the Native Americans, fulfilling the promises of the Book of Mormon.

These are not small things. They are proof that the graft was thriving in the Lord's Vineyard, that His Servant was accomplishing the errand, and that the fruit of the harvest was sweet. They show the graft alive, rooted, and bearing fruit.

## The Opposition to the Graft

Every vineyard faces storms. Every planting meets resistance. That is why the Lord in His parables commands hedges, towers, and watchmen. For where the Lord labors, the adversary presses in.

The graft Joseph planted bore fruit, but it also drew fire. From the beginning, the Saints learned that the vineyard would not thrive without opposition.

> **Kirtland.** The temple in Kirtland was built with sacrifice.[22] Farmers sold land to fund construction; families offered what little they had. Men labored through the nights, and women organized meals, sewing, and song to strengthen weary hands. Angels were seen there,[23] and visions unfolded. But almost as soon as it was dedicated, storms arose.
> Speculation and financial schemes entangled the Saints. The collapse of the Kirtland Safety Society ruined many[24], and bitter division spread. Apostasy followed. Within a few short years, the temple that had cost so much was lost to debt,[25] and soon the very Saints who built it were driven from their homes.
>
> **Missouri.** Violence in Missouri was sharp and unrelenting. Neighbors feared the Saints' rapid growth, their unity, and their bold claims of revelation. Old prejudices flared into hatred. Mobs burned homes and fields, destroyed printing presses, and forced families into the cold with nothing.[26]

> At Haun's Mill, men, women, and children were massacred.[27] Governor Boggs issued the infamous extermination order, declaring the Saints must be *"exterminated or driven from the state."*[28] Thousands fled in terror, leaving behind farms, graves, and the labor of years.
>
> **Nauvoo.** Out of a swamp on the Mississippi the Saints built a city that flourished with commerce, culture, and industry.[29] But as it grew, suspicion and political resentment grew with it. Accusations and slanders filled the newspapers. Lawsuits and threats pressed Joseph constantly.[30] Betrayals from within compounded pressure from without.[31]
> By the 1840s, Nauvoo was both a marvel and a powder keg—a city of hope and unity, but also a target for mobs and militias who circled it with envy and fear.

Things were not perfect. The Saints endured hardship upon hardship. But this was the reality of the vineyard: fruit and storms, growth and opposition, triumph and tragedy woven together.

The parables had already warned of it: wild grapes, corrupt branches, towers neglected, enemies breaking in by night. The Saints in Joseph's day lived those parables in flesh and blood.

## The Servant in the Vineyard

Joseph himself embodied both realities. Through his labor the vineyard flourished; through his suffering it endured its fiercest storms. The revelations, the temple, the scriptures, the gifts, the missions—all of it came through his labor.

The same life that produced abundance was relentlessly attacked.

He was ridiculed in the press, betrayed by friends, and hounded by lawsuits. He was dragged into court more than once, often on false charges. He was beaten, tarred and feathered,[32] and narrowly escaped assassination attempts.

In Missouri he shared the Saints' chains,[33] imprisoned in Liberty Jail. And in Nauvoo he faced constant suspicion, accusation, and unrest.[34]

Still he labored. He preached, he organized, he built, he translated, he dictated revelation. He poured out his strength until his life itself became the offering.

The vineyard allegories always pointed to such a servant: one who would plant, nourish, and prune, but also suffer for the sake of the graft.

Joseph's life was that pattern. He bore fruit in abundance, and experienced opposition in equal measure.

## The Burden of a Stiff-Necked People

One of Joseph's greatest challenges was the burden of a stiff-necked people.

This is one of the oldest patterns in scripture. From the beginning, those called of God have labored not only against outside opposition, but against resistance from their own people.

> **In the Bible,** Moses cried out: *"Ye have been rebellious against the Lord from the day that I knew you"* (Deuteronomy 9:24). Isaiah declared: *"This is a rebellious people, lying children, children that will not hear the law of the Lord"* (Isaiah 30:9). Stephen, in the New Testament, bore the same witness: *"Ye stiffnecked and uncircumcised in heart and ears, ye do always resist the Holy Ghost: as your fathers did, so do ye"* (Acts 7:51).
>
> **In the Book of Mormon,** Nephi grieved: *"They will not search knowledge, nor understand great knowledge, when it is given unto them in plainness"* (2 Nephi 32:7). Jacob lamented: *"Ye are a stiffnecked people ... hearts are set so much upon the things of this world"* (Jacob 2:13). Mosiah warned that when the people forgot their God, *"their hearts were set upon riches ... and they began to persecute those that did prophesy"* (Mosiah 11:14–15). Mormon summarized generations of the same cycle: *"How slow to remember the Lord their God, and to give ear unto his counsel ... because of their iniquity the church had begun to dwindle, and there had been slain many of their brethren"* (Helaman 4:21–23).

From Bible to Book of Mormon, the pattern is plain: when the Lord sends truth, many rejoice—but many resist. Prophets labor, but their own people are often their greatest grief.

So it was with Joseph.

The storms he faced did not come only from mobs and militias. Again and again, his greatest struggle was with his own people

The Saints who gathered to hear the word were often the first to resist it.

Joseph lamented:

> *"I have tried for a number of years to get the minds of the Saints prepared to receive the things of God; but we frequently see some of them, after suffering all they have for the work of God, will fly to pieces like glass as soon as anything comes that is contrary to their traditions: they cannot stand the fire at all." (HC 6:183)*

At another time he confessed: *"If you brethren knew what I know, you would seek to take my life"* (HC 6:317). He bore knowledge too heavy for a people not yet willing to receive it.

The Lord Himself condemned the Church for neglecting the very scripture He had given them:

> *"Your minds in times past have been darkened because of unbelief, and because you have treated lightly the things you have received—Which vanity and unbelief have brought the whole church under condemnation."* (D&C 84:54–55)

And the calls to repentance were not only to the body of the Church. Revelation after revelation corrected individual Saints—and Joseph himself.

The Lord rebuked entire councils:

> *"Behold, there are many called, but few are chosen. ... Their hearts are set so much upon the things of this world, and aspire to the honors of men, that they do not learn this one lesson—That the rights of the priesthood are inseparably connected with the powers of heaven."* (D&C 121:34–36)

He warned leaders in Kirtland:

> *"Ye have sinned against me a very grievous sin, in that ye have not considered the great commandment in all things."* (D&C 95:3)

Even still in Nauvoo He cautioned:

> *"If my people will hearken unto my voice, and unto the voice of my servants ... they shall not be moved out of their place. But if they will not hearken ... they shall be moved out of their place."* (D&C 124:45)

Joseph himself always stood under the Lord's correcting hand. To the young prophet the Lord commanded, *"Say nothing but repentance unto this generation"* (D&C 11:9).

Why? Because *"all flesh is corrupted before me"* (D&C 38:11). Even Joseph himself heard the rebuke: *"Behold, thou hast not kept the commandments, and must needs stand rebuked before the Lord"* (D&C 93:47).

Even the loss of the first 116 pages of the Book of Mormon drew a sharp chastening:

> *"You should not have feared man more than God. ... You have lost your gift."* (D&C 3:7–14)

Repeatedly, the Lord reminded Joseph that receiving revelation did not excuse him from obedience. His calling did not place him above correction; it bound him more tightly to accountability.

The Lord's Vineyard has always been tended with both nourishment and pruning. Comfort and correction came side by side. The same voice that opened heaven also cut down pride, exposed sin, and commanded repentance.

The Lord explained it this way: *"I, the Lord, have suffered the affliction to come upon them ... in consequence of their transgressions"* (D&C 101:2).

Why? Because, *"there were jarrings, and contentions, and envyings, and strifes, and lustful and covetous desires among them; therefore by these things they polluted their inheritances"* (vs. 6).

But the Lord's promise was sure: *"They shall be mine in that day when I make up my jewels"* (vs. 3).

And to shape those jewels, *"They must needs be chastened and tried, even as Abraham"* (vs. 4), for *"all those who will not endure chastening ... cannot be sanctified"* (vs. 5).

*"They were slow to hearken unto the voice of the Lord their God; therefore, the Lord their God is slow to hearken unto their prayers, to answer them in the day of their trouble"* (vs. 7).

Why would the Lord allow such chastening? Because, *"In the day of their peace they esteemed lightly my counsel; in the day of their trouble, of necessity they feel after me"* (vs. 8).

They were *"set to be a light unto the world, and... saviors of men"* (D&C 103:9), but to do that the Lord knew He had to chasten His people *"until they learn obedience... by the things which they suffer"* (D&C 105:6).

> ***Jewels*** *are not made in ease; they are cut, polished, and refined in fire.*
> ***Branches*** *are not made fruitful in ease; they are dug about, pruned, and nourished in patience.*

These are two metaphors saying the same thing. And, so it was with the Saints. In good times they treated lightly the things of God; in tribulation they cried out for Him. And in both, the Lord labored still—unwilling to abandon His Vineyard.

## Joseph's Life Cut Short

And then, in June of 1844, the vineyard lost its Servant.

Joseph and Hyrum were taken to Carthage Jail under false charges. That evening, a small band of armed men broke into the jail while a mob surrounded the building. Gunfire erupted at the top of the stairs. In the chaos, both brothers were shot and killed in cold blood.[35]

Together the two brothers sealed their testimony with their blood.[36] Joseph was only thirty-eight years old; Hyrum, forty-four.

The men who had prayed together, labored together, and carried the burden of the Restoration together now fell side by side.

Their deaths silenced their voices, but not their work. The graft they tended remained.

> *The scriptures they brought forth.*
> *The revelations they received.*
> *The pattern they lived.*

All these stand as witness that God had planted His true graft anew.

In the spring of 1844, Joseph moved with increasing urgency—organizing, teaching, preparing the Saints for what was to come. He knew the price of restoration would be high. His death did not end the work; it confirmed it. The blood he shed stood as heaven's witness that the true graft had been restored.

Joseph's and Hyrum's deaths were a tragedy, but not the end of their labor. Their voices still speak from the dust. Their example still shows us how to walk with God: to seek, to ask, to receive, and to live by the word of the Lord.

*"Joseph Smith, the Prophet and Seer of the Lord, has done more, save Jesus only, for the salvation of men in this world, than any other man that ever lived in it. ... He lived great, and he died great in the eyes of God and his people; and like most of the Lord's anointed in ancient times, has sealed his mission and his works with his own blood; and so has his brother Hyrum. In life they were not divided, and in death they were not separated."* (D&C 135:3)

## Invitation to Live the Pattern

The story of the vineyard is not only about hillsides in Isaiah's day, olive trees in Zenos' vision, or towers in Joseph's revelations. It is about the Lord's work and His glory—His care, His labor, His expectation of fruit.

The pattern is about the Lord of the Vineyard's persistence with a people who often fail Him, and His love that refuses to abandon His Vineyard.

In our day, Joseph Smith was the servant sent into the vineyard.

He prayed, he asked, he received, he acted—and the heavens were opened.

Through him the graft was set, scripture was multiplied, and the tree began to bear fruit once again. His life was cut short, and though the graft he planted did not reach its full potential, the Lord of the vineyard keeps watch over His vineyard.

This book is not about everything that followed. It is about what Joseph learned from the Lord, and what he taught to those who would hear.

His pattern was simple, but powerful: seek God, ask in faith, receive by revelation, and live what is given. That pattern is the Gospel of Jesus Christ. It is the graft. It worked for Joseph. It can work for us.

The invitation is plain: let us learn what Joseph learned, and live what he lived. For the same God who answered him will answer us.

Come back to the vineyard. Taste again the fruit of the graft. Learn the pattern, and live it.

## Chapter 1 Notes

1 Isaiah 5:1–7
This section explicitly lays out the parable of the vineyard, the failed harvest, and the Lord's grief at bringing forth *"wild grapes."*

2 Jacob 5 (esp. vv. 11–77)

3 D&C 101:43–62

4 History of Joseph Smith by His Mother, chap. 1–2

5 D&C 76:16–19

6 Consecration: vv. 30–39
Teaching: vv. 12–13
Healing: vv. 43–48
Community law: vv. 11, 22–29

7 D&C 89:19

8 Resurrection & sanctification vv. 14–35, 85–98,
School of the Prophets / House of Learning vv. 117–137

9 Richard Anderson's Joseph Smith's Testimony of the First Vision

10 Joseph Smith—History 1:29–54 (first visits, 1823–1827).
Later angelic instructions noted in History of the Church, esp. Vol. 1.

11 First Vision: Joseph Smith—History 1:15–20. 1832
Vision of the Degrees of Glory: D&C 76:20–24.

12 2 Nephi 29:11–13

13 D&C 1:38

14 Historical compilation (1851, Franklin D. Richards)

15 D&C 45:60–61

16 D&C 109 (dedicatory prayer)

17 D&C 88:3–5 (promise of comforter; *"seal upon you to prepare you"*).

18 Historical anchor: History of the Church 4:187 (arrival at Commerce/Nauvoo, 1839).

19 D&C 124:1–3, 60

20 D&C 46:8–26

21 D&C 1:30 (Church called to spread abroad). D&C 112:21 (keys given to Twelve for nations). Historical fulfillment: History of the Church 2:489–492 (1837 mission to England).

22 History of the Church 2:427–428 (accounts of women donating glass, china, labor).

23 *"We... saw the Lord standing upon the breastwork of the pulpit, before us; and under his feet was a paved work of pure gold... and his eyes were as a flame of fire."*
– Joseph Smith Journal, 1 April 1836, in Dean C. Jessee, Papers of Joseph Smith, Vol. 2, p. 427.
*"Great manifestations of the power of God were seen and felt, and angels administered unto many."* (History of the Church 2:432)

24 History of the Church 2:471–482 (Kirtland Safety Society failure, 1837).

25 History of the Church 3:2–3 (creditors seized temple).

26 History of the Church 3:175–209.

27 History of the Church 3:183–190; also Joseph Young's affidavit (Nov. 1838).

28 Governor Lilburn Boggs, Oct. 27, 1838. Official Missouri Executive Order 44 *("must be exterminated or driven from the state").*

29 History of the Church 4:187 (arrival at Commerce/Nauvoo, 1839).

30 History of the Church 5:280–282 (arrests, slanders, political attacks in 1842).

31 William Law, dissenters' Nauvoo Expositor (June 1844). History of the Church 6:408–412.

32 *"I was dragged out of bed by an armed mob, my body naked, and then tarred and feathered."* (History of the Church 1:261–262

(March 24, 1832, Hiram, Ohio).
Painesville Telegraph, March 1832, reported the incident.

33 D&C 121–122

34 HC 6:408–412 (Nauvoo Expositor + unrest).

35 *"Account of the Martyrdom of Joseph and Hyrum Smith,"* Warsaw Signal, July 3, 1844; see also Dallin H. Oaks and Marvin S. Hill, Carthage Conspiracy (Urbana: University of Illinois Press, 1975), 66–74; Illinois State Journal reports, July 1844.

36 D&C 135:3—*"Joseph Smith, the Prophet, and Hyrum Smith, the Patriarch... did seal their testimony with their blood."*

# The Church of the Lamb of God

Sanctified by the Holy Ghost and Born Again as His People

---

### The Fork in the Road

There are only two churches.

Let that sink in.

To be clear, I'm not talking about the Church of Jesus Christ of Latter-day Saints or any other denomination for that matter. There are literally thousands of churches on the earth today. And I'm not talking about a single one of them.

Nephi didn't leave us guessing either. He didn't offer a spectrum of belief systems or a marketplace of spiritual options. He said it plainly:

> *"Behold, there are save two churches only: the one is the Church of the Lamb of God, and the other is the church of the devil."* (1 Nephi 14:10)

There is no third option. No middle ground. No *"trying your best"* category for those caught in between. You are either in the Church of the Lamb of God, or you are not. And if you have not entered that church according to Christ's definition, you remain—by default—in the other one.

That may sound harsh. But it is one of the most hopeful doctrines in all of scripture.

Because the Church of the Lamb of God is not a brand. It's not a building. It's not a line on a record in some database. It is a spiritual reality. It is the body of Christ—composed of those who have come to Him and been born of Him.

So, to be clear, it's not about denomination. It's about identity—*your* identity. It's about alignment—*your* alignment. It's personal, not institutional. It's about the kind of being you're becoming, and which church—spiritually—you belong to.

And the door is still open.

## What Joseph Had to Learn

Imagine you're Joseph Smith—young, rough around the edges, trying to follow God the best you know how—and you're translating the Book of Mormon—something you've never done before. And then right there in 1 Nephi you read that piercing line:

*"There are save two churches only."* (1 Nephi 14:10)

Two?

If it were me, I'd stop cold. I'd be asking the Lord what on earth that meant. Two churches? Where does that leave everyone else? Where does that leave *me*? Especially when I'd already been told—face to face in a grove of trees—that none of the churches on the earth were His. So then... what *is* His church? And how does someone actually join it?

The amazing part is—Joseph did exactly what you'd hope a prophet would do. He asked. He sought. And the Lord began teaching him, line upon line, what it actually means to become a member of the Church of the Lamb of God.

But it wasn't simple.

Joseph encountered a wave of divine vocabulary: born again, baptism of fire and the Holy Ghost, Church of the Firstborn, mighty change of heart, Second Comforter, calling and election made sure, and the Holy Spirit of Promise.[1]

If your head's spinning already, you're not alone. His probably was too. Mine certainly was.

But the Lord taught Joseph directly—line upon line—so he could teach it. And that's exactly what I'm trying to do right now: teach you what the Lord taught him. To take all those seemingly separate ideas and tie them into one clear reality.

Let's make sense of it—right here, right now.

## Christ Defines His Church

If Joseph Smith was going to be the one to restore the Lord's church to the earth, he first had to learn what the Lord's church actually was.

That question wasn't left to guesswork or tradition. It was answered by the Lord Himself:

> *"Behold, this is my doctrine—whosoever repenteth and cometh unto me, the same is my church." (D&C 10:67)*

According to the Lord, His church is made up of those who repent and come to Him. That's it. Period.

That single sentence would have shattered every assumption Joseph had inherited—and probably many of yours as well. So Joseph, being Joseph, didn't just quote it. He had to *understand* it. And to understand it, he had to ask:

> *What does it mean to repent?*
> *What does it mean to come to Christ?*
> *What does it mean to be received by Him?*
> *To receive His gospel?*
> *To be born again?*

And—perhaps most urgently—what does it mean to be baptized with water, and then with fire and the Holy Ghost?

Joseph had to learn what each of these terms meant. So do we.

Let's take them one at a time.

## Two Foundational Questions

If the Lord said that His church is made up of those who *repent and come unto Him*, then Joseph would have had to ask two foundational questions:

> *What does it truly mean to repent?*
> *And what does it mean to come unto Christ?*

Let's start with repentance.

Because if repentance itself has been watered down, then the doorway into the Church of the Lamb of God becomes like a wet threshold—slippery, and more likely to make people fall than enter. We can't have that. We've got to lay down firm footing from the very start.

Modern interpretations have softened the word to the point that it barely resembles the scriptural standard. Some have suggested that we should repent *daily*—as if repentance is just a routine check-in, like brushing your teeth or updating your to-do list.

But that's not the kind of repentance the Lord is talking about.

He's not inviting us into a cycle of endless apology. He's calling us to stop sinning. To change our hearts. To become the kind of people who no longer *desire* to sin.

Repentance always begins with truth-telling. *"He that covereth his sins shall not prosper: but whoso confesseth and forsaketh them shall have mercy"* (Proverbs 28:13).

To repent is not only to forsake sin but also to name it—to confess it openly before God, and where needed before the one we have wronged. Joseph's revelations made it simple:

> *"By this ye may know if a man repenteth of his sins—behold, he will confess them and forsake them."* (D&C 58:43)

Confession is not a ritual or a performance; it is the honest recognition of wrong-doing before God joined with the resolve to abandon it and never return to it—never. Only then can the forsaking be real.

That's not my interpretation. That's the pattern:

> **The sons of Mosiah** experienced such a change that they could not even bear the thought of returning to sin.
> **The people of King Benjamin** entered a covenant so deep that they said, *"we have no more disposition to do evil, but to do good continually"* (Mosiah 5:2).
> **Alma** described the truly penitent as those who *"look upon sin with abhorrence"* (Alma 13:12).

This is the repentance Joseph had to understand. Not just remorse—but confession, followed by an absolute forsaking, leading to complete transformation.

Not a spiritual treadmill. Repentance is a complete turn of the heart.

## Come Unto Christ

Once Joseph understood what it meant to repent—not just to feel sorrow, but to confess, to forsake, and be transformed—he had to ask:

What does it mean to come unto Christ?

That phrase gets used so often in sermons and slogans that we think we already know. But Joseph had to strip it down to the core. Because coming to Christ isn't the same as believing in Him. It's not even the same as following Him.

Coming unto Christ means moving toward Him in every way.

It is reaching for Him with the heart, surrendering our will, and yielding our whole soul unto Him—*"to come unto Christ, and offer your whole souls as an offering unto him"* (Omni 1:26).

It is seeking His presence with honesty and trust, learning of Him as He said, *"Take my yoke upon you, and learn of me"* (Matthew 11:29). It is listening to His voice and walking in His Spirit, until He becomes the center and the source of our life.

It means we stop reaching for approval from others and start reaching for *Him*. It means surrendering control. Letting go of old beliefs. Letting go of our own righteousness. Letting go of the version of God we've been taught—and seeking to know Him for real.

It's not a performance. It's a yielding. It's surrendering yourself completely.

It's Moses removing his sandals at the base of the mountain[2]—because even *his understanding* wasn't worthy of the ground he was about to walk on. The Lord was asking him to take off what was under the place he was standing. In other words: *take off your understanding.* Lay aside what you think supports you. Come to Me without pretense or preconceived ideas is what the Lord is asking us to do.

Coming to Christ begins with reverence, but it requires release – absolute release. Not partial.

It's the soul saying: I want truth more than I want to be right.

Joseph had to come to Christ the same way we do: with questions. With weakness. With hunger.

And the promise is the same today as it was then:

> *"Draw near unto me and I will draw near unto you."* (D&C 88:63)

Coming to Christ is more than a single step. It is an orientation of soul—a continual turning of the heart. It leads to forgiveness. It leads to fire. And ultimately, it leads into His mercy.

The way is plain: He invites all to come, and the promise is sure—He will draw near to you in your seeking.

## A Broken Heart and a Contrite Spirit

If repentance is the first condition, and coming unto Christ is the movement, then a broken heart and a contrite spirit are the posture of the soul.

Joseph had to learn that power with God does not come from strength—it comes from yielding, or surrendering.

A broken heart isn't about sadness. It's not an emotion. It's not just being sorry for sin or feeling emotional about your wrongdoings. It's the deliberate shattering of your pride. It's the conquering of your ego. It's when your heart breaks open enough to let God in—and stay in.

A contrite spirit is not self-loathing. It's not passive guilt. It's the deep spiritual humility that says: *I know I can't do this without Him, and I'm not going to try to fake it anymore.*

This isn't superficial sorrow—it's godly sorrow refined. As scripture states, it is the kind of sorrow Paul described in 2 Corinthians:

> *"For behold this selfsame thing, that ye sorrowed after a godly sort, what carefulness it wrought in you, yea, what clearing of yourselves, yea, what indignation, yea, what fear, yea, what vehement desire, yea, what zeal, yea, what revenge! In all things ye have approved yourselves to be clear in this matter"* (2 Corinthians 7:11)

Paul taught that godly sorrow doesn't lead to shame—it leads to action. To purification. To transformation.

The words he chose are not the words we might use today. Let's open the dictionary of Joseph's day[3] and see them with greater clarity:

> **Carefulness**—*"Concern; anxious desire; attention to the matter; solicitude."*
> Repentance awakens a deep concern to set things right, never casual indifference.
> **Clearing of yourselves**—*"To free from imputation or charge; to justify; to vindicate."*

> True repentance makes restitution, removes the offense, and stands clear before God and man.
> **Indignation**—*"Displeasure, anger excited by something unjust, unworthy, or mean."*
> The repentant soul burns with hatred for sin itself, not just its consequences.
> **Fear**—*"A holy awe and reverence of God."*
> Repentance deepens reverence, awakening the soul to God's majesty and justice.
> **Vehement desire**—*"Ardent, fervent longing; intense wish or inclination."*
> The soul yearns passionately to be reconciled and to remain in His favor.
> **Zeal**—*"Warmth of passion for a cause; fervor in pursuit of a goal."*
> Repentance sets the heart ablaze with devotion to live differently and serve God fully.
> **Revenge**—*"Vindication of right; retribution against wrong; inflicting deserved punishment."*
> Here it means a holy resolve to root out sin, to take corrective action even against oneself, until it has no more place.

With this clarity, Paul's meaning becomes plain: repentance is not resignation but resolve. Not passivity but purification. This is how the Kingdom is entered.

The Lord has always required this posture for repentance:

> *"Behold, I require the heart and a willing mind, and him that is contrite in spirit I will receive."* (D&C 64:34)

Scripture shows us that when hearts truly turn, the body follows.

> ***Alma the younger*** *fell to the earth, prostrate before God, crying out from the depths of his soul (Mosiah 27:29).*
> ***Nephi*** *bowed himself before the Lord, wrestling in mighty prayer for his people (2 Nephi 33:3).*
> ***The brother of Jared*** *raised his hands to the heavens, calling on the Lord until the veil parted (Ether 3:6).*
> ***Enos*** *knelt in prayer, and poured out his whole soul (Enos 1:4).*

These outward postures were not empty gestures—they revealed inward brokenness and yielding of the heart.

When that yielding is real, it becomes the beginning of transformation.

This is the posture required to submit to the Lord—and be changed by Him.

> *"For the natural man is an enemy to God... and will be, forever and ever, unless he yields to the enticings of the Holy Spirit... and becometh as a child—submissive, meek, humble, patient, full of love."* (Mosiah 3:19)

That, my friend, is how one becomes a Saint, and how sanctification happens. When the heart truly breaks, and the soul finally lets go, heaven begins to draw near—not only because of heaven moving toward us, but because in repentance we rise nearer to heaven.

### Receive Him

Once Joseph learned what it meant to repent and come unto Christ, the next question naturally followed:

What does it mean to receive Him?

It's a phrase we hear often—spoken in prayers, songs, and sacramental rituals. But for all its repetition, few truly understand what it means.

To receive Christ is not to merely accept His story. It's not passive belief. It's not intellectual agreement. It's not joining a church or adopting a label. It's not even being baptized. These only swat at the idea, but are woefully insufficient to get the job done.

To receive Christ is to be changed by Him.

The Lord defined it with unmistakable clarity:

> *"Whoso receiveth my gospel receiveth me... and shall be called the sons of God. And whoso receiveth not my gospel, receiveth not me."* (D&C 39:5–6)

That's not a metaphor. It's a dividing line.

And then He told us right where that line is:

> *"And this is my gospel—repentance and baptism by water, and then cometh the baptism of fire and the Holy Ghost..."* (D&C 39:6)

Let that settle deep.

Because many who have been baptized by water and *confirmed* by the laying on of hands believe they've already fulfilled this commandment.

But if there has been no power, no fire, no spiritual rebirth—then the ordinance was incomplete.

The baptism of fire is not conferred by words or ritual—it comes from God. The record makes it plain:

> *"when they were all baptized and had come up out of the water, the Holy Ghost did fall upon them, and they were filled with the Holy Ghost and with fire"* (3 Nephi 19:13)

No mention is made of confirmation, because the Spirit came directly from heaven. The true baptism of fire requires no ritual formula—it is heaven's own act, when the Spirit is poured out upon one who has first been baptized with water.

Without the actual *receiving* of the Holy Ghost by power, the promise remains unfulfilled. And according to the Lord's own words, that is not just missing a step—it's rejecting Him.

> *"He that receiveth not my gospel, receiveth not me."* (D&C 39:5)

And this is not just semantics.

> *"The baptism of fire and the Holy Ghost is a vital component of the gospel. Until one receives each and every one of these elements—including the baptism of fire—one has not received Christ. Those who reject His gospel, or any part of it, actually reject Jesus Christ."*[4]

> *"The remission of sins comes only through the baptism of fire. It's through that fire that Christ's Atonement becomes fully effective. So when Jesus says those who reject His gospel also reject Him—He's saying they've rejected the Atonement itself."*[5]

Sobering, isn't it?

This isn't just about church attendance. This is about whether the power of the Atonement has actually been applied to your soul.

You can go down into the water and come up exactly the same as when you went in. You can be baptized a hundred times and never be born again.

Water is the beginning. A witness. Proof you are willing.

But fire is the fulfillment. The evidence. The power to make it stick – forever. And if you haven't received that power—you haven't received the gospel. And if you haven't received the gospel—you haven't received Him.

And He warned us plainly:

> *"Whoso shall declare more or less than this... the same cometh of evil."* (3 Nephi 11:40)

So, if you've been led to believe it means anything else—you've been misled. Because when more is required, the invitation gets buried. And when less is offered, the power gets lost. In either case, the result is the same: You miss Him.

He is the gospel.

And He's still waiting to be received.

No more. No less.

### Born Again by Fire

So what does it mean to be born again?

Nicodemus asked the same question.

When Jesus told him, *"Except a man be born again, he cannot see the kingdom of God,"* Nicodemus was baffled. *"How can a man be born when he is old? Can he enter the second time into his mother's womb?"* (John 3:3–4)

Jesus didn't back down. He said, plainly:

> *"Except a man be born of water and of the Spirit, he cannot enter into the kingdom of God."* (John 3:5)

Water *and* Spirit. Both are necessary. But also blood.

Because being born again isn't just a poetic phrase—it mirrors literal birth:

> **Water**—like the amniotic fluid that surrounds and cushions new life.
> **Spirit**—like the moment the spirit joins the body and the child begins to live.
> **Blood**—always present at birth, a symbol of the mother's sacrifice to bring forth life.

In the same way, your spiritual birth requires all three: Water, Spirit, and the blood of Christ, who labored and bled to give you a new life.

The Lord taught this clearly in His command to Adam:

> *"By the water ye keep the commandment; by the Spirit ye are justified, and by the blood ye are sanctified."* (Moses 6:60)

And He added:

> *"Inasmuch as ye were born into the world by water, and blood, and the spirit... even so ye must be born again."* (Moses 6:59)

This wasn't just for Adam—it was to be passed on:

> *"Therefore I give unto you a commandment, to teach these things freely unto your children..."* (Moses 6:58)

That was the Lord's instruction to Adam. Through Joseph Smith, the Lord restored this same divine pattern in the Restoration.

And the commandment remains: it is to be taught to our children, so they may know the true terms of entrance into the kingdom of God—by water, by the Spirit, and by blood.

Because the terms are still binding: Water. Spirit. Blood.

All three are required.

Let's break them down.

### Water is the witness.

It represents your willingness to obey. Even Jesus Christ—perfect and without sin—submitted to baptism by water to *"fulfill all righteousness"* (Matthew 3:15).

As Nephi taught:

> *"If the Lamb of God, he being holy, should have need to be baptized by water... O then, how much more need have we, being unholy... even by water!" (2 Nephi 31:5)*

Water is the beginning. The sign. The covenant act that says, *"I'm ready to be changed."*

### Spirit is the power.

It's the actual force that causes rebirth. Through the Holy Spirit, Christ sanctifies—He doesn't just inspire, He transforms. It is through the fire of the Spirit that your sins are purged. That's what remission of sins means:[6] not erased from memory, but burned out of your being. This is what makes you holy. This is what prepares you to receive Him.

> *"...they must be born again; yea, born of God, changed from their carnal and fallen state, to a state of righteousness, being redeemed of God, becoming his sons and daughters; And thus they become new creatures; and unless they do this, they can in nowise inherit the kingdom of God."* (Mosiah 27:25–26)

But the Spirit cannot dwell where uncleanness remains.

> *"Know ye not that ye are the temple of God...? If any man defile the temple... him shall God destroy."* (1 Corinthians 3:16–17)

The baptism of fire makes you clean enough for Christ to abide in you.[7]

### Blood is the price.

This is a direct reference to the Atonement of Jesus Christ. It is the cost He paid so your nature could change—so your sins could be burned out and your heart made holy. And it is applied by the Spirit. Not just to forgive, but to transform.

So that, like the people of King Benjamin, *"we have no more disposition to do evil, but to do good continually."* (Mosiah 5:2)

It is only through this process—repentance, water, Spirit, and fire—that His sacrifice, His blood, becomes active in your life.

> *"Then cometh a remission of your sins by fire and by the Holy Ghost."* (2 Nephi 31:17)

This isn't metaphor - this is the real baptism. It is the refining crucible of sanctification, and every soul—alive or dead—must pass through it.

There is no alternate route.

Water prepares your heart, it proves your willingness to obey, but it cannot change you. Only fire can purify your heart. Only fire transforms you. Only fire remits your impurities and makes your soul holy.

And this baptism—this holy fire—is given by Jesus Christ Himself. It is His gift, His ordinance, His witness, His covenant. No hand but His can bestow it, for only He can sanctify, only He can seal, and only He can make a soul holy in His presence.[8]

> *"They shall be mine... in the day when I shall come to make up my jewels."* (D&C 101:3)

To make a jewel, you need gold. But gold doesn't begin as something beautiful. It starts as raw ore—hard, rough, buried deep, and full of dross.

You can't just wash that kind of rock. You have to crush it.

Tribulation does that. So does sin. And sometimes, God allows you to be broken—crushed under the weight of His loving chastisements and the consequences of your own transgressions—because He knows what it will uncover.

Once it's crushed, it's washed. Not to polish it, but to clear away the dust and debris that surface breaking reveals. That's what repentance really looks like—letting the filth fall away, not clinging to what cracked you.

Then comes the fire.

Gold is only gold once it's been through heat. A furnace hot enough to burn away everything false. Everything extra. Everything that cannot abide the presence of God.

> *"He is like a refiner's fire... and he shall purify the sons of Levi, and purge them as gold and silver..."* (Malachi 3:2–3)

When you are refined as gold, you are no longer just a believer. You become something new.

You become His.

His son.
His daughter.
Spiritually begotten.
Sanctified.
Sealed.
Born of God.

That's the only way it happens.

Joseph had to be crushed before the light came.

So will you.

### The Real Gate. The Only Gatekeeper

We've misunderstood the gate—and imagined things the Lord never required.

According to Him, the real gate is not confirmation. It is not an interview. It is not being welcomed into a group or assigned a duty.

The real gate is made of fire.

> *"Then cometh a remission of your sins by fire and by the Holy Ghost."* (2 Nephi 31:17)

That line matters. Because the scriptures are plain: *"The keeper of the gate is the Holy One of Israel; and he employeth no servant there"* (2 Nephi 9:41). The Lord Himself is the one who opens the way. No one else can take His place.

But when in all of scripture does the Lord ever say: *"Come unto me, all ye that labour and are heavy laden—but first, speak to the attendant at the gate"?* When does He ever say: *"My yoke is easy, and my burden is light—once you've passed another's test"?*

He said it plainly: *"I am the door: by me if any man enter in, he shall be saved"* (John 10:9).

And He still stands there—alone—watching for the humble, the repentant, the childlike seeker. No lines. No passwords. No certificates. Just an invitation: Come unto me.

## Have You Been Born Again?

This is where it gets personal. This is going to require some deep introspection.

Because once you've seen the pattern—crushing, washing, Spirit, and fire—you have to ask the question Joseph asked. And the question Christ still invites: Have you been born again?

That's the real process. It begins with a breaking—tribulation, chastisement, or deep repentance that brings you low. Then comes the water, where you surrender and let go. Then the Spirit comes, and with it, fire. Not metaphor, but real purification. That's what sanctifies. That's what makes you new.

So the question isn't, *"Have you been baptized?"* Or, *"Do you go to church?"* It's not, *"Do you sit in a congregation?"* And it's not even, *"Do you believe in Jesus?"*

Stated plainly, it's this: Have you been changed? Has your heart actually been made new? Has the old creature been crushed—and a new one truly born again? A new creature. An infant in a new way of being.

The scriptures are not vague about this moment. They don't describe it as a long, slow fade into holiness. They describe it as a distinct, undeniable experience. Not just a process, but a point. A moment. A mighty change. You were this. Now you are that. Period.

Alma didn't say, *"Did you gradually improve over time?"* He said: *"Have ye spiritually been born of God? Have ye experienced this mighty change in your hearts?"* (Alma 5:14).

Birth is the event that follows pregnancy, but don't confuse the two. Pregnancy is not birth. You are either still waiting in the womb of the natural man, or you have been delivered—delivered by Christ into new life, a new creation in Him. You have been born His child, and taken upon you His name.

This is about identity—your identity. It's about what kind of being you've become. It's about whether He recognizes you as one of His children.

## The Signs That Follow

*"But I've been baptized,"* some may say. *"I was confirmed and told to receive the Holy Ghost. Don't I now have the constant companionship of the Holy Ghost?"* That's what we're taught. That's what we hope. But now—after all you've read—can you still believe that's true without question? Has the fruit matched the promise? Have the signs followed?

The scriptures describe unmistakable evidences of the real thing.

Nephi taught that when we receive the Holy Ghost, we can now *"speak with the tongue of angels"* (2 Nephi 31:13). That's not poetic fluff—it's a description of what happens when the Spirit truly takes hold.

So, ask yourself: Do you speak with the tongue of angels? Can you testify with power, clarity, and heavenly authority?

In scripture, when people received the Spirit, they did not merely feel peaceful—they were filled with light. They prophesied. They spoke with power. They knew. Moroni promised: *"By the power of the Holy Ghost ye may know the truth of all things"* (Moroni 10:5).

Not just believe. Know.

If you had truly received the Holy Ghost, you would know the truth of this very message. Do you?

Enoch said that those who receive the Holy Ghost receive the record of heaven, the peaceable things of immortal glory, and understanding so expansive that *"all things [are] made known unto them"* (Moses 6:61). Is that your experience?

These are not lofty ideals. They are fruits—scriptural, sacred, and promised to every soul who truly receives the Holy Ghost and the baptism of fire.

If you've been told you already have the *gift of the Holy Ghost*—but the change never came, the fire never burned, the voice never spoke—then the issue is not you. It's the pattern you were taught to expect.

Because the gift of the Holy Ghost is not a promise sealed on you by men. It's a gift given to you, even power conferred on you by Christ.

It doesn't come just because a priesthood holder laid hands on your head. No one laid their hands on Jesus' head when He was baptized. No, *"the Holy Ghost descended in the form of a dove, and rested upon him"* (John 1:32).

That's how it happens—it comes by divine sending, when God Himself bears witness and confers power.

If you've never felt that fire—if you've never known that cleansing, purifying, soul-altering rebirth—then you have not yet received the gift.

> *Seek it.*
> *Ask for it.*
> *It is yours to receive.*

Because anything less is not fire. Anything less is not the gate. Anything less is not from Him.

### Entry Into the Holy Order

Joseph learned that being born again wasn't the end of his progression—it was only the beginning. It opened the way to the next level of discipleship—a holy order where sanctified souls are entrusted with greater knowledge, responsibility, and spiritual power. But what does that mean?

It means progression—not promotion among men, but adoption by God. Understand this: every stage of that progression is part of a sacred path.

The scriptures call them estates. Each one is a graduation to the next level. A spiritual transition. And each one marks the same milestones:

> *A **birth***
> *A **body***
> *A **parent***
> *A **name***
> *An **inheritance***
> *A **death***

This isn't just the cycle of mortality. It's the divine path of eternal ascent.

Let's walk through just a few to help you understand how beautiful the Plan of Salvation truly is.

### First Estate—Pre-Mortal Life

> **Birth:** You were born as a spirit child of God
> **Body:** A spirit body—glorious, but incomplete
> **Parent:** Heavenly Parents
> **Name:** You were called sons and daughters of God
> **Inheritance:** The opportunity to enter mortality, and receive a body
> **Death:** A willing separation from God's presence—a descent into the veil of forgetfulness, to walk by faith and grow by choice

### Second Estate—Mortal Life

> **Birth:** You were born into a physical body
> **Body:** Flesh and blood, vulnerable and aging
> **Parent:** Earthly parents
> **Name:** Given by family; recorded in earthly records
> **Inheritance:** Agency, conscience, and the chance to ascend into the presence of Deity
> **Death:** Physical death—the end of your mortal probation

### Third Estate—Born Again

Just like our mortal birth followed a divine path—so does being born again. The Third Estate mirrors the same structure: there's a birth, a body, a name, a parent, an inheritance... and yes, even a death. But this time, it's spiritual.

> **Birth:** By fire and by the Holy Ghost
> **Body:** A sanctified vessel, made clean through the Spirit
> **Parent:** Christ Himself—*"Ye shall be called the children of Christ"* (Mosiah 5:7).
> **Name:** You take upon you the name of Christ
> Just like a child who is adopted into a new family is given the family name, so are you. The name you carried in sin doesn't follow you. When you're born again, you take on a new identity—His. You are now known by His name
> **Inheritance:** Citizenship in the Church of the Lamb of God.

> **Death:** Death of the old creature, rebirth into a new one to ascend to the next estate

This isn't poetry—this is doctrine. To be born again is not a mere figure of speech. It is an actual spiritual rebirth. You receive a new parent, a new name, and a new spiritual inheritance. You are no longer the same creature you were before—that old creature dies, and a new life begins in Christ.

One writer recognized the shape of this transformation when he said: *"The fulness isn't a checklist—it's a compound gift. It includes a personal visit, a revealed name, a heavenly endowment."*[9]

He saw the shape. And he was right—it's not a title, it's a transformation. It's not a ceremony, it's a birthright. You don't just get instruction. You get a name. A body. A parent. And a place in His house.

## Higher Rungs on the Ladder

Once that gift has come, you are on the straight and narrow way that leads to eternal life. Lehi saw it in vision: a path pressing onward beside the river of water, through mists of darkness, to the tree of life (1 Nephi 8:20).

That path does not begin at the gate—it begins after it opens. Only then do your feet touch the way. As Nephi says: *"Then are ye in this strait and narrow path which leads to eternal life"* (2 Nephi 31:18).

Joseph Smith was taught the same truth. He once explained it in the simplest of ways:

> *"When you climb up a ladder, you must begin at the bottom, and ascend step by step, until you arrive at the top; and so it is with the principles of the gospel—you must begin with the first, and go on until you learn all the principles of exaltation."*[10]

The gospel doesn't end at remission of sins—it rises from there. And here is why: none of the higher rungs on the ladder are accessible if you are still unclean. They would destroy you. You would not be able to endure them. The scriptures warn that impurity would burn you up, or you would cry for the mountains to cover you (D&C 50:55; 84:54; Revelation 6:16).

God, in His love, will never force such glory upon you until you are sanctified enough to bear it.

Joseph gave this assurance: *"God hath not revealed any thing to Joseph, but what he will make known ... even the least Saint may know all things as fast as he is able to bear them" (Joseph Smith, TPJS, p. 149).*

In other words, the Lord unfolds the climb step by step, never withholding what He is willing to give, but granting it as His children are ready to receive.

And so it was with Joseph himself. He was taught about the Church of the Firstborn—a higher order of sanctified beings who are brought into the presence of God, sealed by Him, and made inheritors of eternal life.

These are they who are not just spiritually begotten by Christ, but adopted fully into His eternal household, as sons and daughters of God, joint-heirs with Christ Himself.

And still the ladder rose higher.

Joseph was shown that beyond the gate lay higher ascents—further rungs on the ladder:

> ***The Church of the Firstborn,*** where sanctified souls are received into God's presence and numbered as His sons and daughters (Hebrews 12:23; D&C 76:54).
> **The Second Comforter,** when Jesus Christ Himself appears face to face (John 14:21, 23).
> ***Calling and Election made sure,*** when the promise of eternal life is confirmed to you in mortality (2 Peter 1:10).
> ***The more sure word of prophecy,*** when He seals your exaltation by His own voice (2 Peter 1:19).
> ***The sealing of the Holy Spirit of Promise,*** when your inheritance in eternal life is ratified in heaven (D&C 76:53).

These aren't detours or side paths. They are successive steps—higher rungs of the same ladder, each one built on the last, each one lifting the faithful nearer to God's own presence.

This isn't symbolic. It's not an impression, a warm feeling, or an abstract *"relationship with Jesus."* This is a face-to-face visitation with Jesus Christ Himself.

> *Just like Lehi.*[11]
> *Just like Nephi.*
> *Just like Jacob.*
> *Just like Enos.*

> *Just like Alma.*
> *Just like the Brother of Jared.*
> *Just like Mormon.*
> *Just like Moroni.*

And just like Joseph Smith.

The Book of Mormon testifies of it again and again—from the first page to the last.[12] And the Doctrine and Covenants is laced with invitations from the Lord for His Saints to prepare to receive Him in like manner.[13] Not just believe in Him—but meet Him—face to face.

> *"Then shall ye know that I have seen Jesus, and that he hath talked with me face to face, and that he told me in plain humility, even as a man telleth another in mine own language, concerning these things."* (Ether 12:39)

This is not the end of the road. It's the next step of eternal progression—the continuation of the same pattern that was restored to the earth through Joseph Smith.

In that holy interview, the Lord declares who you are. And where you're going.

This is what it means to have your *calling and election made sure*—when the Lord Himself says, *"Son, thou shalt be exalted."*[14] Joseph taught that this moment is sealed by what he called *the more sure word of prophecy*—the Lord's own voice declaring your exaltation, not a feeling, not an ordinance, not a man-made assumption.

He also learned that this same divine sealing is called being *sealed by the Holy Spirit of Promise.*

> *"Though [the apostles] might hear the voice of God and know that Jesus was the Son of God, this would be no evidence that their election and calling was made sure, that they had part with Christ, and were joint heir with him.*
> *They then would want that more sure word of prophecy, that they were sealed in the heavens and had the promise of eternal life in the kingdom of God.*
> *Then, having this promise sealed unto them, it was an anchor to the soul, sure and steadfast.*
> *Though the thunders might roll and lightnings flash, and earthquakes bellow, and war gather thick around, yet this hope and knowledge would support the soul in every hour of trial, trouble and tribulation.*
> *Then knowledge through our Lord and Savior Jesus Christ is*

> *the grand key that unlocks the glories and mysteries of the kingdom of heaven." (Joseph Smith, TPJS, p. 298)*

This is the anchor of the soul. It is the personal promise from Christ Himself that you are His. That your faith, repentance, and obedience have been accepted by Him. You are given a new name by Him, a name written in the Lambs Book of Life and that your exaltation is assured.

> *"Whoso believeth in God might with surety hope for a better world... which hope cometh of faith, maketh an anchor to the souls of men." (Ether 12:4)*

> *"Ye receive no witness until after the trial of your faith." (Ether 12:6)*

These aren't separate doctrines. They are all the same promise—taught with different language at different times.

> *Second Comforter*
> *Calling and Election Made Sure*
> *Holy Spirit of Promise*
> *Sealed up to Eternal Life*
> *Church of the Firstborn*

They are all different ways of describing the same holy moment. The day Christ calls you His, and seals you His unto eternal life.

These truths were not invented by Joseph—they were restored through him. And when Joseph received them, they were part of the same living pattern we've been learning here. It has always begun the same way:

> *With faith.*
> *With repentance.*
> *With baptism of water.*
> *With sanctification.*
> *With being born again by the baptism of fire and of the Holy Ghost.*

These are not new systems. They are higher rungs of the same ladder.

> *A new birth.*
> *A new body.*
> *A new name.*
> *A greater inheritance.*

But make no mistake, these truths are deep. And we've only just entered the gate.

For now, let's set them on the shelf—knowing the Lord will unfold them when we're ready.

But first—we must be born again. By fire and by the Holy Ghost.

Only then can the next ascent begin.

## What Must We Repent Of?

If entering the Church of the Lamb of God requires repentance and coming unto Christ, then we ought to be asking the obvious follow-up:

Repent of what?

We've already touched on the modern tendency to water down repentance—to treat it like a daily checklist or vague spiritual attitude. But real repentance is specific. It's exacting. And it requires more than regret.

So, the question is: what exactly are we repenting of?

Let's walk through just a few of the things the Lord has said must be left behind:

### 1. All sin.

That seems obvious—but it must be said. Not just the big sins. Not just the public ones.

All sin. All rebellion. Every time we say, *"My will be done,"* instead of His. And every time we pretend it's not sin instead of confessing it for what it really is.

The Lord has no tolerance for half-hearted repentance. The path is narrow. And the price is the whole heart.

> *"I, the Lord, cannot look upon sin with the least degree of allowance." (D&C 1:31)*

This doesn't mean He expects instant perfection, but it does mean He expects real forsaking.

Repentance is not a casual nod to God, repeated day after day, saying, "*Oops, I slipped again—sorry,*" while we go right back to the same behaviors. True repentance is a break, a confession and a forsaking—a turning so complete that the old life dies, and a new life is born.

As Paul wrote, *"our old man is crucified with him, that the body of sin might be destroyed"* (Romans 6:6). We are *"buried with him by baptism into death,"* that we might also rise to *"walk in newness of life"* (Romans 6:4).

In Paul's words again, *"I am crucified with Christ: nevertheless I live; yet not I, but Christ liveth in me"* (Galatians 2:20).

> *"and they were changed in their hearts... and they humbled themselves and put their trust in the true and living God."* (Alma 5:13)

It is the command to stop sinning. Period. The call of the gospel is not *"sin and repent, sin and repent,"* but to turn and forsake—to leave the old life behind.

The Book of Mormon is clear: *"Whosoever repenteth and forsaketh his sins, the same is forgiven, and I, the Lord, remember them no more"* (Mosiah 26:29–30). Forsaking is the key.

Anything less—not naming the sin, not confessing and forsaking—is not repentance at all.

The revelations say the same with equal force:

> *"Go your ways and sin no more; but unto that soul who sinneth shall the former sins return"* (D&C 82:7)

In other words, if sins return, it is because repentance was never complete in the first place.

This is why the idea of *"repenting daily"* is such a dangerous wresting of scripture. If we think we are repenting but continue in the same sins, we are never fully repenting. And if we never fully repent, we are never forgiven. And if we are never forgiven, then we cannot receive the remission of sins and become holy without spot.

The truth about repentance is simple and unbending: *stop sinning.*

> *"...inasmuch as you strip yourselves from jealousies and fears, and humble yourselves before me, for ye are not sufficiently humble, the veil shall be rent and you shall see me and know that I am..."* (D&C 67:10)

We're not talking about perfection overnight. We're talking about genuine turning. Real forsaking. Real fruit.

And here is the promise: when sin is truly forsaken, forgiveness is real. The Spirit comes. The heart is cleansed. And sanctification begins. This is the joy of repentance—not endless struggle with the same chains, but release, freedom, and the power to walk in newness of life.

## 2. Pride.

The Book of Mormon makes it plain: pride is the great stumbling block of the last days. It is the root sin of the devil. The armor of the natural man. It is the attitude that says, *"I already know enough. I'm doing fine. I don't need to be told. I don't need to change."*

Nephi warned:

> *"Because of pride, and because of false teachers, and false doctrine, their churches have become corrupted... they have all gone out of the way." (2 Nephi 28:12)*

Pride shuts the ears and hardens the heart. It blinds us to our own need for God.

Isaiah saw the same condition: *"The whole head is sick, and the whole heart faint. From the sole of the foot even unto the head there is no soundness in it"* (Isaiah 1:5–6).

Avraham Gileadi observed, these wounds and bruises are like those of a slave cast off, left untended and unhealed. That is the state of Jehovah's people when they rebel and alienate themselves from Him.

Yet Isaiah also shows us the antithesis: though the wicked are left without ointment or healing, Jehovah does not deny His balm to the righteous. He promises to heal, restore, and anoint those who repent (Isaiah 30:26; 57:18–19; 61:3).[15]

Judgment is real, but it is not the end. For the humble, healing still waits.

The Book of Mormon echoes the warning:

> *"The pride of this nation, or the people of the Nephites, hath proven their destruction."* (Moroni 8:27)

It was never just wealth or war that undid them—it was pride at the core.

That is why true repentance begins with brokenness. *"Behold, he that is humbled shall be made strong, and shall not be confounded"* (D&C 136:32).

Pride insists, *"I can manage on my own."* Brokenness cries out, *"I need Thee every hour."* Only the second can be received.

And here is the promise: *"Yea, come unto Christ, and be perfected in him, and deny yourselves of all ungodliness... then is his grace sufficient for you"* (Moroni 10:32). Where pride leaves the soul sick and untreated, humility opens the way for Christ's healing touch. The proud are left wounded, but the repentant are anointed, healed, and made strong in Him.

### 3. Trusting in the arm of flesh.

This is one of the hardest to see—especially for religious people. We say we trust God. But in practice, we often lean on systems, credentials, or traditions. We measure safety by the strength of leaders, the opinions of peers, or the approval of men.

Trusting in the arm of flesh is subtle, because it wears a cloak of devotion. It sounds like loyalty, but in reality it is dependence—or worse, idolatry.

Isaiah warned of this again and again: *"They lavish gold out of the bag, and weigh silver in the balance, and hire a goldsmith; and he maketh it a god: they fall down, yea, they worship"* (Isaiah 46:6).

What begins as reverence for something good can become worship of something lesser.

The prophets declare that idols never save: *"They cannot answer, nor save him out of his trouble"* (Isaiah 46:7).

As Avraham Gileadi observed, whether carved from wood and clay in ancient days or fabricated from modern materials and systems, all such inventions are powerless.

The very moment a person looks to them for saving power, he repudiates the only Savior-God. To supplant Jehovah with manmade objects, structures, or ideas is mockery—a desecration of His reality, which resembles nothing made by human hands (Deuteronomy 4:23–25).[16]

The Book of Mormon echoes this warning: *"Cursed is he that putteth his trust in man, or maketh flesh his arm, or shall hearken unto the precepts of men, save their precepts shall be given by the power of the Holy Ghost"* (2 Nephi 28:31).

Dependence on the arm of flesh is not trust in God, no matter how pious it appears.

And here is the promise: *"Fear thou not; for I am with thee: be not dismayed; for I am thy God: I will strengthen thee; yea, I will help thee; yea, I will uphold thee with the right hand of my righteousness...*

*For I the Lord thy God will hold thy right hand, saying unto thee, Fear not; I will help thee"* (Isaiah 41:10, 13). To trust in men is to fall with them. But to trust in God is to be upheld by His own arm, strengthened, helped, and secured in His presence.

### 4. Not Receiving the Holy Ghost.

This one stings. Because many who believe they've received the Holy Ghost have not. They've been confirmed by men—but not baptized by fire. They've been told they have the gift—but show none of the gifts.

My friend, I have said this at least a dozen different ways in this chapter.

The Lord said plainly:

> *"He that rejecteth me, rejecteth my gospel; and he that rejecteth my gospel, rejecteth me. And he that rejecteth me is not my disciple."* (D&C 84:57)

I can't say it any more plainly than this: to not receive the baptism of fire is to not receive Him—to reject the baptism of fire is to reject Christ Himself.

Please, understand that's why repentance matters.

And here is the promise: Alma declared to his people at the waters of Mormon: *"Now I say unto you, if this be the desire of your hearts, what have you against being baptized in the name of the Lord... that he may pour out his Spirit more abundantly upon you?"* (Mosiah 18:10). And when the disciples in Bountiful prayed in faith, *"they were filled with the Holy Ghost and with fire... and angels did come down out of heaven and did minister unto them"* (3 Nephi 19:13–14).

The witness is unmistakable. When repentance is real and faith is exercised, the Lord answers tangibly—with power, with gifts, with His Spirit poured out.

Repentance isn't just about sin, it's about confessing and forsaking, it's about a complete returning.

> *Returning to Christ.*
> *Returning to graft.*
> *Returning to truth.*
> *Returning to the only gate.*

It's not just stopping bad behavior. It's laying down every false tradition, every bad habit, every addiction, every hollow ritual, every false assurance that says, *"I'm good enough."*

If you want to be born again—if you want to be numbered among the Church of the Lamb of God—then you must turn your back on Babylon and fully turn toward Christ.

Confess and forsake—there is no other way.

Everything else must go. Everything.

## You Are Not a Saint Unless You Do This

We've used the word Saint so casually, so automatically, that we've forgotten what it means. Too often it's become just a label, a title, a box you check—something claimed by membership, not proven by holiness.

According to scripture, you are not a Saint because you attend meetings, keep a calling, or wear a name tag. You are not a Saint because you were born into the Church.

You are not a Saint unless you have been sanctified. That's what the word means.

> *"And again we bear record—for we beheld and bear record—that he cannot receive the kingdom of God unless he be sanctified by the Holy Spirit." (D&C 76:116)*
>
> *"There were many... who were pure and spotless before God. Therefore, we call them holy, for they were sanctified." (Moroni 6:4)*
>
> *"For the natural man is an enemy to God, and has been from the fall of Adam, and will be, forever and ever, unless he yields to the enticings of the Holy Spirit, and putteth off the natural man and becometh a saint through the atonement of Christ the Lord, and becometh as a child, submissive, meek, humble, patient, full of love, willing to submit to all things which the Lord seeth fit to inflict upon him, even as a child doth submit to his father." (Mosiah 3:19)*

To be a Saint is to be made holy. To be holy is to be sanctified. To be sanctified is to be cleansed, purified, and filled by the power of the Holy Ghost—not just in symbol, but in reality.

You may say, *"I'm trying. I'm doing my best."* And that's good.

But let's be honest: effort alone does not sanctify. Ordinances alone do not sanctify. Christ sanctifies, through fire and His Spirit. And if that fire hasn't come—if you haven't been changed, if you haven't been cleansed—you haven't yet become what He calls a Saint.

Again, that's why repentance must go deeper. That's why being born again matters. Because you are not a Saint until you are sanctified. Period.

### Conclusion: Enter the Gate

The doctrine is simple. The implications are eternal. Before you are born again, you will be broken. Before you are clean, you will be crushed. Before the fire burns your sins away, the weight of them will fall on you. You are not a Saint until you are sanctified by His Spirit—His fire.

This is not extremism. This is the standard that He set. And it has always been the standard—from Adam to Joseph Smith to you.

But here's the hope:

You don't need to be perfect. You don't need to earn your way into His presence. You don't need man's approval. But you do need one thing—Him.

This is the gate.
This is the Church of the Lamb of God.
And the invitation is still open.

Come to Him.

## Chapter 2 Notes

1 These phrases appear across scripture and Joseph's revelations: *"born again"* (John 3:3; Mosiah 27:25), *"baptism of fire and the Holy Ghost"* (2 Nephi 31:13–14), *"Church of the Firstborn"* (D&C 76:54), *"mighty change of heart"* (Mosiah 5:2), *"Second Comforter"* (John 14:21–23), *"calling and election made sure"* (2 Peter 1:10; D&C 131:5), *"Holy Spirit of Promise"* (Ephesians 1:13; D&C 76:53).

2 Exodus 3:5 – The Lord commands Moses to remove his sandals, for he stands on holy ground.

3 Noah Webster, American Dictionary of the English Language (New York: S. Converse, 1828).

4 Hal M. Wilcox, Experiencing the Mighty Change (Foothill Pub., 1993)

5 Hal M. Wilcox, Experiencing the Mighty Change (Foothill Pub., 1993)

6 2 Nephi 31:17

7 2 Nephi 31:17; Mosiah 4:3; Mosiah 5:2; 3 Nephi 27:20; Romans 8:9–10.

8 Matthew 3:11; 3 Nephi 11:11

9 Robert B. Warcup, Lost Doctrines of the Restoration: Recovering the Fulness of the Gospel of Jesus Christ from Joseph Smith (2022), 30. *"The fulness isn't a checklist—it's a compound gift. It includes a personal visit, a revealed name, a heavenly endowment. That's why it was so rarely received, and so quickly lost."*

10 Joseph Smith (TPJS, p. 348; HC 6:306–307

11 Each of these prophets testified of a personal encounter with the Lord: Lehi (1 Nephi 1:8–14), Nephi (2 Nephi 11:2–3; 31:13–15), Jacob (2 Nephi 2:4; Jacob 2:4; 7:5), Enos (Enos 1:5–8), Alma the Elder (Mosiah 26:14–20), Alma the Younger (Mosiah 27:11–24; Alma 36:22), the Brother of Jared (Ether 3:13–20), Mormon (Mormon 1:15; 3:20), and Moroni (Ether 12:39; Moroni 10:1–2).

12 1 Nephi 1:8; 2 Nephi 2:4; Mosiah 27:25–26; Ether 3:13–16; Moroni 7:48; Moroni 10:31-32

13 D&C 50:45; D&C 67:10; D&C 93:1

14 Joseph Smith, Teachings of the Prophet Joseph Smith, p. 150. *"In answer to the question—'What is the meaning of the sealing power?'—Joseph explained that it was the power by which one's exaltation could be made sure. He said: '...when the Lord has thoroughly proved him, and finds that the man is determined to serve Him at all hazards, then the man will find his calling and election made sure. Then it will be his privilege to receive the*

*other Comforter... When any man obtains this last Comforter, he will have the personage of Jesus Christ to attend him... and the Lord will teach him face to face... and he will say unto him, Son, thou shalt be exalted.'"*

15 Avraham Gileadi, IsaiahExplained.com, "Apocalyptic Commentary," Isaiah 1:5-6

16 Avraham Gileadi, IsaiahExplained.com, *"Seven Spiritual Levels of Humanity"* Paraphrase: Gileadi points out that man-made inventions—whether ancient idols carved from wood or clay, or modern systems and ideas—are powerless to save; when one looks to them for salvation, one repudiates Jehovah.

# Interlude

## TEACH THE CHILDREN

### Guiding Them to the Gate—and to the Keeper of It

I held my grandson's hand during a quiet walk after Thanksgiving dinner—his small fingers wrapped around mine, his steps uncertain but full of wonder.

Little children enter the world without pretense or assumption. Everything is new. Everything is honest. A passing car captures their attention. The rumble of a distant train becomes an event. Even a drifting leaf can hold their entire imagination.

As we walked, I tried to see the world the way he does. To slow down. To notice. To remember what it's like to encounter life with unfiltered eyes.

And in that moment—simple, quiet, unforced—something pressed upon my heart with unmistakable clarity:

***"Teach the children."***

It didn't come as a rebuke.
It didn't come as a burden.
It came as a reminder.

Every parent begins with a sincere desire to bless their children. We share what we've learned, what anchored us, and what we believe will help them navigate life with faith and confidence. Our motives are loving and our efforts genuine.

But each of us has inherited traditions alongside truth. Sometimes we pass on ideas that feel familiar rather than revealed—tradition not anchored in truth—hoping they'll help, not realizing they may cloud what God intended to be clear.

A sincere belief can still be incomplete. A cherished tradition can still be untrue. And even the smallest misunderstanding—planted early—can grow roots deep inside a child's life.

James Allen described this with piercing clarity more than a century ago. In *As a Man Thinketh* (1903), he taught that a single errant thought, if accepted and repeated, crystallizes into habit. Habits become character. Character becomes destiny.

What we plant in the soil of a child's mind will grow—whether we meant to plant that seed or not.

That's why the impression came with such weight:

***"Teach the children."***

Teach them clearly.
Teach them early.
Teach them truth.

The question eventually reaches every parent and grandparent, every teacher and mentor, every soul who has ever placed their hand in the life of a child:

**Will you pass on truth—or will you pass on tradition?**

The next morning the impression returned, only stronger.

It felt less like a passing thought and more like a reminder of something ancient and essential—something woven into the very fabric of God's dealings with His people.

As I sat with it, a scripture I've known for years came quietly to mind:

> *"We talk of Christ, we rejoice in Christ, we preach of Christ, we prophesy of Christ... that our children may know to what source they may look for a remission of their sins."* (2 Nephi 25:26)

In that moment, the meaning of the prompting became clear.

Teaching the children isn't merely passing along stories or traditions. It's giving them a true knowledge of the One who can cleanse them, guide them, and redeem them. It's helping them know where to turn when they need Him most.

The prompting wasn't simply about nurturing a grandchild or enjoying a quiet walk. It was about the responsibility God places upon every parent and grandparent—to speak of Christ in such plainness that our children know exactly where to look when the time comes for them to seek forgiveness, cleansing, and new life.

It struck me with sobering clarity that children don't automatically inherit truth. They inherit whatever we teach them—whether it's accurate or not, whether it lifts or misleads, whether it points them to Christ or simply gives them comforting assumptions.

And the more I considered this, the more I understood why the Lord pressed *"Teach the children"* upon my heart with such insistence.

When we pass on truth clearly, the next generation stands on solid ground. They know where to turn. They know whom to trust. They know where life begins and where healing comes.

But when truth is clouded—or mingled with tradition, or replaced with assumptions that sound right but aren't—a child grows up believing something their parent never intended to distort. The parent believes they're helping. The child believes they're safe. But the path tilts slightly, almost imperceptibly, and years later that small deviation becomes a canyon.

That's why the impression felt so weighty.

The Lord wasn't merely reminding me to love my grandson. He was reminding me to **father** him, to **instruct** him, to **hand him truth** in a world overflowing with inherited ideas that feel comfortable but lack power.

What we teach becomes the foundation they build their life upon.

What we fail to teach leaves them on sand when the storms come.

The wise man built on a rock, and when the rains fell and the winds beat upon his house, it did not fall. But the man who built on sand had no foundation beneath him, and when the same storms came, the fall of his house was great. (3 Nephi 14:24–27)

> *"And now, remember... it is upon the rock of our Redeemer, who is Christ, the Son of God, that ye must build your foundation; that when the devil shall send forth his mighty winds... it shall have no power over you."* (Helaman 5:12)

If we want to build the strongest foundation of Christ in a child's life, Nephi gave us the clearest counsel. We talk of Him, we rejoice in Him, we teach of Him, and we center our lives on Him.

And this has been God's way from the very beginning.

When He taught Adam about repentance, baptism, the remission of sins, and being born of the Spirit, He also gave a command that still stands today: *"Teach these things freely unto your children."* (Moses 6:58)

That word—freely—carries a world of meaning.

It means:

> **Openly,** not in secrecy.
> **Plainly,** not in complexity or obscurity.
> **Generously,** without holding anything back.
> **Naturally,** as effortlessly as a parent breathes.
> **Without coercion,** for truth offered freely carries its own power.

This ancient mandate reveals something essential about God's order: **What He gives to a parent becomes the inheritance of their**

**children.** Truth is meant to pass from one generation to the next with clarity and love.

When we pass truth down *freely*—openly, plainly, and without distortion—the next generation stands on solid ground.

They know where to turn. They know whom to trust. They know how to come unto Christ.

But when tradition replaces plain truth—even unintentionally—a fog settles over the rising generation, a veil God never placed upon them.

Lehi saw these as the mists of darkness: subtle influences that blind the eyes and harden the hearts of the children of men, leading them away into broad roads where they are lost. (1 Nephi 12:17)

History is full of examples.

For centuries, the Bible was taught mainly in Latin—spoken by priests but not understood by most believers. Ordinary men and women longed to know God's word for themselves, yet were told they could not read it (a condition that remained until reformers like Wycliffe and Tyndale fought to place the scriptures in the hands of the common people).

Good parents in those generations taught their children the little they had been told, believing it was enough. But the plainness of truth was still lost—not because they hated the scriptures, but because a tradition had grown up around them that kept the word of God closed.

No malice was required. Just a long chain of inherited assumptions. A small shift, repeated over time, became a wide departure.

This is how fountains become polluted—not by sudden corruption, but by gradual accumulation. Precepts of men mingle with scripture. Traditions pass forward with love but without light.

And so the command stands unchanged from the days of Adam until now:

> Teach these things freely.
> Teach them plainly.
> Teach them openly.
> Teach them without adding or withholding.
> **Let truth flow through you to your children as naturally as breath.**

When parents teach truth clearly, their children inherit clarity. When they don't, their children inherit confusion they never deserved.

Even with sincere hearts and the best intentions, clarity fades across generations unless truth is preserved. Scripture warns us that revealed doctrine must remain pure, because over time even small shifts in teaching and understanding can cloud what God intended to be plain.

Plain doctrine handed down with plainness stays sharp. But when it mingles with tradition—even slightly—its edges begin to blur.

The Book of Mormon describes this with sobering precision. It speaks of *"the traditions of the fathers"*—beliefs passed down with love, but not always with accuracy. These traditions shaped entire peoples and influenced choices for centuries.

But the scriptures make clear that such drift is never neutral. The adversary works through small errors and subtle assumptions, gently leading souls away from what God intended to be plain, until light is lost and blindness sets in—long before rebellion ever enters the heart.

Joseph Smith received a revelation that pulls back the curtain on how this happens. The Lord said:

> *"Every spirit of man was innocent in the beginning; and God having redeemed man from the fall, men became again, in their infant state, innocent before God.*
>
> *And that wicked one cometh and taketh away light and truth, through disobedience, from the children of men, and because of the tradition of their fathers."* (D&C 93:38–39)

In just a few lines, the Lord describes the whole story of a soul.

Every child begins innocent before God—clean, unburdened, full of light. Heaven sees them as redeemed from the fall, ready to receive truth. That's the starting point.

And then comes the warning**: the wicked one comes to take away light and truth.**

> He doesn't take it by violence.
> He doesn't take it by open rebellion.
> He doesn't take it by some dramatic, obvious act of evil.
>
> **He takes it by tradition.**

Through inherited misunderstandings. Through beliefs passed from one generation to the next without being weighed against the word of God. Through teachings that sound right, feel familiar, and are offered with love—yet lack the clarity that protects a child's soul.

The wicked one doesn't need to appear to the child. He only needs someone to teach the child something God didn't say.

**Light** is taken away, not usually by hatred, but by **mis-teaching** or **incomplete teaching**.

**Truth** is lost, not always by deliberate rejection, but by inherited **unbelief** and doctrine that is **incomplete** or **watered down**.

**The Book of Mormon gives living examples of this pattern.**

Nephi saw it among the Jews. They had the scriptures, but *"because of the precepts of men"* (2 Nephi 28:14), they stumbled when the Messiah stood before them. Their hearts were sincere, but their understanding had been shaped more by tradition than revelation.

Alma saw it in the Lamanites, who *"were taught to hate"* by traditions so old their origin was forgotten (Alma 9:16–17). That hatred didn't begin with the children who carried it—it began generations earlier and was simply handed down.

Even the righteous Nephites struggled with this drift. Alma warned that his own people had begun to *"teach the children of men"* things that were *"not correct"* (Alma 31:17), and that these errors would lead them into pride and unbelief if left uncorrected.

The pattern is consistent throughout the record:

> *a misunderstanding becomes an assumption, an assumption becomes a tradition, and a tradition becomes the lens through which generations interpret the word of God.*

None of this happens because parents want to harm their children. On the contrary—parents teach what they sincerely believe will help. They pass down the light they have, even when that light has dimmed from what God gave in the beginning.

This is why the command given to Adam still stands with such urgency:

> Teach these things freely.
> Teach them plainly.
> Teach them openly.
> Teach them without adding or withholding.
> **Let truth flow to the next generation in its purity, without mixture.**

When parents teach truth clearly, their children inherit clarity. When they don't, their children inherit confusion God never intended them to bear.

## A Beloved Tradition That Deserves Plainness

And when I speak of children, I also mean every soul who is newly baptized—whether they are eight or eighty—because all of us inherit what we are taught long before we are born again by fire.

There is a tradition almost every Latter-day Saint child receives with joy: when they are baptized, they *"join the Church."*

In one sense, this is completely true. Their name is added to the records. Their membership becomes official. They are welcomed and celebrated as part of a believing community, and there is nothing dishonest or harmful about any of that.

In fact, during the confirmation ordinance itself, hands are placed upon their head and it is declared plainly that they are now a member of the Church.

## What Confirmation Does Not Give

But here is where plainness must replace tradition.

In every baptism service—whether the person is eight or eighty—there is always a talk about baptism and a talk about confirmation. And in almost every talk about confirmation, the same familiar line is spoken with sincerity and confidence:

*"Today, hands will be placed on your head and you will receive the Holy Ghost."*

It is spoken by parents, leaders, teachers, and friends.

It is repeated so often, and with such certainty, that it becomes the living belief of nearly every member of the Church.

**But it is not true.**

No ordinance of man can bestow the Holy Ghost. No phrase spoken in a circle of priesthood holders can deliver the fire of God. The ordinance invites, it blesses, it counsels—but it does not, and cannot, give the gift itself.

> ***Only Christ bestows the Holy Ghost.***
> ***Only Christ baptizes with fire.***

When a newly baptized soul is told—without hesitation—that they *"got the Holy Ghost"* during confirmation, they naturally assume the journey is complete, even if nothing inside them has changed.

They believe they already received the gift, not realizing scripture teaches no one can receive the Holy Ghost until their sins are remitted by fire. That fire comes only through Christ. He alone grants the remission; He alone gives the gift.

But if a soul believes all of that already happened, they assume they already possess the greatest gift God can give. And that is the tragedy: why would anyone seek a gift they're convinced they already received?

This is where tradition quietly steals what scripture teaches so plainly. They have not received the fire. They have not received the remission. They have not received the Holy Ghost. Yet because tradition told them they did, they may never realize there is still a gift Christ stands ready to give.

Tradition can blind a soul to its own need—and the gate Nephi taught remains closed.

Once that belief settles into the heart, they may never seek the real baptism of fire that Christ promised to give.

## Membership Cannot Open the Gate

From the time they are very young, nearly every Latter-day Saint is shaped by three quiet traditions that create the feeling of belonging long before baptism ever takes place—a feeling that becomes crystallized into hard certainty at confirmation.

**First, the baby blessing.**

In that sacred circle the father gives the child a name and a blessing, and speaks the words, *"the name by which the child will be known on the records of the Church"*—and at that moment their beautiful child is placed among the Saints.

**Second, the child-of-record entry.**

Once a child has been named and blessed, their name is added to the Church's records and they become a *"child of record."* This official addition to Church records gently reinforces the idea that something meaningful began at birth.

**Third, the phrase *"born under the covenant."***

Children of sealed parents are told they were born within the covenant and belong to an eternal family from the beginning, adding spiritual weight to their sense of unconditional belonging.

And **there's a fourth tradition**—so familiar, so often repeated, that almost no one pauses to hear what the words actually say.

At baptism and confirmation, hands are placed upon the head and the officiator speaks:

*"...and confirm you a member of The Church of Jesus Christ of Latter-day Saints, and say unto you, receive the Holy Ghost."*

Pay close attention to those words.

They make clear where the tradition goes off course. The officiator is confirming one thing and one thing only: that the newly baptized individual is now a member of The Church of Jesus Christ of Latter-day Saints.

But the officiator is not confirming that they have received the Holy Ghost. He's giving an invitation—an injunction—to the individual:

*"Seek for and receive the Holy Ghost."*

This receiving may come immediately, as it often does in the Book of Mormon. It may come soon after. It may come later. But it doesn't come simply because hands were placed upon the head or because the words were spoken.

Yet so many Latter-day Saints instinctively hear something very different:

*"...and confirm that you have received the Holy Ghost."*

The mind fills in the meaning automatically. The heart accepts it wholeheartedly. And so the conviction forms quietly—and the tradition solidifies in their hearts as actual lived fact.

**But this is where plainness must be spoken.**

> Membership is not the gate.
> Confirmation is not the cleansing.

No earthly tradition, no matter how beautiful or sincere, writes a name in the Lamb's book of life.

John saw that only those whose names *were "written in the Lamb's book of life"* would enter the holy city (Revelation 21:27).

A clerk may record a name on earth, but only Christ can write a name in His book. His record isn't a list of participants—it's a record of the redeemed. Those who have repented, received remission through His grace, and been made new by the baptism of fire and the Holy Ghost.

> One record marks community—the other record marks cleansing.
> One welcomes a soul among the Saints—the other welcomes a soul through the gate.

Nephi's words are unmistakable:

> *"For the gate by which ye should enter is repentance and baptism by water; and then cometh a remission of your sins by fire and by the Holy Ghost."* (2 Nephi 31:17)

This is the beginning. This is the gate. This is the moment a soul enters the Church of the Lamb of God.

If a person grows up believing they've been *"inside"* since childhood—because of a blessing, a record, a sealing, or the familiar words of confirmation—they may never look for the very gate God Himself provided.

Tradition may place a name among the Saints, with records that welcome you in. But only fire can open the gate and let you enter the way.

---

Baptism at eight is a joyful moment. A child chooses faith, family gathers, and they're welcomed with love. Nothing about that moment should be diminished.

But because it's so sacred, many children grow up assuming everything God promises in the doctrine of Christ happened the day they were baptized and confirmed.

The wording of the ordinance reinforces this assumption. Hands are placed on their head, they're confirmed a member of the Church, and then they're invited to *"receive the Holy Ghost."*

Most hear this as something completed rather than something the Lord will give after repentance and remission.

But scripture teaches a clear order: **remission of sins first, then the Spirit.**

Mosiah taught that when a people received forgiveness, *"ye shall be called the children of Christ... and ye are made free"* and numbered among His people (Mosiah 5:7).

Nephi taught that this remission comes only after baptism by water and the baptism of fire and the Holy Ghost.

Christ alone brings that fire. He alone grants the remission. He alone writes the names of the redeemed in His book, for He is the keeper of the gate, and *"He employeth no servant there"* (2 Nephi 9:41). No ritual can do what He alone performs.

But when a child is taught that all of this already happened—that they *"got the Holy Ghost"* at eight years old—they naturally assume they already possess the greatest gift God can give. And this is the quiet tragedy: why seek what you think you already have?

These assumptions don't come from rebellion. They come from tradition that spoke warmly but not plainly enough. And clarity matters, because when a child understands the order of things, their expectations shift. They begin to look forward with hope for what the Lord Himself will do—not automatically because of a ritual, but personally and intentionally.

When the Holy Ghost truly comes, the change is unmistakable. A soul feels clean. The pull of old desires weakens. Something new begins to live inside them. This is the spiritual rebirth Christ promised—the moment when forgiveness becomes real and a name is written in the Lamb's book of life.

When children understand this, their view of the journey changes. They no longer see baptism at eight as the end, but the beginning of something deeper. They feel a desire to repent more sincerely. They want to be changed, not simply counted. They want to become new creatures in Christ, not the old person with a new status. They begin to hope for the new life Christ alone can give.

There is also a truth about teaching that humbles every parent. We can explain the doctrine plainly and clear away misunderstanding. We can point a child toward Christ with sincerity and love.

But we cannot give them the Holy Ghost. We cannot produce the fire. We cannot write their name in the Savior's book. Only Christ can do that.

Our stewardship is to teach plainly and trust that Christ will meet them when they seek Him.

This truth is both humbling and liberating. It means our responsibility isn't to persuade or pressure—it's to prepare and invite.

Paul understood this when he wrote that his preaching was *"not with enticing words of man's wisdom,"* but in the power of God, *"that your faith should not stand in the wisdom of men, but in the power of God"* (1 Corinthians 2:4–5). The same holds true in our homes. A parent's words aren't enough unless the Lord makes them so.

I've learned that the preparation of the teacher matters as much as the teaching itself.

If I speak truth but live in contradiction to it, I place a veil between heaven and my children. But when I speak with sincerity, when I teach with meekness, and when I seek Christ before I speak of Him, something changes. Christ joins the conversation. He confirms what is true. He carries the message to places my words cannot reach.

This is how simple moments become sacred. A child suddenly understands. A heart softens. A question opens the way to something deeper—not because the parent was eloquent, but because Christ was present.

This, too, is part of our stewardship: helping our children recognize His voice.

I point it out when it comes. When peace settles after reading scripture, I say, *"Do you feel that? That is the Lord confirming what we just read."* When a prompting comes to them and they act on it, I acknowledge it: *"You listened. That is how He guides you."*

My hope is that they learn to trust His voice more than mine, more than tradition, more than the noise of the world.

Because the day will come when they stand on their own before Him. And in that moment, the question won't be, *"What did my parents tell me?"* but *"What has the Lord Himself made known to my heart?"*

> My part is to teach plainly. His part is to make truth alive. And I trust Him to meet them when they seek Him.

This brings us to something that must be faced honestly. Even sincere teaching, if grounded in an inherited assumption, can send a child in a direction the Lord never intended.

This is how a warm tradition, spoken with love, can unintentionally obscure the path a child must walk to come to Christ. It doesn't diminish the sincerity of parents or leaders—it simply reveals how powerful an unexamined assumption can become over time.

This is why God commanded Adam to teach the doctrine of Christ freely and plainly. It's why He warned Joseph that light and truth are taken from children *"because of the tradition of their fathers"* (D&C 93:39). And it's why the impression to teach the children carried such weight.

He's calling us to clarify the path so the next generation can seek Him with open eyes and open hearts—so they can find the real gate, experience the real rebirth, and enter the real Church of the Lamb.

### The Church of the Lamb

The Church of the Lamb isn't defined by earthly records or membership rolls. It's not complicated, but it is deeply spiritual. Those who belong to Christ are those who have been changed by Him.

King Benjamin taught that after his people cried out for mercy, *"the Spirit of the Lord came upon them"* and they received a remission of their sins. Only then did he say they had become the children of Christ and were numbered among His people (Mosiah 4:1–3; Mosiah 5:7–9). Their belonging didn't rest on a date, a record, or ritual—it rested on what God had done within them.

Alma asked his people whether they had *"been spiritually born of God,"* whether they had received His image in their countenance, and whether they felt to sing the song of redeeming love (Alma 5:14, 26). These were the marks of true belonging—not lineage, not community standing, not a name on a roll, but spiritual rebirth and a heart made clean.

Christ Himself declared that those who are *"baptized with fire and with the Holy Ghost"* are His (3 Nephi 9:20). He taught that those not yet born again must come unto Him and be converted (3 Nephi 18–19).

To Nicodemus He said plainly that unless a person is *"born of water and of the Spirit,"* they cannot enter the kingdom of God (John 3:5). The Spirit gives life. The power comes from above.

Nephi taught the same doctrine with unmistakable clarity. The *"gate"* into the way of Christ is repentance, baptism by water, remission of sins, and reception of the Holy Ghost (2 Nephi 31:17–18). This sequence—always this sequence—opens the path of discipleship and places a soul in Christ's church.

John the Revelator described the heavenly record that matches this transformation. Only those who overcome through the Lamb, who keep His commandments, and who are purified through His atoning blood are written *"in the Lamb's book of life"* (Revelation 3:5; Revelation 21:27). This book is not an earthly ledger. It is the record of those made clean by Christ and sealed to Him by His Spirit.

Every one of these witnesses—Benjamin, Alma, Nephi, Jesus Christ, and John—teaches the same truth:

> **Those** who belong to the Church of the Lamb are those who have been redeemed by the Lamb.
> **Those** whose names are written in His book are those who have been cleansed by His power.
> **Those** who are His are those who have experienced the rebirth He alone can give.

This is why teaching our children plainly matters so deeply.

> These experiences cannot be inherited.
> They cannot be assumed.
> They cannot be conferred by tradition.
> They cannot be transferred by ritual alone.
> They cannot be bestowed by any mortal hand.

A parent may prepare a child, guide a child, pray for a child, and place their hands upon a child in blessing. But only Christ can remit sins. Only Christ can pour out His Spirit. Only Christ can change a heart, purify a soul, and write a name in His book.

When we teach doctrine clearly, a child understands where to look. When we teach truth plainly, a child knows Whom to seek. And when they seek Christ with full purpose of heart, He opens the gate.

To teach the doctrine of Christ freely is to give a child something priceless: a straight path, an honest invitation, and the confidence to come to the One who alone can save.

### My Invitation

All of this settled on me with unexpected weight. The walk with my grandson, the quiet impression, the scriptures I'd loved for years—they came together with a clarity I hadn't felt before.

I realized the Lord wasn't simply reminding me to cherish the little ones in my family. He was reminding me of the responsibility I carry as a father and a grandfather. The truths God revealed through Joseph were always meant to be taught in the home, passed from heart to heart, one generation at a time.

Whether my child is two or thirty-three, I'm still a father. A father's stewardship doesn't expire with age or circumstance. My calling is to teach what is true, not merely what is familiar—to pass on what God has revealed, not what tradition has handed down.

I've also learned to pause and examine my own assumptions. Sometimes I've taught things simply because they were familiar, or because they were spoken by people I trusted, without realizing they were tradition rather than truth. With time, the Lord has taught me to ask a simple question whenever I speak of Him: "Is this something God has revealed, or something I inherited?"

That question has become a safeguard. It slows me down just enough to listen. It helps me separate what the Spirit confirms from what has merely been repeated. And it's given me the courage to let go of ideas that once felt comfortable but didn't rest on the word of Christ.

My purpose in this is clear: to give my children and grandchildren the chance to seek Christ for themselves with open eyes and honest hearts.

I can't repent for them, believe for them, or be reborn for them. But I can prepare them. I can guide them. I can pray for them. I can give them the plainness I didn't always receive. And I can show them the way through my living example—just as Lehi did for his sons, who later testified that they themselves had seen the Redeemer (2 Nephi 11:2–3).

This is the pattern from the beginning. Adam was commanded to teach his children freely. Nephi taught Jacob. Mothers taught their little ones in the wilderness. Alma taught his son with tears. The Restoration was always meant to be carried in families, not just institutions.

I can't choose Christ for my children, but I can make sure the path before them is clear. I can clear away the fog tradition placed in front of them. And I can offer them a straight course to the One who opens the gate, pours out His Spirit, writes the names, and claims His people as His.

This is why the impression mattered.

This is why it wouldn't leave.

This is why this Interlude exists.

This is my invitation to you.

The heart of a child is precious. Their beginning is innocent. And the stewardship to teach them truth—plain, unclouded, and centered in Christ—is one of the holiest trusts God gives to a parent.

As I considered all of this, my thoughts turned to my own children—and to every child who looks to a parent with trust and expectation. It doesn't matter whether they're small and learning to walk, or grown and navigating their own lives; a parent's stewardship doesn't end with age.

Whenever a child comes to us with sincere questions about God, about repentance, or about what it means to follow Christ, something sacred is taking place. Their heart opens. Their mind begins to search. And what we teach in those moments can either clear their path or cloud it.

I cannot walk their path for them, but I can give them truth. I can't live their discipleship, but I can show them the way through my own example. I can't force belief, but I can offer them the plainness I didn't always receive.

That's what the Lord impressed upon me—that my responsibility isn't to control outcomes, but to pass on light without mixture.

And when I discover that I've already passed on a tradition not grounded in truth, I've learned not to despair. Children respond to humility. They recognize sincerity. A gentle correction is often more powerful than the original teaching ever was.

Christ can correct misunderstandings as easily as He heals hearts, and He can fill in the gaps where my words have fallen short. It's never too late to teach plainly.

Every parent knows the desire we carry for our children: that they be protected, that they be guided, that they be clean, and that they come to know Christ for themselves. We want them to recognize His path when they see it. We want the truths we teach to lift and clarify. And we want our teaching to point them directly to the One who saves.

These thoughts have stayed with me, shaping how I see my role as a father and grandfather. The Lord's invitation was simple and unmistakable:

> *Teach the children.*
> *Teach them freely.*
> *Teach them truth.*

I offer this Interlude not as a scholar or expert, but simply as a parent who has seen how easily tradition can cloud the path to Christ.

If you're reading these words, you carry your own stewardship—whether over children, grandchildren, students, or anyone who looks to you for light. Their hearts trust you. Their minds listen to you. And what you teach may shape how they understand God for the rest of their lives.

You don't need to be perfect to teach them. You don't need a title or position. What they need from you is plainness, honesty, humility, truth, and love.

They need to see you seeking Christ.

They need to hear you speak of Him without fear or hesitation.

They need to watch you walk toward Him with real intent.

And they need truth taught clearly, so they know where to look when the time comes for them to seek a remission of their own sins. You know as well as I do that time will come. As surely as the sun will rise tomorrow, they will need to know how to find Him.

This is the purpose behind every scripture we've read, every example we've considered, and every warning about tradition we've uncovered. The Lord entrusted these little ones to us. Their journey begins with what we place in their hands.

So speak of Christ. Rejoice in Christ. Teach of Christ.

Show them the way to Him by your own steps upon the path.

For the scriptures testify:

> *"We talk of Christ, we rejoice in Christ, we preach of Christ, we prophesy of Christ... that our children may know to what source they may look for a remission of their sins."* (2 Nephi 25:26)

This is the calling. This is the stewardship. This is the way we prepare the next generation to come unto Him.

*We teach the gate,*
*the water, fire—*
*the path the Lord*
*Himself requires.*

*And as they seek,*
*His love is shown.*
*He leads them in,*
*and makes them His own.*

# True Priesthood & True Keys

## The Power of God Made Manifest

---

### A Great Question

A few days ago, my son asked me a question I didn't have an immediate answer for.

He said, *"Dad, I get what you're saying about being born again—but then why does the Book of Mormon and Doctrine and Covenants say we have to be baptized by someone with authority?"*

It stopped me cold. Not because I didn't believe there was an answer. But because I realized in that moment how much baggage is wrapped around that word—authority.

I'd just spent all this time showing him how the real gospel is about transformation, not performance. That the Church of the Lamb is made up of those who repent and receive the Holy Ghost. That being baptized by water alone doesn't make someone a Saint—being baptized by fire and being sanctified by the Spirit does.

And now here he was, asking the perfect follow-up.

Who has the authority to baptize someone in the name of Jesus Christ?

It's a question that sits right at the center of everything Joseph Smith taught.

This chapter is about finding that answer. Not through speculation. Not through tradition. But by going back to the scriptures and revelations the Lord gave through Joseph Smith—starting with what priesthood really is, and what it's for.

### What Is Authority?

So, what is this thing the scriptures call authority? Is it a title, or a calling, or a certification, or a credential? Is it being set apart by men? Is it holding an office? Is it something only men can have? Is it the power some men hold over other men?

That's often how people think of it—that a person is *"authorized"* when someone lays hands on their head and declares it so. But that only raises another question: how was that person authorized in the first place?

Let's cut to the chase. If we're going to take the scriptures seriously—especially the ones revealed through Joseph—we have to let go of quite a few of those kinds of assumptions.

Many of us first heard the story that John the Baptist visited Joseph Smith and Oliver Cowdery to restore priesthood.

For many, that account is woven deeply into memory and devotion.

I understand that, because I was a wide-eyed deacon once, taught from my youth to believe this story as a pillar of my faith. Those moments felt sacred, and I hold them tenderly even now.

That is why it deserves to be approached with gentleness and care. And I promise to do so—with honesty, but also with empathy.

So if what follows feels different from what you've always heard, know that I am not dismissing the faith you've carried. I am walking the same path you are—seeking to set aside assumptions, to let scripture and Joseph's own words teach us what authority really is.

As I studied the record for myself, I was surprised to discover that Joseph never wrote or preached the account we now know so well.

The earliest appearance of the John the Baptist story comes not from Joseph, but from Oliver Cowdery in 1834–35. And the short verse now printed as D&C 13 wasn't added to the Doctrine and Covenants until 1876—more than thirty years after Joseph's death.[1]

That realization made me pause.
It wasn't easy to hear.

But then I found something that helped me understand more clearly.

In Joseph's lifetime revelations and sermons, the words *Aaronic priesthood* never appear at all.

And when I searched the Book of Mormon, I realized the same thing: not once does it mention an Aaronic priesthood or an order after Aaron.

That silence wasn't an oversight. It was a witness. It showed me what Joseph had really learned and taught.

And what he taught was something far greater.

He taught that all priesthood is one—after the order of the Son of God. That authority doesn't come from lineage, or office, or even from men laying hands.

Because real authority doesn't come from ordination. It comes from God. It always has.

It comes from God Himself, bearing witness and conferring power on the sanctified.

When I read Alma's words, I could see Joseph's pattern clearly:

> *"They were called and prepared from the foundation of the world... on account of their exceeding faith and good works."* (Alma 13:3)

They were sanctified, and their garments were washed white through the blood of the Lamb (Alma 13:11). That is priesthood.

When I read Moroni's record, it struck even deeper:

> *"They ordained them by the power of the Holy Ghost, which was in them."* (Moroni 3:4)

Authority came not from men, but from God bearing witness and conferring power.

That was the way in Nephite days, and Joseph testified of the same in his own revelations.

When I came again to Joseph's words in D&C 121, I realized how consistent it all was:

> *"The rights of the priesthood are inseparably connected with the powers of heaven, and... cannot be controlled nor handled only upon the principles of righteousness."* (D&C 121:36)

Titles, offices, or structures could never substitute for that righteousness. If unrighteousness appeared, the Spirit—and the authority—would withdraw.

This is what Joseph understood: priesthood was never a ladder of offices; it was a living current of power from heaven, given by God's voice to those prepared through faith, sanctification, and holiness.

Without it, as Joseph's revelation declared, *"no man can see the face of God, even the Father, and live"* (D&C 84:22).

Israel was offered that gift once, but they shrank back in fear. Instead of standing in His presence, they received a lesser portion—outward ordinances instead of open vision, shadows instead of fulness. We will return to that story shortly, because it reveals not just their choice, but the very mandate God places on His prophets in every generation.

But the question becomes: Will we prepare ourselves to endure His presence, as Enoch and Joseph did? Or will we, like Israel at Sinai, shrink back in fear and ask another to go in our place?

That is why Joseph's witness matters so deeply to me: priesthood is not structure, it is presence. Not men conferring titles, but God conferring power.

That is where Joseph always pointed—away from hierarchy, and into the arms of the living God who calls, sanctifies, and reveals Himself.

Right there, is where we'll begin.

## Priesthood from Heaven

Just like my son, Joseph had questions.

He wasn't given a handbook. He didn't have a church to guide him. He had no titles, no mentors, no training—only the plates before him and a command from heaven to begin.

But where do you even begin?

He must have asked: What is faith? What is power? What does it mean to act in God's name? How do I know if I'm authorized? How does anyone receive that kind of trust from heaven?

And then—over time, and almost always through the very words he was translating—Joseph began to learn.

The first record he worked on was Lehi's.

Those pages are now lost. But we know how they must have ended—because Nephi preserved the key detail on page one of his own record.

Right there we learn that Lehi saw God sitting upon His throne.

> *"He thought he saw God sitting upon his throne, surrounded with numberless concourses of angels... And it came to pass that he saw One descending out of the midst of heaven..."* (1 Nephi 1:8–9)

He saw angels. He received commandments. And he left Jerusalem.

The voice of the Lord called him to preach repentance (1 Nephi 1:18). The same voice warned him to flee (1 Nephi 2:1–2). The same voice commanded him to retrieve the brass plates (1 Nephi 3:4). Do you see how the sequence unfolds?

There was no structure around him. No visible ordination. No earthly authority giving permission. Just God—and a man who obeyed Him. That's the pattern.

That obedience became authority.

Joseph must have seen it. Because the same thing was happening to him.

As he continued translating, he watched Lehi's son Nephi, walk the same path.

Nephi sought revelation. He believed in the voice of the Spirit. He obeyed when others mocked. Eventually, Nephi himself would see the Lord.

His record says it plainly: *"I have seen my Redeemer"* (2 Nephi 11:2). And later, *"My brother Jacob also has seen him"* (2 Nephi 11:3).

This was the pattern Joseph was seeing. Authority from God came by voice. It was confirmed by obedience. And it led to the Lord.

Next came King Benjamin.

He labored with his own hands. He taught his people with boldness. He gave his life not to rule—but to prepare them for something higher.

He called them together at the end of his ministry to deliver one final message. He taught of Christ. He taught of the coming redemption. And then something astonishing happened.

The entire group fell to the ground.

They cried aloud with one voice. They said they believed in Jesus Christ, and that His Spirit had changed them. They said their hearts had been purified and they had no more desire to do evil (Mosiah 5:2, 5, 7).

King Benjamin told them they had been spiritually begotten of God.

This was the baptism of fire. And it came not through structure—but through a man whose voice had authority because it carried the power of heaven.

Then Joseph met Abinadi.

Abinadi stood before an evil king who ruled over false priests. He taught truth. He spoke boldly. He testified of Christ. And he was killed (Mosiah 11–17).

But one man believed him.

Alma heard the words of Abinadi. He fled from King Noah's court. He was moved by the Spirit to write down everything he could remember. And then he began to teach others the truths he had learned.

He brought them to the waters of Mormon. And he baptized them *"having authority from the Almighty God"* (Mosiah 18:13).

Notice he didn't say, *"Having authority from King Noah."* There was no visible ordination. No administrative line. Only a voice that had pierced him—and a people willing to follow it.

Joseph must have seen this pattern building.

Next came Alma's son. And the sons of Mosiah.

They rebelled against the church. They fought against the truth. Until others—righteous men and women—began to fast and pray for their redemption (Mosiah 27:14).

An angel came (Mosiah 27:11–17). He called Alma to repentance. And for three days, Alma lay in darkness until he called upon Christ to redeem him:

> *"Nevertheless, after wading through much tribulation, repenting nigh unto death, the Lord in mercy hath seen fit to snatch me out of an everlasting burning, and I am born of God."* (Mosiah 27:28)

He was changed. He was born of God. And he spent the rest of his life trying to bring others to the same moment.

The sons of Mosiah followed. They gave up everything to preach the gospel. Not because they were assigned—but because they were called by the Spirit of God (Mosiah 27:32–35).

Then Joseph translated 3 Nephi.

Christ descended. He appeared to the people. And He gave authority with His own voice.

He said: *"I give you power to baptize"* (3 Nephi 11:21). Not through hands. Not through ordination. But by command of His own voice.

And when they baptized, they said it like this: *"Having authority given me of Jesus Christ, I baptize you in the name of the Father, and of the Son, and of the Holy Ghost. Amen"* (3 Nephi 11:25).

Joseph must have heard the echo. It matched what he had just read from Alma, and it became the same pattern he restored among the Saints.

At the end of his translation work, Joseph received more. A revelation from Genesis that no one else had ever seen.

It spoke of Melchizedek.

He was a man of righteousness. He established peace. His people were translated.[2] And the priesthood he held came directly from God.

It was *"after the order of the Son of God"* (JST Genesis 14:28).

And it was given to sanctify others. To prepare them for the presence of the Lord.

This is what Joseph was learning all along.

Priesthood is not about authority to govern. It is about power to sanctify. It is given by voice. Confirmed by obedience. And fulfilled in the presence of Christ.

Every servant of God whose story Joseph encountered during the translation shared this same pattern: they were called by God, they obeyed, and they labored to bring others into the rest of the Lord.

And yet, most were never called prophets. They didn't need to be.

Because the Lord had called them. And that was enough.

## The Purpose of Priesthood Power

Joseph had seen the manner of heaven—priesthood came by voice, by obedience, by sanctification.

> *"And this is the manner after which they were ordained: being called and prepared from the foundation of the world according to the foreknowledge of God." (Alma 13:3)*

But what actually was it? The Lord answered that directly in one of the most important revelations Joseph ever received:

> *"This greater priesthood... holdeth the key of the mysteries of the kingdom, even the key of the knowledge of God."* (D&C 84:19)

That's the definition.

Priesthood is the key that unlocks the knowledge of God. It is the power by which the gospel is administered in its fullness. And it is the means by which individuals are prepared to stand in the presence of the Lord.

This is what Joseph learned through revelation.

And it's what he had already seen play out again and again in the records he was translating.

When a servant of God was called by revelation—and obeyed that call—they were given access to light, knowledge, and power. The kind of power that purified. That changed people. That made them holy.

Nephi received it. King Benjamin carried it. Alma used it to invite others into a sacred relationship with Christ. The sons of Mosiah taught by it. Christ conferred it with His voice. Every time, the effect was the same—people were sanctified.[3]

That's what priesthood power does.

It brings people into alignment with heaven. It prepares them for the presence of the Lord.

This was the real power Joseph was being taught to seek.

In later revelations, the Lord would explain it again:

> *"Sanctify yourselves, and ye shall be endowed with power from on high."* (D&C 43:16)

This power wasn't about status. It wasn't for display. It wasn't about rituals. It was given to righteous people for the purpose of preparing others to see the Lord.

D&C 88 expands it even further. The Lord instructs the Saints to be taught things in heaven and on earth, to gain a knowledge of countries and kingdoms and laws, to be instructed by the Spirit.

Why?

> *"That they may be prepared in all things... to be prepared for the presence of the Lord."* (D&C 88:80, 85)

Truth was only the beginning. The end goal was sanctification—real change through Christ.

The priesthood was the power to elevate. To purify. To refine hearts. To prepare the mind and spirit to endure glory.

That's what Joseph was learning.

And that's what priesthood power was always meant to do.

## Authority to Baptize—What Really Matters

As Joseph translated the Book of Mormon, he came across a commandment he couldn't ignore.

Nephi had seen in vision that the Lamb of God would be baptized. He saw the heavens open. He saw the Spirit descend—and heard the Father's voice bear record of His Son (1 Nephi 11:26–27).

And Nephi taught that if Christ needed baptism, then every person needed it too.

It wasn't just baptism as a ritual. It was baptism as a gate—the beginning of a sanctifying process. The path toward being born again—of water and of Spirit.

The question, then, wasn't whether baptism was necessary. The question was: *Who had authority to perform it?*

The Book of Mormon answers that not with offices, but with a pattern.

Alma had once been a priest under a corrupt king. But when he heard the words of a prophet, he repented, fled, and was changed. At the waters of Mormon, he stood with boldness and declared:

> *"I baptize thee, having authority from the Almighty God..."* (Mosiah 18:13)

No office. No lineage. No structural ordination. Just obedience to a voice—and fruit that proved it came from God.

As we saw earlier, when Christ visited the Nephites, He chose twelve disciples and gave them power:

> *"I give unto you power that ye shall baptize this people..."* (3 Nephi 11:21)

And those who performed baptisms in water said it plainly:

> *"Having authority given me of Jesus Christ..."* (3 Nephi 11:25)

That phrase was never tradition. It was always a declaration—spoken by one who had heard the Lord's voice and been sent to act in His name.

Sometimes that call came by the voice of Christ Himself. Sometimes by the whisper of the Spirit. Sometimes by angelic command. But always, it was heaven doing the calling.

And the heavens always confirmed it with power.

Baptism with water, then, is not just a symbol. It is the commanded ordinance that witnesses repentance and prepares the soul for what only heaven can give. For remission of sins comes through fire—the baptism of the Holy Ghost, which no man can bestow.

And unless even the water is performed by one who is truly called and empowered of God, it cannot fulfill its purpose. Jesus warned of this Himself:

> *"Many will say to me in that day, Lord, Lord, have we not prophesied in thy name? and in thy name have cast out devils? and in thy name done many wonderful works? And then will I profess unto them, I never knew you."* (Matthew 7:22–23)

Heaven will not honor what heaven has not authorized.

This is what Joseph came to understand—not from a messenger, but from the manner preserved in scripture.

And it's what Christ taught every time He gave power to baptize in water.

## What Did Joseph Teach About Keys?

At some point, Joseph must have asked: *What are keys?*

He had already received priesthood power. He had witnessed the Holy Ghost manifest. But now the revelations introduced a new word—*keys*. And Joseph, who sought divine meaning in every word, wanted to know exactly what that meant.

D&C 84 gave him the first clue:

> *"This greater priesthood administereth the gospel and holdeth the key of the mysteries of the kingdom, even the key of the knowledge of God."* (D&C 84:19)

Notice the grammar. The verse has two clauses:

> ***What the priesthood does:*** *"administereth the gospel"* (to dispense/minister the gospel).
> ***What it holds:*** *"the key of the mysteries... the knowledge of God."*
>
> The keys are not "administration"; they open access—they unlock the knowledge of God.

That was the definition Joseph worked with. Keys weren't tokens or titles. They were functional. Like a key that unlocks a door, priesthood keys granted access to what was sealed: the mysteries of the kingdom—the knowledge of God.

This is how Joseph came to see priesthood: one divine opening at a time. Keys were gifts of access from heaven, pointing beyond themselves to the real end: the knowledge of God.

Joseph saw in scripture this same manner: keys as gifts of access that open the way to God. In his inspired revision of Genesis, Melchizedek held this priesthood, and those who entered it had *"power, by faith, to break mountains... to stand in the presence of God... and [were] translated and taken up into heaven"* (JST Genesis 14:30–32).

Keys, then, are about revelation. They open the way to God's presence. As Jesus said, *"Ye have taken away the key of knowledge: ye entered not in yourselves, and them that were entering in ye hindered"* (Luke 11:52). The true key is knowledge of Him, opening the way for every soul.

And that invitation is universal:

> *"He inviteth them all to come unto him and partake of his goodness; and he denieth none that come unto him, black and white, bond and free, male and female; and he remembereth the heathen; and all are alike unto God, both Jew and Gentile."* (2 Nephi 26:33)

Joseph's understanding of keys was not confined to men alone. He taught that the Spirit could open gifts of prophecy, healing, and discernment among the daughters as well as the sons of God. These openings were part of the same pattern: keys unlock knowledge, and God pours it out on all who are prepared to receive it.

That is what keys are for:

> *To open the way into God's mysteries.*
> *To unlock the knowledge of God.*
> *To guide a soul step by step—until Christ Himself appears.*

## What Did Joseph Teach About Ordinances?

When Joseph used the word *ordinance,* he meant something very different than most of his Christian contemporaries. In his day, the word was usually tied to ceremonies such as baptism or communion. But Joseph pressed into the root meaning.

Webster's 1828 defined ordinance as: *"A rule established by authority; an observance commanded; an appointment; or an established rite or ceremony."*[4] In Joseph's time, most Christians leaned heavily on the last sense—rites and ceremonies. But Joseph deliberately emphasized the older and broader sense: *appointments* ordained by God.

To him, ordinances were not rituals devised by men but living thresholds—moments ordered by God Himself where His power is revealed. They were divine appointments, not man's inventions—moments when God reached out to His children with instruction and command.

Think of them as assignments from God, each with a beginning, a middle, and an end.

Every ordinance was a threshold—an appointed crossing where heaven touched earth. If obeyed, that moment became a channel of further light and knowledge. The individual was aided by the Lord to accomplish the very thing He had ordered, and in experiencing such manifestations, their confidence in God increased.

Scripture puts it this way: *"thy confidence wax strong in the presence of God"* (D&C 121:45). In this way each ordinance drew the faithful closer to His presence.

An ordinance, then, was never the outward act alone. It was the whole process: God's command, the individual's obedience, and the manifestation of His power to accomplish that which He ordered.

Sometimes it came as a word whispered to the heart. Sometimes as a charge. Sometimes as an assignment. Sometimes as a task impressed by the Spirit, or a command to go, do, speak, or refrain.

However it came, the hallmark was always the same: heaven ordered it, and heaven honored it with power.

Every ordinance follows a living order. It is not static or ceremonial, but dynamic and personal. The steps are simple:

1. Problem—a need arises, a weakness is exposed, or a task is set that cannot be solved alone.

2. Instruction—the Lord gives direction, often quiet but unmistakable.
3. Obedience—the individual acts, sometimes with uncertainty, but with faith that the Lord will honor the command.
4. Manifestation—heaven responds. Power flows. God shows Himself, whether by deliverance, revelation, or sanctifying presence.
5. Increased Confidence—with each appointment kept, trust grows stronger. As scripture says, *"thy confidence [shall] wax strong in the presence of God"* (D&C 121:45).

This is what ordinances are: divine appointments where God orders the moment, man responds, and heaven opens.

Scripture is full of such ordinances.

> ***Lehi:*** *Problem*—his life was threatened after a prior ordinance, when the Lord commanded him to call Jerusalem to repentance. *Instruction*—flee the city with his family. *Obedience*—he departed into the wilderness. *Manifestation*—he was carried away in vision and saw *"God sitting upon his throne"* (1 Nephi 1:8–9). *Increased Confidence*—Lehi trusted the Lord's guidance for the journey ahead.
> Alma: *Problem*—he served as a priest under wicked King Noah, bound to a corrupt system. *Instruction*—separate himself and gather believers. *Obedience*—he fled, gathered the people, and baptized at the waters of Mormon. *Manifestation*—the Spirit descended and gave him "authority from Almighty God" (Mosiah 18:12–13). *Increased Confidence*—Alma became a true shepherd of God's flock.
>
> ***The Brother of Jared:*** *Problem*—darkness filled the barges, vessels he had constructed under a prior ordinance where the Lord gave the design. *Instruction*—the Lord asked, "What will ye that I should do?" *Obedience*—Mahonri molten stones, carried them to the mount, and prayed with faith that the Lord would touch them. *Manifestation*—the Lord touched the stones, showed His finger, and then His full presence (Ether 3:6, 13). *Increased Confidence*—his faith grew so strong that the veil could not withhold the Lord.
>
> ***Enos***: *Problem*—a soul burdened with sin. *Instruction*—a stirring within his heart compelled him to wrestle before God.

> *Obedience*—he prayed "all the day long." *Manifestation*—the Lord's voice declared, "Thy sins are forgiven thee" (Enos 1:5). *Increased Confidence*—Enos gained assurance in God's mercy and covenant.

What do these stories teach us? That ordinances are divine appointments—moments where heaven and earth meet.

They are God's way of teaching His children step by step, weaving confidence into the soul through lived experience with Him, and building a bond with Deity that cannot be destroyed when the fiery darts and tempests of the adversary blow:

> *"for behold, it is upon the rock of our Redeemer, who is Christ, the Son of God, that ye must build your foundation... a foundation whereon if men build they cannot fall."* (Helaman 5:12)

Each appointment carries the same promise: the Lord gives a charge, the humble obey, and He manifests Himself. Over time, these crossings accumulate until the heart is anchored in trust, the mind filled with light, and the soul prepared to stand in His presence.

This is why Joseph spoke of ordinances not as man's inventions, but as heaven's appointments. They are the meetings God Himself orders and sets on our calendar—and when we keep them, we are never the same.

## The Prophetic Pattern—Why Joseph Was Different

If we've been paying attention, we can see it clearly now.

Joseph Smith wasn't inventing something new. He was being shown a very old prophetic path that had been walked by holy men in every dispensation.

It always started the same way:

> *A voice.*
> *A revelation.*
> *A call to repentance.*
> *And then a command: go and prepare others to meet Me.*

This is what happened with Lehi. He saw the throne of God. He heard the voice. He was sent to warn Jerusalem. And then he was commanded to gather his family and leave everything behind. Not just to escape—but to prepare them to receive what he had received.[5]

Nephi followed the same pattern. So did Alma. So did King Benjamin. So did Melchizedek. So did Enoch. Each of them heard the Lord. Each of them obeyed. And each of them was tasked with sanctifying a people—elevating them until they were ready to enter the rest of the Lord.[6]

That's the path Joseph was stepping into.

He was fourteen when the voice first came.[7] And like all true prophets before him, he was changed by it. He began to seek. To hunger. To ask. To obey.

And one by one, the same steps unfolded:

> *He was given power to translate a sacred record.*
> *He was taught from heaven, line upon line.*
> *He was baptized. Ordained. Commanded.*
> *He was sent to preach repentance and establish a church—*
> *but even that wasn't the end.*

Because the real path was still unfolding step by step to Joseph.

He was shown a temple, a place where God would come. He was commanded to gather a people, to teach them what he was learning, and to prepare them for real ordinances—appointments with the Lord Himself.

His mission was clear: to prepare a people to see the Lord. And that's what set him apart.

Unlike many others in scripture, Joseph didn't just receive the call—he answered it.

> *He didn't merely warn; he built.*
> *He didn't just teach; he revealed.*
> *He didn't simply promise; he prepared.*

And even though he faced opposition, betrayal, and ultimately death, he laid the foundation for the Lord to come.

That was the prophetic path that Joseph walked faithfully.

## The Mandate—Prepare a People to See the Lord

If priesthood means access, and keys open knowledge, and ordinances reveal the power of godliness—then the process of sanctification comes into full view.

This has always been the mandate the Lord has given His prophets: prepare a people to see the Lord.

Enoch was given that charge—and he fulfilled it.

He gathered a people in faith, taught them repentance, and led them into such unity that *"the Lord called his people Zion"* (Moses 7:18). They were sanctified, of one heart and one mind, dwelling in righteousness with no poor among them. Their holiness became so great that *"Zion was taken up into heaven"* (Moses 7:21).

This was not the success of a single prophet alone, but of an entire people willing to rise. Enoch's mandate was realized. He prepared a people to endure the presence of God, and they did not shrink.

They walked with Him until He brought them into His own dwelling place.

That was the work given to Moses.

He led Israel out of bondage. He brought them to the mountain. He taught them the commandments and pled with them to prepare their hearts. But when the Lord came to offer them His presence, the people pulled away. Their hearts were hard. Their ears were closed. They were afraid of His voice.[8]

And so, the Lord took away the higher priesthood—the power to bring the people fully into His presence—and gave them a lesser law.

> *"They hardened their hearts and could not endure His presence; therefore, the Lord in His wrath... took Moses out of their midst, and the Holy Priesthood also; and the lesser priesthood continued."* (D&C 84:24–25)

It was not the law of appointments with the Lord, but a law of carnal commandments. A schoolmaster, pointing to what they had rejected.

That story wasn't about Moses failing. It was about the people refusing to rise. D&C 84 tells it plainly: the higher priesthood, the one that holds *"the key of the mysteries of the kingdom, even the key of the knowledge of God"* (v. 19), *"was taken from among the children of Israel... because of the hardness of their hearts"* (v. 25).

And that mandate didn't end there. It was repeated again and again—through prophets who heard the Lord, gathered a people, and tried to sanctify them:

> **Lehi** saw God enthroned (1 Nephi 1:8–13).

> **Nephi** testified of seeing the Lord and of his people pressing toward the tree (2 Nephi 11:2–3; 31:13–15).
> **Alma's** people covenanted at the waters of Mormon until their hearts were changed (Mosiah 18:10–11).
> **King Benjamin's** people fell to the earth, no more disposition to do evil (Mosiah 5:2).
> **Melchizedek** gathered a city of righteousness (Alma 13:14–19).
> **Enoch** saw Zion taken up into heaven (Moses 7:18–21).
> And **Joseph Smith** stood in their same line, declaring: *"Now this Moses plainly taught to our fathers, saying: A prophet shall the Lord your God raise up unto you of your brethren, like unto me; him shall ye hear in all things whatsoever he shall say unto you"* (D&C 84:23).

Each of them held priesthood power—an appointment from the Lord.

Each of them invited others to receive it too—and did all that they could to prepare them for it.

They didn't say, *"Follow me."* They said, *"Prepare yourselves. Come and see Him."*

And that's what Joseph Smith was doing.

His revelations make it clear. The priesthood is for sanctification. For revelation. For elevation. It is to bless, to empower, to anoint, to heal, and to prepare.

And this preparation wasn't just for men.

Joseph taught that all who come unto Christ can receive His Spirit, speak in His name, and minister with His power.

Joseph taught that all who come unto Christ can receive His Spirit, speak in His name, and minister with His power. The gifts of the Spirit—healing, prophecy, visions, discernment—were given to all believers.

He affirmed that all who had faith to heal the sick should go forward and bless,[9] and let all others hold their peace. And he declared that *"the same Priesthood which administers in heaven... is the last law... to prepare [God's children] for the presence of the Lord."*[10]

This is the mandate, and it is the same in every generation. The question is never whether God desires to reveal Himself, but whether His people are willing to rise and receive Him.

## The Sabbath and Sacrament—The First Step

Repentance and baptism of water are the first steps into the fold of Christ, as the Lord revealed in His doctrine. But once a people have entered His church, the first step toward becoming Zion and preparing to be sanctified by fire is the rhythm He commanded of Sabbath and Sacrament.

This weekly appointment is His way of keeping a people unspotted, filled, and ready to receive Him.

Here's why:

From the creation of the world, the Sabbath was hallowed as holy time. Six days are given for labor, but the seventh belongs to the Lord. To cease from labor, to gather, to worship—that they may know who they worship (D&C 93:19)—and to delight in His presence was the pattern.

Isaiah promised that those who honored the Sabbath would *"delight in the Lord"* and inherit the blessings of Jacob (Isaiah 58:13–14). Alma commanded his people at the waters of Mormon to *"observe the sabbath day, and keep it holy"* (Mosiah 18:23).

Through Joseph Smith the Lord renewed the same command:

> *"That thou mayest more fully keep thyself unspotted from the world, thou shalt go to the house of prayer and offer up thy sacraments upon my holy day."* (D&C 59:9)

The Sabbath was commanded as a delight, a day of rejoicing, thanksgiving, and renewal. It is one of the Lord's appointed ways of keeping His people unspotted—and being unspotted is not an end in itself. Moroni taught the reason:

> *"Come unto Christ, and be perfected in him, and deny yourselves of all ungodliness... then is his grace sufficient for you, that by his grace ye may be perfect in Christ... unspotted from the world."* (Moroni 10:32)

The Sacrament stands beside the Sabbath as its companion command.

In every age the Lord has provided a witness meal. Melchizedek brought forth bread and wine to bless Abraham. Israel ate the Passover lamb with unleavened bread, their loins girded, their staff in hand. They were commanded to mark their doorways with the lamb's blood so that the destroying angel would pass them by (Exodus 12:7, 22–23).

Too many readers of scripture assume the destroyer is the devil. This is simply not the case. The Lord Himself is the destroyer when He comes in judgment. He sets the conditions of His law. If His people keep it, they are blessed. If they rebel, they suffer the consequence (see D&C 19).

In like manner, the Sacrament symbolizes marking the doorway of our lives with the blood of the Lamb. His blood is the shield that protects us when judgment falls.

In the wilderness Israel ate manna, bread from heaven. And at Jerusalem Jesus took bread, broke it, and gave His disciples the cup: *"This cup is the new covenant in my blood."* (Luke 22:20)

After His resurrection, He gave the same ordinance to the Nephites.

> *"And when the multitude had eaten and were filled, he said unto the disciples: Behold there shall one be ordained among you, and to him will I give power that he shall break bread and bless it and give it unto the people of my church."* (3 Nephi 18:4–5)

They were not filled with crumbs of bread. They were filled with Him. He is the Bread of Life: *"He that cometh to me shall never hunger; and he that believeth on me shall never thirst"* (John 6:35).

He is the Living Water: *"Whosoever drinketh of the water that I shall give him shall never thirst"* (John 4:14). When disciples eat His bread and drink His cup, they are filled—not by portion, but by Person.

The symbols Joseph was given to preserve speak this plainly.

The bread, broken, witnesses His body broken for us. But it also points to our own hearts, broken before Him. *"Behold, the Lord requireth the heart and a willing mind"* (D&C 64:34). He does not ask for shattered lives, but for yielded, willing hearts—disciples who offer themselves fully to Him. Therefore every disciple who comes to Him must be broken.[11]

The broken bread placed in our hands is not only His gift—it is also our offering. His body broken, our hearts broken, joined together in one witness meal.

And the Lord's command to Joseph was never meant to be locked behind walls or offices. He gave it to His people—all His people.

And this command is not dependent on a building, a congregation, or a chain of earthly authority. The Lord's voice to Joseph was simple: keep His day holy, remember Him in the sacred meal. If you don't have an official congregation, honor the Sabbath anyway. Set it apart as holy. Partake of bread and wine—or water if that is what you have—in remembrance of Him. Do it in purity, with real intent.

Even if no one with an appointment from heaven is present, the command still stands. A mother, a father, a single man or woman, a youth, or even a soldier far from home—all may keep it with exactness.

A single parent with or without children alike are invited into His rest. Imagine a mother with her children, stranded far from any congregation. Is she forbidden to obey the Lord's command because no one but her is there to pronounce words over bread and wine?

Nowhere in scripture does the Lord say, *"You cannot access these blessings unless a male priesthood holder is present."* He says simply: honor the Sabbath, and partake of His Sacramental meal. When done with sincerity, His Spirit sanctifies the act.

And I would add my solemn feelings about this as well. Even if you do not have the scriptures, or access to the exact words of the Sacrament prayers, that should not stop you from partaking of emblems that represent the body and blood of Christ.

The Lord Himself declared:

> *"It mattereth not what ye shall eat or what ye shall drink when ye partake of the sacrament, if it so be that ye do it with an eye single to my glory."* (D&C 27:2)

If all you had were a chocolate chip cookie and a cup of orange juice, and you partook with a broken heart and contrite spirit, the Lord would not be offended. In truth, He would be pleased.

Say something simple, from your heart: *"In the name of God, I partake of this cookie in remembrance of His body that was broken for me, to remind me that I must be broken for Him. And I do so in the holy name of Jesus Christ, Amen."*

Then take the cup and say likewise: *"In the name of God, I drink this in remembrance of His blood that was shed for me, to remind me that I must forsake my sins and live in Him. And I do so in the holy name of Jesus Christ, Amen."*

The power is not in a polished form. The power is in remembrance of Him.[12]

Thus the two stand together, Sabbath and Sacrament—not as rites invented by men but as ordinances, appointments from the Lord, after the manner He taught His apostles in Jerusalem, and the same manner He taught Joseph.

The witness is consistent across scripture:

> ***In Jerusalem—Jesus to His apostles***
> *"This do in remembrance of me"* (Luke 22:19–20).
> ***Among the apostles after His resurrection***
> *"They continued stedfastly... in breaking of bread, and in prayers"* (Acts 2:42, 46).
> ***In the promised land—Jesus to the Nephites***
> *"This shall ye always do... in remembrance of my blood... that ye may witness unto the Father that ye do always remember me"* (3 Nephi 18:11).

From Jerusalem to the New World to Joseph's day, the manner is the same: the Lord ordains, and His disciples remember.

The Sabbath sanctifies time. The Sacrament sanctifies the soul. One teaches us to rest from our labors and consecrate a day to Him. The other teaches us to rest from our sins and receive His life within us.

Both are types of the eternal promise: that God's people will enter into His rest forever (Alma 13:12; Hebrews 4:9–10).

When obeyed in humility, He manifests Himself in marvelous ways:

> *He keeps His people unspotted from the world (D&C 59:9; Moroni 10:32).*
> *He fills them with His Spirit so they hunger and thirst no more (3 Nephi 18:4–5; John 6:35).*
> *He grants light, healing, and guidance (Isaiah 58:8–11).*
> *He restores joy and gladness (Isaiah 58:13–14).*
> *He pours out the fulness of the earth—temporal and spiritual abundance (D&C 59:16).*
> *He sanctifies their labors and consecrates their time (D&C 59:13).*
> *He prepares them to enter His rest for eternity (Alma 13:12; Hebrews 4:9–10).*

For disciples who have been born again, who have taken His name upon them as adopted children of Christ, the Sabbath magnifies that adoption into a day wholly consecrated to Him.

As Paul wrote:

> *"Ye have received the Spirit of adoption, whereby we cry, Abba, Father."* (Romans 8:15)

The word *Abba* is not formal—it is the tender cry of a child to a parent, the equivalent of saying *"Dad"* or *"Papa."* And who is this Abba? It is Christ Himself, the Father of our new birth.

To eat His bread and drink His wine is to proclaim with body and spirit: Christ is Abba Father; He is my life.

For as these emblems enter our bodies, they are broken down and become part of us.

So too, when we are broken and contrite, we remove all barriers of the natural man that separate us from Him. He can enter our mind and our heart, and spiritually dwell within us (D&C 8:2).

He becomes part of us. That is the truest description of becoming one heart and one mind found in all of scripture.

This is the Lord's commanded beginning. A people who keep His Sabbath with delight, who eat and drink of Him until they are filled, who remain unspotted from the world and wholly consecrated to Him—such a people will be prepared to see His face.

Weekly holiness through Sabbath and Sacrament was the Lord's beginning. Yet Joseph's charge reached further: to build a people sanctified not just in rhythm, but in order—a Zion people prepared by the High Priesthood, after the order of the Son.

## The High Priesthood—After the Order of the Son

By 1832, Joseph had already been translating, preaching, and organizing for nearly three years. And every effort pointed back to the same divine assignment: to prepare a people to receive the Lord.

That was the mandate.

He wasn't gathering people just to form a church. He wasn't restoring scattered truths for their own sake. He was laying a foundation for Zion. A people of one heart, one mind, and pure in heart—ready to be visited, instructed, and sanctified by God Himself.

So the Lord began to reveal more.

While translating the Book of Genesis, Joseph was shown an entirely new dimension to priesthood. The name Melchizedek had always been there in the Bible, but now the Lord revealed who he really was—and what kind of power he held.[13]

This wasn't an earthly priesthood. It wasn't a system of governance. It was *"the Holy Priesthood, after the Order of the Son of God."* (D&C 107:3)

Melchizedek had received it. He had been called by the voice of God. He had been ordained to a holy calling. He had received power and authority to enter into the presence of the Lord—and teach others how to do the same.

The revelation made it clear: this kind of priesthood came to those who were sanctified. Who *"were made pure,"* who *"entered into the rest of the Lord,"* and who were *"after the order of His Son."* (JST Genesis 14:27–32)

It was not given lightly, or by tradition.

It was given by God's own voice. It was sealed by His Spirit. And it was confirmed by real, heavenly power.

Later, the Lord would confirm this pattern again in D&C 107. The Melchizedek Priesthood was said to hold *"the keys of all the spiritual blessings of the church,"* including *"to have the heavens opened," "to commune with the general assembly and church of the Firstborn,"* and *"to enjoy the communion and presence of God the Father, and Jesus the mediator"* (D&C 107:18–19).

This wasn't theoretical language.

It was a description of what the priesthood was always meant for.

Joseph saw it. He wrote it. He lived it. And he taught it.

He was not seeking position. He was answering a divine commission. He was doing everything in his power to prepare others to receive this same ordination—not from men, but from heaven.

This was the high priesthood he was restoring.

Not the priesthood of titles and offices. But the priesthood of ascension and encounter. The priesthood after the order of the Son of God (JST Genesis 14:27–32).

And Joseph believed that if the people were sanctified, and willing, and ready—they too could receive it, and be prepared to enter Zion, the New Jerusalem.

### Prophets, Seers, and Revelators—What Joseph Actually Taught

In the scriptures Joseph translated, the terms "Prophet, Seer, and Revelator" carried specific meanings, and this is what those words must have meant to him:

**A prophet:** The word prophet is derived from the Greek word *prophētēs*, meaning *"one who speaks for another,"* specifically for God. A prophet is one who speaks with God—and for God. He receives revelation for the salvation of mankind. He hears the voice of the Lord and is given power to teach, warn, and sanctify.[14]

His primary work is to prepare a people for a divine encounter.

Joseph Smith personified this role. He was not simply a messenger of future events, but one who conversed with God and acted as His mouthpiece.

Through Joseph, the Lord revealed truths that were vital for salvation, including the restoration of lost doctrines, the principles of the gospel, and the plan of salvation.

Joseph didn't just prophesy; he lived the revelations he received, preparing the way for others to have their own encounters with the divine.

**A seer:** The root word seer comes from the Old French *cere,* meaning *"to see,"* and refers to one who perceives through divine revelation. A seer is one who sees what is hidden—knowledge that cannot be obtained by human means.[15]

Ammon in the Book of Mormon explained it clearly: *"A seer is a revelator and a prophet also; and a gift which is greater can no man have."* (Mosiah 8:16) Seers are given the power to read sealed writings, translate ancient records, and unlock mysteries that only God can reveal (Mosiah 8:17).

Joseph's life was a testament to this role. He translated the Book of Mormon, bringing forth a hidden record that was sealed for centuries.

Through the power of God, Joseph uncovered truths from the past, from ancient prophets, and revealed them to the world. His translation of the Book of Mormon, along with the Pearl of Great Price and his translation of the Bible, exemplified his role as a seer, seeing what others could not and bringing it into the light.

**A revelator:** The word revelator comes from the Latin *revelatio,* meaning *"an uncovering"* or *"a disclosure."* A revelator is one who receives pure knowledge from heaven by direct communication with God via revelation.[16]

This knowledge is personal, real, and life-changing.

Joseph Smith didn't invent this term—he received it and magnified it.

Joseph embraced the title of revelator by continually receiving and delivering profound revelation to guide the church.

Joseph restored the true doctrine of Christ, bringing to light essential truths that had been lost. His revelations were not mere interpretations of scripture or ideas—they were direct messages from heaven, intended to build the kingdom of God on earth.

And, he taught that others could do the same, by following his example.

Joseph was a prophet because he received the voice of the Lord. And he believed that others could, too.

As Moses once said:

> *"Would God that all the Lord's people were prophets, and that the Lord would put his spirit upon them!"* (Numbers 11:29)

Joseph taught the same. He believed that all people—male or female, ordained or not—could receive revelation, speak with God, walk in the gifts of the Spirit, and be prophets, seers, and revelators.

That's what he taught.

That's what he modeled.

And that's what a prophet truly looks like.

## The Priesthood Joseph Taught: Power Shared by Sons and Daughters

Joseph Smith didn't set out to build a priesthood system.

He set out to fulfill a divine mandate—to prepare a people to receive the Lord.

That calling shaped everything he taught about priesthood, authority, and spiritual power. And what the Lord revealed through him wasn't hierarchy. It was access.

From the very beginning, Joseph learned that real authority doesn't come from men. It comes from heaven. It is confirmed by the Spirit and sealed by power. It is given to those who obey the voice of God and are willing to sanctify themselves so they can prepare others to be sanctified.[17]

That's how priesthood began for Joseph—by voice, by vision, by calling.

And that's what he read in scripture.

From Lehi to Nephi, from Alma to King Benjamin, from Melchizedek to Enoch—the pattern was always the same. God called. They obeyed.

Power followed. And with that power came a responsibility: to prepare a people to enter the presence of the Lord.[18]

This is the purpose of priesthood. It is the power to teach by the Spirit, act in the name of Christ, and minister with divine approval. But more than anything, it is the power to lift others—men and women—into sanctifying relationship with God.

And Joseph would soon make this even clearer—not only in words, but in action. The daughters of Zion were to share fully in this same work, building Wisdom's house through prophecy, healing, and the beautifying gifts of the Spirit.

Priesthood is not exclusive. It is not inherited by bloodline or office. It is extended to the humble, the obedient, and the willing. Joseph taught that it was after the Order of the Son of God—meaning it was patterned after Christ Himself.[19] It is a priesthood of revelation. A priesthood of sanctification. A priesthood of invitation.

And its fruits are unmistakable.

The keys it carries are not to control, but to unlock—to open access to divine knowledge, where ordinances of real transformation occur, and to guide souls to where the veil becomes thin and the Lord draws near.

This is what Joseph taught. And it gives us the clearest possible answer to the question my son asked at the very beginning of this chapter:

If the scriptures say baptism must be done by someone with authority—what does that really mean?

It means the person must be called of God. Not by ordination, but by revelation. Their authority must be confirmed by the Holy Ghost, sealed by obedience, and recognized by heaven. It's not enough to hold a title or trace a line of hands.

The question is: Has God called this servant? Has heaven approved their ministry? Have they been authorized to administer the gospel of Jesus Christ—and has the Lord Himself confirmed it with power from on high?

Because that's the baptism that matters.

And that's the authority Joseph taught.

He lived it. He walked it. And he pointed others to it—not just so they could be baptized, but so they could receive the real gift: sanctification, transformation, and the power to enter the presence of the Lord.

This is the priesthood Joseph taught.

Not a priesthood of offices, but a priesthood of power.

Not a hierarchy of men, but a path to God.

The invitation remains. It is offered to you now—if you will receive it as Joseph did: by righteousness, by revelation, and by real encounter with Christ the Redeemer.

## Chapter 3 Notes

1 Oliver Cowdery, Messenger and Advocate (Oct. 1834–Oct. 1835), letters to W. W. Phelps describing priesthood restoration.
D&C 13 (first included in the 1876 edition).
Compare Joseph Smith—History 1:68–72 (later compiled).

2 JST Genesis 14:33–34

3 Nephi: 2 Nephi 11:2–3
King Benjamin: Mosiah 5:2, 5, 7
Alma: Mosiah 18:13
Sons of Mosiah: Mosiah 27:32–35
Christ: 3 Nephi 11:21, 25

4 Noah Webster, American Dictionary of the English Language (1828), s.v. "ordinance."

5 Lehi: 1 Nephi 1:8–14; 1 Nephi 2:1–2

6 Nephi: 2 Nephi 11:2–3
Alma: Mosiah 18:12–13
King Benjamin: Mosiah 5:2, 5, 7
Melchizedek: JST Genesis 14:28, 33–34
Enoch: Moses 7:69

7 JS–H 1:14–19 "I retired to the woods to make the attempt... I saw a pillar of light... I saw two Personages... One of them spake unto me, calling me by name..."

8 Exodus 19:16–25; Exodus 20:18–21; Deuteronomy 5:22–27.

9 TPJS, p. 224 "Respecting the female laying on hands, there could be no devil in it if God gave his sanction by healing... the time had not come for the organization of the Church completely."

10 TPJS, p. 322 "The same Priesthood which administers in heaven will be with the faithful in eternity... It is the last law, and the last ordinance, and the last covenant... to prepare men for the presence of the Lord."

11 2 Nephi 2:7; 3 Nephi 9:20; Moroni 6:2; D&C 59:8; Psalm 34:18; Psalm 51:17.

12 This principle was lived under Joseph Smith. When the Saints worried that wine might be unsafe, the Lord revealed: "It mattereth not what ye shall eat or what ye shall drink when ye partake of the sacrament, if it so be that ye do it with an eye single to my glory" (D&C 27:2). In practice, the Saints sometimes used water in place of wine. The focus was always remembrance of Christ, not the form of the emblems.

13 JST Genesis 14:27–32

14 Prophet—from *prophētēs*, Greek: *"one who speaks for another, especially for a god"*—Liddell & Scott, Greek–English Lexicon, s.v. "προφήτης"; see also Strong's Concordance, G4396.
General description of prophets: Numbers 12:6; Jeremiah 1:7; Amos 3:7; D&C 1:38. *"one who speaks for another,"* specifically for God. A prophet is one who speaks with God—and for God. He receives revelation for the salvation of mankind. He hears the voice of the Lord and is given power to teach, warn, and sanctify.

15 Seer—from Old French *seere / cerre ("to see"),* ultimately from Latin *sedere ("to sit, look, perceive"*); see Oxford English Dictionary, s.v. *"seer."*
Scriptural use: 1 Samuel 9:9 *("he that is now called a Prophet was beforetime called a Seer"*); Mosiah 8:13, 17 (a seer can know of things past and things to come, revealed by God). *"to see,"* and refers to one who perceives through divine revelation. A seer is one who sees what is hidden—knowledge that cannot be obtained by human means.

16 Revelator—from Latin *revelātiō ("an uncovering, disclosure"),* from *revelare ("to lay bare, reveal");* see Lewis & Short, Latin Dictionary, s.v. *"revelatio";* Oxford English Dictionary, s.v. "revelator."

Scriptural use: Amos 3:7; Daniel 2:28–30; D&C 28:2; D&C 43:2. *"uncovering"* or *"a disclosure."* A revelator is one who receives pure knowledge from heaven by direct communication with God via revelation.

17 John 1:12–13—authority *("power to become the sons of God")* comes from God, not men.
Mosiah 18:12–13—Alma baptizes *"having authority from the Almighty God."*
D&C 121:36–37, 41–42—priesthood authority is inseparably connected with heaven, confirmed only by righteousness, persuasion, long-suffering, meekness, love.

18 Lehi: 1 Nephi 1:8–14; 1 Nephi 2:1–2
Nephi: 2 Nephi 11:2–3
Alma: Mosiah 18:12–13
King Benjamin: Mosiah 5:2, 5, 7
Melchizedek: JST Genesis 14:28, 33–34
Enoch: Moses 7:69

19 D&C 107:2–4 "Why the first is called the Melchizedek Priesthood is because Melchizedek was such a great high priest... But out of respect or reverence to the name of the Supreme Being, to avoid the too frequent repetition of his name, they... called it the Melchizedek Priesthood."

# The Two Strands of the Image of God

## Builder and Beautifier in the Restoration

---

### The Witness of Heaven and Earth

> *"The heavens declare the glory of God; and the firmament sheweth his handywork."* (Psalm 19:1)

From the beginning, creation itself has borne witness to the image of God. Genesis declared: *"So God created man in his own image... male and female created he them."* (Gen 1:27). The image of God is not solitary but composed of two strands—masculine and feminine, equal and necessary, distinct yet united.

This pattern is written into the heavens themselves:

> **The masculine Sun** rises in constancy, radiant with strength, light, and warmth.
> **The feminine Earth** receives that light, nourishes the seed, and brings forth life.
> **The feminine Moon** moves in her cycles, waxing and waning, mirroring fertility and renewal.
> **The masculine planets**—Mercury swift with speech, Mars fierce with strength—move as herald and warrior.
> **The feminine constellations**—Virgo the virgin, nurturing

> life; Cassiopeia the enthroned queen—lift the witness of womanhood into the stars.[1]

The same witness is heard in language:

> In Hebrew, *ruach*—Spirit, breath, wind—is feminine.
> In Greek, *sophia*—wisdom—is feminine, while logos—word, pattern—is masculine.
>
> In Latin and the romance tongues:
> *sol* (sun) is masculine.
> *terra* (earth), sapientia (wisdom), *ecclesia* (church), and *Sion* are feminine.[2]

Even grammar itself bears testimony: the masculine conveys order, word, and strength; the feminine conveys life, wisdom, and nurture. Together, they form a dance written into speech itself.

The heavens declare in type what Genesis declared in word: the image of God is twofold, masculine and feminine, each distinct yet united in purpose, together revealing His handiwork.

This is the pattern of creation: two strands, equal and necessary, distinct yet united. One builds structure, the other fills it with life. One provides order, the other adorns it with beauty. Together they reveal the wholeness of God's image on earth.

In this chapter we will trace both strands—the masculine as builder and guardian of structure, the feminine as life-bearer and beautifier. Each has its place in scripture and in Joseph's Restoration. Each is essential. Without either, the house collapses. With both, the Church of the Lamb flourishes in strength and glory.

## The Eden Pattern: Adam and Eve

The first testimony of the two strands is found in Eden. Genesis does not present Adam as complete in himself, but as a beginning awaiting fullness. *"It is not good that the man should be alone,"* the Lord declared. *"I will make him an help meet for him."* (Gen 2:18). Only when Eve was formed and brought to Adam did the image of God appear whole: *"male and female created he them."* (Gen 1:27).

Adam's roles reveal the masculine strand.

> **Tiller and Keeper of the Ground**—*"The Lord God took the man, and put him into the garden of Eden to dress it and*

> *to keep it."* (Gen 2:15). The Hebrew words are *ʿābad* = to work, serve; *šāmar* = to guard, preserve.[3] Adam was not called to rule by domination, but to serve and guard creation, to cultivate and protect what God had made. His role was stewardship: to establish structure, preserve order, and ensure that life could flourish.
> **Naming and Ordering Creation**—*"And whatsoever Adam called every living creature, that was the name thereof."* (Gen 2:19). Naming is an act of order and identity. By giving names, Adam grounded creation in language and structure. His role was to discern boundaries, provide order, and set creation in its proper place.

Eve's roles reveal the feminine strand.

> **Helper "Meet"**—Corresponding Power—*"I will make him an help meet for him."* (Gen 2:18). The Hebrew phrase is *ʿēzer kenegdô,* literally.[4] Elsewhere *ʿēzer* is used of God Himself as deliverer and helper. Eve is not presented as subordinate, but as a co-equal power—a counterpart who completes what is lacking, mirroring God's own sustaining role.
> **Mother of All Living**—*"And Adam called his wife's name Eve; because she was the mother of all living."* (Gen 3:20). Her identity was life-bearing and life-nourishing. Eve embodies vitality, continuance, and the generative beauty of creation.
> **Perception and Discernment**—*"And when the woman saw that the tree was good for food... pleasant to the eyes... and to be desired to make one wise, she took of the fruit thereof."* (Gen 3:6). Eve is described as seeing and discerning. Though her choice carried consequence, the role itself reveals the feminine strand of seeking wisdom, perceiving beauty, and awakening awareness.

Together they reveal the image of God.

> ***Adam*** = *ground/order/guard.*
> ***Eve*** = *life/beauty/wisdom.*

Builder and beautifier, protector and perceiver, cultivator and life-bearer. Neither was sufficient alone. Remove either strand, and Eden collapses. But together they embodied the wholeness of God's image.

And, the Restoration mirrors Eden.

Adam's strand appears in Joseph Smith's calling: to guard, to structure, to name and to order Zion through scripture, organization, and temple building. Eve's strand reappeared in Emma and in the sisters of Nauvoo: to beautify Zion with hymns, to heal and prophesy, to receive the key of Wisdom through the Relief Society.

The Restoration did not restore one strand without the other; it restored the image of God in type—both masculine and feminine, builder and beautifier, working together for the church of the Lamb.

## The Masculine Strand in Scripture and Restoration

From Eden forward, the masculine strand appears wherever God calls men to build structure and guard life. Its purpose is never self-glory but stewardship—creating order so that life can be preserved and God's presence can dwell among His people.

**Noah: Structure Preserving Life**
In an age of violence and corruption, Noah was commanded to build an ark.[5] This was more than a vessel of wood; it was a structure to safeguard seed, to shelter creation, and to carry a remnant into a new world. In Noah we see the masculine strand as guardian: he built a frame in which life could survive judgment and begin again.

**Abraham: Ordering the Household**
Abraham was chosen not simply to receive promises but to order his house after God. The Lord declared of him, *"For I know him, that he will command his children and his household after him, and they shall keep the way of the Lord, to do justice and judgment."* (Gen 18:19). Abraham's calling was to establish structure at the most basic level: the household. His masculine stewardship showed that order begins in the family, where faith and justice are taught and transmitted.

**Moses: Law and Tabernacle**
Moses was raised up to bring a people out of bondage and give them both law and structure. At Sinai he received commandments that defined their worship, their time, their relationships, their identity as a nation. He was also shown the heavenly construction of the tabernacle: a portable edifice where God's presence could dwell among them. Moses reveals the masculine strand as steward of order, shaping a community where holiness could flourish.[6]

**Joseph Smith: Restoring Zion's Structure**
In the last days, Joseph Smith carried the same imprint. His ministry was not only to reveal truth but to set things in order. He organized quorums, gathered scattered Saints into communities, built temples,

translated and published scripture.[7] Each of these was a structure—frames where heaven's power could be received, preserved, and transmitted. Joseph embodied the masculine strand by restoring Zion's structure: not a monument to men, but a dwelling place prepared for God.

The Traits of the Masculine Strand

> **Structure:** building frames where life can thrive.
> **Guardianship:** protecting and preserving, shielding what is precious.
> **Provision:** ensuring the conditions for growth and flourishing.
> **Sacrifice:** laying down strength for others, as Christ said, *"Greater love hath no man than this, that a man lay down his life for his friends."* (John 15:13).

The masculine strand is not hierarchy or domination. It is humble stewardship. When it functions by the Spirit, it creates order so that life may flourish. When it forgets its purpose, it hardens into control and collapses into tyranny. Joseph warned against this distortion: *"No power or influence can or ought to be maintained by virtue of the priesthood, only by persuasion, by long-suffering, by gentleness and meekness, and by love unfeigned."* (D&C 121:41).

The true masculine strand, then, is not loud or domineering. It is steady, humble, and sacrificial—a strength that builds and guards, so that creation may thrive.

## The Masculine Strand Incomplete Without Its Counterpart

The record of scripture and Restoration never presents the masculine strand as sufficient on its own. Wherever God calls a man to build or to guard, there is a corresponding witness of women who nurture, beautify, and sustain. Structure without life cannot endure, and life without structure cannot take root.

Together the two strands form the wholeness of God's image.

### Noah and His Household

Noah built the ark,[8] but without the women aboard it would have been an empty frame. They nurtured the animals, gave tenderness to their young in birth, and carried the music and beauty that made the ordeal bearable.

Without the women, the ark would have been a prison of toil and fear. With them, it became a vessel of hope. The masculine strand preserved the structure, but the feminine preserved the seed and the spirit that kept them alive.

**Abraham and Sarah**

Abraham ordered his household and looked to the stars for God's promise,[9] but Sarah was no less a star reader. For the promise to be fulfilled, she had to attend to the cycles of the moon and of her own body. Each month she must have weighed hope against disappointment, anxiously searching heaven and earth for the fulfillment of God's word.

In her long waiting, she faltered and gave Hagar to Abraham, a decision born of desperation rather than unbelief. Even in her struggle, Sarah bore the cost of promise in her own flesh.

When Isaac was finally conceived, it was through her faith that seed was carried forward. Abraham built the household, but Sarah bore the heir.

**Moses and Miriam**

Moses raised the staff at the Red Sea,[10] but Miriam lifted the song of deliverance. While Moses gave law and pattern, Miriam gave voice and joy, leading the women with timbrels and dances: *"Sing ye to the Lord, for he hath triumphed gloriously"* (Ex 15:21).

Moses structured the nation, but Miriam helped sustain its spirit, turning deliverance into worship. Where law provided the frame, song filled it with beauty and courage.

**Joseph and Emma**

Joseph restored Zion's structure—quorums, scriptures, and temples—but Emma adorned it with beauty and bore it with suffering. She chose hymns that gave the Saints a voice of worship. She nursed her husband back to life after he was tarred and feathered. She endured the loss of children, taught their surviving ones when Joseph was in prison, and stood by him when mobs and betrayals surrounded them.

Without her nurture, her faith, her quiet teaching and steadfast love, Joseph's labors could not have endured. He built; she beautified. He revealed; she preserved. Together they mirrored Eden's pattern of builder and life-bearer.

**Takeaway**

The witness of scripture and the Restoration is clear: masculine strength alone is never enough. Noah's ark, Abraham's household,

Moses' nation, and Joseph's Zion each required the feminine strand—nurturing, discerning, beautifying, sustaining.

Where one strand is silenced, the image of God collapses. Where both move in harmony, creation is preserved, promise fulfilled, law rejoiced in, and Zion rises.

## The Feminine Strand in Scripture and Restoration

The feminine strand is woven through scripture as clearly as the masculine. Wherever God raises up builders and guardians, He also raises life-bearers, perceivers, and beautifiers to complete the image of His work. Their stories remind us that wisdom, nurture, and beauty are not ornament but foundation.

**Ruth: Loyalty that Preserves the Line**
Ruth was a Moabite, a foreigner with no claim on Israel's inheritance. Yet by her loyalty she preserved the lineage of David and, through him, the lineage of Christ. *"Thy people shall be my people, and thy God my God"* (Ruth 1:16). Her covenant faithfulness grafted her into the tree of Israel. The masculine strand establishes households; the feminine strand sustains them with fidelity. Ruth's witness is that beauty and life come from loyalty, even when all else seems barren.

**Mary: Overshadowed by the Spirit**
Mary's story is the center of the New Testament. Overshadowed by the Holy Ghost, she bore the Son of God (Luke 1:35). Her humble consent—*"Be it unto me according to thy word."* (Luke 1:38)—opened the way for salvation itself to enter the world. No masculine power could have fulfilled that role. Mary embodies the feminine strand as life-bearer, the one through whom the Word became flesh and dwelt among us.

**Deborah and Anna: Prophetic Voices**
Deborah judged Israel under the Lord's voice (Judges 4:4–5). Anna, the prophetess, bore testimony of Christ in the temple (Luke 2:36–38). Their lives show that the Spirit's gifts of discernment, prophecy, and vision are poured upon women as fully as upon men. Without their witness, Israel's story and the story of Christ would be impoverished. The masculine strand brings structure; the feminine strand brings prophetic voice.

**Emma Smith: Elect Lady, Partner in Restoration**
Joseph could not have carried Zion's labors without Emma. She was named *"elect lady"* and charged to expound scripture and select hymns (D&C 25). Her hymnbook gave the Saints their worship, their song, their beauty of holiness. She endured mobs, tar and feathering, the loss

of children, and seasons of loneliness when Joseph was imprisoned. She carried burdens of suffering with a dignity that made her her husband's equal partner in faith. Emma embodies the feminine strand as beautifier, nurturer, and sustainer of Zion.

The Traits of the Feminine Strand

> ***Life:*** *breath, vitality, oil, motherhood, healing.*
> ***Awareness:*** *wisdom, perception, prophetic vision.*
> ***Beauty:*** *harmony, song, adornment, restoration of joy.*

Where the masculine strand provides frame and order, the feminine strand breathes life, awakens awareness, and adorns creation with beauty. Together, they restore the image of God.

## The Feminine Strand Incomplete Without Its Counterpart

The feminine strand is never presented as self-sufficient. Her work brings life, beauty, and wisdom into the structures built by the masculine strand. Together the two strands reveal the image of God; apart, the pattern collapses.

**Ruth and Boaz**
Ruth's loyalty and faith preserved the seed,[11] but without Boaz's household her devotion had no shelter. His role as redeemer gave structure to her life, and her role as life-bearer gave continuity to his line. The two together carried forward the promise that led to Christ.

**Mary and Joseph**
Mary bore the Son of God,[12] but Joseph shielded her. His obedience to the angel's command spared her life and preserved the Child. He provided a household and protection in Egypt while she nurtured and sustained. Mary gave life; Joseph guarded it.

**Deborah and Barak**
Deborah judged Israel and prophesied victory,[13] but she called Barak to lead the army. He refused to go without her, and she agreed to accompany him. Deborah's wisdom gave voice; Barak's strength gave structure. Together they delivered Israel.

**Anna and Simeon**
Anna prophesied of the infant Christ in the temple,[14] but her testimony is paired with Simeon's. Both awaited the consolation of Israel, and both bore witness together. Her perception and his blessing revealed the Messiah to Israel's faithful remnant.

**Emma and Joseph**
Emma sustained and beautified, but Joseph built the frame she adorned. His translations, revelations, and structures of Zion were strengthened and humanized by her song, nurture, and endurance. Her witness would not have survived without his, nor his without hers.

**Takeaway**
The feminine strand without the masculine is like beauty without foundation, or life without shelter. It can move hearts, but it cannot endure unless framed. Just as the masculine is sterile without the feminine, so the feminine is fleeting without the masculine. Only together do they reveal the full image of God.

## The Dance of the Strands Together

The image of God is never revealed in isolation. It comes only when the two strands move in harmony.

Structure without life is sterile. Life without structure is fleeting. The masculine provides the frame; the feminine fills it with breath, light, and song. One builds, the other beautifies. One guards, the other gives life. Each alone is partial, but together they embody wholeness.

As we have shown, scripture reveals this dance again and again. Adam tilled and named, but Eve gave life and discernment. Moses gave law and pattern, but Miriam gave song and prophetic voice. Joseph Smith built Zion's frame, but Emma gave it beauty and nurture.

Nature itself testifies of the same image.

> **Butterflies:** the chrysalis holds structure, the butterfly brings life and color. Without the chrysalis there is no transformation; without the butterfly the chrysalis is an empty shell.
>
> **Trees and Fruit:** the trunk and branches give order and rootedness, the blossoms and fruit provide fragrance, nourishment, and continuance. Without trunk the fruit withers; without fruit the trunk is barren.
>
> **Nests and Hatchlings:** the nest offers boundaries and shelter, the chicks bring breath, sound, and renewal. A nest without life is meaningless; life without a nest is exposed and fragile.

> **Music:** notes and meter provide rhythm and order, melody and harmony fill it with beauty. Structure without song is mechanical; melody without order dissolves into chaos.

Everywhere the witness is the same: structure and life, order and beauty, frame and fullness. This is the image of creation itself—the true image of God. All of creation is preaching the same sermon: that the two strands must move as one.

Nephi declared: *"All things which have been given of God from the beginning of the world, unto man, are the typifying of him"* (2 Nephi 11:4).

And Alma added: *"...all things denote there is a God; yea, even the earth, and all things that are upon the face of it... do witness that there is a Supreme Creator"* (Alma 30:44).

The dance of the strands points us to Him. All things testify of Christ.

## Defining Wisdom's House

The language of scripture gives us the pattern: *"Wisdom hath builded her house, she hath hewn out her seven pillars"* (Proverbs 9:1).

Wisdom is not a mere abstraction, but a living presence—a feminine figure who builds, sustains, and adorns creation. She is described as a master-worker beside the Lord in the beginning:

> *"The Lord possessed me in the beginning of his way, before his works of old. I was set up from everlasting, from the beginning, or ever the earth was. ... Then I was by him, as one brought up with him: and I was daily his delight, rejoicing always before him; rejoicing in the habitable part of his earth; and my delights were with the sons of men."* (Proverbs 8:22–23, 30–31)

Here Wisdom is not a symbol but a personified presence—rejoicing at creation, delighting in humanity, standing beside God as a partner in His work. Ancient Israel understood her as the Lady of the Temple: a feminine counterpart who represented life, discernment, and prophetic vision.

Modern readers may be less familiar with this Lady, because she was later removed from Israel's worship. Scholar Margaret Barker has written extensively on this. A Cambridge-trained biblical scholar, Barker has shown that Josiah's reform (2 Kings 23) purged the older symbols of Israel's temple, removing the Lady—Wisdom—from its heart. She explains:

> *"The Lady in the Temple was Wisdom, and she was removed when the reformers purged the symbols of the older faith. The loss of Wisdom was the loss of the Mother from the temple, and with her the loss of vision and the gift of prophecy."* (The Mother of the Lord, vol. 1, pp. 93–96)

When Wisdom was silenced, prophecy waned. When she was erased, the gifts of vision and healing dried up. Israel's worship became all structure with no life—a temple without its Lady, a house without breath.

To speak of *"Wisdom's House Restored,"* then, is to speak of the return of this strand—not as ornament, but as essential. Proverbs gives the blueprint: a house, built on pillars. The masculine strand orders and frames; the feminine strand fills with life, wisdom, and beauty. Together they create a house in which God's presence can dwell.

And in 1842, Joseph Smith turned to the daughters of Zion and restored that house among the Saints.

## Joseph builded her house

On March 17, 1842, Joseph Smith met with a gathering of women in Nauvoo. In that upper room above the red brick store, he organized what would become known as the Relief Society. But to understand what happened that day, we must hear it in Joseph's own words:[15]

As we discussed in Chapter 3 on Priesthood and Keys, to turn a key is to unlock a door—to grant access to a realm of knowledge and power. By turning the key to the sisters, Joseph did not place them under the order of men; he invited them into a house that had been prepared for them from the beginning: Wisdom's house.

The Relief Society was thus born as more than a society of service. It was the restored dwelling place of the feminine strand in Zion—a house where women would heal the sick, prophesy, discern, speak in tongues, and adorn Zion with song and beauty.

Emma Smith was sustained as president, fulfilling her earlier charge to *"expound scriptures and to select hymns"* (D&C 25). And the minutes of those early meetings record the Spirit poured out upon the daughters of Zion in power.

The Relief Society was therefore not an auxiliary tacked onto the structure of the Church—like an extra bedroom or annex added to a house. It was woven into the very DNA of the Restoration.

From the beginning, the work carried two strands—knowledge and wisdom, structure and life—and only together do they reveal the true image of God. Through Joseph, the Lord revealed what was already integral; Joseph simply opened the door for that understanding to flow.

## Women Manifesting Gifts in Nauvoo

When the key was turned, the Spirit moved. The sisters immediately began to breathe life into Nauvoo. Wherever they gathered, the gifts of God were manifest.

Women laid hands on the sick and they recovered. They prophesied of things to come and spoke in tongues as a sign of the Spirit's presence. They exercised discernment, guarding Zion from deception. Their meetings recorded dreams, visions, and revelations—living proof that the Spirit was poured out upon the daughters of Zion, just as Joel and Peter had promised: *"Your sons and your daughters shall prophesy"* (Joel 2:28; Acts 2:17).

Emma Smith presided as president, fulfilling her earlier charge to *"expound scriptures and to select hymns"* (D&C 25). Her hymnbook gave the Saints their voice of worship—a gift of beauty that adorned Zion's order with song.

Where Joseph provided frame and structure, Emma and her sisters filled it with harmony and life.

These manifestations were not marginal. They were central. The Relief Society was Wisdom's house in action—a living testimony that the feminine strand was restored alongside the masculine. Zion was meant to rise not only by law and order, but by prophecy and beauty, healing and song.

## The Most Explicit Feminine Restoration

The Relief Society was Wisdom's house restored—the most explicit embodiment of the feminine strand in Joseph's ministry. In that upper room in Nauvoo, the Lord revealed what had always been integral to the very life of His work: the life-bearing, discerning, beautifying strand without which the Church of the Lamb could never flourish.

Through Joseph, the key was turned. Knowledge and wisdom, structure and life, law and prophecy were joined together. In the Relief Society, the daughters of Zion stepped into their place as healers, prophets, and builders alongside their brethren.

This was not a temporary flourish, but the very DNA of the Restoration revealed. Where the masculine frames, the feminine fills. Where one guards, the other gives life. Together they reveal the image of God.

The Relief Society therefore stands as a living witness: the Church of the Lamb cannot be whole until both strands move in harmony.

## When Either Strand Is Suppressed

The image of God is revealed only when both strands move together. To silence one is to weaken the other. To suppress either is to distort the whole.

**When the masculine strand is suppressed**
Without guardianship and structure, chaos follows. A house without frame cannot stand. Israel in the days of the Judges bore this witness: *"Every man did that which was right in his own eyes"* (Judges 21:25). Without order, families unravel and communities dissolve. What should have been preserved perishes for lack of protection.

**When the feminine strand is suppressed**
Without life and wisdom, structure collapses into sterility. Prophecy fades, vision is lost, healing withers, and beauty turns to silence. Josiah's purge of the First Temple stripped away the Lady of Wisdom, and with her the gift of vision.[16] Worship continued, but the Spirit was absent. A temple remained, but it was hollow.

## The Restoration bears the same witness

In Joseph's ministry both strands were alive. He built, ordered, and guarded; Emma and the sisters discerned, beautified, and healed. Together they revealed the DNA of the Church of the Lamb—the DNA of the Restoration itself. But after Joseph's death, the feminine strand was suppressed. The Relief Society was disbanded, women no longer laid hands upon the sick, and the voice of Wisdom was muted. What remained was structure without life, order without song.

The lesson is plain:

> *Masculine without feminine = a frame with no breath.*
> *Feminine without masculine = life with no shelter.*
> *Only together do they reveal the image of God.*

Where one strand is silenced, the Church of the Lamb falters. Where both are honored, the Restoration flourishes.

### The Image of God Restored in Type

From Eden to Nauvoo, the witness is consistent: the image of God is revealed only when both strands move as one. Adam tilled and named, but Eve gave life and discernment. Together they embodied the beginning. Joseph built Zion's frame, but Emma and her sisters adorned it with beauty and breathed it with prophecy. Together they revealed the Restoration's DNA.

The Relief Society was Wisdom's house restored—the daughters of Zion rising into their place as prophets, healers, and life-bearers alongside their brethren.

This was not a flourish or an experiment. It was the Lord revealing what had always been integral to the very life of His work: that the Church of the Lamb cannot be whole without both strands in harmony.

Suppress either strand and the house collapses. Structure without life becomes sterile; life without structure cannot endure. But where the masculine and feminine move together, the image of God shines forth in fullness.

This chapter has shown the strands in type—builder and beautifier, steward and life-bearer, knowledge and wisdom. In the chapter that follows, we will step beyond type into the very heart of eternity, where the Godhead itself is revealed. What Joseph restored in pattern will open in fullness, preparing us to see the image of God more clearly than ever before.

## Chapter 4 Notes

1 Classical astronomy and ancient mythology consistently associate Mercury with eloquence, Mars with strength or war, Virgo with purity and harvest, and Cassiopeia with queenship. These symbolic pairings appear across Greek, Roman, and medieval Christian traditions and serve here as poetic witnesses to creation's dual testimony.

2 Ruach (רוּחַ) in Hebrew is grammatically feminine and used throughout the Old Testament to denote *"Spirit," "breath,"* or *"wind"* (e.g., Genesis 1:2; Ezekiel 37:5). In Greek, sophia (σοφία, "wisdom") is feminine, while logos (λόγος, *"word"* or *"reason"*) is masculine. In Latin, sol (*"sun"*) is masculine, whereas terra

(*"earth"*), sapientia (*"wisdom"*), ecclesia (*"church"*), and Sion (*"Zion"*) are feminine. These grammatical genders are consistent across the Romance languages and reinforce the symbolic pattern of masculine and feminine expression in creation and theology.

3 The Hebrew verbs in Genesis 2:15, *ʿābad* (עָבַד) and *šāmar* (שָׁמַר), carry rich nuance: *ʿābad* means *"to work, serve, or cultivate,"* while šāmar means *"to keep, guard, or preserve."* Together they describe Adam's divine commission not of domination but of stewardship and care.

4 The Hebrew phrase *ʿēzer kenegdô* (עֵזֶר כְּנֶגְדּוֹ) in Genesis 2:18 is commonly rendered *"an help meet for him." ʿĒzer* means *"help"* or *"one who assists,"* a term also used for God as deliverer and protector (e.g., Deuteronomy 33:26, Psalm 33:20). *Kenegdô* means *"corresponding to him," "opposite him,"* or *"equal to him."* Together the phrase signifies a counterpart or co-equal partner, not a subordinate.*"a help corresponding to him."*

5 Genesis 6:14

6 At Sinai the Lord declared His law through Moses, establishing Israel's covenant identity and order (Exodus 19–20). He then revealed the pattern for the tabernacle, saying, *"According to all that I show thee, after the pattern of the tabernacle, and the pattern of all the instruments thereof, even so shall ye make it."* (Exodus 25:9). The law defined their worship and relationships; the tabernacle embodied divine order and presence among them.

7 Joseph Smith's ministry reflected the same divine impulse to build and order. He organized priesthood quorums (D&C 107), gathered the Saints into stakes and cities of refuge such as Kirtland and Nauvoo (D&C 101:20–21; 124:25–36), directed the building of temples (Kirtland 1836; Nauvoo 1841), and produced sacred translation and publication projects including the Book of Mormon (1830), the D&C (1835), and the inspired revision of the Bible (Joseph Smith Translation).

8 *"Thus did Noah; according to all that God commanded him, so did he"* (Genesis 6:22). Noah's obedience in constructing the ark preserved every form of life, establishing the first recorded house of refuge—a type of salvation through obedience and divine design.

9 The Lord said of Abraham, *"For I know him, that he will command his children and his household after him, and they shall keep the way of the Lord"* (Genesis 18:19). Earlier, the Lord brought Abraham forth and said, *"Look now toward heaven, and tell the stars, if thou be able to number them... So shall thy seed be"* (Genesis 15:5). Abraham's stewardship joined earthly order with heavenly promise.

10 At the shore of the Red Sea, *"Moses stretched out his hand over the sea; and the Lord caused the sea to go back by a strong east wind all that night, and made the sea dry land"* (Exodus 14:21). The raised staff became a symbol of divine authority—order commanding chaos, structure prevailing over the deep.

11 Ruth's devotion to Naomi preserved the covenant line through which David and, in time, Jesus would be born. *"And Ruth said, Entreat me not to leave thee... for whither thou goest, I will go"* (Ruth 1:16). Her loyalty and faith made her the great-grandmother of David (Ruth 4:17–22), a witness that steadfast love sustains the living seed.

12 *"The angel of the Lord appeared unto Joseph in a dream, saying, Joseph, thou son of David, fear not to take unto thee Mary thy wife: for that which is conceived in her is of the Holy Ghost"* (Matthew 1:20). Mary bore the Son of God; Joseph shielded and sustained her, fulfilling the divine pattern of life joined with guardianship.

13 *"And Deborah, a prophetess, the wife of Lapidoth, she judged Israel at that time... And she sent and called Barak... Hath not the Lord God of Israel commanded?"* (Judges 4:4–6). Deborah's leadership joined wisdom with courage; she governed Israel and prophesied their deliverance, standing as a living witness of the feminine strand empowered by God's Spirit.

14 *"And there was one Anna, a prophetess... which departed not from the temple, but served God with fastings and prayers night and day. And she coming in that instant gave thanks likewise unto the Lord, and spake of him to all them that looked for redemption in Jerusalem"* (Luke 2:36–38). Anna's temple

prophecy testified that the Spirit of revelation rests equally upon the daughters of God.

15 Minutes of the Nauvoo Female Relief Society, March 17, 1842. Joseph Smith said to the assembled sisters, *"I now turn the key to you in the name of God, and this Society shall rejoice, and knowledge and intelligence shall flow down from this time"* (Relief Society Minutes).
Book, Nauvoo, Illinois, 1842, in History of the Church, 4:607.)
This declaration marked the formal organization of the Relief Society and Joseph's acknowledgment of the women's divine commission.

16 Biblical historian Margaret Barker identifies King Josiah's temple purge (2 Kings 22–23) as the moment when the older First Temple traditions were suppressed—including the figure she calls the Lady of Wisdom or the Lady of the Temple. In removing her symbols—the Asherah, the Tree of Life, and the heavenly host—the reformers erased Israel's older vision of divine Wisdom.
See Margaret Barker, The Mother of the Lord, Vol. 1: The Lady in the Temple (London: T&T Clark, 2012), pp. 75–96.

# The Godhead

## The Breath of Heaven Within Us

*"For this is life eternal, that they might know thee..."* (John 17:3)

### Knowledge—The Power of God unto Salvation

In the beginning, before a single star took shape, there was only light and matter unorganized. God the Father went out into that chaos and began to give it form. He organized the elements, set them in order, and prepared a foundation where life could dwell.

When His work was ready, Heavenly Mother came forth and breathed life into that structure.

> *Her breath made it living.*
> *Her wisdom made it aware.*
> *Her love made it beautiful.*

Together They filled the heavens with light and motion. When all was ready, They brought forth Their children—sons and daughters of glory, made in Their image, each one a spark of Their own intelligence.

But in time They looked upon Their children and saw something that stirred Their compassion.

Some were radiant and strong, but others were troubled—gentle souls held captive by those who had learned to use power without love.

The Prophet Joseph explained:

> *"Before the foundation of the earth, the spirits of all men were subject to oppression, and the express purpose in God giving it a tabernacle was to arm it against the powers of darkness."*[1]

The Father and the Mother could not leave Their family in that condition. They knew that for Their children to become like Them, they must be free—free to act, to learn, to love, and to grow.

So They convened a great council in heaven to prepare a way.

Each child would come to an earthly home, receive a body, and enter a world of opposites where agency could be tested and experience gained.

This would become their second estate—a time of proving and progression, where light and darkness would both be present so that choice might be real.

Yet the plan carried a price.

A world of opposition would mean a world where weakness and imperfection could take root. Through disobedience and deception, some would fall into sin; others into sorrow. The very earth itself would be marked by decay, and death would enter as a necessary gate.

Without divine help, no soul could pass through that gate and return clean. Imperfection would stain the very children They longed to bring home and help obtain their later estates—life with Them in eternal glory.

Therefore, redemption had to be built into the plan from the beginning. Someone pure, willing, and capable would need to descend below all things, bear the weight of that fall, and open a path of return.

It was here that two voices arose in the Council.

One—the voice of love and order—belonged to Jehovah, the Firstborn of the Father and the Mother. He offered Himself as Redeemer, saying, *"Here am I, send me"* (Abraham 3:27).

His plan honored agency and upheld the law of mercy, allowing every child to choose and to learn through experience.

But another voice sought to alter that plan. lucifer, filled with ambition, offered a counterfeit: he would save all but by taking away choice. He promised glory without growth, safety without struggle, and demanded that all honor be his.[2]

His offer sounded compassionate but was rooted in control. If accepted, it would have destroyed the very freedom that makes love possible.

Then came the great division.

Some aligned with light, others with the shadow of compulsion. Thus began the opposition in all things,[3] the process by which every soul would learn the difference between fear and love, ignorance and understanding, death and life eternal.

The Father and the Mother honored Their Firstborn's offering. Jehovah would descend as the Son, the Redeemer of the world. Through Him, mercy would satisfy justice, and every child willing to learn truth and walk in love could return home.

This was the purpose of the Council—to make redemption possible so that none of Their children need be lost.

And so four divine gifts were prepared for the journey of the soul: **a body, knowledge, wisdom, and redemption.**

Each is a portion of Their own power, shared with Their children.

> **A body** grants the right to act in the worlds of matter.
> **Knowledge** grants understanding of truth.
> **Wisdom**—Mother's eternal gift—shows how to use that knowledge with love.
> **Redemption**—through the Son—restores what weakness and sin would otherwise destroy.

Together these gifts make us free.

Joseph taught:

> *"Knowledge is necessary to life and godliness. ... Knowledge is revelation. Hear all ye brethren, this grand key: knowledge is the power of God unto salvation."*[4]

But knowledge alone is not enough. Knowledge must be warmed by love and shaped by wisdom, or it hardens into pride. That is why our Parents sent us here—to learn not only truth, but how to live it.

He warned again:

> *"As far as we degenerate from God, we descend to the devil and lose knowledge; and without knowledge we cannot be saved."*[5]

To lose light is to lose liberty:

> *"Wherefore, men are free according to the flesh ... they are free to choose liberty and eternal life, through the great Mediator of all men, or to choose captivity and death."* (2 Nephi 2:27)

The adversary's power has always rested on ignorance and fear, while God's power flows through understanding and compassion. lucifer's plan remains unchanged: control through deception, fear, and confusion.

But the Father and the Mother teach liberty through light, inviting all to know for themselves. When truth enters a heart, darkness loses its hold.

That is why the Prophet said, *"A man [or woman] is saved no faster than he gets knowledge; for if he does not get knowledge, he will be brought into captivity by some evil power in the other world, as evil spirits will have more knowledge and consequently more power."*[6]

You see, our Parents' plan was never a test of worthiness—it was a school of light. This world was designed to be a place of discovery and refinement, where experience would teach what instruction alone never could.

> *Every truth received expands our capacity to love.*
> *Every principle learned enlarges our power to serve.*
> *And every act of genuine love increases the wisdom that ties us back to Them.*

Mortality, then, is not punishment—it is opportunity. It is the sacred classroom where knowledge is tested, refined, and made wise through experience, and where redemption gives every failure a second birth.

Here we learn what our Parents already know: that all power flows through love, and all love flows through understanding.

Each truth embraced brings us a little nearer to Them, until the day when Their light and ours become one.

## O My Father

There are truths so ancient, so woven into the fabric of creation, that they can never be fully erased—only obscured and tarnished by the evil one, who seeks above all to blot them from our collective memory.

When the Restoration began, the Lord whispered these truths back into the hearts of His people, one by one. Some came through revelation. Others came through song.

In 1843, Eliza R. Snow—sister to Lorenzo Snow and secretary to the Relief Society—penned words that carried more light than perhaps even she realized at the time.

She wrote:

> *O my Father, thou that dwellest*
> *In the high and glorious place—*
> *When shall I regain thy presence*
> *And again behold thy face?*
> *In thy holy habitation,*
> *Did my spirit once reside?*
> *In my first primeval childhood*
> *Was I nurtured near thy side?*[7]

Her words swept through Nauvoo like the sound of memory awakening. Saints who had long spoken only of *"Father"* suddenly felt something stir within them—an echo of Mother.

It was as though the Spirit itself was testifying: "*You have not only a Father in heaven, but also a Mother who loves you still.*"

Eliza continued:

> *For I learned to call thee Father,*
> *Through thy Spirit from on high,*
> *But until the key of knowledge*
> *Was restored, I knew not why.*
> *In the heavens are parents single?*
> *No, the thought makes reason stare;*
> *Truth is reason—truth eternal*
> *Tells me I've a mother there.*[8]

These lines became scripture in song—a hymn of remembrance, carrying the essence of what Joseph had taught and lived.

This was Wisdom restored through the feminine, by the Divine Feminine Herself.

Through Eliza's pen, the Mother at last found voice again among Her children. The long-banished Lady of the Heavens, who had been erased from temples and texts since the days of Josiah, returned quietly in a hymn sung by women.

She came not with thunder, but with remembrance.

Joseph had restored the key of knowledge; Eliza turned it in the lock. And through that small act of faith, a flood of divine memory poured forth. From that time forward, those who had eyes to see and hearts to feel could no longer think of heaven as solitary.

The image of God was whole again—Father and Mother, joined in eternal union, revealed through the Son.

The early Saints sang it by candlelight and on dusty roads, their voices rising like prayer: "In the heavens are parents single?"

That single question answered centuries of silence.

It declared that God is not a lonely sovereign but a living union of love—Father and Mother, the image of all creation. In that knowledge, hearts were healed, families were sanctified, and Zion's foundations grew a little stronger.

The hymn gave voice to what Joseph had already restored—the truth that heaven's image is never solitary.

## God Is Not Solitary

From the beginning, the scriptures have borne quiet witness that God is not solitary. The very first page of Genesis opens the mystery:

> *"Let us make man in our image, after our likeness: ... So God created man in his own image, in the image of God created he him; male and female created he them."* (Genesis 1:26–27)

Here, in the first breath of creation, the plural voice of heaven speaks. It is the voice of unity—Father and Mother, speaking as one. The image of God has never been a single figure standing alone; it has always been the harmony of two divine Beings whose love brings life to all creation.

Together They formed Adam and Eve to mirror Themselves—two becoming one flesh, distinct yet inseparable, male and female, life and law, heart and mind, light and love.

The masculine and feminine strands of divinity are not competing forces; they are complementary currents of the same eternal light. Father orders and sustains; Mother quickens and beautifies.

Father establishes law and boundary; Mother breathes wisdom and mercy into all that law protects. He builds the frame; She fills it with living color.

From Their union all creation flows.

This image has echoed through every world and every dispensation. The sun and the moon, the sea and the shore, the seed and the soil—all testify of partnership. Every act of true creation requires two powers joined as one.

When one dominates and the other is dismissed, the result is distortion and death. When both are honored and united, life flourishes in abundance.

The ancient writers knew this.

Long before the Lady of Wisdom was silenced, she was praised in Israel's earliest songs:

> *"Doth not wisdom cry? and understanding put forth her voice? ... The Lord possessed me in the beginning of his way, before his works of old."* (Proverbs 8:1, 22)

Wisdom—*ḥokmâ* in Hebrew, *Sophia* in Greek—was always described in the feminine.[9] She was not a metaphor for intellect; She was the living breath of the Divine Feminine—the awareness, love, and adornment of creation itself.

It was She who stood beside the Father when the foundations of the earth were laid, rejoicing before Him and delighting in the sons and daughters of men (Proverbs 8:30–31). When Josiah's reform purged Her from the temple,[10] Israel lost more than a symbol; they lost the understanding of how heaven and earth were meant to work together.

The world forgot that the Godhead is not masculine alone.

## The Prayer of Oneness—How the Lord Revealed the Godhead

When the disciples asked Jesus how to pray, He did not give them a formula to memorize. He gave them a revelation—a window into the relationship of heaven itself. Each line of what we now call *The Lord's Prayer* reflects the harmony of the Father and the Mother, the mediation of the Son, and the indwelling Spirit that makes heaven's order alive within us.

---

### 1. Abwoon d'bwashmaya

**Common translation:** *"Our Father who art in heaven."*
**Revealed sense:** *"O Source of all life—Father and Mother of the shining realms."*

The Aramaic word *Abwoon* joins *Abba* (Father) with *Woon* (Womb, or Birther). It calls upon both aspects of the Divine as one creative power—the Father's structure and the Mother's vitality, united in love. *Bwashmaya* means *"in the heavens,"* literally *"in the realms of light."* The Lord began His prayer by addressing the full Godhead, showing that creation is born of divine partnership between Father and Mother, not solitude.

In short, the Savior knew His eternal Parents.

---

**2. Nethqadash shmakh**

**Common translation:** *"Hallowed be Thy name."*
**Revealed sense:** *"Let Your name—Your nature—be made holy within us."*

In the ancient tongue, *"name"* meant character or essence. To hallow His name is to awaken Their likeness within the heart. Holiness is not distance; it is transformation.

When Their name is sanctified in us, heaven begins to rise from within.

---

**3. Tete malkuthakh**

**Common translation:** *"Thy kingdom come."*
**Revealed sense:** *"Let Your divine order and harmony arise within us."*

The Pharisees searched for a kingdom built with walls and crowns, but Jesus declared, *"The kingdom of God cometh not with observation... behold, the kingdom of God is within you"* (Luke 17:20–21). The word *malkutha* carries both governance and relationship. The kingdom comes when the Father's structure and the Mother's wisdom reign together in the soul—when divine love governs from within.

---

**4. Nehwey sebyanach aykanna d'bwashmaya aph b'arha**

**Common translation:** *"Thy will be done, on earth as it is in heaven."*
**Revealed sense:** *"May the unity that reigns in heaven be reflected in the earth—within us."*

Heaven and earth are not separate spheres but reflections of the same creative order. The will of God is that what is whole above may be restored below. When the Spirit brings the Mother's wisdom into the form the Father has prepared, heaven touches earth, and the two move as one.

---

**5. Hawvlán lachma d'sunqanan yaomana**

**Common translation:** *"Give us this day our daily bread."*
**Revealed sense:** *"Grant us this day the nourishment of Your wisdom and life."*

In Aramaic, *lachma* means more than bread—it means sustenance, understanding, and life-energy. Jesus was not merely asking for food; He was inviting daily revelation. This bread is the Mother's gift—wisdom that descends like manna from heaven. Through the Son, the Bread of Life, that wisdom becomes living truth within us.

---

**6. Washboqlan khaubayn aykana d'aph khnan shbwoqan l'khayyabayn**

**Common translation:** *"Forgive us our debts, as we forgive our debtors."*
**Revealed sense:** *"Release the cords that bind us, as we release those bound to us."*

The Aramaic *shboqlan* means *"loosen"* or *"release."* Forgiveness is not a transaction—it is the restoration of flow. When we forgive, we create space for the Son's redeeming power to move through us. The same current that frees us also frees those we forgive.

---

**7. Wela tahlan l'nesyuna, ela patzan min bisha**

**Common translation:** *"Lead us not into temptation, but deliver us from evil."*
**Revealed sense:** *"Do not let us be overtaken by the test; rescue us from the bondage of error."*
Here the Lord acknowledges the Holy Spirit's role as protector and guide. Temptation is the pressure that reveals our alignment; deliverance comes through light. The Spirit's

indwelling presence teaches discernment, steadies the heart, and strengthens the will. It is the voice that says, *"This is the way; walk ye in it"* (Isaiah 30:21).

---

**8. Metol dilakhie malkutha wahayla wateshbukhta l'ahlam almin**

**Common translation:** *"For Thine is the kingdom, and the power, and the glory forever."*
**Revealed sense:** *"For Yours is the kingdom (Father), the power (Son), and the glory (Spirit and Mother) throughout all ages."*

This closing unites the Godhead in one harmonious triad. *Malkutha*—the Father's order. *Hayla*—the Son's redeeming strength. *Teshbukhta*—the radiance of the Spirit, the glory of the Mother reflected in all creation. In these three, heaven's circle is complete.

Christ's prayer begins and ends in oneness.[11]

## Closing Reflection

The Lord's Prayer is more than a set of petitions—it is the Lord Himself showing us how heaven breathes. Every phrase unveils relationship: Father and Mother giving life, the Son mediating between light and flesh, the Spirit drawing both into one heart.

When we speak this prayer with understanding, it becomes more than words—it becomes a reunion. Heaven and earth meet within, and the Godhead—the divine family—finds expression again in the soul of man.

## The Living Order of Heaven

As we learned earlier, all creation runs by law. *"All kingdoms have a law given."* (D&C 88:37), and every law and kingdom has a steward of light assigned to it.

From the smallest atom to the greatest kingdom, the order of heaven is one of love—organized, purposeful, and alive within every realm of glory. Paul glimpsed this when he wrote, *"There are also celestial bodies, and bodies terrestrial, and bodies telestial; ... one glory of the sun, and another glory of the moon, and another glory of the stars"* (1 Corinthians 15:40-41).

Joseph later saw the same panorama in vision and recorded it in Doctrine and Covenants 76. Each glory differs in light and law, and each is ministered to by a member of the Godhead who perfectly embodies that order of divine life.

## The Three Realms of Glory

**The Holy Ghost** ministers to the *telestial* world—the realm in which we now live. Here the Spirit works as conscience and comforter, whispering truth, softening hearts, and testifying of Christ. This is where each of us begins—learning by faith to hear the whisper of truth amid the noise of mortality.

His influence is the first light that pierces mortal darkness, the gentle schooling that prepares souls for a higher law.

**The Son—Jehovah, Jesus Christ**—presides over the terrestrial kingdom.

When He said, *"I will pray the Father, and he shall give you another Comforter,"* He promised a progression. The Holy Ghost is the first Comforter, the One who abides with us in this fallen sphere. But the Savior Himself is the *Second Comforter,* the One who appears to the pure in heart and whose presence transforms the faithful into beings of greater light.

His reign defines the Terrestrial order—the glory of those who *"receive the presence of the Son, but not of the fullness of the Father"* (D&C 76:77).

It is to this order that Zion must rise, for Zion is the Terrestrial condition on earth—the society of those who dwell with Christ in peace.

Above these stands the Celestial realm, the dwelling place of the Father and the Mother.

They are the Third Comforter, the culmination of the promise Christ gave His disciples:

> *"If a man love me, he will keep my words: and my Father will love him, and we will come unto him, and make our abode with him."* (John 14:23)

In this final union, Their children receive the fullness of Their glory, becoming one with Them in mind and in heart.

The progression of comfort is also the progression of presence:

> *First Comforter—Spirit*
> *Second Comforter—Son*
> *Third Comforter—Father and Mother*

## The Law of Glories

Each degree of glory operates by its own law (D&C 88:22). To abide a higher law, a soul must first be quickened by a higher light.

> **The Holy Ghost** entices and inspires us toward telestial obedience—truth received by faith.
> **The Son** tutors us in terrestrial transformation—truth lived through faith, hope, and charity.
> **The Father and Mother** bestow celestial fullness—truth perfected in love.

As Joseph taught, *"You have got to learn how to be Gods yourselves... by going from a small capacity to a greater capacity."*[12]

Progression through these glories is the very path of exaltation: from belief to companionship to unity.

## The Functional Godhead

The *Lectures on Faith* describe the Godhead not as a closed mystery but as a living relationship of divine Beings working together in perfect unity:

> *"These three constitute the Godhead and are one: the Father, the Son, and the Holy Spirit. The Father being a personage of spirit, glory, and power; the Son a personage of tabernacle...; the Holy Spirit the mind of the Father and the Son."* (Lectures on Faith 5, 1835 Doctrine and Covenants)

Joseph further clarified this:

> *"There are two personages who constitute the great, matchless, governing and supreme power over all things—by whom all things were created and made, that are created and made, whether visible or invisible; whether in heaven, on earth, or in the earth, under the earth, or throughout the immensity of space. They are the Father and the Son: the Father being a personage of spirit, glory, and power; possessing all perfection and fullness. The Son, who was in the bosom of the Father, a personage of tabernacle, made or fashioned like unto man, or being in the form and likeness of*

> *man, or rather, man was formed after his likeness and in his image. He is also the express image and likeness of the personage of the Father, possessing all the fullness of the Father, or the same fullness with the Father; being begotten of him, and was ordained from before the foundation of the world to be a propitiation for the sins of all those who should believe on his name, and is called the Son because of the flesh."* (Lectures on Faith 5:2, 1835 Doctrine and Covenants)

This teaching removes all confusion. Joseph revealed two distinct, sovereign, exalted Beings—separate in person yet perfectly united in purpose. The Father stands as the eternal Source of glory and power; the Son embodies the living revelation of that glory within creation. Their unity is not a blending of identity but the perfect harmony of will, mind, and love.

Within this divine order, creation itself bears witness to the Divine Feminine—*the Mother*, the co-Creator and eternal companion of the Father. Together They form the fountain of life from which all worlds spring. She and the Father are the Creators; the Son is the Redeemer; and the Holy Ghost is the Testator.

From this we discern the three eternal functions that govern all creation:

> ***Creator—The Father and the Mother:*** *They bring order out of chaos, breathe life into form, awaken awareness, and crown all things with beauty.*
> ***Redeemer—The Son:*** *He descends below all things to bridge law and mercy, offering deliverance and resurrection to every child who will come.*
> ***Testator—The Holy Ghost:*** *He bears record of truth, comforts the sorrowful, and sanctifies the willing heart.*

These roles operate in perfect unity. Wherever one labors, the influence of the others is felt—for Their work is one eternal round: creation, redemption, and sanctification—law, love, and life moving together through every world and every soul.

## The Vision and the Law of Glory

As a young man searching for forgiveness and light, Joseph walked into the woods near his home one spring morning.

He had read the simple promise in James 1:5: *"If any of you lack wisdom, let him ask of God, that giveth to all men liberally, and upbraideth not; and it shall be given him."* Those words struck his heart like living fire. He believed them. And because he believed, he acted.

Kneeling alone among the trees, he poured out the prayer of an honest soul who desired to know which church he should join and how his sins might be forgiven.

It was then that the heavens opened.

What followed was not called the first *visitation*, but the First Vision—and the word itself reveals the law behind it.

Joseph's physical body remained on earth, yet his spirit was carried upward to behold things of a higher order. He was caught up into the realm of light that his current estate could bear, much as prophets before him had been *"carried away in the Spirit."*[13]

There, within that field of brilliance, he saw the glory of the Second Comforter—the Redeemer of this world.

And as at the Jordan, when a voice from heaven proclaimed, *"Behold my beloved Son, in whom I am well pleased"* (Matthew 3:17), and again in the land Bountiful, when the same voice declared the same words to the Nephites (3 Nephi 11:7), so in the grove the Father's voice bore witness of the Son.

The scene was the same pattern of heaven: the Father's voice introducing, the Son revealing.

Joseph later described the light as brighter than the sun, descending gradually until it enveloped him.[14] It was a lawful manifestation, precisely suited to his light and estate, and it marked the beginning of his long ascent toward the higher glories.

In the years that followed, Joseph communed with angels, conversed with translated beings, and beheld visions of worlds and dispensations beyond number.[15] Though he never left a written testimony of it, the pattern of his life suggests that in vision, he ascended through each estate until he at last beheld the realm of the Father and the Mother themselves.

He became the exemplar in this dispensation of that very progression: from the voice, to the Son, to the fullness of the Father's presence.

Each encounter enlarged his capacity to bear light, just as it can enlarge ours.

For the law of heaven is constant—glory received prepares the soul for greater glory yet to come.

Joseph's *first* vision was the beginning of that eternal education, the moment when the heavens once again reached down to lift the earth, one child at a time.

## The Path of Progression

Many yearn for celestial fullness without walking the steps of sanctification that lead to it. But there is no sudden leap from the telestial to the celestial; there is only faithful ascent.

The Second Comforter must first be received before the Third can be endured.

The calling in this generation is to rise to the Terrestrial order—to live so that the Son may dwell among us and prepare us for the presence of the Father and the Mother. That is the call to Zion itself.

Each step is a gift of grace; each glory a greater capacity for Their love.

## Who I Thought God Is

Joseph's story does more than recount a vision; it invites us into one of our own. And as I walked his path—reading, asking, wrestling—I began to notice that the same God who opened the heavens for him was quietly opening my eyes too.

For most of my life, I thought I already knew who God was. But when I began to follow Joseph's witness rather than inherited tradition, the picture started to change.

I began to see God not through creeds or repetition, but through the unfolding reality of who He truly is.

One afternoon, while sitting in a courthouse lobby, my gaze drifted to a mural of the Ten Commandments.

As I read the familiar words, one phrase seemed to lift from the stone itself:

> *"Thou shalt have no other gods before me."* (Exodus 20:3)

He did not say before us.

In that moment, the commandment itself bore witness: there is one sovereign God to be worshiped, not a panel or a council of equals.

I remember thinking, *"No way. I haven't been obeying that commandment. Ever."*

That simple realization became a turning point for me.

Just as the Lord opened my understanding line upon line through those words etched in stone, He opened Joseph's understanding line upon line through sacred encounter. Different paths, same Teacher. Both fulfilled Paul's promise that *"the eyes of your understanding [would be] enlightened"* (Ephesians 1:18).

And when you read Joseph's accounts closely, you notice something almost everyone overlooks: he never names the heavenly figures he saw.

He doesn't call one *"Heavenly Father,"* or the other *"Jesus Christ."* He never even labels one as *"the Son."* He simply describes what happened—a divine Being appeared, spoke, and forgave.

Joseph wasn't mapping theology; he was recounting a sacred encounter. Understanding, for both of us, came not from the definitions learned by the culture around us, but from revelation.

That is how the Lord teaches still—one light-filled still-small-voice at a time.

When we seek Him in humility, the same unfolding order appears: first the whisper, then the witness, then the dawning comprehension that the One we worship is infinitely more than we imagined.

And in time, as the veil thins, we begin to recognize that the image revealed in the Son reflects not only the Father, but also the Mother, whose love and wisdom are inseparably one with His.

## Jehovah—God of This System

From Joseph's vision in the grove to every revelation that followed, one truth stands constant: *Jehovah is the God of this system.*

He is the living bridge between heaven and earth—the Son who stepped forward in the Grand Council, saying, *"Here am I, send me"* (Abraham 3:27). In that moment He wasn't only volunteering to atone for sin, but accepting stewardship over an entire order of creation.

The Father and the Mother placed the care of this system in His hands. Every law, every orbit, every soul within it moves under His light.

The scriptures speak this plainly. The Lord told Moses, *"By the word of my power have I created them, which is mine Only Begotten Son. Worlds without number have I created; and by the Son I created them"* (Moses 1:32–33).

When He appeared to the Nephites, He declared, *"I am the God of Israel, and the God of the whole earth"* (3 Nephi 9:15).

These are not metaphors—they describe administration. Jehovah governs this system as the appointed heir of the Father and the Mother. Through Him that Their law, love, and life flow to every soul, every world, every system They have created.

When He came in the meridian of time, He entered His own dominion. John wrote of Him, *"He was in the world, and the world was made by him, and the world knew him not"* (John 1:10).

The Creator walked among His creations, veiled in flesh. He came not only to redeem but to reveal—to show us what the God of this system is truly like: love embodied, law made merciful, light joined with compassion.

As Redeemer, He holds the keys of both death and life. He descended below all things so that He might lift all things.[16] Through His suffering and resurrection, He reconciled this system to higher systems of glory, linking the Telestial and Terrestrial realms back to the Celestial order of the Father and the Mother.[17]

By Him, the fall of Adam and Eve was answered and the gulf between mortality and eternity bridged.[18] No soul can ascend except through His mediation, for He is the ladder itself—the living way by which every child of God returns home.

Joseph bore constant witness of this truth.

From the earliest revelations to the last, he declared that Jesus Christ is *"the Great I Am, the beginning and the end, the Redeemer of the world"* (D&C 19:1). All priesthood, all light, and all truth flow through Him.

Through Him we come to know the divine order of relationship—the way love governs heaven and earth alike, for He is Their perfect reflection—the Son who makes the Father and the Mother known. To know Him is to begin to know Them.

When Joseph taught of the Melchizedek Priesthood, he said it was "*the channel through which all knowledge, doctrine, the plan of salvation, and every important matter is revealed from heaven*" (History of the Church, 5:555).

That channel flows directly from Christ, for He is both High Priest and King.[19] Through Him, men and women are anointed to act in His likeness—as builders, healers, comforters, bringers of light and life. Every ordinance, every revelation, every sacred endowment ultimately points back to Him.

He is the God of this system because He embodies every law by which it lives.

And yet His work is never separate from the Father and the Mother. Everything He does is to bring Their children home. He reigns until all enemies are subdued, until death is swallowed up in victory, and until every willing soul is gathered into the embrace of Their divine love.

Then, as Paul wrote, He will deliver the perfected kingdom to the Father and the Mother, *"that God may be all in all"* (1 Corinthians 15:28). The circle of creation will close; the light will be one.

For now, this earth remains His stewardship—His vineyard, His classroom, His kingdom in training. Through Him we receive every measure of light; through Him we learn to walk the path of sanctification.

And when He returns to reign personally upon the earth, it will mark the Terrestrial day—the dawning of Zion in her fullness.[20] Then the prophecy will be fulfilled: *"The Lord shall be king over all the earth"* (Zechariah 14:9). In that reign we will finally see what Joseph only began to glimpse—Christ in His glory, the God of this system, revealing in Himself the heart of both the Father and the Mother.

## The Right Hand of Power—David's Lord and David's Son

When Jesus asked the Pharisees, *"What think ye of Christ? whose son is he?"* they answered, *"The son of David"* (Matthew 22:42). They were thinking in terms of lineage, structure, and hierarchy. But Jesus exposed the flaw in their thinking.

He quoted Psalm 110:1:

> *"The Lord said unto my Lord, Sit thou on my right hand, till I make thine enemies thy footstool."*

To the Pharisees, this sounded like a conversation between two Beings. But they missed the point.

In ancient courts, the right hand wasn't just a place to sit beside the King. It was the seat of the acting sovereign—the one invested with full authority to execute the King's will.

You see, to *"sit at the right hand"* meant to be the active arm of power, not a second throne occupant.

Jesus wasn't describing a hierarchy of Gods. He was revealing that He Himself—the Sovereign Jehovah—was filling two roles at once.

David's Lord (Jehovah) would descend as David's Son (Jesus Christ) to redeem Israel.

> *The same Being.*
> *Two divine roles.*

The Pharisees couldn't answer Him. They couldn't reconcile a Messiah who was both David's Creator and David's offspring. Yet the scriptures testify plainly.

*"I am the root and the offspring of David."* (Revelation 22:16)

> ***Root*** = *Father role (Creator)*
> ***Offspring*** = *Son role (Redeemer)*

When David, speaking by the Spirit, said *"The Lord said unto my Lord,"* he wasn't documenting a conversation between two Gods. He was bearing witness of One Sovereign being, fulfilling two roles—Father and Son.

The right hand of power is not a seat beside God. It is the position of executive dominion—the acting role of God Himself in mortality.

Jesus is Jehovah.
Jehovah is the Father.
And the Father, in descending, became the Son.

The Pharisees couldn't answer Him. But now, you can.

### Let Him Tell You Who He Is

Take a moment. Stop reading for just a second and think about what you've just read.

Joseph wasn't given a theological model. He wasn't diagramming a Godhead. He met a Person.

> *The same Being the Brother of Jared saw through the veil.*[21]
>
> *The same God Abinadi testified would come down among men.*[22]
>
> *The Holy One of Israel. The One True God.*[23]

And He tells us who He is.

When Jesus descended to visit the Nephites, He didn't begin with titles or theology. He simply said:

> *"Behold, I am Jesus Christ, whom the prophets testified shall come into the world."* (3 Nephi 11:10)

Then He made it unmistakable:

> *"I am the light and the life of the world; and I have drunk out of that bitter cup which the Father hath given me, and have glorified the Father in taking upon me the sins of the world, in the which I have suffered the will of the Father in all things from the beginning."* (3 Nephi 11:11)

Not a diagram. A testimony. The Redeemer fulfilling the will of the Father, while Himself being the Father of their deliverance.

When Philip asked to see the Father, Jesus responded:

> *"He that hath seen me hath seen the Father." (John 14:9)*

And again:

> *"Believe me that I am in the Father, and the Father in me."* (John 14:11)

He never divides them. He never sets them apart.

Standing before Thomas, He said simply:

> *"Behold my hands and my feet, that it is I myself."* (Luke 24:39)

No titles. No filters. Just: *"It is I myself."*

This is His witness. He tells us plainly who He is—not what tradition claims, not what men declare, but in His own words.

Abinadi taught it the same way. He didn't cloak it in philosophy. He said it straight.

> *"I would that ye should understand that God himself shall come down among the children of men, and shall redeem his people.*
> *And because he dwelleth in flesh he shall be called the Son of God,*
> *and having subjected the flesh to the will of the Father, being the Father and the Son—*
> *The Father, because he was conceived by the power of God; and the Son, because of the flesh; thus becoming the Father and Son—*
> *And they are one God, yea, the very Eternal Father of heaven and of earth."* (Mosiah 15:1–4)

Abinadi couldn't have been clearer. The God who created them was the same God who would redeem them. Not two beings. One sovereign God, fulfilling both roles.

But they couldn't hear it. They were too steeped in their own traditions to see what Abinadi was showing them.

Centuries earlier, the Brother of Jared had a similar encounter. He pleaded with the Lord for guidance across the ocean. When the Lord touched the stones to give them light, the Brother of Jared saw His finger. Startled, he heard these words, *"Because of thy faith thou hast seen that I shall take upon me flesh and blood"* (Ether 3:9). Then he was brought into the Lord's full presence.

And the Lord declared:

> *"Behold, I am he who was prepared from the foundation of the world to redeem my people.*
> *Behold, I am Jesus Christ.*
> *I am the Father and the Son."* (Ether 3:14)

The Brother of Jared wasn't seeing two beings. He was seeing the One. The same God who created him. The same God who would redeem him.

Joseph's encounter in the grove followed that same heavenly sequence—invocation, revelation, and transformation. He wasn't introduced to a theological model.

He met the One.

> *The same Being the Brother of Jared saw through the veil.*[24]
>
> *The same God Abinadi testified would come down among men.*[25]
>
> *The Holy One of Israel. The One True God.*[26]

When Moses was called to lead Israel out of bondage, he stood before a burning bush and heard these words:

> *"I am the God of thy father, the God of Abraham, the God of Isaac, and the God of Jacob."* (Exodus 3:6)

When Moses asked for His name, the Lord replied:

> *"I AM THAT I AM."* (Exodus 3:14)

Later, the Lord declared to Moses:

> *"I am the Lord [Jehovah]: and I appeared unto Abraham, unto Isaac, and unto Jacob, by the name of God Almighty." (Exodus 6:3)*

The Book of Moses (Pearl of Great Price) removes all doubt about who this Jehovah is. When Moses sees God face to face, the Lord introduces Himself plainly:

> *"Behold, I am the Lord God Almighty, and Endless is my name; for I am without beginning of days or end of years; and is not this endless?" (Moses 1:3)*

And when Moses pleads for strength to continue, the Lord says:

> *"I am the Beginning and the End, the Almighty God; by mine Only Begotten I created these things."* (Moses 2:1)

> *The same God.*
> *The same voice.*
> *The same identity.*

Jehovah—the God of the Old Testament—declaring His creative power, His redeeming role, and His eternal name.

So when Jesus stood before the Nephites and said, *"I created the heavens and the earth,"* (3 Nephi 9:15). He wasn't introducing a new God. He was revealing Himself—the same Being who spoke to Moses, to Abraham, and to all the prophets of old.

I was stunned when I noticed the words of Joseph's own prayer in the Kirtland Temple dedication. In that prayer, *"Lord God of Israel," "Holy Father," "Jehovah,"* and *"Jesus Christ"* are all addressed as the same sovereign Being (D&C 109:1, 10, 34, 73–77).

Joseph wasn't dividing Deity into separate gods. He was bearing witness of the one true God who reveals Himself under many names and titles.

And notice too his plea that the Saints might *"receive a fulness of the Holy Ghost"* (D&C 109:15). Joseph understood that fulness not as a partial influence, but as the reality of Christ's presence—when His Spirit no longer comes in part, but in fulness, face to face.

It was the very same truth I had first glimpsed staring at the courthouse mural: *"Thou shalt have no other gods before me"* (Exodus 20:3). Not *"before us."* Words matter.

The commandment itself affirms what Joseph knew and declared in his prayer—that there is one sovereign God, the Holy Father, Jehovah, Jesus Christ, the Lord God of Israel.

And the Book of Mormon seals the witness in unmistakable words.

When Zeezrom asked Amulek, *"Is the Son of God the very Eternal Father?"* (Alma 11:37), the answer came clear and unflinching:

> *"Yea, he is the very Eternal Father of heaven and of earth, and all things which in them are; he is the beginning and the end, the first and the last. And he shall come into the world to redeem his people; and he shall take upon him the transgressions of those who believe on his name; and these are they that shall have eternal life, and salvation cometh to none else."* (Alma 11:38–40)

There is no stronger testimony in all of scripture.

After years of study, prayer, and searching the scriptures, I can testify: what Joseph saw that day in the grove was not a hierarchy of heavenly beings—it was Him. The One. My Redeemer. My God.

I wrestled with this. I tried to fit it into the framework I was raised with. But the closer I've come to Him, the clearer it has become: He is both the Father and the Son—one Being, two divine roles.

The more I have released my assumptions, the more real He has become—not distant, not divided, but present and near. My God. Your God. The only One who can save.

## The Holy Ghost—The Unfinished Revelation

When the Savior departed, He promised His disciples that they would not be left comfortless. *"I will pray the Father, and he shall give you another Comforter, that he may abide with you for ever."* (John 14:16.)

That promise has never been withdrawn. It remains the quiet miracle of every believing soul—the continuing voice of heaven, whispering light into the dark corners of mortality.

This Comforter we call the Holy Ghost remains one of the great mysteries of the Restoration. Joseph spoke often of this presence but never fully defined it. He taught that the Holy Ghost is a personage of spirit—real, intelligent, and independent—yet so united with the Father and the Son that the same divine life moves through all three.

In the fifth Lecture on Faith, Joseph taught that the Holy Spirit is *"the mind of the Father and the Son,"* the channel through which They commune with all creation.

Beyond that, Joseph said little. He had begun to unfold what heaven had revealed, but his life was cut short before the teaching was complete. Like the unfinished walls of the Nauvoo Temple, this truth remains partially built—its foundation sure, its upper chambers waiting to be revealed.

Still, what Joseph did gave us is enough to guide the humble seeker.

The Holy Ghost was never meant to be an abstraction or a theological puzzle. The Spirit is the living breath of God moving through the hearts of men and women—the Comforter, the Witness, the Teacher of all things.[27] Through the Holy Ghost, our Divine Parents and the Son make Their abode with us. Through the Holy Ghost, knowledge becomes understanding and revelation becomes relationship.

And though the full mystery has not yet been revealed, Joseph left us enough to begin discerning and understanding the mystery. He gave us a key distinction that helps untangle centuries of confusion about the light that fills creation and the fire that sanctifies it.

Before we can understand the Holy Ghost, we must first discern the voice behind the words—the way heaven speaks through spirit and light.

## Through the Holy Ghost: The Voice and Presence of Heaven

The Holy Ghost **does** guide, speak, teach, and testify—as we have already shown. The Spirit's work is not limited to carrying the words of Deity; it also bears independent witness of truth, brings comfort, gives warning, and moves upon the heart with life-giving power. It is heaven's living presence already within us.

Yet there are also times when the Lord—or even the Father or the Mother—desires to speak directly to Their children. When They do, They may send angels, or They may speak by means of the Holy Ghost. In those moments, the Spirit functions not only as comforter, but as conduit—carrying the voice and mind of Deity to the receptive soul.

Doctrine and Covenants 8 gives the key. Speaking to Oliver Cowdery, the Lord identifies Himself as the source: *"I say unto you..."* (v. 1). Then He explains the **means:** *"I will tell you in your mind and in your heart, by the Holy Ghost, which shall come upon you and which* *shall dwell in your heart"* (v. 2). The distinction is elegant and simple: there is a **Speaker** ("I will tell you") and there is a **delivery** ("by the Holy Ghost"). The message originates with God; it is conveyed through the Spirit.

This is how heaven maintains nearness without confusion. The Holy Ghost isn't presented as merely an independent origin of doctrine or a simple courier—the Spirit is both teacher and **messenger**—the divine medium through which the Lord communes with His children, clarifies, persuades, and seals truth upon the soul. And when heaven wills it, this same order can carry the voice of the **Father** or the **Mother** to Their children—still through the Holy Ghost. Different divine Speakers; one living, holy means.

Recognizing this helps discipleship. It is natural shorthand to say, *"The Spirit told me,"* yet mature hearing remembers Who is speaking through that Spirit. The more precisely we discern the **source** (the Lord, or the Father and the Mother) and the **means** (the Holy Ghost), the more faithfully we can respond to the voice that matters most.

This is why truth carries the same signature wherever it is found: *"whatsoever is truth is light, and whatsoever is light is Spirit, even the Spirit of Jesus Christ"* (D&C 84:45). When light reaches your mind and heart, you are not being left to an intermediary in place of God; you are being addressed **by** God, *through* the Holy Ghost—so that His word can be known, recognized, and obeyed.

## Whose Voice Are You Hearing?

Let me share a simple parable.

Imagine you're on a phone call with your dearest friend. You're pouring out your heart—listening, receiving comfort, direction, and peace. You know their voice. You recognize their tone. The conversation feels alive and deeply personal.

But halfway through, you stop and say, *"I'm so thankful Verizon is speaking to me right now. Verizon is comforting me."*

Your friend pauses. *"It's me. I'm the one talking to you. Verizon is just the carrier."*

But you keep going. You thank Verizon. You tell others how clearly it speaks. You even bear testimony that Verizon has blessed your life.

How do you think your friend would feel?

This is what often happens in our relationship with heaven. We rightly honor the Holy Ghost, yet sometimes forget that the voice we hear through the Spirit often belongs to the Lord—or, at times, to the Father or the Mother. The Spirit is the living carrier, but the voice is Theirs.

That does not diminish the Holy Ghost—it reveals the majesty of this sacred work. For what higher calling could there be than to carry the words of divine love and truth? The Spirit is not merely a signal; it is the living channel through which heaven reaches the heart.

And still, there are moments when the Holy Ghost speaks directly—bearing witness of truth, warning of danger, comforting in sorrow, or teaching from within. Whether the Spirit speaks in its own voice or carries Theirs, every message bears the same signature: peace, clarity, and light.

I once saw this principle illustrated in a small, homely way.

When my mother was alive, she had a dear friend named Peggy who came each morning to help her with the day. Peggy would tidy up, fix breakfast, and then sit and visit awhile. One morning she came to me, nervous and apologetic. *"I think I broke your brand-new washing machine,"* she said.

I followed her to the laundry room. She explained that she had washed a bathroom rug, but the rubber backing had disintegrated and now the machine wouldn't start. *"Something told me I shouldn't put that rug in,"* she added.

Without thinking, I replied, *"Oh, that's what we're calling Him now? Something?"*

She looked puzzled, and I smiled. *"Peggy, wasn't it the Lord who told you not to put that rug in the washing machine?"*

We do it all the time. We downplay it. We call it something or a feeling or the Spirit, forgetting that it is the living God speaking through the Spirit. When we learn to recognize that voice—to honor both the Messenger and the Source—we can say with confidence, *"I have heard His voice and know His words."* (D&C 18:36)

Because those words are truth, and *"whatsoever is truth is light, and whatsoever is light is Spirit, even the Spirit of Jesus Christ."* (D&C 84:45)

Whether the Holy Ghost speaks in its own capacity as witness and comforter, or whether it carries the word of the Lord—or even the united voice of the Father and the Mother—it is always the same holy current of light.

And when we discern it clearly, heaven ceases to feel far away. We realize that we are not straining to hear across the veil at all.

They are speaking—right here, right now—through the very breath of the Spirit that already lives within us.

This is the mystery and the mercy of divine communication—one Spirit, many voices, all working together to make the light of heaven intelligible to the heart of man.

## Restoring Clarity: The Voice Behind the Words

We've used a lot of terms over the years—*"the Spirit," "the Holy Ghost," "the Gift of the Holy Ghost,"* and *"the Comforter."* But when you look closely, a thread becomes clear—one that weaves a beautiful tapestry, with Christ Himself at the center.

It begins with the Light of Christ.

This is the universal conscience given to every soul that comes to this earth. It's the innate ability to discern good from evil.

> *"The Spirit of Christ is given to every man, that he may know good from evil."* (Moroni 7:16)

This Light isn't earned. It's not given through any earthly ordinance. It's simply part of who we are as children of God—a gift granted the moment we enter this mortal estate.

But its influence depends on how we respond to it. It speaks to everyone, but not everyone chooses to listen. If ignored, rejected, or silenced long enough, the heart can become *"past feeling,"*[28] and the Light grows dormant.

Quite truthfully, it's the first touch of the Master's pure love for us. The whisper. His way of saying, *"Come to Me."*

Then comes the Power of the Holy Ghost.

This is the revelatory witness of truth extended to every sincere seeker. Regardless of creed, religion, or race—this power reaches out to every single soul on earth.

> It's how **Martin Luther** found the courage to stand against a corrupt religious system.[29]
> It's how **C.S. Lewis**, who once mocked faith, came to know Jesus Christ and teach of Him with brilliance and clarity.[30]

> It's how **Hannah Whitall Smith,** though never part of the Restoration, came to understand sanctification by faith and lived it.[31]
> It's how **reformers, thinkers, and humble believers** throughout history have been guided to do good in the name of the Lord.

The power of the Holy Ghost isn't something you only find in church or formal religion. It's Christ's voice calling out to His children, inviting them to come to Him—anytime, anywhere, if they will listen.

And Moroni's promise applies to them too:

> *"By the power of the Holy Ghost ye may know the truth of all things." (Moroni 10:5)*

But this power is not an abiding presence. It's not a permanent companion. It's an invitation to come closer.

It's how He gives us the ordinances we spoke of in the prior chapter on Priesthood. Remember? Those appointments? He speaks to us by the Holy Ghost—inviting us to come to Him, to walk with Him, and to receive what He has ordered for us.

The Gift of the Holy Ghost is different.

First, you must understand this: it isn't automatically conferred by men. We often use the phrase *"receive the Holy Ghost"* as if it's a switch flipped by ordinance. But Joseph never taught that. The scriptures never teach that.[32]

What is confirmed by men is membership; what is offered by God is His Spirit. And the invitation to receive His Spirit comes after, on His terms.

That truth was clear even in the Kirtland Temple dedication.

Joseph prayed that the Saints would *"receive the Holy Spirit"*—not as a title or delegation, but as God's own presence and power (D&C 109:15).

It is not a guarantee automatically bestowed by men. It is a command to seek, to prepare, and to live so that heaven can ratify His presence in your life.

As Nephi declared, *"If ye will enter in by the way, and receive the Holy Ghost, it will show unto you all things what ye should do"* (2 Nephi 32:5). When that seeking is real, the promise is sure: you will hear His voice and be led by it.

That act of obedience is the ordinance—the appointment—where the power of godliness is manifest.

Not in the ritual. Not in the formality. But in the moment when you hear Him, and you respond by obeying Him, and He manifests Himself—His love, His power, His grace, His Godliness.

Here's another crucial distinction: The Gift is not granted by man.

No person, through priesthood or position, can force the gift. The laying on of hands is an ordinance only in the sense that it invites you to hear His voice.

But the true ordinance—the one that manifests the power of godliness—happens when you hear Him and obey. Only then will heaven bestow the Gift.

It's ratified by heaven through sanctification. Remember what we talked about this in Chapter 1—the baptism of fire and remission of sins? Until a heart is cleansed, the Lord's Spirit cannot dwells there.

When someone receives a remission of sins by fire and by the Holy Ghost (2 Nephi 31:17–18), their heart is purified, making it a dwelling place for Him. That's the Gift.

Moses described it this way:

> *"It is given to abide in you; the record of heaven; the Comforter; the truth of all things; that which quickeneth all things."* (Moses 6:61)

Imagine it.
All of it.

> *The record of heaven abiding in you.*
> *The peaceable things of immortal glory.*
> *The truth of all things—living in your heart.*
> *His quickening power flowing through you.*
> *Life-giving power, not as a future promise, but as a present reality.*

This is not symbolic. This is what the Gift of the Holy Ghost is.

And here's the line most people miss: If you haven't received these gifts, you haven't yet received the Gift of the Holy Ghost.

So you see, it's not about a confirmation ordinance.
It's about Him.
Abiding in you.

We've called the Holy Ghost *"He"* for so long that we've started thinking of Him as someone else—an individual, sovereign being with his own personality and agency, distinct from Christ.

But Joseph never taught that, and the scriptures never teach it. The Holy Ghost is not a third God. The Holy Ghost is His Spirit. It is the mind of Christ. The light of Christ. The power of Christ.

> *When you feel that whisper, it's Him—Christ.*
> *When you feel that burning clarity, it's Him—Christ.*
> *When you are comforted in your deepest grief—that is not an agent of heaven sent on His behalf; it's Him—Christ.*

It is Jesus Christ Himself, through His Spirit, ministering to you.

When Jesus promised His disciples, *"I will not leave you comfortless: I will come to you"* (John 14:18), He wasn't sending a substitute. He was telling them that He Himself would return to them through His Spirit.

Earlier, He had said:

> *"And I will pray the Father, and he shall give you another Comforter, that he may abide with you for ever;*
> *Even the Spirit of truth; whom the world cannot receive, because it seeth him not, neither knoweth him:*
> *but ye know him; for he dwelleth with you, and shall be in you."* (John 14:16–17)

Did you catch that?

> *"Ye know him."*
> *"Dwelleth with you."*
> *"Shall be in you."*

He's not introducing someone new. He's describing Himself.

While He was physically present with them, they didn't need His Spirit to dwell within them. He was already there—with them in the flesh.

But He promised that after He left, He would return—not in body, but through His Spirit—abiding within them as the Comforter.

He made this even clearer later:

> *"Nevertheless I tell you the truth; It is expedient for you that I go away:*

> *for if I go not away, the Comforter will not come unto you; but if I depart, I will send him unto you."* (John 16:7)

If the Comforter were a separate sovereign being, why did Jesus need to leave for the Comforter to come? Why couldn't they both be present at the same time?

The answer is simple. They are not two beings. They are one. He wasn't abandoning them. He was returning to them—through His Spirit.

## The Living Image in Us

All creation bears the same divine signature. This image that governs the heavens also governs the soul. Everything God builds outwardly, He mirrors inwardly. The same triad that rules worlds—the Creator, the Redeemer, and the Testator[33]—exists within each of us, whispering the story of our own becoming.

The Father and the Mother gave us bodies—vessels of structure, law, and potential. Within that frame They placed the breath of life: the capacity to feel, to think, to create. From Them flows the power to organize, to nurture, and to beautify—echoes of the masculine and feminine strands of Their own image.[34]

Through our mortal parents, They continue that divine work, forming tabernacles of clay where Their spirit children might dwell and learn.

The Son gave us redemption—the bridge that unites flesh and spirit, matter and light. He enters every broken place, every weakness, every longing. Through Him, the scattered parts of our nature begin to gather; through His mercy, we learn harmony.

Each time we forgive, sacrifice, or choose love over fear, we act in His name—reflecting the life of the Redeemer. His light refines the body into a temple and the soul into a melody that carries the Holy Ghost's voice.

The Holy Ghost completes the divine triad within us—the abiding witness of truth and the quiet teacher of wisdom. This presence turns knowledge into understanding, and understanding into living light.

It is the breath of our Divine Parents moving invisibly through the chambers of the heart, teaching the tongue to speak kindness, the hands to heal, and the mind to discern light from shadow. Wherever truth is welcomed, the Spirit confirms it; wherever love is offered, the Spirit magnifies it.

Together, these three divine influences—body, redemption, and spirit—reproduce in miniature the harmony of the Godhead. The

Father and Mother create and give life; the Son redeems and binds life back together; the Spirit testifies, sanctifies, and brings all to remembrance. When these powers move in resonance within us, the image of God begins to reappear in its fullness.

This is the mystery of godliness that Joseph labored to restore: Christ in you, the hope of glory.[35]

To know the Son is to awaken to the indwelling presence of the Father and the Mother. Their unity becomes our unity; Their light, our light. The journey through the glories of heaven mirrors an inner ascent—from the telestial pull of the natural man, to the terrestrial life of Christlike love, to the celestial consciousness where perfect charity reigns.

As we ascend inwardly, we ascend outwardly, for heaven is not only a place—it is a state of being.

In the end, the image of God is not something far away or beyond reach. It is written into our very design—woven into our flesh, our breath, and our light. When those elements unite in love and truth, the divine image within us awakens, and heaven is born again upon the earth.

## The Godhead—and the Comforter—I Have Come to Know

I once believed the Holy Ghost was a separate person—an unseen messenger whose role was to carry revelation and comfort while Jesus Christ Himself remained distant. That's what I was taught, and for years I accepted it without question. But the more I searched, prayed, and wrestled with God, the more the truth began to unfold.

He is not far. He is not handing His love and care to another. Jesus Christ Himself is the Comforter. He is the Prince of Peace,[36] and peace is the one gift the adversary can never counterfeit.

I know this because His peace has come to me when I needed it most—in moments of betrayal, grief, and crushing loss, when fear and despair should have swallowed me whole. And yet, in those very moments, I found myself wrapped in a calm that could not be explained. It wasn't an impression passed along by another. It wasn't an abstract force. It was Him. His nearness. His Spirit.

Looking back, I can see that every whisper of truth, every moment of comfort, every spark of inspiration, every revelation that has pierced my heart has come from the Lord Jesus Christ Himself. This is how I know He loves me—not because of a theory about His nature, but because He has walked with me through my darkest hours.

When He said, *"I will not leave you comfortless: I will come to you"* (John 14:18). He meant it. He has come. He has been with me. That peace—the Comforter—is not a third being sent on assignment. It is Christ Himself, the God of Israel, my Redeemer, ministering to me through His Spirit.

This is how I have come to know Him, and with all that I am, I bear witness that it is true. The same divine rhythm that opened heaven to Joseph continues to play its beautiful melody and awaken heaven within us still.

For all creation bears His signature.

This is the image that governs the heavens and also governs the soul.[37] Everything God builds outwardly, He also builds inwardly. The same triad that rules worlds—the Creator, the Redeemer, and the Testator[38]—moves within each of us, whispering the story of our own becoming.

From the beginning, the purpose of creation has been relationship—light joined to light until all things are one, *"brighter and brighter until the perfect day"* (D&C 50:24).

The Father and the Mother brought forth Their children in love, the Son offered Himself to redeem them, and the Holy Ghost continues to teach and testify of truth. Each works in perfect unity, not as separate powers, but as one heart moving through the eternity.

This is the harmony Joseph Smith labored to restore. Through his life and his teachings, he showed that godliness is not hierarchy—it is union. It is the mind of Christ filling the soul until the will of heaven and the will of man are indistinguishable from each other.

For years I searched the scriptures, thinking I'd find the clue that would unlock the mystery of the Godhead. But the Godhead is not an enigma to be decoded, nor a hierarchy to be charted or diagrammed. They can only be known through love—by entering a living relationship with Them. They invite us to know Them as a child knows a parent—not by contracts or covenants, but through love, trust, and daily nearness.

And when that relationship becomes real, something begins to awaken within us. The same love that unites Father, Mother, and Son starts to shape our own nature, turning knowledge into life and life into light. The God we sought in heaven begins to live and move within our own hearts.

That image now calls to each of us. Within the smallest acts of creation, in every offering of forgiveness, and in every whisper of the

Spirit, the same triad of divine love continues its work. The Creator shapes us, the Redeemer heals us, and the Holy Ghost seals what is true. As these move in harmony, heaven is not something distant—it is born within.

When that harmony is restored in the heart, the image of God begins to shine again in its fullness. Father and Mother, Son and Spirit, creation and creature—each reflects the other until separation dissolves. This is both the end and the beginning of all things: the great at-one-ment of heaven and earth—the harmony restored. The Godhead.

## Chapter 5 Notes

1 Teachings of the Prophet Joseph Smith, comp. Joseph Fielding Smith (Salt Lake City: Deseret Book, 1976), p. 181.

2 Moses 4:1–3; Abraham 3:27–28 lucifer's plan to destroy agency and demand God's honor.

3 2 Nephi 2:11 *"For it must needs be, that there is an opposition in all things."*

4 TPJS, 217—Joseph Smith taught that knowledge, being revelation, is the very power of God unto salvation.

5 TPJS, 217—Knowledge is inseparable from salvation; to degenerate from God is to lose knowledge.

6 TPJS, 217–218—Joseph Smith: Salvation progresses in proportion to knowledge.

7 Eliza R. Snow, *"O My Father,"* verse 1, Times and Seasons 6, no. 17 (Nov. 15, 1845): 1039. Later appeared as hymn no. 292 in the 1985 Hymns of The Church of Jesus Christ of Latter-day Saints.

8 Eliza R. Snow, *"O My Father,"* verse 3, Times and Seasons 6, no. 17 (Nov. 15, 1845): 1039. Later appeared as hymn no. 292 in the 1985 Hymns of The Church of Jesus Christ of Latter-day Saints.

9 Margaret Barker, The Mother of the Lord: Volume 1, The Lady in the Temple (London: Bloomsbury T&T Clark, 2012), 21–23.

10 Josiah's reform, as recorded in 2 Kings 23, removed the Asherah from the temple. Barker argues this act suppressed the Lady or Wisdom—the feminine presence of the divine—and with it, the ancient Israelite understanding of heaven and earth in union. (Mother of the Lord, 90–95.)

11 Aramaic transliterations and interpretive renderings adapted from Neil Douglas-Klotz, Prayers of the Cosmos: Meditations on the Aramaic Words of Jesus (San Francisco: Harper San Francisco, 1990), 3–14. Additional contextual insights drawn from Matthew 6:9–13 (KJV) and the Peshitta (Eastern Aramaic NT). The composite phrases reflect the unitive aspects of the Divine—Father, Mother, Son, and Spirit—as expressed in the original Aramaic roots.

12 Joseph Smith, Discourse, 7 April 1844, Nauvoo, Illinois (commonly

known as the King Follett Sermon), reported by Wilford Woodruff, History of the Church 6:305–312; see also Teachings of the Prophet Joseph Smith, comp. Joseph Fielding Smith (Salt Lake City: Deseret Book, 1976), 346.

13 See Revelation 1:10; 4:2; 2 Nephi 3:20–21; 1 Nephi 11:1; Moses 1:11. In each case the prophet is "carried away in the Spirit" or caught up into a heavenly vision according to what their mortal frame could bear.

14 Joseph Smith—History 1:16. "*I saw a pillar of light exactly over my head, above the brightness of the sun, which descended gradually until it fell upon me.*"

15 Joseph Smith—History 1:30–49; D&C 76; 128:20–21; and History of the Church 4:536–541.

16 See Revelation 1:18—"*I am he that liveth, and was dead; and, behold, I am alive for evermore... and have the keys of hell and of death.*"; and D&C 88:6—"*He that ascended up on high, as also he descended below all things, in that he comprehended all things, that he might be in all and through all things.*"

17 1 Corinthians 15:40–42; D&C 76:70–92; 88:18–20. These passages describe the gradations of resurrected glory—telestial, terrestrial, and celestial—and Christ's role in reconciling all things to the Father (Colossians 1:20), restoring order and unity among the realms of glory.

18 1 Corinthians 15:21–22—*"For since by man came death, by man came also the resurrection of the dead. For as in Adam all die, even so in Christ shall all be made alive.";* and 2 Nephi 9:6–11, whichs describes how the infinite atonement of Christ overcomes the fall and bridges the gulf between mortality and eternity.

19 Hebrews 4:14–15; 5:5–6—*"Seeing then that we have a great high priest, that is passed into the heavens, Jesus the Son of God... Thou art a priest for ever after the order of Melchizedek.";* and Revelation 19:16—"And he hath on his vesture and on his thigh a name written, KING OF KINGS, AND LORD OF LORDS."

20 D&C 88:17–20, 25—describing the earth's sanctification and its transition to a Terrestrial glory when Christ reigns personally upon it; and Articles of Faith 1:10—"We believe that Christ will reign personally upon the earth; and, that the earth will be renewed and receive its paradisiacal glory.

21 Ether 3:6–16

22 Mosiah 15:1–4

23 2 Nephi 9:41

24 Ether 3:6–16

25 Mosiah 15:1–4

26 2 Nephi 9:41

27 John 14:26; 15:26; Genesis 2:7

28 1 Nephi 17:45

29 Martin Luther—See Luther's Works, 32:112–113 (Luther at the Diet of Worms, 1521).

30 C.S. Lewis—See C.S. Lewis, Mere Christianity (1952), Preface; and Surprised by Joy (1955), esp. chap. 14.

31 Hannah Whitall Smith—See Hannah Whitall Smith, The Christian's Secret of a Happy Life (1875), esp. chap. 5 *"Difficulties Concerning Faith."*

32 Acts 8:14–17—The apostles laid hands on believers, but the Spirit came from God, not through human agency.
2 Nephi 31:12–13; Mosiah 18:12–13—The Holy Ghost comes after repentance and baptism, by fire and the Spirit.
D&C 35:6; 39:6—The Spirit is given directly by Christ.
TPJS 199–200—Joseph Smith taught: *"You might as well baptize a bag of sand as a man, if not done in view of the remission of sins and getting of the Holy Ghost."*

33 Teachings of the Prophet Joseph Smith, 190; cf. D&C 20:28; Lectures on Faith 5:2

34 Genesis 1:26–27—*"Let us make man in our image, after our likeness... male and female created he them."*; Moses 2:26–27; Abraham 4:26–27

35 Colossians 1:27; D&C 93:1

36 Isaiah 9:6

37 Genesis 1:26–27; Moses 2:26–27

38 Teachings of the Prophet Joseph Smith, 190; cf. D&C 20:28; Lectures on Faith 5:2

# The Voice of God

## Revelation is the Only True Governance

---

### Christ Governs Through His Voice

This is what Joseph Smith learned. The government of God is not built on ranks, offices, or positions. It is built on the voice of Jesus Christ. That living voice is the same breath that moved upon the waters in the beginning—the Word and the Breath joined as one to quicken all creation.

From the very first page of the Book of Mormon, Joseph was shown this manner of heaven's work. Lehi governed his family by revelation, not compulsion. He taught his son Nephi to seek the Lord for himself—Jacob too. He showed them how to follow the Spirit, recognize the Lord's voice, and obey it.

Such guidance reveals the manner of heaven—order balanced by nurture, structure joined with compassion. The wisdom that governs worlds also teaches children how to hear.

This is how heaven governs. This is the order Joseph would come to live and teach.

Joseph's own journey followed the same course. As a boy, the Light of Christ stirred his conscience. He wrestled with the confusion of his day, the contradictions of churches, and the hypocrisy of men who professed holiness yet lacked power.

He wanted to know which of them was right, and how he could come to God for himself. That inner light is the same Wisdom who calls to every soul, leading each toward the love that created them.

The more Joseph read, the more the Spirit unfolded, line upon line, precept upon precept. The whisperings from the Lord's own voice awakened a desire to seek forgiveness. He wanted to know which church was right, but more than that, he wanted to know if God would forgive him.

That light eventually guided him into the grove. He didn't go to start a church. He went to pray. He went to seek mercy. He went to ask God for himself.

And there, he heard it—the voice of the Lord, calling him by name.[1] In that moment, heaven and earth breathed together; the Voice that formed worlds spoke within a mortal frame. Speaking truth. Giving commandments. Personal commandments. Ordinances and appointments that, if obeyed, would allow the Lord to reveal more of Himself to Joseph.

That's the manner of heaven's work.

This is how Christ governs His people. He governs by speaking to them. His voice is not a metaphor or a theological idea. When He speaks, His words are alive.

> *They are truth.*
> *They are light.*
> *They are Spirit.*
> *They are power.*

The very power that created you and me, and the earth upon which we live.

The Lord explained this pattern to Joseph in revelation:

> *"You shall live by every word that proceedeth forth from the mouth of God. For the word of the Lord is truth, and whatsoever is truth is light, and whatsoever is light is Spirit, even the Spirit of Jesus Christ."* (D&C 84:44–45)

These are not separate things. The Word of God is truth. Truth is light. Light is Spirit. Spirit is Jesus Christ. Do you see it? It's a simple equation. A=B, and B=C, therefore A=C. It's all the same flow. It's all Him.

This is the manner of heaven Lehi saw in his vision. The Rod of Iron was Christ. The Path was Christ. The Fountain of Living Water was Christ. The Tree of Life was Christ. Everything in the vision flowed to Him, and from Him.[2]

There were no man-made supports along that path.

> *No programs.*
> *No intermediaries.*

Just a pure, direct way to the presence of God.

The only structure in the dream that resembled a man-made monument was the great and spacious building—floating in the air, without foundation.[3] It was filled with people pointing fingers, mocking those who clung to the Rod. It represented the pride of the world—those who sought power, influence, and validation through man-made systems.

The mist of darkness wasn't random, either. It was a deliberate barrier—a smokescreen designed to blind the eyes and cause souls to lose their grip on the Rod. It represents every deception, distraction, and counterfeit that clouds the flow of Christ's voice.[4]

Lehi's vision was not subtle.

The path to God was simple and direct. The barriers were not placed there by Him. They were the works of men. They were the strategies of the adversary.

Those who reached the Tree did so by holding fast to the word of God, ignoring the voices from the great and spacious building, and pressing through the mist of darkness. They reached the Tree because they refused to let go of the Rod.

They reached the Tree because they knew whose voice they were holding onto.

Joseph saw this same manner of heaven. The government of God is not found in the institutions floating in the air. It is found in the living word that flows to every heart willing to receive it.

Christ governs by light. He calls through His Spirit. He teaches through His word. As we obey, His power is made manifest.

Priesthood power does not begin with ordination. It begins when a person hears the Lord's voice and obeys it.

Authority to act in Christ's name is not conferred by a mortal laying hands, but by the Lord's own command.

Joseph taught that no man stands at the gate. Christ is the gatekeeper. His sheep hear His voice and follow Him because they know Him—they know how to recognize His voice.[5]

This is the government of God Joseph restored. A living flow of Light, Spirit, Voice, and Power—administered directly by Jesus Christ.

## The Light of Christ: The First Invitation to Be Governed

Long before a person receives the Holy Ghost, the Lord is already speaking.

Every soul is born with the Light of Christ. It is the first voice that stirs the conscience. A whisper that teaches right from wrong. This light is not reserved for the baptized or ordained. It is given freely to all. It is the first invitation to come to Him.

Joseph learned that the Light of Christ is not passive. It is alive. It seeks to enlighten every person who is willing to listen. He received this truth by revelation:

> *"The Spirit giveth light to every man that cometh into the world; and the Spirit enlighteneth every man through the world, that hearkeneth to the voice of the Spirit."* (D&C 84:46)

This is the foundation of divine governance. Christ does not begin His work through programs, offices, or rituals. He begins with light.

> *Light that calls.*
> *Light that reveals.*
> *Light that flows into those who receive it.*

Joseph learned that every soul who responds to this light is being governed by Him.

The promptings of conscience, the subtle nudge to choose right over wrong, the desire to seek after truth—these are not mere feelings. They are acts of governance.

Nephi testified that no servant stands at the gate. It is Christ Himself who gives this light. No man controls it, and no officeholder dispenses it.

Every person who hearkens to it draws closer to Him. Every person who ignores it finds the light beginning to dim.

That's how it works.

Joseph taught that this is the first law of divine relationship. The Light of Christ invites. It calls every soul to come unto Him, but it will never force. It offers itself freely and waits for a response.

Those who respond are given more.
Those who reject lose even what they had.

Alma testified of this same principle. He said, *"He that will not harden his heart, to him is given the greater portion of the word, until it is given unto him to know the mysteries of God in full."* But *"they that will harden their hearts, to them is given the lesser portion of the word until they know nothing concerning his mysteries"* (Alma 12:10–11).

The Light of Christ waits.
It waits to see what a soul will choose.

This is why Joseph understood that governance in heaven does not begin in a church.
It begins in the heart.

As a boy, Joseph felt a deep yearning to know what was right. The religious confusion around him wasn't just noise—it unsettled his soul. The Light of Christ was already working in him, telling him that something was wrong. *"It was impossible for a person young as I was, and so unacquainted with men and things, to come to any certain conclusion who was right and who was wrong,"* he said (JS-H 1:8).

But that confusion was not left to fester. The Light of Christ stirred him to act. It led him to the scriptures. *"I was one day reading the Epistle of James, first chapter and fifth verse... If any of you lack wisdom, let him ask of God"* (JS-H 1:11).

The moment Joseph read those words, they struck him with greater force than any verse had before. It was the voice of the Lord speaking to him through the scriptures. *"Never did any passage of scripture come with more power to the heart of man than this did at this time to mine"* (JS-H 1:12).

He knew what he had to do. He would go and ask God. Not a preacher. Not a congregation. He would ask God for himself.

This is how the governance of heaven begins. The Light of Christ awakens the soul. If that light is followed, it leads to greater revelation. If it is rejected, the heart becomes hardened, and the voice becomes faint.[6]

Joseph's life was a testimony of what happens when a person follows that light. It led him to the scriptures. It led him to pray. It led him to hear the Lord's voice. And it prepared him to receive the greater gifts that would come.

Christ's government begins here—with light that calls every soul home.

### The Gift of the Holy Ghost: Governance Through Sanctification

Joseph learned that the Lord's governance does not stop with the Light of Christ. That light is the invitation. The next step is sanctification.

When a person responds to the Light, the Lord offers them His Spirit in greater measure. Joseph taught that receiving the Holy Ghost is not just a ritual performed by hands. It is a living reality—a baptism of fire that purifies the heart. We've gone into this in great detail in Chapter Two. Remember?

Nephi said, *"Then cometh a remission of your sins by fire and by the Holy Ghost"* (2 Nephi 31:17).

Joseph understood that this is not symbolic. The baptism of fire is a literal cleansing. A real transformation. Until a person's heart is purged of sin and impurity, the Holy Ghost cannot abide. The Gift of the Holy Ghost is not a token blessing—it is the presence of the Lord's Spirit dwelling within a sanctified vessel.

We have seen this pattern before. Moses described it as the *"record of heaven," "the Comforter," "the truth of all things"* (Moses 6:61). Joseph taught that these are not titles of a distant messenger. They are descriptions of Christ's own Spirit abiding in a purified heart.

When a person is sanctified, the Lord governs them from within.

> *His Spirit teaches.*
> *His Spirit comforts.*
> *His Spirit reveals.*

The heart becomes a temple where His presence dwells.

Moroni extended this invitation with a powerful plea: *"Awake, and arise from the dust, O Jerusalem; yea, and put on thy beautiful garments, O daughter of Zion; and strengthen thy stakes and enlarge thy borders forever, that thou mayest no more be confounded"* (Moroni 10:31).

He continued, *"Yea, come unto Christ, and be perfected in him, and deny yourselves of all ungodliness; and if ye shall deny yourselves of all ungodliness, and love God with all your might, mind and strength, then is his grace sufficient for you, that by his grace ye may be perfect in Christ; and if by the grace of God ye are perfect in Christ, ye can in nowise deny the power of God"* (Moroni 10:32).

This is the promise of true governance. The Lord's Spirit sanctifies, purifies, and perfects those who come unto Him. Joseph taught that this is what it means to receive the Gift of the Holy Ghost—to become holy, without spot, prepared to stand in His presence.

Joseph did not teach that this comes by office or title. It comes by obedience. It comes by purity. It comes by the real cleansing power of the baptism of fire.

Nephi said, *"If ye will enter in by the way, and receive the Holy Ghost, it will show unto you all things what ye should do"* (2 Nephi 32:5).

This is governance—Christ leading His people through the abiding presence of His Spirit, sanctifying them, teaching them, guiding them.

The Gift of the Holy Ghost is not the end. It is the threshold. It is the beginning of a life where Christ governs the individual soul directly, preparing them for even greater manifestations of His presence.

Nephi taught this pattern with clarity: *"For the gate by which ye should enter is repentance and baptism by water; and then cometh a remission of your sins by fire and by the Holy Ghost"* (2 Nephi 31:17).

The baptism of fire is not the destination—it is the gate. It is the entrance into a life where the Lord begins to teach and guide His disciples personally.

Nephi foresaw the question that would naturally arise: *"Brethren, I suppose that ye ponder somewhat in your hearts concerning that which ye should do after ye have entered in by the way"* (2 Nephi 32:1).

Receiving the Holy Ghost is not a resting place—it's a beginning. There is still a path to walk, a rod to hold, a voice to follow.

*"Do ye not remember that I said unto you that after ye had received the Holy Ghost ye could speak with the tongue of angels?"* Nephi asked. *"And now, how could ye speak with the tongue of angels save it were by the Holy Ghost?"* (v.2).

Angels speak by the power of the Holy Ghost. They speak the words of Christ. So Nephi's counsel is clear: *"Feast upon the words of Christ; for behold, the words of Christ will tell you all things what ye should do"* (2 Nephi 32:3).

Joseph taught this same progression. The Gift of the Holy Ghost is the gate. His words become the connection. His voice becomes the guide. And the destination is not a concept—it is Christ Himself.

The journey is designed to bring every soul into His presence.

## The Voice of Christ: The Rod of Iron Leading to Life

Joseph learned that Christ's governance is not static. It flows.

He taught that when a person fills their heart with charity, they are drawing closer to the very nature of Christ. Moroni invited, *"Pray unto the Father with all the energy of heart, that ye may be filled with this love, which he hath bestowed upon all who are true followers of his Son, Jesus Christ; that ye may become the sons of God..."* (Moroni 7:48).

Charity is not just an attribute. It is the process of becoming like Him. When charity fills the heart, it changes who we are. We begin to love as He loves. We begin to see as He sees.

Joseph taught that as charity works in the heart, virtue begins to garnish the thoughts. Virtue purifies. It refines the inner vessel. [7]

Virtue is not about outward appearance. It is about inner alignment. When thoughts are filled with virtue, the heart becomes pure. And it is the pure in heart who shall see God.[8]

As charity and virtue take root, a transformation occurs.[9]

The soul becomes ready—not just to feel His Spirit, but to hear His voice. The Lord's voice distills gently. It does not shout. It does not compel. But to the heart that has been prepared, it comes with clarity.

Confidence begins to grow. Not arrogance. Not presumption. But a quiet confidence that comes from familiarity.

A person who has been taught of God—line upon line, appointment after appointment—begins to know His voice. They do not cower when He speaks. They do not shrink back in fear. They have learned, through many small manifestations, that His voice brings life. It invites. It empowers.

This is what Joseph learned when the Lord said, *"Then shall thy confidence wax strong in the presence of God"* (D&C 121:45). This confidence is not manufactured. It is earned through a relationship that has been built, one faithful step at a time.

In this state, *"the doctrines of the priesthood shall distill upon thy soul as the dews from heaven"* (D&C 121:46). Revelation flows easily because the heart has been made a ready vessel.

> *The Spirit finds no resistance.*
> *The mind is clear.*
> *The will is aligned.*
> *The doctrines do not need to be shouted.*

They settle upon the soul naturally, like dew upon the morning grass.

It is in this condition that dominion begins to flow. Not because of a title. Not because of a position. But because of who the person has become. Dominion flows as a natural extension of their oneness with Christ. Their influence expands—not through compulsion, but through the quiet, constant flow of the Spirit within them.

This is the governance of heaven. It is not imposed. It is not delegated by office. It is the living flow of Christ's own Spirit filling a purified vessel.

This is how Joseph understood priesthood power.
It is not something a person wields.
It is something they become.

Do you see it? That is how Christ governs.

Let's return for a minute to Lehi's vision of the Tree of Life, where he reveals this flow in vivid detail.[10]

Joseph taught that every symbol in Lehi's vision flows in one direction—to Christ, who was both the source and the destination.[11]

**The Rod of Iron is Christ.**

John declared, *"In the beginning was the Word, and the Word was with God, and the Word was God"* (John 1:1). To hold to the Rod is to hold to Him.

**The Path is Christ.**

Jesus said, *"I am the way, the truth, and the life: no man cometh unto the Father, but by me"* (John 14:6). The path leading to the Tree is not a metaphorical road—it is Christ Himself.

**The Fountain of Living Waters is Christ.**

Jesus promised, *"Whosoever drinketh of the water that I shall give him shall never thirst"* (John 4:14). The living water flowing beneath the Tree is His life-giving Spirit.

**The Tree of Life is Christ.**

When Nephi asked about the meaning of the Tree, the angel showed him Mary bearing the Son of God, and Nephi beheld *"the love of God, which sheddeth itself abroad in the hearts of the children of men"* (1 Nephi 11:22).

The Tree, its fruit, the joy it brings—are all Christ.

Every element in Lehi's vision flows to Him and from Him. The Rod. The Path. The Water. The Tree. It is all Jesus Christ.

This is why Joseph taught that Christ governs by voice. His word is not confined to scripture alone.

His word is alive. It speaks today.

> *It reveals.*
> *It leads.*
> *It flows.*

Nephi invited all to *"feast upon the words of Christ; for behold, the words of Christ will tell you all things what ye should do"* (2 Nephi 32:3).

The Rod of Iron is not a checklist. It is not a program. It is a beautiful living connection between the Lord and the soul. When a person clings to the Rod, they are clinging to Him. When they let go, they are letting go of Him.

Joseph learned that Christ's governance flows in deeply personal ways.

The Lord speaks. The individual listens. His words guide, correct, and empower. There is no middleman. There are no intermediaries. The flow is direct.

No one stands between the Lord and a soul who is willing to hearken to His voice.

Nephi also promised that *"if ye will enter in by the way, and receive the Holy Ghost, it will show unto you all things what ye should do"* (2 Nephi 32:5). The path to the Tree of Life is not revealed by institutions or stewards—it is shown by the Spirit—His Spirit.

Joseph's life demonstrated this reality. From the First Vision to the revelations he received, every step of his journey was directed by the living word. He did not wait for men to authorize him to act. He waited upon the Lord. He held to the Rod.[12]

This is the pattern of governance Joseph restored and tried in everything he did to model for us, so that we could learn these principles too.

Christ governs His people by speaking to them. His voice is the Rod. His voice is the path. His voice is the source of life. When someone holds fast to that voice, they are safely guided to the Tree of Life.

## Priesthood Power Flows Through Righteousness, Not Position

Joseph continued to teach that priesthood power is inseparably connected to the powers of heaven. He had already revealed that this power flows into a soul filled with charity and virtue, where the doctrines of the priesthood distill gently, like dews from heaven (D&C 121:45–46).

But Joseph also made it clear that this power cannot be controlled or handled in any other way. *"The powers of heaven cannot be controlled nor handled only upon the principles of righteousness"* (D&C 121:36).

Joseph embodied this pattern in every aspect of his life and leadership.

> *He had no family heritage of priesthood authority.*
> *He had no ecclesiastical title when he was called.*
> *His authority came because God spoke to him.*

But it didn't happen all at once.

The Lord mentored Joseph in this very manner—line upon line, appointment by appointment. Angels visited him. He was taught, corrected, and prepared.

Authority wasn't conferred in a single moment. It was cultivated through one small inspiration, one personal commandment, one ordinance of the Lord at a time.

The true ordinances—the ordered appointments and divine acts that the Lord administers to prepare His servants to come unto Him. You've already seen this. It's the manner of heaven we learned in an earlier chapter.

Joseph did not wake up one morning and suddenly become a prophet. He became a prophet by following the voice—step by step—until heaven entrusted him with more.

It was the voice of the Lord that conferred power—not the laying on of mortal hands.

Joseph recognized this same truth in the scriptures. Every true servant of the Lord—male or female, prophet or foreigner, rich or poor—received power directly from His voice.

> **Ruth,** a Moabite outsider, became the great-grandmother of David and an ancestor of Jesus Christ by her loyalty to God (Ruth 1:16; 4:17–22).
> **Nephi** recorded, *"The Lord commanded me, wherefore I did make plates of ore"* (1 Nephi 19:1).
> **Anna,** the prophetess, bore witness of Christ in the temple (Luke 2:36–38).
> **Alma** testified, *"They are made known unto me by the Holy Spirit of God"* (Alma 5:46).
> **Amos,** a shepherd and no prophet's son, was called to cry repentance (Amos 7:14–15).
> **Mary** was overshadowed by the Holy Ghost and carried the Son of God (Luke 1:35).
> **Enoch,** slow of speech and despised by the people, was lifted by the Lord's voice (Moses 6:31).
> **Paul** declared, *"The gospel which was preached of me is not after man... but by the revelation of Jesus Christ"* (Galatians 1:11–12).
> **Deborah** judged Israel by the Lord's direction (Judges 4:4–5).
> **The Brother of Jared** received his ministry when *"the Lord stretched forth his hand and touched the stones"* (Ether 3:6).
> **Lehi, Nephi,** and **Jacob** were commissioned directly by God, not by men (1 Nephi 1:18; 2 Nephi 5:19; Jacob 1:17).
> **Isaiah, Mormon,** and **Moroni** each recorded their direct charge from heaven (Isaiah 6:5–9; Mormon 1:15–17; Moroni 8:1–2).

All these received their authority by revelation from Christ Himself—through righteousness and obedience.

This is how heaven has always governed.

> *The Lord calls.*
> *The Lord prepares.*
> *The Lord empowers.*

Priesthood power flows when Christ speaks and a servant obeys.

It flows to all who are willing to receive it.

> *Male or female.*
> *Black or white.*
> *Bond or free.*
> *Rich or poor.*

The priesthood is not a male-exclusive stewardship. It is the living power of God, extended to any soul who will hearken to His voice and follow Him in righteousness.

Each of these servants received their calling and authority by direct revelation from the Lord, not by mortal appointment. None waited for a mortal intermediary to lay hands on their head and declare them qualified.

> *The Lord called.*
> *The Lord prepared.*
> *The Lord empowered.*

Joseph taught that priesthood power is not maintained by position. *"No power or influence can or ought to be maintained by virtue of the priesthood,"* the Lord revealed, *"only by persuasion, by long-suffering, by gentleness and meekness, and by love unfeigned" (*D&C 121:41).

The Lord governs His people through influence that flows—to those who are pure in heart, to those who act in meekness. to those who listen best.

Joseph taught that priesthood is not a rank—it is a relationship.

Power is given when a person's life is aligned with heaven. Authority is manifest when the Spirit is present. Titles and offices do not confer power. The Spirit does.

He also learned that ordinances themselves do not hold power. They are only vehicles. *"In the ordinances thereof, the power of godliness is manifest,"* the Lord declared, *"and without the ordinances thereof, and the authority of the priesthood, the power of godliness is not manifest unto men in the flesh" (*D&C 84:20–21).

But that manifestation is not automatic. It is conditional. Ordinances become dead works when performed without the Spirit. The power of godliness is revealed only when the individual is obedient, when the flow of heaven is open, when the ordinance is alive with the Spirit of Christ.

Joseph learned that priesthood power isn't stored in offices or passed through lines of authority. It's manifest through revelation and obedience.

The priesthood is alive. It flows.

It flows into those who are prepared to receive it.

## The Second Comforter: Christ's Personal Governance

Joseph learned that the culmination of Christ's governance is not simply receiving His Spirit, but receiving Him.

The promise of the gospel is not just to be guided by the Holy Ghost, but to be ministered to by the Lord Himself.

In Chapter Two we spoke of the higher rungs on the ladder of progression—the steps by which faith, repentance, and sanctification lift a soul nearer to Him. The Second Comforter is one of those higher rungs. It is not reserved for prophets or apostles alone. It is not a mystery held back for a select few. It is a promise extended to all who love Him and keep His commandments.

Joseph said, *"The other Comforter is no more nor less than the Lord Jesus Christ Himself; and when any man obtains this last Comforter, he will have the personage of Jesus Christ to attend him, or appear unto him from time to time"* (TPJS, p. 150).

The Lord declared this directly to His disciples:

> *"He that hath my commandments, and keepeth them, he it is that loveth me... and I will love him, and will manifest myself to him" (John 14:21).*

Joseph understood that the path of governance begins with the Light of Christ, increases through the Gift of the Holy Ghost, and reaches its fulfillment when the Lord Himself ministers personally.

In D&C 93 the Lord revealed that even He, as a mortal, progressed by receiving *"grace for grace"* (D&C 93:12). Grace for grace is reciprocal—it's an exchange. As we extend grace through humility, obedience, and faith, the Lord extends grace back to us.

This is how the flow begins. One act of offering. One act of receiving. Each response of grace given by the soul opens the way for grace received from Him.

But this beautiful principle doesn't stop there.

The next verse introduces a crucial shift. Christ *"received not of the fulness at the first, but continued from grace to grace, until he received a fulness"* (D&C 93:13).

Grace to grace is not an exchange—it is a progression. Once the flow is established (grace for grace), the soul is invited to ascend, moving from one grace to the next, appointment after appointment, until it is filled with His fulness.

This is not a passive process. It is an active journey of being governed by Christ.

The Lord teaches by word. The soul responds. He gives more. Each grace received expands the soul's capacity to receive more. It is an upward flow, until the fulness is attained.

And what is that fulness?

The Lord defined it plainly:

> *"Verily, thus saith the Lord: it shall come to pass that every soul who forsaketh his sins and cometh unto me, and calleth on my name, and obeyeth my voice, and keepeth my commandments, shall see my face and know that I am."* (D&C 93:1)

Joseph summarized this process with clarity:

> *"Here, then, is eternal life—to know the only wise and true God; and you have got to learn how to be Gods yourselves, and to be kings and priests to God, the same as all Gods have done before you, namely, by going from one small degree to another, and from a small capacity to a great one; from grace to grace, from exaltation to exaltation, until you attain to the resurrection of the dead, and are able to dwell in everlasting burnings, and to sit in glory, as do those who sit enthroned in everlasting power."* (TPJS, p. 346)

This is the law of governance Joseph restored.

> ***It begins with grace for grace***—a reciprocal flow of giving and receiving.
> ***It progresses grace to grace***—a living ascent into His fullness.
> And it is fulfilled when Christ Himself governs the soul, personally, face to face.

This is not a theological abstraction. It is the literal reality of the gospel. Christ governs His people by His voice. And He seals His people by His own presence.

Joseph taught that calling and election, the more sure word of prophecy, the Holy Spirit of Promise, and the Second Comforter all refer to the same event—the higher rungs of spiritual progression, the fullness where the Lord Jesus Christ personally declares a person's standing before Him.

He did not present this as a rare or unreachable blessing. He taught it as the natural progression for those who live by every word that proceeds from the mouth of God. Those who endure in obedience, purified by His Spirit, are prepared to receive Him.

> *This is the purpose of priesthood.*
> *This is the purpose of ordinances.*
> *To prepare a person to stand in the presence of God.*

Joseph didn't invent this doctrine—it's a beautiful principle laid out in scripture. Enoch walked with God (Genesis 5:24). Moses spoke with Him *"face to face, as a man speaketh unto his friend"* (Exodus 33:11). The Nephite disciples were ministered to by Christ after His resurrection. Paul, though he described himself as one born out of due time, testified that the Lord appeared to him as well.[13]

Because of Joseph, this beautiful principle is no longer hidden but taught openly to the world.

The Second Comforter is not a hidden ordinance. It is the fulfillment of Christ's promise to govern His people personally.

## Zion: A People Governed by His Voice

The crowning result of Christ's governance is Zion. Joseph learned that Zion is not built by gathering people into an organization. Zion is built by gathering people to the Lord.

The Lord defined Zion simply: she is the pure in heart. Purity is not achieved through policy, structure, or ritual. It comes through sanctification—when individuals are governed by the voice of Christ, taught by His Spirit, and filled with His love.

Joseph saw that Zion is a community of people who have learned to be governed by God directly. In Zion, the Lord is their King. His word is their law. His Spirit is their guide.

This truth was revealed in the city of Enoch: they were of one heart and one mind, and dwelt in righteousness, with no poor among them (Moses 7:18). Their unity did not come through external compulsion or institutional hierarchy. It came because every individual had been taught of God.

The Nephites lived this way after the Savior's visit. Their record describes a people who became one because the love of God filled every heart. There were no contentions among them. Every man dealt justly with one another. They held all things in common, and there were no poor among them (4 Nephi).

Their unity was not structured by policy or regulated by office. It was the natural fruit of being governed by Christ's Spirit.

Christ Himself declared, *"Be one; and if ye are not one, ye are not mine"* (D&C 38:27). This is not a demand for conformity. It is a promise: to follow His voice is to become one with Him. And those who are one with Him will become one with all who hear that same voice.

Zion is not created by external scaffolding. Zion emerges when individuals are sanctified. When Christ governs His people directly, Zion becomes inevitable.

## Joseph Smith's Testimony Regarding Zion

Everything Joseph Smith did was to prepare a people fit to become citizens of Zion.

Joseph's mission was never about outward ordinances, rituals, or organizational structure. He was not simply organizing a church. His entire ministry was aimed at preparing a people who could receive the Lord and be gathered into Zion.

The City of Enoch, taken up into heaven (Moses 7:21), will return in the last days and join the City of the New Jerusalem (Moses 7:62). Joseph's work was to prepare a people fit to receive them.[14]

Zion is not built from heaven downward. It is built from the earth upward—by hearts that are sanctified and governed by the voice of Christ.

The Lord declared through him:

> *"For Zion must increase in beauty, and in holiness; her borders must be enlarged; her stakes must be strengthened; yea, verily I say unto you, Zion must arise and put on her beautiful garments."* (D&C 82:14)

Joseph's vision of Zion was not a utopian dream. It was a living pattern. A divine mandate. He was building a people God could join with Enoch's city, creating a Zion that spans heaven and earth.

In a discourse on the Second Comforter, Joseph taught that after a person has been thoroughly proved and found determined to serve God *"at all hazards,"* the Lord would say, *"Son, thou shalt be exalted."* He then added, *"When the Lord has thoroughly proved him... it will be his privilege to receive the other Comforter"* (TPJS, p. 150).

This was the ultimate preparation for Zion—a people who would see the Lord and be sealed by His voice.

Joseph's vision of Zion was a sanctified people, each ascending individually and merging into a community where the Lord Himself could dwell and reign among them.

This is the mandate of every servant God has ever called. From Enoch to Nephi, from Alma to Mormon, from Joseph Smith to the present day—the commission has always been the same: Prepare a people.

### My Personal Witness

I know these things are true.

I know that Zion is not a distant, symbolic idea. It's a living reality the Lord is preparing right now. I know that Joseph Smith's mission was to restore these profound truths about governance by revelation—to prepare a people who could walk with God, not merely as members of a church, but as sons and daughters of Christ.

This governance is personal.
It is alive.
It is direct.

It begins with His Light. It flows through His Spirit. It is confirmed by His voice. And it culminates when He seals you His.

Zion will not be built by men holding offices. It will be built by hearts filled with His Spirit. It will be gathered by His voice.

Zion is not an institution. Zion is a people. And when the people are prepared, He will come.

This is the pattern Joseph restored.

This is the pattern that will yet be fulfilled.

# Chapter 6 Notes

1 D&C 3:9–11; D&C 5:21–22; D&C 24:1–3; D&C 28:2; D&C 35:4, 18

2 1 Nephi 8:10–13, 19, 24; 1 Nephi 11:21–25.

3 1 Nephi 8:26–27; 1 Nephi 11:35–36.

4 1 Nephi 8:23; 1 Nephi 12:17.

5 John 10:2–4, 7, 27; 2 Nephi 9:41.

6 Moroni 7:12–19; D&C 84:46–48; D&C 93:28–32.

7 D&C 121:45–46; Matthew 5:8; Moroni 7:47–48.

8 D&C 121:45–46; Matthew 5:8; Moroni 7:47–48.

9 D&C 121:45–46; Matthew 5:8; Moroni 7:47–48.

10 1 Nephi 8; 1 Nephi 11; Joseph Smith, Teachings of the Prophet Joseph Smith, p. 196.

11 1 Nephi 8; 1 Nephi 11; Joseph Smith, Teachings of the Prophet Joseph Smith, p. 196.

12 Joseph Smith—History 1:11–20; D&C 1:17; 2 Nephi 31:20; 1 Nephi 11:25.

13 3 Nephi 26:13–14 (Nephite disciples ministered to by Christ); 1 Corinthians 15:8 (Paul, *"last of all he was seen of me also, as of one born out of due time"*).

14 Ether 13:3–10 (prophecy of the New Jerusalem and the meeting of the two holy cities).

# The Wheel of Consent

## God Governs by Law and Agreement

### Consent is the Lord's Government

In every age when the Lord has gathered a people, He has done so by two unchanging principles: His law, and the willing agreement of those who follow Him.

When law and willing hearts move together, heaven's order becomes life among the people—principle joined with choice, authority exercised without compulsory means.

Law is the eternal standard—unchanging, perfect, and revealed by God. Agreement is the people uniting their hearts, voices, and actions to that standard.

When divine law and human accord meet, heaven's order takes form on earth—justice balanced by mercy, and truth expressed through love.

Joseph taught that in the Lord's church, *"all things shall be done by common consent"* (D&C 26:2).

It was the Lord's way of ensuring His will was not only made known, but also received and embraced together.

In heaven's order, authority is never enforced by compulsion. It flows from His voice, is confirmed by His Spirit, and is sustained by the free acceptance of His people. When that happens, the law becomes binding—not because it was imposed, but because it was embraced.

Such consent is the language of creation itself—the same yielding by which light first entered the world and life was breathed into humankind.

We see this principle in Enoch's day, when a people were gathered and taught until their hearts were knit together in the word of God. Their unity was not the product of rigid control, but the fruit of individuals who willingly embraced the Lord's voice.

We see it again in the New Testament. When the needs of the early church grew, the apostles called upon the body of disciples to choose seven men of honest report, full of the Holy Ghost and wisdom, to oversee the daily ministrations (Acts 6:3–6).

The whole multitude agreed, laid hands upon them, and the work went forward in harmony.

This is the wheel of consent—revelation given, confirmed by witnesses, and willingly sustained by all, so the Lord Himself may dwell in the midst of His people.

## The Scriptural Foundation for Law and Agreement

In the Lord's revelations to Joseph Smith, law is never merely a set of instructions. It is the sustaining power of creation itself, given by revelation. And agreement is the act of the people joining their hearts and actions to that standard.

This is not merely a way of running meetings or filling callings—it is the very pattern by which heaven itself operates.

D&C 28 establishes that the order of the Church flows by revelation from the Lord through those He appoints. These appointments are themselves revelations, confirmed so the truth is known not merely assumed.

D&C 42 expands this into the *"law of the Church,"* given for the benefit of all—not as a static code, but as a living framework, sustained by continuing revelation and confirmed by the Spirit.

We see this principle in Kirtland when the Lord commanded the building of His first latter-day temple. In December 1832, He revealed:

> *"Organize yourselves; prepare every needful thing; and establish a house... a house of prayer, a house of fasting, a house of faith..."* (D&C 88:119)

Joseph presented the commandment before the Saints in conference. Many lived in poverty, still struggling to establish themselves, yet they covenanted together to build. There was no compulsion—only the call of the Lord and the willing agreement of His people. When the work lagged, the Lord spoke again with reproof and clear direction:

> *"If you keep not my commandments, the love of the Father shall not continue with you."* (D&C 95:12)

The law was revealed, the people gave their voice, and the labor moved forward in unity.

The same pattern appears years later in Nauvoo.

In D&C 124, the Lord gave detailed instructions for building the Nauvoo Temple and organizing the work. Every assignment—from construction to appointing officers—came by revelation, confirming that both the law and the labor flowed from Him.

He set the boundaries—what to build, who would oversee it, and how it would be done—*"by my own voice and by the voice of my servants"* (D&C 124:45–46).

The precision of these instructions made clear that the Lord Himself directs His work. It does not begin with human initiative; it begins with His word, delivered through those He appoints.

And the same Lord who gives specific instructions to His people also governs the whole of creation by law.

In D&C 88, He gives perhaps the clearest description of what that means:

> *"That which is governed by law is also preserved by law and perfected and sanctified by the same... The light which is in all things, which giveth life to all things, which is the law by which all things are governed."* (D&C 88:34–35, 13)

This *"light which is in all things"* is the Light of Christ—the living energy that sustains every particle, every truth, every kingdom. It proceeds from the presence of God, filling the immensity of space.

And then comes a sweeping statement that changes how we see everything:

> *"All kingdoms have a law given; and there is no space in the which there is no kingdom; and there is no kingdom in which there is no space." (D&C 88:37)*

Wherever there is space, there is law.

Every kind of space is governed by something—physical, spiritual, cultural, emotional.

Think of a bathroom. It has its own customs. You act differently there than you would in a kitchen.

The kitchen carries its own norms and unspoken rules—a different set of "laws" than a bathroom.

And both differ from a chapel. The way you dress. The way you speak. Even the way you think shifts, because the space itself carries a kind of order.

These are all *"kingdoms"* in the broadest sense. Each one operates by laws.

And within every space, there are smaller spaces.

> *Molecules.*
> *Atoms.*
> *Subatomic structures.*

Each governed by its own laws.

It's all the same pattern. From the largest to the smallest, there is no space where there is no law.

Physical law follows this same principle too. Gravity holds you to the floor in the kitchen, in the bathroom, in the chapel. But in outer space—an entirely different kingdom—gravity does not hold sway in the same way.

> *Law fits the space.*
> *Space reveals the law.*

The Book of Mormon ties this truth directly to the greatest choice we face:

> *"Men are free... to choose liberty and eternal life, through the great Mediator of all men, or to choose captivity and death, according to the captivity and power of the devil." (2 Nephi 2:27)*

The same God who sets the bounds of galaxies also sets the bounds of your life—not to trap you, but to preserve you.

## Freedom in the Law

Liberty is not living outside of structure.

It is life lived within God's structure—where His law sets the bounds and His Spirit makes you free.

> *It is the ability to act without coercion.*
> *To choose without fear.*
> *To grow without being restrained by unrighteous control.*

Captivity begins when that same outward structure is twisted into a tool of compulsion. When trust is replaced with fear. When persuasion gives way to force.

The law of God doesn't fence you in—it gives you ground to stand on. Without it, everything dissolves into chaos.

Obedience to that order is not bondage. It is the same creative force by which worlds are organized, sustained, and filled with life.

And under God's government, obedience is always voluntary. Forced obedience would destroy the very purpose of creation (D&C 58:26; Moroni 7:36).

If you think about it, the freest Being in eternity—Christ—was also the most obedient.

As Jehovah, He had power over the elements, over life and death itself (John 10:17–18). Yet the greatest use of His freedom was to yield it completely to His own divine will as the Eternal Father.

In Gethsemane,[1] serving in the role of the Son, He did not act from compulsion or loss of identity. He chose—deliberately and lovingly—to bring every desire, thought, and action of His mortal will into perfect harmony with His eternal will.

This was not the erasure of His agency. It was the highest and most deliberate use of it.

Christ's will as the Son being *"swallowed up"* in His will as the Father (Mosiah 15:7) was not defeat—it was the ultimate expression of freedom.

Think of it like this:

**The Aspen Grove:** On the surface, each aspen tree looks like an independent life.

But underground, they share one living organism, connected by a single root system.

Each tree stands upright, distinct, and whole—yet all draw life from the same source, moving in the same rhythm through the seasons.

Above ground, they sway to the same breeze, are washed by the same rain, and reach tall toward the same sky.

In this same way, Christ retained His full individuality in mortality—but every decision, every breath, was nourished by and aligned with His eternal will as the Father.

**True Identity:** When the Savior was asked who He was, His answer was simple and profound: *"I am"* (Exodus 3:14).

He knew exactly who He was. To be so certain of identity that nothing more needs to be added—that is power.

Our true identity is revealed in the same way: when we hear and respond to the voice of God. His voice defines who we really are, because when we yield our will to His, we discover ourselves.

This was the Savior's life. As both the Father and the Son in this world, His identity as Redeemer was inseparable from fulfilling the work He Himself had set to accomplish before the foundation of the earth.

To act outside that mission would have been to step outside of who He truly was, for His role and His being were one.

**The River and the Sea:** A river is free to carve its own course, winding where it will. But the river that willingly flows into the sea becomes part of something infinitely greater.

The Savior's mortal will was the river—full and strong. His eternal will as the Father was the vast, life-sustaining ocean.

When Christ yielded, it was not the end of His flow. It was the fulfillment of its purpose.

This is what Mosiah 15:7 means. His will was *"swallowed up"* not because one Being overpowered another, but because the mortal and eternal wills of the same Being were united in perfect purpose—to bring to pass the immortality and eternal life of man.

And because He perfectly governed Himself in unity with the divine will, He could show us—by word and by example—how heaven governs everything else.

## Captivity as the Converse

Rejecting God's law doesn't set you free. It simply puts you under another law.

Paul called it *"the law of sin and death"* (Romans 8:2).

Captivity is not the absence of governance—it is life under a ruler whose order produces decay.

> *The devil has a government.*
> *He has laws.*
> *But every law in his system is designed to deform and dismantle God's creation.*

Helaman said it bluntly: even dust obeys God, but human beings often refuse (Helaman 12:7–8).

When that happens, they don't escape law. They simply start living under one that was never meant to preserve them.

Captivity is just governance under a destructive master.

## Two Outcomes of the Same Law

The same law that gives life to the righteous also sustains the wicked. But the experience of that law is entirely different (Doctrine and Covenants 88:35).

For the obedient, it flows as liberty, light, and creation—like sap through a fruitful branch.

For the disobedient, it still flows... but not for their good. It becomes the fuel of captivity, the slow ripening of iniquity toward an inevitable harvest.

Law is impartial.

It doesn't have to *"switch modes"* to bless one and condemn another—it simply is. Its blessings and its judgments are both the natural results of alignment or resistance.

This is why scripture says that God's goodness leads a soul to repentance...or that the same goodness can become a witness against them in the day of wrath (Romans 2:4–5).

Christ, the root of all creation, upholds every breath, every heartbeat, every realm—even those who fight against Him. Their strength is not proof of His approval. It is proof of His sustaining mercy... until the day He prunes.

## King Benjamin's Farewell: A Living Example

King Benjamin understood this law. He had seen it work both ways.

After a lifetime of service, he gathered his people—not to announce new taxes or to enforce decrees, but to remind them of the One who gave them life.

He spoke of the God who creates and sustains all things. The same God who blesses every effort to obey Him... and who allows the wicked to *"dwindle in unbelief"* when they choose another path (Mosiah 1:5).

Benjamin's counsel was simple.

> Keep God's commandments and you will *"prosper in the land"* (Mosiah 2:22).
> Break them, and you *"withdraw yourselves from the Spirit of the Lord"* (Mosiah 2:36).

The prosperity he described wasn't about gold or armies. It was about living under the life-giving flow of God's law—aligned with Him in word, thought, and deed.

He warned that stepping outside that flow meant cutting yourself off from its source. Not because God abandons you, but because you choose to disconnect.

> *This is the same choice every soul faces.*
> *Liberty and life... or captivity and death.*
> *Both outcomes carried by the same sustaining law (2 Nephi 2:27).*

## Judges Chosen by the People

When Benjamin's reign ended, his son Mosiah stepped into the role of king.

But years later, Mosiah made a choice that would change the nation.

He saw the dangers of a wicked king—how one man, set above the law, could drag an entire people into captivity.

Righteous kings were rare. Under a wicked ruler, repentance and reform were nearly impossible unless the king himself changed.

Mosiah refused to leave that risk to the next generation. So he laid the choice before them:

> *"Choose you by the voice of this people, judges, that ye may be judged according to the laws..." (Mosiah 29:25)*

He didn't force the change. He taught them the principle, trusted their agency, and let them give their voice.

Under God's law, leaders were not imposed from above—they were recognized from among the people.

The same law that governed the king would govern the judges. And the same law would govern the people who gave their sustaining voice.

Mosiah warned them: if the majority chose righteousness, the nation would be blessed. If they turned to wickedness, the Lord's judgments would follow—not because of a tyrant's will, but because the people themselves had chosen the path (Mosiah 29:27).

In other words—the law itself wouldn't change. Their experience of it would.

A righteous people would prosper. A wicked people would collapse under the weight of their own choices.

We see the same principle years later when Alma served as chief judge.

It was a time of growing pride among the people. The laws were still in place, the system of judges still functioning—but Alma could see that something deeper was at risk. The outward structure meant little if hearts were drifting from the word of God (Alma 4:6–11).

So when the weight of both civil judgment and spiritual leadership began to pull him in two directions, Alma made a choice.

He relinquished the judgment seat, entrusting it to Nephihah, a man of integrity.

Alma then devoted himself fully to his calling as high priest, "*bearing down in pure testimony against them*" (Alma 4:19).

It was a living demonstration of the same principle Mosiah had taught: leadership was not about clinging to position, but about keeping the people anchored to the Lord's law. Alma understood that a society's safety came from a living connection between God's word and the hearts of His people—and he was willing to lay aside political power to strengthen that bond (Alma 4:16–19).

Both Mosiah and Alma modeled the same pattern: law revealed, confirmed by witnesses, and embraced by the willing. When this structure holds, liberty flourishes. But when the center shifts or the spokes weaken, the wheel can't bear the weight—and bondage creeps in.

### 4 Nephi *"The Happiest People"*

Centuries later, the Book of Mormon gives us the clearest picture of what it looks like when an entire people live by that pattern.

After the risen Lord visited the Americas, everything changed.

When a soul has seen and spoken with the Lord, they are never the same. They no longer have a disposition to be selfish or proud.

They love as He loves. They act as He acts—because His image has formed in them.

And in that generation, all were converted unto the Lord—both Nephites and Lamanites (4 Nephi 1:2). There was no partial peace, no uneasy truce. The change was complete.

They *"had all things common among them; therefore there were not rich and poor, bond and free, but they were all made free, and partakers of the heavenly gift"* (4 Nephi 1:3).

> *There were no "-ites."*
> *No divisions.*
> *No contentions.*

The record says they were *"in one, the children of Christ, and heirs to the kingdom of God"* (4 Nephi 1:17).

And it adds this simple line:

> *"Surely there could not be a happier people among all the people who had been created by the hand of God" (4 Nephi 1:16).*

It didn't happen by accident.

> *They chose it—day after day, year after year, generation after generation.*
> *They kept the law of Christ.*
> *They stayed aligned with His Spirit.*
> *They resolved disputes in peace, lived without pride, and gave freely of what they had.*

As long as they remained in that unity, the law preserved them. No enemies overpowered them. No famine swept them away. The same law that blessed the individual in liberty blessed the whole society in abundance.

### The Wheel That Holds Everything Together

In every true system the Lord establishes, there is a center, a rim, and spokes.

> *The center—the hub—is where the motion begins.*
> *The rim is what holds everything together in one whole.*
> *The spokes connect the two, carrying strength and alignment from the center out to the rim.*

In heaven's pattern, the hub is Christ—the living source of light and law. Everything flows from Him. His voice is the law. His Spirit is the power. His life is the light in every spoke.

The rim is the unity of the people—*"of one heart and one mind"*—moving together as one body. Without the rim, the wheel collapses. Without unity, the law loses its power among the people.

The spokes are the revealed laws, the inspired leaders, and the mutual agreements that bind the people to Christ and to each other. The spokes keep the rim aligned with the hub. If the spokes break, the wheel cannot carry the weight it was built for.

And this pattern is everywhere.[2] Once you see it, you start spotting it in places you never noticed before:

> *The bloom of* ***a daisy****, petals radiating from the golden heart.*
>
> *The cross-section of an orange, each segment bound to the center by thin white spokes.*
>
> *The design of* ***a bicycle wheel****, carrying the weight of the rider over rough ground.*
>
> *Even the turning* ***gears of a fine watch****—each spoke-like tooth in perfect proportion, transferring motion from the core to the outer edge.*

The wheel is efficient. Strong. Beautiful. It keeps balance while allowing motion. It carries weight without collapsing. It connects every point on the rim to the same source of strength.

> *You see it* ***in the heavens****—planets orbiting the sun, bound by invisible spokes of gravity.*
>
> *You see it* ***in the smallest life****—a cell's nucleus anchoring the organism, with channels radiating outward, holding the whole in order.*

> *You see it* ***in the design of temples and gathering places****, where all movement and meaning converge toward a central point.*

And here is the wonder of it: the wheel is one—but it has two layers that fit perfectly together.

In heaven's layer, Christ Himself is the hub from which all law and authority flow. In the earth's layer, that same law is confirmed and set in motion by the willing voice of the people—the hub of common consent.

### Two layers. One wheel.

The first reveals the source. The second shows how it moves among us.

When both layers are aligned—heaven's hub and earth's hub—the wheel rolls forward with strength and purpose. When either layer slips out of place, the wheel wobbles, and the work slows or stops.

Ancient cultures understood this. They wove the wheel into their sacred symbols.

Among many indigenous peoples, the medicine wheel[3] represents the circle of life—four directions, four seasons, four stages of being—all bound together around a sacred center.

In these wheels, every direction carries meaning, every spoke has its place, and the circle is never broken.

> *The wheel works because it is connected.*
> *Every spoke pulls its weight.*
> *Every part stays in its place.*
> *The rim moves because the hub holds steady.*

And so it is with the Lord's governance. The eternal wheel—in heaven and on earth—turns in perfect balance when the center holds, the spokes are sound, and the rim moves in unity.

And now here's the part that catches your breath.

### Heaven and Earth

This isn't just a design of nature or human ingenuity. It's the Lord's own blueprint for how heaven and earth are meant to work together.

From the smallest particle to the mightiest kingdom, the design remains the same:

> *Life flows from the center.*
> *Strength is carried through the spokes.*
> *Unity holds at the rim.*

In creation, the hub is Christ. In the governance of His people, that same life is confirmed by the voice of the willing—the sacred gift of common consent.

And because it is His pattern, it cannot be improved by human invention. It cannot be replaced by the clever systems of men without losing the very power that makes it work.

This is why, when the Lord restored His church through Joseph Smith, He did not hand down a rigid corporate chart. He revealed a living wheel—heaven's hub aligned with the earth's—and then showed His people how to keep it rolling forward.

### The D&C Structure: A Wheel in Revelation

In *D&C 20*, the Lord outlines how the Church is to function—not through blind hierarchy, but with the voice of the people confirming every decision (D&C 20:63–66).

In *D&C 26:2*, He makes it plain: *"All things shall be done by common consent in the church, by much prayer and faith."* That's the hub—the place decisions join with revelation, where the whole body agrees together before moving forward.

In *D&C 28:13* and *D&C 42:11*, He reinforces that no one acts alone in directing His people. Spokes of connection—multiple witnesses, united voices, confirming the same Spirit—give the wheel its strength.

In *D&C 107:27–30*, even the highest councils are bound by the same order: nothing is decided without unity, without every spoke holding fast to the hub.

The rim—the outward work—appears in passages like *D&C 84:109–110*, where every member has a place, every gift is needed, and all parts move together *"that the whole body may be edified."*

And at the very heart of it all—the Lord and His people—joined in one purpose by common consent. It's the unshaken hub that keeps the whole moving forward.

This is not just a structure for Christ's Church. It's the structure of heaven itself.

Once you see it, you begin to see it everywhere—in creation, in ancient wisdom, even in the design of your own soul.

### Beyond the Rim

You thought the wheel was a powerful way to see how the Lord's government works—and it is. But that's only two dimensions.

Now let's step into something bigger. Let me show you the Lord's universal structure in *three dimensions*.

Picture the wheel you've been imagining—the hub, the spokes, the rim. Now lift it, turn it, and set it in motion. As it moves forward, the path it traces isn't flat anymore. It rises. It twists. It forms a living spiral—a helix.

This is the Lord's true, universal pattern. You see it in the double helix of DNA, carrying the code of life.

> *You see it* ***in the spiral arms of galaxies****, turning like vast wheels of light.*
>
> *You see it* ***in the curling of a fern frond****, the winding of a seashell, the pattern of a sunflower's seeds, the growth of a ram's horn.*
>
> *You see it* ***in ocean currents, whirlwinds, and hurricanes****—forces of both life and cleansing.*
>
> *You even see it* ***in the paths of planets and comets*** *as they dance through the heavens.*

This design appears everywhere because it comes from Him. It is His signature—the shape of life, creation, and progression.

In this living helix, one strand is Christ—the constant, eternal source of light and truth. The other strand is His people, moving forward through time. The rungs that join them are the moments of revelation and willing consent—the living "spokes" that bind heaven and earth together.

Just as a single DNA molecule contains billions of rungs, the Lord's living government is built from countless direct connections between Christ and His people—individual to Christ, family to Christ, quorum to Christ, congregation to Christ.

Remember how we described the DNA of the Restoration? This is where that design becomes visible. Here the two strands work seamlessly together under Christ's direction: the masculine frames, the feminine fills.

One establishes order and protection; the other nurtures, beautifies, and gives life. Each depends on the other, and both draw their strength from Him who is the Source of all life.

When the two move in harmony, revelation flows freely and the whole body grows. The structure of heaven and the compassion of heaven join—justice and mercy, strength and gentleness, form and fullness—woven together through the living Christ..

These bonds carry His life, light, and direction upward, turn by turn, in an endless spiral of increase.

The wheel shows us balance and unity. The helix shows us motion and destiny.

This isn't just about keeping order—it's about moving God's people along a path of eternal progression until they are ready to dwell with Him forever.

But there's also a counterfeit. The adversary twists the same pattern downward. His spiral is just as real—but it pulls toward darkness, confusion, bondage, and death.

One helix ascends into the presence of Christ; the other descends into the pit. The pattern is the same; the direction and the destination make all the difference.

## Scriptural Witnesses of the Wheel of Consent

The Lord has never governed His people by fiat.

A "fiat" is an order issued from a position of authority that must be obeyed simply because it was declared. In earthly kingdoms, kings and rulers often say, "Do this," and the people must do it—whether they agree, understand, or believe it's right. It is law by decree, not by unity of heart.

But the Lord's government works differently. He reveals His will and then allows His people to choose it—freely, willingly, without compulsion. It is never *"because I said so."* It is always *"this is My word... will you receive it? Will you obey it?"*

That is the Wheel of Consent—the two-dimensional view of a deeper, living structure the Lord uses to govern both heaven and earth. In its simplest form, it shines through scripture like sunlight through stained glass—each example a different color of the same Light.

### Enoch's City (Moses 7)

Long before "Zion" became a dream for the latter days, it was a living, breathing city.

The Lord called Enoch to cry repentance.[4] He taught the people the law of God, invited them to walk in His ways, and promised His presence if they would. The record says they were *"of one heart and one mind"* and that *"there was no poor among them."*

That kind of unity is never accidental. It is the fruit of each soul personally agreeing with God's word and with each other. They did not become one because of force. They became one because each heart consented to the same Light. And when the city was ready, the Lord gathered them into His presence—literally.

### King Benjamin's Assembly (Mosiah 2–5)

Few moments in scripture reveal the Wheel of Consent more vividly than King Benjamin's farewell address.[5]

The people gathered—families in tents, doors facing the temple, a living symbol of turning their hearts toward God. Benjamin stood before them, not to demand their loyalty to him, but to bear witness of the true King.

He reminded them that he had never taxed them, never sought gold or silver, never made them slaves. He had worked with his own hands to serve them. Then he taught them of Jesus Christ—His atoning blood, His resurrection, His role as the source of salvation.

And here is the key: when the people responded, they did not pledge loyalty to Benjamin or to any earthly institution. They entered into agreement with God Himself.

The record is clear: *"The Spirit of the Lord Omnipotent... has wrought a mighty change in us, or in our hearts, that we have no more disposition to do evil, but to do good continually"* (Mosiah 5:2).

They experienced a baptism of fire and of the Holy Ghost. Their sins were remitted. They were spiritually reborn, sealed by the Spirit as His people (Mosiah 5:5–6). This was not political unity—it was the unity of sanctified hearts knit together.

## The Nephite Zion (4 Nephi)

After the risen Christ ministered at Bountiful, something happened that the world had never seen.

They didn't just hear His voice—they saw Him, sat at His feet, and felt the prints in His hands, His feet, and His side.

They watched Him bless their children one by one. They saw angels descend and encircle them with fire. He taught them His doctrine, broke bread with them, and prayed in words so holy they could not be written.

They were invited by Him to be baptized again, and each of them entered the waters of baptism. Then they sought for the baptism of fire and the Holy Ghost—and He gave it to them. They were sanctified, made holy without spot.[6]

When you have experienced that, you are never the same. You are born again. You are a new creature.

That is why they lived in peace. Their hearts had been sanctified, and the adversary had no foothold among them. They chose to remain in that unity for nearly two hundred years, living as one because they were one with Him.

## The Jerusalem Council (Acts 15)

This principle held even in the early Church after Christ's ascension.

A dispute arose over whether Gentile converts must keep the Law of Moses. The apostles and elders gathered—not to vote on a policy, but to seek the Lord's will. They heard witnesses, searched the scriptures, and prayed.[7]

When the answer came, they sent word to the Saints with this phrase: *"It seemed good to the Holy Ghost, and to us"* (Acts 15:28) .

That is the Wheel of Consent in a single sentence—the Spirit confirmed the revelation, and the people agreed together to follow it.

From Enoch's city to the Jerusalem Council, the design holds true—heaven's hub and earth's hub turning together as one strand in the same living structure.

And when they do, something more than unity happens.

They are protected. The same law that binds the people to Christ also shields them from deception, abuse, and corruption.

This is why the Lord revealed that *"every decision... must be by the unanimous voice of the same"* (D&C 107:27).

It is why *"every member... must be tried before the body of the church"* and confirmed *"by the voice of the church"* (D&C 20:63–66).

Not because He needs procedure for its own sake, but because when the whole body hears, weighs, and confirms the truth together, falsehood cannot slip in unnoticed.

The Wheel of Consent—or, seen in three dimensions, the Lord's living helix of revelation and agreement—is not only His way of moving His people forward. It is His way of keeping them safe.

## The Structure That Protects

The Lord's way of governance is not fragile. It was never meant to hang on the will of one man or even a small circle of leaders.

It is layered, balanced, and self-correcting—a system designed to protect the body of believers from being led into error, bondage, or destruction.

At its heart, the protection is simple: no one advances the work of God alone.

Every law, every calling, every decision is rooted in revelation from Christ and confirmed by the willing agreement of His people.

When both strands of the helix are in place—heaven's hub and earth's hub spiraling upward together—the spokes hold firm, and the rim moves as one.

A strand that binds God and His willing people in the same living structure cannot be quietly severed or replaced. Spokes that carry revelation cannot be silenced without the rest of the wheel knowing something is wrong. False doctrines are stopped before they take root.

Personal agendas are checked by the Spirit and by the voice of the body. The gifts of the Spirit are recognized and confirmed, not hidden or suppressed.

In every age, this pattern has been the Lord's defense against unrighteous dominion.

It is not guarded by gates or walls, but by the living bond between heaven's word and the hearts of the Saints.

It thrives where there is light, unity, and choice—and it withers where those are taken away.

History shows what happens when this balance is kept. And history shows what happens when it breaks.

When one strand weakens, the other is forced to carry a weight it was never meant to bear—twisting the structure, throwing the whole upward motion off balance. Spokes splinter. The wheel wobbles. The people become vulnerable to the very dangers the Lord's pattern was given to prevent.

The Pattern That Protects is not just a principle for church governance. It is an eternal safeguard—the same law by which all things are preserved (D&C 88:34)—woven like a double helix into the heavens, the earth, and the Kingdom of God alike.

### The Lord's Safeguard Against Unrighteous Dominion

In every age, this pattern has been the Lord's defense against unrighteous dominion.

It is not guarded by gates or walls, but by the living bond between heaven's word and the hearts of the Saints—two strands of the same helix, each dependent on the other to stay aligned. It thrives where there is light, unity, and choice—and it withers where those are taken away.

So what is this thing called *unrighteous dominion*?

The words come straight from the Lord's own mouth in D&C 121. He warns that when anyone in a position of influence begins to *"exercise control or dominion or compulsion upon the souls of the children of men"* in any degree of unrighteousness, the Spirit of the Lord is grieved, and that person's authority is gone.

The Lord's definition is razor-sharp:

> ***Control*** *that replaces persuasion.*
> ***Compulsion*** *that overrides agency.*
> ***Dominion*** *that seeks its own will instead of God's.*

A hub shared between God and His willing people—the very axis where the strands of the helix meet—cannot be quietly replaced. False doctrines are stopped before they take root.

Spokes that carry revelation—the connecting rungs of the helix—cannot be silenced without the rest of the structure sensing something is wrong.

This safeguard works because the same law that governs in heaven must also be received on earth by the voice of the people (D&C 107:27–30; D&C 20:63–66).

In the Lord's order, decisions that affect the whole body are confirmed by the whole body.

He appoints leaders, but their voice does not stand alone—it is established in the presence of witnesses, sustained by the Spirit, and embraced by common consent.

### How to Spot It Anywhere

If you see these patterns, you are seeing the early stages of unrighteous dominion:

> **Voice without listening:** leaders speak, but do not receive. Decisions without consent—choices are made for the group without seeking their agreement.
> **Power without accountability:** no one can question the decision without being punished or removed.
> **Fear instead of faith:** compliance is secured by threat, shame, or fear of loss.
> **Loyalty without love:** worthiness measured by allegiance to a church or organization rather than devotion to the Lord, breeding pride, virtue-signaling, and an "us vs. them" spirit.

The danger is subtle because these patterns can be dressed in the language of care, duty, or even doctrine. But at its core, unrighteous dominion replaces the Lord's safeguard—the living consent of the people—with control from above.

This structure is not only for the Church, but for Zion itself—the eternal helix that links heaven's government with earth's willing hearts.

> *This is the way heaven governs.*
> *This is the way freedom endures.*

### When the Wheel Goes Out of Balance

When the Lord's order is intact, everything moves in harmony.

> **The hub:** Christ in heaven and the willing consent of His people on earth—stays aligned at the axis, keeping the two strands of the helix turning upward together.

> **The spokes:** revelation, inspired leaders, and mutual agreement—remain strong.
> **The rim:** the unity of the Saints—moves in perfect rhythm, spiraling upward in step with the Lord's purposes.

But when the wheel goes out of balance, the signs are unmistakable. The hub begins to shift. Revelation is replaced by policy. Persuasion gives way to pressure. Consent becomes a formality. The wheel may still turn for a while, but it wobbles, strains, and eventually grinds to a halt.

History and scripture are full of the wreckage left behind when this happens. Without the living safeguard of common consent, the door opens for control from above. Fear replaces faith. Unity is traded for conformity.

The Lord's definition of unrighteous dominion becomes visible—control instead of persuasion, compulsion instead of agency, man's will instead of God's.

And here is the sobering truth: the wheel does not usually collapse overnight. It weakens slowly, spoke by spoke, until one day the hub no longer holds. By then, the imbalance may feel normal—even righteous—to those riding in the cart.

That is why the Lord gave us the pattern in the first place.

> *To keep the hub steady.*
> *To keep the spokes sound.*
> *To keep the rim moving in unity.*

Because when the wheel holds, Zion can move forward.

When it breaks, captivity follows.

## Why the Safeguard Works

The Lord's structure prevents this from the start. His design keeps the center—His revealed will—tied inseparably to the people, like two strands of the same helix winding upward together. No one can insert themselves between the two without it becoming obvious.

In this structure, the people are not passive recipients. They are participants. They hear the word, weigh it, confirm it by the Spirit, and add their sacred yes.

That agreement is not empty assent—it is their willing commitment to live what they have confirmed as true. They have skin in the game.

Their participation locks the wheel to its true center—or in the helix view, keeps both strands anchored to the same axis—making it impossible for a single spoke or rung to dominate the whole.

Every spoke—or rung in the helix—is accountable to the hub/axis and the rim/spiral. Leaders and witnesses must remain in harmony with the revealed will of God and the confirming voice of the people.

No change can be made without agreement. Consent is not assumed—it is sought, voiced, and sustained.

The people retain the right and responsibility to withdraw their consent if what is presented no longer aligns with the Lord's word.

Break any one of those three, and the balance is lost. These are not just good ideas—they are the very laws that keep the wheel aligned with God's design. Keep them all, and the wheel turns steady and strong.

The Lord's design makes it impossible for unrighteous dominion to thrive unnoticed.

In His government:

> **Leaders cannot govern alone.** Their role is to receive and deliver His word—not to compel obedience to their own ideas.
>
> **The people cannot be bypassed.** Their consent is sought and sustained, not assumed.
>
> **The Spirit confirms all things.** If the Spirit withdraws, the authority to act is gone, no matter the position.

Joseph warned the Saints never to place blind trust in any man, reminding them that *"a prophet [is] only a prophet when he [is] acting as such"* (History of the Church, 5:265).

He also cautioned, *"If he should transgress, he should not be sustained by the Saints"* (Times and Seasons, 3:651).

And in counsel to the Relief Society, he taught, *"We are to try our leaders as we try other men; and if they are found in transgression, they should be reproved with justice and mercy"* (Relief Society Minutes, Nauvoo, April 28, 1842).

Safety lies in the Lord's voice, confirmed by the Spirit, not in the assumed infallibility of a leader. No one is above counsel or correction, and no calling exempts a person from the law of God.

It is this living exchange—God speaks, His people confirm, and all move forward together—that keeps the wheel true and the helix aligned, turning upward in balance.

Scriptural Roots of the Safeguard

The Lord has always tied His government to the consent of His people.

> **Moses at Sinai:** The Lord gave the commandments; the people heard them and answered together, *"All that the Lord hath spoken we will do"* (Exodus 19:8).
>
> **King Benjamin's Assembly:** After hearing the word, the people experienced a mighty change of heart, cried out to God for mercy, received a remission of their sins, and entered into a covenant directly with Him (Mosiah 5:2–5).
>
> **The Nephite Zion of 4 Nephi:** Equality reigned because they were all made free and partakers of the heavenly gift.

In each case, the safeguard was not a law code or a procedural checklist. It was a living connection between God's word, His law, and a people willing to receive it and obey it.

### What This Means for Us

Understand this: the safeguard against unrighteous dominion is a relationship, not policy or traditional culture.

It is a relationship—a constant exchange between the Lord and His people—with every participant, male and female, holding a place in the wheel and a strand in the helix.

When that relationship is vibrant, truth moves freely from the hub (Jesus Christ) to the rim (His people) and back again.

When it is neglected or suppressed, the wheel may still turn for a while, but it turns out of balance, gathering momentum in the wrong direction. It becomes rigid, controlling, even weaponized against those who question its drift.

When the masculine strand is suppressed, guardianship and structure falter, and chaos follows. A house without a frame cannot stand. Without order, families unravel and communities dissolve. What should have been preserved perishes for lack of protection.

When the feminine strand is suppressed, life and wisdom retreat, and structure collapses into sterility. Prophecy fades, vision is lost, healing withers, and beauty turns to silence. Worship may continue, but the Spirit is absent. The temple remains, but it becomes hollow.

This is why the structure matters.

It is not about preserving an institution; it is about protecting the living bond between God and His people, so His will is known, embraced, and carried out in unity.

And when that bond holds, the wheel turns strong and true—ready to carry Zion forward.

### Bridging the Structure into Joseph's Day

We've seen this structure in the Lord's dealings with His people from Enoch to the early Saints in Jerusalem. In Joseph's day, it would take on flesh and bone—not just in sermons, but in how a city was built and a people were led.

In Nauvoo, Joseph Smith set divine governance in motion. He would not stop at preaching heaven's pattern—he worked to see it lived.

Zion began on paper, in the plat Joseph drew. But it had to be gathered, organized, and set in motion to become real.

In that gathering, he wove two strands together: law and consent, strength and compassion, the masculine and the feminine. The structure provided order; the spirit within gave life. It was the same harmony he demonstrated when he organized the Relief Society—men and women laboring side by side under the same heavenly authority, each carrying the Spirit's gifts according to divine design.

Joseph invited people from every nation to gather and live under the same law—by invitation, not by force.

> *He preached unity in Christ.*
> *He encouraged mutual support.*
> *He emphasized consecration as a voluntary act of love, not a compulsory tax.*

Early in his ministry, he sent missionaries to the remnant of Israel—the people the Book of Mormon calls Lamanites—believing they had a prophetic role in the Lord's work.

This wasn't a side mission. It belonged to the same vision.

Each soul—from far nations or from the ancient covenant people on this land—was invited to take a living place in Zion's wheel, each one a strand in the upward helix of revelation and willing agreement, joined to the same center in Christ.

To give that vision form, Joseph secured the Nauvoo Charter—a sweeping grant of self-governance that let the Saints elect leaders, form a city council, and maintain courts.[8]

The structure echoed the wheel: a center of guiding principles, spokes of active representation, a rim of united action—and, seen from another angle, the two strands of heaven and earth winding upward together around the same axis.

The Council of the Fifty grew from the same impulse. It wasn't a secret club of elites, but an earthly experiment in heavenly order—a body where men from different nations, languages, and faith backgrounds sat as equals, seeking the will of God for the good of all.[9]

Joseph taught that their charge was nothing less than to prepare the way for the reign of Christ on earth.

He spoke often of the necessity of gathering. *"Come to Nauvoo,"* he urged, *"where we can build up a city that shall be the joy of the whole earth."*[10]

For him, the city was never the goal. It was a living framework for something far greater: a people bound together in faith and love, moving forward like strands in the same helix, prepared to receive the Lord.

Every street, every council, every gathering served that higher purpose—to help the Saints learn how to live as one body under God's law.

In council, in print, and from the pulpit, Joseph pressed the same point: Zion could not be scattered. Its strength came from the living connection between God's word and a people willing to receive it—together—the same unbroken bond that keeps the two strands of the helix turning upward as one.

He was building the bridge between the pattern revealed in scripture and a society that could live it—not in theory, but in the dust and timber and heartbeats of a gathered people.

And when that bond held, the work moved with power. When it slipped, Joseph returned to the Lord—and the Saints returned to their voice.

## The Balance Between Revelation and Agreement

From the beginning, the Lord anchored His Church in a principle both practical and divine—that nothing would move forward without both His word and the people's willing agreement:

> *"all things shall be done by common consent in the church, by much prayer and faith."* (D&C 26:2)

This wasn't a courtesy vote. It was a commandment: the people's voice belongs inside His government.

Every spoke in the Lord's wheel—or rung in His upward-turning helix—depends on balance. Revelation runs from the center, but without the people's sustaining yes, it stalls. Consent rises from the body toward Christ, but without revelation to anchor it, it drifts.

Common consent was more than a raised hand. The people held a real place in the wheel—not as spectators, but as the living rim that gives the hub its motion. And when Joseph applied this in Nauvoo, it looked nothing like a perfunctory tally.

Joseph kept both sides alive. Receiving direction from heaven wasn't passive—it was the very law by which all things are governed. Hear the word by the Spirit. Recognize it. Sustain it. Obey it.

When a proposal came forward—whether to call a new leader, build a temple, or send out a company—it was presented openly. If there were questions or concerns, they were voiced. The body would counsel together until there was unity.

It wasn't about hurrying the process. It was about making sure every spoke was firmly in place before the wheel began to turn.

No one was set apart simply because Joseph said so. Calls, changes, initiatives—all were presented for a sustaining vote. And if a hand rose in dissent, the meeting didn't move on. It paused—because in the Lord's helix, a misaligned rung must be set right before the whole can keep ascending.

> *They stopped.*
> *They talked.*
> *They prayed together.*
> *They listened, and they sought the mind of the Lord until there was unity—not just in form, but in Spirit.*

It wasn't about haste or loyalty tests. It was about protecting trust—and making sure the wheel moved with every spoke in place.

## Revelation Lived in Nauvoo

In Nauvoo, revelation wasn't an abstract principle—it was lived.

We see this clearly at the April 6, 1841 General Conference in Nauvoo.[11]

Long before the conference, Joseph sought the Lord's mind on who should serve. He prayed, counseled with Hyrum and others, weighed the city's needs, and prayed again—waiting until the Lord made the names clear.

These weren't casual picks. Each name came through petition, revelation, and the weight of heaven's direction.

The Saints gathered to sustain the First Presidency, the Twelve, and other presidencies. Names were read aloud from the stand, one by one. Hands went up—not in lockstep, but in the honest, visible voice of the people.[12]

If a hand went up in dissent, it wasn't brushed aside—it was addressed, often right there in the meeting.

Leaders and members alike knew the Lord's will came not only to His people, but through them—and consent was the confirmation.

That day, unity was reached, the quorums sustained, and the Saints moved forward together—the wheel turning strong and true.

The city council of Nauvoo offers another example. As mayor, Joseph didn't sit in a gilded chair issuing decrees. He sat shoulder-to-shoulder with other council members—proposing measures, hearing debate, refining ideas through the counsel in the room.[13]

Even in urgency, the process was patient—unity mattered more than speed. The same principle held in moments of crisis.

On August 8, 1844, after Joseph's death, the Saints faced a wrenching question: who would lead?

The people gathered in Nauvoo to hear from Sidney Rigdon and Brigham Young. They listened, weighed, and then—in a moment many later described as decisive—raised their hands to sustain the direction they believed the Lord was leading them.[14]

Whether the outcome was perfect is another discussion. The process still rested on the same revealed law—the people's voice, seeking the Lord's will together.

Even in contested moments, the wheel turned because the people stood at the center—and the spokes of their consent and witness still ran to the hub, Jesus Christ.

This wasn't theater. It was governance by common consent. And the people knew their role: not spectators, but participants in the Lord's work.

## Joseph Like King Benjamin

Joseph's conduct reinforced this again and again.

He worked beside them on building projects, defended them in court, and walked the same dusty streets. He was no distant ruler.

Joseph never treated common consent as a rubber stamp. It was a safeguard against unrighteous dominion—a living exchange between revelation and the Saints.

Like King Benjamin in the Book of Mormon, Joseph labored beside the people, not above them. He proposed, explained, invited—and then listened. This was governance in the Lord's pattern:[15]

> *The hub received light.*
> *The spokes carried it to the rim.*
> *And in the helix view, the axis received life, the rungs carried it outward and upward, and the spiral advanced only when both strands were joined in the same life.*

The message was clear: the Lord's governance was never about one man's will, but about the whole body seeking His will together.

When that balance held, the work moved forward in strength. But when leaders neglected the people's right to confirm—or when the people ignored the Lord's word—the wheel began to wobble.

Joseph's genius didn't come from ambition or personal brilliance, but from years of the Lord mentoring, teaching, and refining him. He had stumbled, repented, and learned through his own mistakes to trust the Lord completely, to seek His voice above all others, and to obey it without hesitation.

Out of that refining fire came a leader able to hold revelation and relationship in constant harmony.

He taught from what the Lord revealed, but he also listened to the Saints. He governed by eternal principle, yet practiced persuasion, patience, and mutual respect. And because he lived these lessons, he could model them for others—showing not just the words of the pattern, but the way to walk in it.

This structure was never about a single man's control.

It was about the living bond between heaven and earth—a bond kept strong by revelation and agreement turning together, like hub and rim connected by living spokes, or like the twin strands of a living helix—each bound to the same axis, moving upward together in the life of Christ.

### Consent at Work in Nauvoo

When the Lord commanded Joseph to build the Nauvoo Temple, it wasn't just about a structure of stone. It was about a people learning to act together—a process that would prepare them to receive more light and knowledge.

In January 1841, the Lord declared through Joseph:

> *"And ye shall build a house unto me, for the place of your washing, and your anointing, and your solemn assemblies... that I may reveal mine ordinances therein unto my people; for I deign to reveal unto my church things which have been kept hid from before the foundation of the world."* (D&C 124:37–38)

It was an invitation—not a decree forced upon them. Joseph presented the revelation openly. The people heard it, discussed it, and consented to it together. Assignments were given in public settings. Resources were pledged by choice. There was no coercion; the temple would rise only if the people united by choice.

Joseph never separated revelation from relationships. He walked the streets, spoke in meetings, and encouraged workers by name. He modeled that the "how" mattered as much as the "what"—that Zion couldn't be built on forced labor or blind loyalty, but only on willing hearts united in common cause.

This same pattern unfolded across every sphere of Nauvoo life.

By 1842, the principles Joseph had already taught—the two strands of law and consent, strength and compassion—were beginning to take tangible form in the city. One of the clearest examples was the Female Relief Society of Nauvoo. Joseph met with the women, outlined its revealed purpose—to *"relieve the poor"* and to *"save souls"*—and then invited them to choose their own president and officers.

Emma Smith was sustained by the women, not appointed over them. The minutes record the sisters counseling together, voting on initiatives, pooling their resources to aid families, and sustaining one another's efforts.[16]

Though organized separately, the Society moved on the same wheel: revelation at the hub, counselors and officers as spokes, and the united action of the sisters forming the rim. It was the feminine strand of the same living pattern—governed by revelation, ordered by consent, and enlivened by charity.

Education followed the same course. Nauvoo's charter for a university was not a top-down decree but a city-wide aspiration, sustained by vote and then acted upon by the community. Trustees were elected, curriculum discussed, and teachers appointed by common consent.[17]

Even the Nauvoo Legion—the city's defensive militia—reflected the same principle. Officers were nominated and sustained. Service was voluntary. Participation came with a sense of ownership, not subjugation.[18]

In all these efforts, Joseph shared one defining trait: he trusted the people to govern with him, not beneath him. He didn't simply issue instructions and expect silent compliance. Guided by the Lord's voice, he taught, persuaded, listened, and refined—and then acted with them.

The temple project, in particular, shows the seed he was planting. It was more than stone and timber. It was a living rehearsal for Zion—a people laboring together under the Lord's appointments, governed by revelation and bound by willing agreement.[19]

And, as we will see in later chapters, that seed was meant to grow into something far greater. For now, it stands as one of the clearest examples of how Joseph practiced the structure of common consent in every sphere of Nauvoo life.

## Conclusion–This Structure Opens the Way for the Spirit

From the assemblies of ancient Israel to the councils of Nauvoo, the Lord's way has always been the same:

> *Revelation at the center.*
> *Living witnesses as the spokes.*
> *A people united in action forming the rim.*

Joseph didn't just teach this order—he embodied it. In gatherings large and small, he sought heaven's voice first, then brought the Saints into unity through persuasion, patience, and prayer.

In this structure, the two strands move together. Revelation gives direction and structure; consent gives life and harmony. One without the other creates imbalance, but together they form the rhythm of heaven itself.

It was more than a method of governance—it was a spiritual discipline, the heartbeat of the Restoration.

When the Lord's people walk in the order of common consent, they create a living channel for His Spirit to move freely among them. Unity is not abstract—it is the environment where heaven flows into earth.

And bear this in mind: this resonance exists for one express purpose—to prepare a people, one heartbeat at a time, to become like Them: Father, Mother, and Son.

When hearts are knit together in love and truth flows freely between the Lord and His people, something greater becomes possible—the outpouring of the gifts of the Spirit.

These gifts—prophecy, healing, tongues, discernment, and more—are not tokens of status for the spiritually favored, but gifts given to strengthen the entire wheel.

They are heaven's confirmation that the wheel is turning as it should, that the Lord is truly in the midst of His people.

Where there is agreement in righteousness, the Spirit can move without restraint.

> *We saw it in Nauvoo on March 31, 1842, when Joseph met with the Relief Society. He spoke of their sacred work, urging them to seek the gifts of the Spirit. As the meeting unfolded, Eliza R. Snow recorded that "many spoke in tongues, prophesied, and bore testimony of the truth."*[20]

In that room, hearts were knit together. There was no hierarchy, no distance—only a shared bond in Christ expressed through the free exercise of His gifts.

The structure of common consent does more than keep a community in harmony. It opens the channels through which the Lord blesses, directs, and empowers His Saints.

And when those channels are clear, the same Spirit that governed the early Saints will govern us—not by compulsion, but by living power.

That is the wheel in perfect balance: revelation at the center, carried by willing hearts to every part of the body, returning in gratitude and testimony—like the two strands of a living helix, Christ and His people, bound to the same axis and moving upward together toward His fullness.

It is a foretaste of what happens when the Saints live in agreement with God—His Spirit is poured out, His gifts are manifest, and His people grow stronger together.

As we move into the next chapter, we will look more closely at those gifts—the very manifestations that signal God's presence among a united body, and the means by which He builds, refines, and empowers His people to prepare them for His presence.

## Chapter 7 Notes

1 Matthew 26:39; Luke 22:42

2 *"The course of the Lord is one eternal round"* (1 Nephi 10:19; Alma 7:20; D&C 3:2).

3 Paula Gunn Allen, The Sacred Hoop: Recovering the Feminine in American Indian Traditions (Boston: Beacon Press, 1986); Beverly Hungry Wolf, The Ways of My Grandmothers (New York: Quill, 1980). Both describe the medicine wheel as a unifying circle of life, directions, and seasons around a sacred center.

4 Moses 6:26–27 (Enoch called to cry repentance); Moses 7:16–21 (the Lord's presence among Zion and the city taken up to heaven).

5 Mosiah 2–5 (King Benjamin gathers his people, teaches of Christ, and they experience a mighty change of heart before entering into a covenant to be called the children of God).

6 3 Nephi 19:9, 11–15, 20–22, 28–29 (disciples baptized again, praying for the Holy Ghost, and filled with fire and sanctified in Christ's presence).

7 Acts 15:1–29 (dispute over circumcision, apostles and elders in council, testimony of Peter and James, and decision confirmed by the Holy Ghost).

8 *"An Act to Incorporate the City of Nauvoo,"* Laws of the State of Illinois, 12th General Assembly, 1840–1841, pp. 52–57 (approved December 16, 1840). The Nauvoo Charter granted broad powers of self-governance, including the election of leaders, city council authority, and the establishment of courts.

9 Joseph Smith Papers, Administrative Records: Council of Fifty, Minutes, March 1844–January 1846, ed. Matthew J. Grow and R. Eric Smith (Salt Lake City: Church Historian's Press, 2016). These minutes document Joseph's establishment of the council as a political body to prepare for the kingdom of God, emphasizing equality and deliberation among men of varied nations and faiths.

10 Joseph Smith, discourse, Oct. 1841, Nauvoo, IL, in History of the Church, 4:272. Joseph urged the Saints to gather to Nauvoo to build a city of strength and joy.

11 Minutes of the General Conference of the Church of Jesus Christ of Latter-day Saints, April 6–11, 1841, Nauvoo, Illinois, in History of the Church, 4:341–352. At this conference, the cornerstones of the Nauvoo Temple were laid, the Nauvoo Legion was discussed, and Joseph emphasized the necessity of gathering.

12 Minutes of the General Conference, April 6, 1841, Nauvoo, Illinois, in History of the Church, 4:341–342. The record shows the congregation sustaining Joseph Smith and his counselors in the First Presidency, the Quorum of the Twelve, and other presiding quorums by uplifted hands.

13 Minutes of the Nauvoo City Council, Feb. 1841–June 1844, in Joseph Smith Papers, Documents and Administrative Records. As mayor (elected Feb. 1, 1841), Joseph participated actively in council deliberations, proposing measures and engaging in debate alongside other members rather than ruling unilaterally.

14 *"Special Meeting,"* August 8, 1844, Nauvoo, Illinois, in History of the Church, 7:229–241; see also Minutes of Meeting, Aug. 8, 1844, in Joseph Smith Papers, Administrative Records: Council of Fifty, Minutes, March 1844–January 1846, ed. Matthew J. Grow and R. Eric Smith (Salt Lake City: Church Historian's Press, 2016), 242–248. These accounts describe Sidney Rigdon's appeal to act as

guardian, followed by Brigham Young's speech and the sustaining vote of the Saints.

15 King Benjamin *"labored with mine own hands"* so he could serve without burdening the people (Mosiah 2:14)

Minutes of the Nauvoo City Council, Feb. 1841–June 1844, in Joseph Smith Papers. Joseph participated in council debate and decision-making, emphasizing consent and collaboration over unilateral command.

16 *"Nauvoo Relief Society Minute Book,"* March 17, 1842, in The First Fifty Years of Relief Society: Key Documents in Latter-day Saint Women's History, ed. Jill Mulvay Derr et al. (Salt Lake City: Church Historian's Press, 2016), 19–25.

17 *"An Act to Incorporate the University of the City of Nauvoo,"* Laws of the State of Illinois, 12th General Assembly, 1840–1841, 131–134 (approved Feb. 21, 1841). See also Minutes of the Nauvoo City Council, Feb. 1841–June 1844, in Joseph Smith Papers.

18 *"An Act to Incorporate the Nauvoo Legion,"* Laws of the State of Illinois, 12th General Assembly, 1840–1841, 55–57 (approved Dec. 16, 1840); see also Minutes of the Nauvoo City Council and Nauvoo Legion records in Joseph Smith Papers.

19 *"My people are always commanded to build temples unto my holy name"* (D&C 124:39).
*"If ye labor with all your might, I will consecrate that spot that it shall be made holy"* (D&C 124:44).
See *"Minutes of the Nauvoo Temple Committee,"* 1841–1845, in Joseph Smith Papers, which documents the cooperative labor, donations of goods, and volunteer organization of the Saints in building the Nauvoo Temple.

20 Nauvoo Relief Society Minute Book, March 31, 1842, in The First Fifty Years of Relief Society: Key Documents in Latter-day Saint Women's History, ed. Jill Mulvay Derr et al. (Salt Lake City: Church Historian's Press, 2016), 41–43. The record notes Joseph Smith's counsel and the spiritual manifestations among the women, including speaking in tongues, prophecy, and testimony.

# Peaceable Followers, Mighty in Power

## The Ascent of Faith, Hope, and Charity

---

### Heaven's Gifts for Peaceable Followers

When Jesus first called Simon, He did not summon him with lofty decrees. He stood on the shore, stepped into Simon's boat, and spoke in the language of his life.

> *"Launch out into the deep, and let down your nets for a draught."* (Luke 5:4)

It was familiar work, yet with unfamiliar results: *"they enclosed a great multitude of fishes: and their net brake"* (Luke 5:6).

The catch was so abundant that both ships were filled to overflowing. Simon fell at Jesus' knees, overwhelmed, knowing he had been met by the Lord on his own ground, in his own terms, in a way he could not deny. From that moment, he left all to follow Him.

This is how the Lord works with His disciples still.

When He called Joseph Smith, it was not with one thunderclap, *"You are a prophet, now lead my people."* It was seed by seed, line by line, gift by gift.

The Lord met Joseph where he was, taught him in language he could understand, and gave him experiences he could bear. The Lord's way is never to overwhelm, but to lovingly mold and prepare, until His servant is ready to do the same for others.

And to do this, He pours out gifts—provisions of heaven to bring His peaceable followers nearer to Him. These gifts are not ornamental, nor reserved for leaders alone. They are His daily provisions for discipleship: power to heal, strength to discern, courage to speak, comfort to endure.

To be peaceable is more than to be calm; it is to be whole. It is to yield without losing strength, to carry firmness within gentleness. The peaceable follower is one whose heart has been softened by the Spirit of Christ—charity itself—that divine love which tempers zeal with mercy and conviction with compassion.

This charity is experienced not as an abstraction, but as a presence. It teaches from within. It consoles. It binds. In scripture and in life, it has often been described in feminine terms—not because it is separate from Christ, but because love that heals, gathers, and nurtures speaks in that register to the human soul.

She is the quiet teacher who dwells within—the unseen companion who whispers truth when words fail and brings tears when the mind cannot grasp what the heart already knows. She is the way charity is felt: the influence that turns memory into knowing, knowledge into love, and love into rest. When this Spirit comes, the heart recognizes it. It was there all along—the comfort in sorrow, the steadiness in fear, the warmth that lingered after prayer.

Through this harmony of strength and peace, Christ equips His people step by step, so that ordinary men and women may rise in His strength and reflect His light.

## Who Receives These Gifts and Powers

Moroni describes the recipients of these powers as *"the peaceable followers of Christ... who have obtained a sufficient hope by which ye can enter into the rest of the Lord"* (Moroni 7:3).

These peaceable followers are not merely passive or polite—they are those whose hearts have been transformed by the Spirit we have just spoken of. Her touch softens their nature until they are no longer divided within themselves. They have been taught by Her whisper and refined by His fire.

To be peaceable is to be reconciled—to have the will of the flesh yield to the will of the Spirit, the mind of man to the mind of God. It means you have been born again by fire and the Holy Ghost, as we discussed earlier. These are they who have become members of the Church of the Lamb of God. They have received a remission of sins. They have laid down the natural man, been changed, and become new creatures in Christ.

Their hearts are knit together in love, and their hope rests in Them.

A sufficient hope is not wishful thinking. It is a confident expectation, rooted in real encounters with God's power. When His Spirit has changed you, hope ceases to be fragile. It becomes steady, settled, certain.

That kind of hope points toward one great promise: to enter into the rest of the Lord.[1] Rest does not mean idleness; it is the assurance of His presence with you, the peace of being reconciled to Him, and the confidence that you are welcome before His face.

This is why Moroni places hope between faith and charity. Faith is where we begin—choosing to trust His word enough to act. Charity is where we end—filled with His love that never fails.

But hope is the bridge between them—stronger than faith alone, because it matures into certainty. It is not a wish, drifting and unsure. It is an anchor that holds in every storm because it is fastened to Christ Himself.

> **Paul** described it as *"an anchor of the soul, both sure and steadfast, and which entereth into that within the veil"* (Hebrews 6:19).
>
> **Ether** taught that *"whoso believeth in God might with surety hope for a better world... which hope cometh of faith, maketh an anchor to the souls of men"* (Ether 12:4).

Hope anchors us in Christ and points us toward Their rest. But hope does not stand alone—it rises out of faith and leads onward to charity. Together, these three gifts form the path of preparation. This is the heartbeat by which disciples are made alive in Them..

### Faith—Trust Enough to Surrender

The path of preparation unfolds step by step: faith, then hope, then charity. And it begins with faith.

Joseph taught in the *Lectures on Faith* that faith is not only the moving cause of action in all intelligent beings, but the very principle of power in God Himself.

> *"By faith the worlds were framed—God spake, chaos heard, and worlds came into order."* (*Lectures on Faith 1:15)*

Without faith there can be no creation, no power, no salvation. Faith is not a vague optimism or a mental nod toward belief. It is the assurance that God is who He says He is, and that He will do what He has said.

Joseph pressed the logic further: *"Faith could not exist without a correct idea of God's character, perfections, and attributes"* (Lectures on Faith 3:4)—and we might add, His personality.

We must come to know Them as They truly are—one God in perfect unity: a God of truth who cannot lie, of power that cannot fail, of love that delights to bless Their children.

Only then can our trust mature into certainty, for that certainty rests on real experience.

> *When They answer prayer.*
> *When Their voice speaks to the heart.*
> *When Their peace descends in sorrow.*
> *When Their presence is made manifest through holy appointments.*

Each of these becomes evidence—witness upon witness—that Their word is sure and Their promises stand forever.

Alma described faith as a seed: fragile, unseen, placed in the soil by our willingness to act on God's word.

At first there is nothing to see, only the hidden swell within. But if nourished by patience and belief, the seed pushes upward, breaking through the soil into light. It grows taller, sends down roots, and begins to bear fruit *"sweet above all that is sweet"* (Alma 32:42).

In this way, faith matures through care and constancy, until what was once invisible becomes undeniable.

Ether added the cosmic weight of this truth: *"If there be no faith among the children of men God can do no miracle among them"* (Ether 12:12). Why? Because without faith we do not act. And without action, the law of cause and effect cannot work. Nothing moves. But when faith acts, heaven and earth respond.

As one teacher once said, *"Nothing happens until something moves."*[2] Coupled with faith, that is powerful truth.

> *"They that wait upon the Lord shall renew their strength; they shall mount up with wings as eagles; they shall run, and not be weary; and they shall walk, and not faint."* (Isaiah 40:31)

Hannah Whitall Smith described true faith as learning to fly with *"the wings of surrender and trust"*:

> *"The soul that waits upon the Lord is the soul that is entirely surrendered to Him and trusts Him perfectly. Therefore, we might name our wings the wings of Surrender and of Trust. If we will only completely surrender ourselves to the Lord and trust Him perfectly, we will find our souls mounting up with wings as eagles to the heavenly places in Christ Jesus, where earthly annoyances or sorrows have no power to disturb us."*[3]

Years ago, I walked through the zoo in Salt Lake City and stopped before a majestic eagle. There was no cage around it, no chains on its feet, only open sky. Yet it did not fly.

Its wings had been clipped.

That broke my heart—to see such strength, such power, such ability held captive. This is what happens when surrender and trust are missing. The eagle has wings, but no power to rise.

The soul is meant to soar. One wing is surrender—laying down our will; the other is trust—resting in His will. Both must spread wide or there is no flight.

To try to trust without surrender is like flapping with a broken wing. To surrender without trust is to fall, believing no one will catch you. But when both wings stretch strong, the soul mounts up above the fog and storm into the clear air of His presence.

This is the invitation of faith: let go of the ground and take flight. Do not merely believe God *can* deliver you—surrender into the reality that He *will*. Stop scratching in the dirt with the chickens and rise into the air as the eagle you were born to be.

Practice: Each time fear grips or control tightens, pause and say aloud, *"Lord, I surrender this to You. I trust You will keep Your word."* Then release the matter fully into His hands. Faith grows not by straining harder, but by surrendering deeper.

## Hope—Expectation Anchored in Christ

Faith is the foundation, but hope is its blossoming. Faith reaches for the promise; hope rests in it. Where faith believes that God *can*, hope knows that He *will*.

This kind of hope does not spring up overnight. It matures as faith is tried and proved. Each time God keeps His word in your life, trust ripens into certainty. That certainty becomes an anchor of the soul, holding fast in every storm because it is fastened to Christ.

This is why Peter calls it *a lively hope* (1 Peter 1:3)—not dead or vague, but alive with assurance, pulsing with the very life of the risen Lord.

Moroni described hope as the sure expectation that leads peaceable followers into the rest of the Lord (Moroni 7:3).

Rest is not merely a future promise—it is a present taste of Their presence, a steady heartbeat of assurance that keeps the soul aligned even when storms rage. This is why hope is called an anchor. An anchor does not still the sea, but it holds the soul steady in Their peace until the storm passes.

Ether taught the same:

> *"Whoso believeth in God might with surety hope for a better world... which hope cometh of faith, [and] maketh an anchor to the souls of men, which would make them sure and steadfast." (Ether 12:4)*

Faith plants the seed, but hope grows it into a tree that reaches heavenward, bearing fruit of patience, courage, and endurance. And when such hope matures, miracles follow.

> *"For if there be no faith among the children of men God can do no miracle among them." (Ether 12:12)*

Faith reaches, hope anchors, and miracles flow.

Joseph Smith taught that this kind of hope is more than sentiment—it is the promise of eternal life sealed upon the soul:

> *"Though [the apostles] might hear the voice of God and know that Jesus was the Son of God, this would be no evidence that their election and calling was made sure... They then would want that more sure word of prophecy... Then, having this promise sealed unto them, it was an anchor to the soul, sure and steadfast. Though the thunders might roll and lightnings flash, and earthquakes bellow, and war gather thick around, yet this hope and knowledge would support the soul in every hour of trial, trouble and tribulation."* (TPJS, 298)

Hope does not only look back on promises already kept, but forward to the great fulfillment still to come. It stretches beyond this life to the day when Christ will wipe away every tear, heal every wound, and welcome His people into His embrace. To have such a hope is to taste that rest even now.

But sadly, the world is plagued by an epidemic of hopelessness.

People try countless strategies to fix their broken state, yet still feel empty. They say, *"Hope is not a strategy for success."*[4] And if by hope they mean only a wish, they are right. A wish is powerless. It drifts, uncertain, without anchor. And in the end, it leaves only despair.

To recognize where your hope stands, here's a simple test:

Try this exercise (read it twice):
First time, fill the blank with the word wish. (Notice how you feel.)
Second time, fill the blank with the word expect. (Pay close attention to the difference in feeling.)

"I _______ I get that job, or that raise."
"I _______ my relationships would finally improve."
"I _______ I won't get sick."
"I _______ my children will make good choices."
"I _______ the Lord will forgive me."
"I _______ to enter into the rest of the Lord."

Feel the difference?

"Wish" is wishy-washy. It's unsure. There is no power in it.

"I wish I get that job, or that raise."
"I wish my relationships would finally improve."
"I wish I won't get sick."
"I wish my children will make good choices."
"I wish the Lord will forgive me."
"I wish to enter into the rest of the Lord."

"Expect" feels secure, strong. It stands on evidence. It has power. You can feel it.

"I expect the Lord to open the right door for work."
"I expect Him to heal and strengthen my relationships."
"I expect Him to guard my health—or give me strength to endure."
"I expect Him to guide my children and answer my prayers for them."
"I expect the Lord to forgive me, because He has promised to."
"I expect that through His grace I will enter into His rest."

When you've completed the test, your heart will recognize the difference, as surely as light feels different from shadow.

That shift—from wishing to expecting—is the movement from fragile hope to sufficient hope, from drifting to anchoring, from uncertainty to certainty in Christ.

This is why Paul said, *"Hope maketh not ashamed"* (Romans 5:5). True hope will not disappoint you, because it is anchored in Christ's proven character and His unfailing promises.

Practice: Return to the I_____ test often. Write down a promise of God yet unfulfilled in your life. Next to it, write in bold: EXPECT. Each time you catch yourself drifting back into wishful hope, declare aloud: *"I expect the Lord to keep His word, for He always has."*

This is not self-hype, but confidence in His proven faithfulness. This is the power of hope—not wishful, but certain, alive, and unshakable.

## Charity: The Crown that Never Fails

It is common in our day to hear reference to the *"unconditional love of God."* If by that we mean that God loves all His children in the sense of valuing their worth, that is true.

But the scriptures are clear: not all receive His love in the same degree.

His promises are bound to His conditions. *"I, the Lord, am bound when ye do what I say; but when ye do not what I say, ye have no promise"* (D&C 82:10). And, Peter declared the same: *"In every nation he that feareth him, and worketh righteousness, is accepted with him"* (Acts 10:34–35).

God loves all, but His love is not a flat, unconditional sameness. It is bestowed with power upon those who follow His Son, filling them with His Spirit—Her presence writing His love upon the heart—so that they may become like Him.

This is why Mormon taught:

> *"Pray unto the Father with all the energy of heart, that ye may be filled with this love, which he hath bestowed upon all who are true followers of his Son, Jesus Christ."* (Moroni 7:48)

This is the prayer for Her indwelling. When She rests upon a soul, charity is born—not borrowed, not performed, but given—bestowed.

For years, I misunderstood this passage. I thought it meant to pray for charity so I could stockpile it in my own account, as though the goal were to have more of it for myself at the last day.

But charity is not a possession to be hoarded.

Charity is the pure love of Christ, carried into us by His Spirit, given so that it may flow outward. We do not pray for charity for ourselves, but for others—that we may be filled with His love for them.

This is what makes us like Him: He did nothing for Himself. Every act, every word, every sacrifice was for others.

John Pontius once described a sacred day when, for a few hours, he was given to love as Christ loves. He wrote:

> *"I looked at people and I did not see their failings, their quirks, their mistakes. I only saw their worth, their eternal value, their divine nature. Love overwhelmed me. It was effortless, complete, without condition or judgment. I wept at the beauty of it. For that day, I knew what it meant to have the pure love of Christ."*[5]

That is what happens when She opens the eyes of the heart.

That is charity. It is not earned, it is bestowed. She does not remain where love is hoarded; She moves wherever love is given. And it is given only for others—never as a personal ornament.

Now face yourself in the mirror:

> *Have you ever tried to win an argument by sheer willpower?*
> *Have you ever used guilt or shame to bend someone to your way?*
> *Have you ever played the victim to gain sympathy?*
> *Have you ever dug in your heels in pride, refusing to admit you were wrong?*
> *Have you ever withheld forgiveness, convinced your judgment was justified?*

If so, then you know what it is to walk without charity.

These ways may *"work"* for a time, but they always collapse. They are brittle, fueled by fear, pride, and ego. And ego is nothing more than Edging God Out. When we edge Him out, we may still make noise—but we are nothing more than *"sounding brass, or a tinkling cymbal"* (1 Corinthians 13:1). Powerless. Empty.

Charity never fails. She never manipulates, never dominates, never deceives.

Charity heals, uplifts, and restores because it is Christ's own love, and His Spirit bears it—gentle and sure—into willing hearts.

And He will not fail:

> *To change hearts.*
> *To lift the faint;*
> *To heal the broken.*
> *To bless the humble.*
> *To bind His people together in one.*

This is why Paul declared: *"And now abideth faith, hope, charity, these three; but the greatest of these is charity"* (1 Corinthians 13:13).

Faith reaches, hope anchors, but charity transforms. It is the capstone of discipleship, the crowning attribute by which God's children are revealed as His.

Joseph Smith personified this path. His faith endured mobs, prisons, and betrayal. His hope anchored him in God's promises even when all seemed lost. And his charity overflowed in forgiveness.

When W.W. Phelps, who had once betrayed him and helped send him to prison, sought reconciliation, Joseph wrote back without hesitation: *"Come on, dear brother, since the war is past, for friends at first, are friends again at last."*[6]

He welcomed Phelps as a friend and brother once more. This is the charity that never fails—love that covers betrayal, restores fellowship, and mirrors Christ's own forgiveness.

Practice: Pray with all the energy of your heart, not to be filled with love for yourself, but to be filled with Christ's love for others. Ask for Her witness to rest upon your heart, that you may feel Their love for others. Name the ones hardest to love, and ask for His eyes to see them. When charity is bestowed, you will find yourself loving as He loves—not in theory, but in truth.

And here the helix rises once again:

> *Faith plants and moves.*
> *Hope anchors and endures.*
> *Charity blossoms and transforms.*

Then the cycle begins again, but higher, nearer, holier. Step by step, turn by turn, the ascent continues until at last we see Him as He is—and we are like Him.

## Fasting—Aligning What Faith, Hope, and Charity Can Do Together

When certain things work together, their effect is far greater than what each can do on its own. This is called synergy. Picture a single 2x4 beam. Under pressure, it will bend and eventually snap. Another beam, just the same, will do the same. But bind two 2x4s together, and their combined strength is not just doubled—it is multiplied. The load they can carry rises far beyond what either could have held alone.

Faith, hope, and charity work the same way. Each is strong in itself, but when joined, they multiply. Faith gives trust, hope gives steadiness, and charity gives divine love. Together they form a strength that can bear the weight of life and lift the soul heavenward.

But synergy does not simply happen. It requires something that brings the pieces into harmony and sets the reaction in motion. This is where a catalyst comes in. In chemistry, a catalyst enters the reaction and makes it happen faster, stronger, or more completely, yet remains unchanged itself.

Think of yeast in bread. The flour and water provide substance, but without yeast the dough lies flat and lifeless. Add the catalyst, and the whole is transformed—it rises, filled with life and lightness.

Fasting is that catalyst. It does not replace faith, hope, or charity. It activates them, quickens them, multiplies them. It takes what is present in the soul and makes it rise.

Consider what happens when each virtue stands alone—and then what happens when it joins with the others:

> **Faith on its own** can trust God enough to surrender and rise, like an eagle lifted on the twin wings of trust and surrender. But when faith is joined with hope and charity, it does more than soar—it acts, moves mountains, and opens channels for heaven's power on earth.
> **Hope on its own** anchors the soul when storms rage, fastening it to Christ with steady expectation. But when hope is joined with faith and charity, it does more than anchor—it strengthens endurance, steadies courage, and holds the disciple firm until promises are fulfilled in real life, not just in thought.
> **Charity on its own** softens the heart, filling it with Christlike love. But when charity is joined with faith and hope, it does more than soften—it transforms. Enemies become

> brothers, the natural man yields to the child of Christ, and we become like Him, able to see Him because we are like Him.

This is the synergy that lifts the disciple higher than any single virtue alone. And the catalyst that brings them together, the yeast that makes them rise, is fasting.

If fasting is the catalyst, then why do we need it? Because the flesh is noisy.

The body constantly calls for attention—hunger, thirst, comfort, distraction, desire. These are not evil in themselves, but when they rule, they create static. Cravings can drown the still small voice. Pride can puff up the heart. Restlessness can scatter prayer before it finds heaven.

This is why Jesus warned that *"the spirit indeed is willing, but the flesh is weak"* (Matthew 26:41). The weakness of the flesh is not a design flaw; it is the very condition that forces the soul to choose. Will appetite rule, or will the Spirit? Will the heart yield to craving, or to God?

When the flesh is loud, faith wavers, hope falters, and charity dries up. The channel is blocked, the signal full of static.

This is the problem fasting was given to solve.

Fasting is God's gift to silence the noise. When appetite is set aside, the body remembers its place as servant, not master. Hunger becomes a teacher, reminding the soul to turn upward.

> **Fasting subdues appetite.** Cravings that once shouted are quieted. The body no longer dictates; the Spirit takes the lead.
> **Fasting humbles pride.** The heart bows low, confessing dependence on God for every breath and every crumb.
> **Fasting sharpens prayer.** Each pang of hunger pushes the soul back into petition, deepening desire and focus.

This is why fasting magnifies every virtue. Faith strengthens because unbelief is silenced. Hope steadies because the soul learns to wait on God more than on bread. Charity is unlocked because an emptied vessel can be filled with His love.

Fasting clears the channel. What was static becomes signal. What was blocked becomes flow.

This is how each virtue is magnified:

> **Faith strengthened.** Faith is trust enough to surrender. Yet when the body is noisy, trust wavers and surrender feels impossible. Fasting quiets the body's protest and proves that man does not live by bread alone. Each pang of hunger becomes an act of faith—choosing God's word over the body's craving. In that yielding, faith is refined until it can act boldly and call down heaven's power (Matthew 4:4).
>
> **Hope steadied.** Hope is not wishful thinking; it is confident expectation in Christ. But the flesh pulls the soul toward immediacy: eat now, gratify now, escape now. Fasting teaches the soul to wait, to hunger for promises more than for bread. As the body endures, the soul learns endurance. Hope is no longer fragile—it is anchored, steady through storm and delay (Romans 8:24–25).
>
> **Charity unlocked.** Charity is the pure love of Christ, bestowed from heaven. But when the vessel is full of self, there is no room for it. Fasting empties the vessel. Hunger awakens compassion for the hungry. What would have been eaten can be given to bless the poor. Pride is softened, selfishness yields, and space is made for God's love to be poured in. In fasting, the disciple begins to see others as Christ sees them, and to love with His love (Helaman 3:35).

The scriptures are full of witnesses that fasting changed everything.

> **Moses.** Israel was restless in the wilderness, murmuring and rebelling. Moses climbed Sinai alone and entered into forty days of fasting. The man who went up carried the burden of a rebellious people; the man who came down carried God's own law, engraved in stone, and his face shone with glory so bright the people could not look upon it (Exodus 34:28–29).
>
> **Elijah.** Despairing under a juniper tree, Elijah begged God to take his life. Fed once by an angel, he journeyed into the wilderness and fasted forty days on Mount Horeb. When fire and earthquake passed, Elijah stood still and heard the whisper of God's voice. The prophet who had wanted to die found new strength to live and finish his work (1 Kings 19:4–12).
>
> **Jesus.** Immediately after His baptism, the Spirit led Jesus into the wilderness. For forty days He fasted, and at His weakest Satan came with three temptations: appetite, pride, and power. Each was overcome with the word of God. When the trial ended, angels ministered to Him, and He stepped

forward in full authority to begin His ministry (Matthew 4:1–11).

**Alma the Younger.** Long after his angelic rebuke, Alma testified, *"Behold, I have fasted and prayed many days that I might know these things of myself"* (Alma 5:46). His testimony of redemption was not borrowed from others. It was sealed in fasting and prayer, and it gave him power to preach repentance with piercing clarity.

**The Sons of Mosiah.** They entered their missions with the odds stacked against them—Lamanites who hated them, dangers that threatened their lives. But *"they had given themselves to much prayer and fasting; therefore they had the spirit of prophecy, and the spirit of revelation, and when they taught, they taught with power and authority of God"* (Alma 17:3). Their fasting did more than open their mouths; it opened their hearts with charity so deep they counted their enemies as brothers.

Isaiah described this kind of fasting with exactness. He condemned hollow fasting—those who bowed the head, wore sackcloth, and made a show of sorrow while nothing changed within. Then he described the fast God had chosen, one that carries real power and fruit:

> *"Is not this the fast that I have chosen? to loose the bands of wickedness, to undo the heavy burdens, and to let the oppressed go free... Is it not to deal thy bread to the hungry, and that thou bring the poor that are cast out to thy house?"* (Isaiah 58:6–7)

***Loosens bands of wickedness.*** Appetite and indulgence are dethroned when the body is denied its demand to rule. Chains of addiction and cycles of sin lose their grip because the soul practices yielding to God instead of craving. Fasting is rehearsal for freedom.

***Lifts heavy burdens.*** When pride is broken, the heart bows low and heaven supplies strength. Burdens that once felt crushing are carried in God's power, not our own. In the act of fasting, the disciple learns what it means to yoke with Christ, and His strength lightens the load.

***Feeds the hungry.*** What would have been eaten—or the money that would have been spent—can be given to relieve another's want. Hunger in the body awakens compassion for those who live with hunger daily. When bread is shared, both

> the giver and the receiver are blessed, and the fast becomes outward as well as inward.

Isaiah's promise is sure: when fasting is true, *"then shall thy light break forth as the morning, and thine health shall spring forth speedily"* (Isaiah 58:8). The soul is filled with light, the body renewed, and the glory of God becomes a shield.

At its heart, a true fast is not about deprivation but alignment. It is the yielding of body, soul, and spirit together to God.

The body hungers, but the soul feasts. Appetite is set aside, and in its place prayer deepens, humility grows, and the Spirit flows. What seems like weakness becomes strength, because God fills the empty places.

This is why fasting cannot be reduced to ritual. Sackcloth and ashes, gloomy faces and hollow gestures miss the point. True fasting is freedom—freedom from craving, freedom from pride, freedom from the static of the flesh.

Fasting is fullness. It fills the soul with clarity, steadiness, and love. It breaks chains, lifts burdens, and blesses others. It clears the channel so revelation can flow and heaven can be near.

In fasting, the disciple is not left empty. The vessel is poured out, and then filled—again and again—until faith grows strong, hope holds firm, and charity overflows.

There is an old fable told of a young warrior who longed to receive wisdom from his chief. He begged for instruction, so the chief led him to the edge of a lake. They waded in until the water reached their waists. Then, without warning, the chief thrust the boy's head beneath the surface and held him there.

The boy struggled. His lungs burned. Panic set in as he clawed for air. Just when he thought he would die, the chief pulled him up, and the boy gasped desperately for breath.

*"Why did you do that?"* the boy cried.

*"When you want wisdom as much as you wanted air,"* the chief replied, *"then you will find it."*

That is the spirit of a true fast. It is not a token sacrifice or a calendar duty. It is hungering and thirsting for God as though your very life depends on Him. It is crying out to heaven all day long, not only when your stomach reminds you, but because your soul refuses to let go until He blesses you.

Set apart a time to fast like that. Lay aside the plate, not for misery's sake, but to pursue Him with all your heart, might, mind, and strength. Empty yourself in prayer. Plead for light. Plead for others. Refuse to be satisfied with less than His presence.

This kind of fast will change you. Faith will not only grow—it will move mountains. Hope will not only steady—it will endure any storm. Charity will not only soften—it will transform, until you see others with the eyes of Christ and love them as He loves.

This is the fast that broke chains, lifted nations, brought angels, and opened the heavens. It is not beyond you. It waits for any disciple who will seek God as desperately as breath itself.

## Taking the Next Step

John Pontius often wrote of his striving for *"flawless obedience"*[7]—living so that every whisper of the Spirit found him responsive. Though he never claimed perfection, his heart was bent toward heaven, continually yielding and seeking to be like Christ.

Into that soil of surrender, the Lord once planted a singular gift: for a few sacred hours John was clothed with the pure love of Christ. He had not earned it; it was bestowed. Yet it came because his heart was prepared.

His experience teaches that charity is not stored up like a balance in a bank; it is bestowed from above, often when a soul has surrendered enough that heaven can safely endow it.

I have seen the same love bestowed in my own life.

As I shared in the Preface, after the accident that took my mother's life, I stood in court and asked the judge for leniency toward the man responsible. What I could not have foreseen was the way that charity, once given, would ripple outward. Later his wife wrote to me:

> *"My family and I thank you for allowing us to read your letters to the court. As we read them, we heard the words of God speaking through you. We cried tears of gratitude and hope, knowing an extraordinary family had touched our lives. We felt God's love and comfort. Your extraordinary act of forgiveness and asking for leniency are rare in today's world, especially in the face of tragedy. We are being shown the face of God's goodness, love, forgiveness, and mercy through your family. From your forgiveness of (Name left out), hopefully one day he will be able to forgive himself."*[8]

Her letter went on to describe how my mother's legacy of love, kindness, and forgiveness was shining through that courtroom act—and how it was changing her husband.

He began sharing his story with other inmates, and soon dozens were coming to hear. She wrote, *"The word was, 'You need to hear what this man has to say.' The leader told (Name left out), 'You have a message and a purpose here, and that is to help others.' But it's not just his story, it's your story as well, Michael. This is the story of hope, forgiveness, and God's love."*[9]

That is charity.

It does not stop with one act; it multiplies. It heals beyond the reach of our own strength. It touches families, it spreads into prison walls, it lifts up men who had lost hope. This is the love that never fails—not mine, but His, given and bestowed.

So kneel—tonight or tomorrow morning—and pray with all the energy of your heart to love others as He loves them. Name the people you find hardest to love, and ask for His eyes to see them. Then rise from your knees expecting Him to answer. Begin to live as though His love is already flowing through you. Because when He bestows it—and He will—you will know that charity never fails.

Faith, hope, and charity are not isolated virtues. They are a living sequence—each one preparing and feeding the next.

Peter called it an ascent: *"Add to your faith virtue; and to virtue knowledge... and to godliness brotherly kindness; and to brotherly kindness charity"* (2 Peter 1:5–7). Paul summed it up: *"And now abideth faith, hope, charity, these three; but the greatest of these is charity"* (1 Corinthians 13:13).

This is the way Joseph learned it—trusting the word, surrendering his will, expecting the Lord's promises, and letting God's love fill and remake him.

This is the way I have learned it—scripture by scripture, experience by experience, grace to grace. And this is the way you will learn it too. If you will walk this path, the same Spirit will teach and transform you.

And this is also why peaceable followers become mighty in power.

Faith acts—so heaven has a channel to work. Hope anchors—so miracles can flow without being dashed by fear (Ether 12:4, 12). Charity transmits Christ's own love—so His power can move through clean hands and a pure heart.

Then the gifts follow as naturally as fruit on a living tree: light to discern, words to prophesy, hands to heal, authority to rebuke darkness, courage to witness.

Angels attend such disciples; the wounded are lifted; captives are set free.

This is not about recognition or being seen by others—that would be the very opposite of the nature of these heavenly virtues. They are the Savior's work expressed through His people.

As we learned earlier, the path is not a straight staircase. It is a living ascent—an upward helix, each turn lifting you higher and drawing you nearer to His presence.

Faith is planted, tested, and grows. Hope strengthens, anchoring you in Christ through deeper trials. Charity blossoms, filling your life with the love that never fails. Then the cycle begins again—but on a higher plane. Step by step, turn by turn, the Lord raises you until one day the spiral ends where it has always been leading: into His presence, entering into His rest.

This is the same ascent Jesus Christ walked. It is the same ascent Joseph Smith walked. And it is the same ascent set before you.

The world is growing darker, and the need for light has never been greater. The Lord is hastening His work, and He is inviting you to hasten with Him. Do not delay. Take the next step now, and He will meet you in the climb.

## Chapter 8 Notes

1 Moroni 7:3; Ether 12:4; Hebrews 6:19

2 Commonly attributed to Albert Einstein, though the precise source is uncertain. The quotation circulates in motivational and educational contexts to emphasize action as the catalyst of change.

3 Hannah Whitall Smith, The Christian's Secret of a Happy Life (Philadelphia: J.B. Lippincott, 1875), 67–68. Smith reflects that the *"wings"* in Isaiah 40:31 may be named Surrender and Trust, by which the soul rises above earthly burdens into Christ's rest.

4 The saying *"Hope is not a strategy"* circulates widely in business and leadership literature (e.g., Rick Page, Hope Is Not a Strategy, 2001). Its common use contrasts superficial wishing with active trust and effort.

5 John Pontius, Journey to the Veil (Springville, UT: Cedar Fort, 2013), 93–96.

6 Joseph Smith to William W. Phelps, July 22, 1840, Nauvoo, Illinois, in The Personal Writings of Joseph Smith, ed. Dean C. Jessee, rev. ed. (Salt Lake City: Deseret Book, 2002), 529–531; also in History of the Church, 4:163.

7 John Pontius, Journey to the Veil (Springville, UT: Cedar Fort, 2013), 93–96, 137–140. Pontius describes his repeated recommitments to *"flawless obedience,"* seeking to respond to every whisper of the Spirit.

8 Personal email to author, Sept. 12, 2024

9 Personal email to author, Sept. 12, 2024

Interlude

# THY WILL BE DONE

## Where Your Desire and God's Desire Become One

### The Misunderstanding at the Heart of Christianity

For generations, Christians have spoken as though God's will were a distant force—something unpredictable, hovering above us, deciding outcomes we can't influence. The language sounds humble:

> *"If God wills it."*
> *"Whatever He decides."*
> *"Not my will, but Thine."*
> *"If it serves God's will."*

On the surface, these phrases appear reverent. But beneath them sits something far heavier. Most believers say these words not from lack of faith, but because they have been trained to believe that God's will is entirely separate from theirs—random, unknowable, and unreachable.

They lean on scriptures like:

> *"My thoughts are not your thoughts, neither are your ways My ways..."* (Isaiah 55:8–9)

And without realizing it, they build an entire spiritual worldview around the idea that God's will is forever foreign, inaccessible, and beyond their understanding.

But something deeper happens in the heart.

Christians begin to believe they must continually suppress their own desires to prove devotion. They see themselves as unworthy of wanting anything, so they discipline themselves into a posture of surrender—not as Jesus lived it, but as a lifelong confession of personal deficiency.

This posture produces a kind of spiritual performance:

> *"Look how humble I am."*
> *"Look how deeply I sacrifice."*
> *"Look how willing I am to accept God's will."*
> *"Look how fully I lay myself aside."*

The words sound noble, even beautiful. But beneath the surface, they become a ritual of self-negation. A way of proving faithfulness by expecting nothing. A way of shielding themselves from disappointment by calling resignation *"trust."*

And so they brace themselves for whatever outcome the heavens decide, because they've been taught that God's will might land on either side of the scale without explanation. Prayer becomes a gamble.

They wait and hope, acting as though heaven were a Las Vegas slot machine and God an unpredictable blackjack dealer.

This mindset quietly reshapes God into something smaller than He is: not a loving Father, not a wise Teacher, but an overlord with favorites, a respecter of persons, a divine monarch who may bless one child but not another based on hidden criteria.

Yet scripture teaches the exact opposite: **God is no respecter of persons** (Acts 10:34).

He doesn't withhold blessings arbitrarily.
He doesn't care for one child more than another.
He doesn't deal out miracles like cards from a hand of chance.

And here's the piercing truth:

What masquerades as humility often reflects something far worse—distrust.

> *distrust of our own hearts,*
> *distrust of our own desires,*
> *distrust of our ability to hear God, and even*
> *distrust of God's goodness.*

I carry a memory that still breaks my heart. My mother was eighty-six years old—faithful, devoted, beloved by everyone who knew her. She lived the gospel she was taught with exactness. If anyone could say they'd kept the commandments with full devotion, it was her. She spent her whole life serving others, raising a family, reading scripture, praying, ministering, and doing everything she believed God required of her.

Mom and Dad served several missions together and spent many years as ordinance workers in the temple. Their lives were full of sacrifice and service.

Near the end of her life, she met with an oncologist who recommended an expensive medication. She felt a hesitation inside—a quiet sense that her body didn't need it. She didn't know why. She simply felt it. She turned to my sisters for counsel, and they encouraged her to trust the doctor. Wanting to include everyone, she asked me next.

I asked her a question that seemed simple at the time: *"Have you asked God?"*

Her answer shattered me.

She said, *"I don't know how to hear Him."*

This was my mother—one of the finest women I have ever known, a woman whose life was a hymn of faithfulness. And in that moment, she was telling me she didn't know how to recognize God's voice. Not because He had been silent. Not because He'd withheld His presence. But because she'd been taught her whole life to distrust her own heart, her own desires, her own spiritual instincts. She'd been taught that God's will was something external, distant, and separate from her—something handed down through authority, never awakened within her.

Yet the irony is this:

She did hear Him.
She felt His guidance in her heart that day.
She sensed what her body needed.

But the scaffolding she had lived under—the traditions telling her she couldn't trust her own spiritual impressions—kept her from recognizing that quiet feeling as God's voice.

She had lived inside Their will far more than she ever knew. But the teachings she inherited had convinced her she couldn't hear Them.

This is what happens when people mistake pious resignation for faith. It creates generations of believers who love God deeply and serve Him faithfully, yet doubt their ability to recognize His voice. They surrender their desires, silence their instincts, and suppress their will—not because God asked them to, but because tradition taught them that humility means distrusting themselves.

And that distortion has consequences. It prevents the very relationship God wants with His children.

This is why we must unveil this misunderstanding gently but clearly—so we do not repeat the heartbreak of those who gave God everything but were never taught to recognize the voice already within them.

## The Woman With the Issue of Blood: A True Pattern of Will

If any story in the New Testament exposes how deeply we've misunderstood God's will, it's the woman with the issue of blood.[1] Her story isn't simply a miracle; it's a revelation of how the Lord responds to a heart that refuses to surrender to resignation.

This woman had carried her affliction for twelve long years. Not just pain, not just fatigue, not just isolation—but ritual impurity. Under the religious law of her day, her condition placed her outside the life of

Israel. She was untouchable. Unwelcome. Rendered invisible by commandments the leaders enforced but couldn't heal. The priests who should have ministered to her offered nothing. The men who interpreted the law could recite the reasons she was unclean, but none could lift her burden. Her community learned to avoid her; their purity mattered more than her suffering.

If anyone had reason to believe that God had already spoken His will over her life, she did. If anyone had reason to fold her hands and whisper, *"If He wills it,"* she did. Every authority around her had taught her, through their silence and their distance, that this was simply how her life would remain.

Yet somewhere in her soul, something continued to live. Something refused to bow to the fatalistic religion she had inherited. It wasn't defiance—it was faith. Not pride, but desire. Not arrogance, but a deep, childlike trust in the goodness of God. She understood the nature of the Messiah long before she ever touched His garment.

And when Jesus passed through the crowd that day, she didn't hang back. She didn't ask permission. She didn't cry out for validation or wait for a sign that healing *"served His will."* She moved with intention, with courage, with a will that had already aligned with the heart of God.

> *"If I may but touch His garment, I shall be whole."* (Matthew 9:21)

That sentence reveals everything. Her faith wasn't conditional. Her desire wasn't timid. Her will had become clear, disciplined, and directed—the kind of will that heaven responds to because it mirrors heaven's own nature.

When she pressed through the crowd, she risked public shame. Every person she brushed against would have considered themselves defiled. Even the disciples, tasked with learning the Lord's compassion, would have recoiled had they known who touched Him. They still saw the world through the old law—categories of clean and unclean, worthy and unworthy, acceptable and unacceptable.

But Jesus did not. The moment she touched His clothing, the power flowed. He stopped. He turned. And in that turning, He revealed a kingdom that functions on completely different terms than the one His followers had assumed.

> *He didn't scold her for approaching Him while unclean.*
> *He didn't rebuke her for daring to act without permission.*
> *He didn't remind her of the law she had violated.*

> *He honored her.*
> *He saw her.*
> *He called her "daughter."*

And then He spoke the sentence that should dismantle centuries of Christian fatalism:

*"Thy faith hath made thee whole."* (Luke 8:48)

Not My will. Not divine sovereignty. Not a heavenly calculation of what best served God's purposes.

> *Thy faith.*
> *Thy courage.*
> *Thy will reaching toward My goodness.*

Her miracle didn't come because God finally decided to heal her. It came because her heart had stepped into harmony with His nature. Her will and His will met in the space between them, and power flowed the moment they touched.

This is the template of divine interaction. This is how heaven works. A willing heart—childlike, courageous, sanctified—acts in faith, and the Lord meets it with the fullness of His love.

The woman with the issue of blood wasn't healed because the stars aligned or because God secretly chose her before the foundation of the world. She was healed because she aligned her desire with His goodness and refused to let fear or tradition silence the will He had awakened within her.

> *This is the will God honors.*
> *This is the will He invites.*
> *This is the will that makes miracles possible.*

## The Natural Man: Why Our First Will Cannot Align With His

Before we can understand how our will aligns with God's will, we must understand where our will begins. Like almost everything else in life, there is a spectrum—a growth from a beginning to an end. Our will develops the same way. It starts in one state and matures into another. Scripture gives a name to that beginning stage:

the natural man.

*"For the natural man is an enemy to God..."* (Mosiah 3:19)

This doesn't mean God despises human will. It means the initial condition of our will—will expressed through an unrefined heart—is governed by the impulses of the natural man.

Prophets describe those impulses with unflinching clarity:

> *"carnal, sensual, and devilish"* (Mosiah 16:3)
>
> *"lost... becoming carnal, sensual, and devilish"* (Alma 42:10)

These descriptions aren't accusations; they are diagnoses. They reveal what will looks like when filtered through ego, fear, appetite, pride, and the instinct to protect ourselves at all costs.

This is the will in the hands of the natural man.

> *It reacts instead of listens.*
> *It grasps instead of trusts.*
> *It resists instead of responds.*
> *It clings to insecurity instead of embracing humility.*
> *It seeks applause instead of truth.*
> *It demands safety instead of transformation.*

And here's the truth few are willing to name:

Most people sense they are not where they should be spiritually.

They know their confidence is fragile and their connection with God is thin. And rather than go to Him—as He pleads with us to do—they turn to the only tools the natural man understands: appearance, belonging, and performance.

No one wants to be exposed or alone.

So people reach for allies—friends and family who believe as they do, speak as they do, feel safe as they do. Within those circles, they perform their faith with practiced ease. They share spiritual experiences that may or may not have happened the way they describe. They exaggerate their certainty just enough to seem solid.

> *"Look how strong I am."*
> *"Look how unwavering I am."*
> *"Look how faithfully I endure."*

But beneath the polished words, many feel lost. They feel small. They feel afraid that if anyone saw the truth—the questions, the cravings, the wounds—the whole social structure would collapse.

A dear friend who has learned to recognize the Lord's voice once shared something He told her:

*"No one is where they are supposed to be—and they know it."*[2]

It's a gentle but piercing truth. Most believers feel that gap deep inside. They try. They serve. They love God with all the devotion they know how to give. And yet, somewhere beneath the surface, they sense there's a relationship He desires with them that they have not fully entered.

That sense of not-quite-being-there terrifies the natural man. So he masks it. He leans into familiar phrases, familiar roles, familiar expectations. And because almost everyone else is doing the same, it becomes invisible.

A whole room of believers, each afraid to admit they feel behind—each assuming everyone else must be at peace.

And like my mother, so many live their entire lives hiding a single, aching fear: that they don't know how to hear His voice, even though His voice has been with them from the beginning.

A friend once shared a story that exposes this same quiet fear in an unexpected way:

A bar was built next to a church. The congregation prayed daily that it would fail. Eventually, lightning struck and burned it down. The owner sued the church, claiming their prayers caused the loss. The church denied responsibility. The judge finally said, *"I'm faced with a strange case—one bar owner who believes in prayer, and an entire church that doesn't."*[3]

This is what happens when people have been taught to distrust their own will and their own ability to hear God.

> *Their **prayers** become ritual instead of relationship.*
> *Their **faith** becomes performance instead of partnership.*
> *Their **will** becomes something to suppress instead of something God can awaken.*

This is why Christians so often confuse the natural man's use of will with will itself. They assume that because their impulses are unreliable, their entire capacity for choice is broken. They believe God wants to erase their decision-making altogether, as if the highest form of discipleship is passivity.

But that's not what God desires.

> *He doesn't want to crush our will.*
> *He wants to* ***transform*** *it.*
> *He doesn't want to erase agency.*
> *He wants to* ***elevate*** *it.*
> *He doesn't want children who surrender selfhood.*
> *He wants children whose selves can actually resemble Him.*

Before we go any further, we need to be absolutely clear about what the problem actually is.

**The will is not the enemy.**
**The natural man is.**

The will becomes distorted only when it's governed by ego, fear, appetite, and the inherited reflexes of a fallen world. The natural man bends desire inward until everything becomes about self-preservation and self-importance. Under that influence, even good desires become guarded, anxious, or reactive.

But when the heart becomes sanctified—childlike, humble, trusting—the will becomes something entirely different: reflective, courageous, teachable, and able "to act and not be acted upon."[4]

And now we arrive at the decisive truth:

**The will is not the problem.**
**The natural man is.**

So Mosiah continues:

> *"...and put off the natural man and become a saint..."* (Mosiah 3:19)

The natural must die for the true will to emerge. Only then can alignment begin.

And this is why the scriptures speak so often of rebirth. Being born again is not poetic language—it describes the transformation of the inner person. The old creature passes away, and a new creature is born.

When you're born again, it's not only your heart that changes, but your will. A new will emerges—humble, willing, responsive—a will capable of aligning with His, and eventually becoming swallowed up in His.

## The Childlike Will: The Will God Can Use

If the natural man represents the beginning state of our will, then let's now describe what the first true awakening looks like. Once the natural man is put off, something unexpected begins to rise inside us. A different spirit stirs—quiet, hopeful, almost like waking from a long sleep. We begin to feel and act like little children again, and everything changes.

> *Little children are wide-eyed and curious.*
> *They forgive quickly.*
> *They learn eagerly.*
> *They ask questions instead of pretending to know.*
> *They trust the one who leads them.*
> *They delight in simple goodness.*
> *They hold no grudges and carry no pretense.*
> *They are humble, teachable, open-minded, open-hearted, believing rather than unbelieving.*

And if you look closely, you may notice something more: we are also describing Jesus.

> *These traits are His traits.*
> *This is how He is.*
> *This is who He is.*

From the beginning, He has invited us to become like Him.

Becoming childlike is not immaturity. It is the mark of readiness. It is the softening of the will—the beginning of a heart that can be shaped, taught, lifted, and led. It is the moment strength becomes gentle enough to be guided and desire becomes honest enough to be healed.

The scriptures describe this transition plainly:

> *"...becometh a saint through the atonement of Christ the Lord, and becometh as a child—submissive, meek, humble, patient, full of love..."* (Mosiah 3:19)

And here we must pause, because no one becomes childlike without the Atonement. No one puts off the natural man through willpower or discipline alone. We become childlike through Christ—through His sacrifice, His cleansing, His lifting, His mercy. Without Him, the natural man survives every effort to change. With Him, the natural man finally begins to fall away.

The Atonement doesn't simply erase sin.

> *It transforms the inner person.*
> *It softens what was once hard.*

> *It heals wounds we could never reach ourselves.*
> *It gives birth to a new heart.*

And with that new heart comes a new will.

To understand that new will, it helps to look at a simple moment from the old Rankin/Bass Claymation Christmas classic, *Santa Claus Is Comin' to Town.*[5]

In the story, the Winter Warlock is feared by everyone—cold, bitter, angry, locked inside his own hardness. He is, in every sense, a picture of the natural man: defensive, isolated, convinced that change is impossible. Then Kris Kringle offers him a simple gift—a small wooden toy train. A gift he didn't earn or deserve. A gift given purely out of kindness.

The impossible happens. His heart melts. He becomes gentle and teachable—a new creature in a single moment. But now he faces something unfamiliar. He doesn't yet know how to walk in this new life.

So Kris teaches him with a childlike song—meant for beginners, for those learning goodness one step at a time:

> *"Put one foot in front of the other*
> *And soon you'll be walking 'cross the floor*
> *You put one foot in front of the other*
> *And soon you'll be walking out the door"*

It is innocent.
It is simple.
And it is profoundly true.

This is how the childlike will awakens. Not through grand spiritual leaps, but through small, trusting steps.

A moment of honesty.
A moment of belief.
A moment of choosing.

Where we choose openness instead of hiding, forgiveness instead of resentment, trust instead of fear.

Soon—almost without noticing—we find ourselves moving in a new direction. A path the natural man could never walk, but one the childlike heart recognizes immediately.

Line upon line, step by step, we begin to act instead of react, fulfilling the scripture that we are **to act and not be acted upon** (2 Nephi

2:26). Our will becomes responsive, eager, teachable. It bends toward what is good because it now recognizes goodness. At last, it begins to align.

> *This is the will God can use.*
> *Not the brittle will born of fear.*
> *Not the stubborn will of ego.*
> *But the trusting, responsive will of a child—*
> *the will that naturally reaches for the Father's hand.*

### What God Actually Means by "My Will"

If there is any phrase most misunderstood in all of Christianity, it's this: *"Thy will be done."*[6] Not because the words are wrong, but because the world has spent centuries hearing them through fear, resignation, and uncertainty. Most believers whisper them with folded hands, imagining God's will as something unpredictable, hidden, or potentially painful. They hope for the best but brace for the worst.

But when Jesus spoke of the will of God, He meant something entirely different. He wasn't describing a distant Sovereign making arbitrary choices.

He was revealing who God is.

> *His nature.*
> *His way.*
> *His character.*

God's will is God's character. It is everything Jesus is.

When Jesus healed, forgave, lifted, restored, taught, blessed, and loved—He was showing us God's will in motion. Not as a special instance, not as an exception, but as a revelation of God's eternal nature.

Jesus is Jehovah.
Jesus is the God of this system.
He is the Word, the Life, and the Light.

He embodies the will of the Father and Mother perfectly because He is one with Them in heart, in purpose, and in love.

> *When He acted, They acted.*
> *When He blessed, They blessed.*
> *When He forgave, They forgave.*

Their will was expressed perfectly through Him.

This is why scripture says:

> *"...He is the same yesterday, today, and forever."* (Hebrews 13:8)

God's will isn't moody or unpredictable. It doesn't swing with circumstance or whim. It isn't hidden behind the clouds, waiting to be discovered.

> ***It is goodness, embodied.***
> ***Always, and in all ways.***

Everything Jesus did—every healing, every mercy, every truth spoken, every kindness extended—perfectly demonstrates the will of God. If something doesn't look like Jesus, it isn't Their will.

## God's Will Is Not Opposed to Your Will—Unless Your Will Is Opposed to Theirs

Many Christians imagine their will and God's will as opposites—a cosmic tug-of-war where one must decrease so the other can increase. That's true only when the natural man still rules the heart. The natural man's will opposes God because it's rooted in fear, ego, appetite, and self-preservation.

But once the natural man is put off and the childlike heart awakens, something remarkable happens: our will begins to grow toward Theirs.

As the will becomes sanctified, it begins—

> *to desire what They desire.*
> *To choose what They would choose.*
> *To see as They see.*
> *To love as They love.*

This is why Jesus prayed:

> *"...that they may be one, even as we are one."* (John 17:22)

This isn't the erasing of individuality—it's the fulfillment of it.

> *The natural man's will dies.*
> *A childlike will is born.*
> *A sanctified will grows.*

And in time, the will of the disciple aligns with the will of the Son.

> *Not through force.*
> *Not through fear.*
> *Through likeness.*

### What Is God's Will?

To answer simply:

> *It is His way.*
> *His nature.*
> *His heart.*
> *His character taking shape in you.*

When Jesus said, *"I am the way, the truth, and the life"* (John 14:6), He wasn't giving us a slogan. He was giving us a trajectory. God's will isn't discovered by asking, *"What should I do?"* It's discovered by becoming the kind of person who naturally does what God does—someone whose desires have been reshaped, whose instincts have been retrained, whose heart has been softened, whose mind has been renewed.

God's will isn't something you guess. It's something you grow into.

As the natural man dies and the childlike heart awakens, your will begins to change. It starts to recognize goodness. It starts to delight in truth. It starts to desire what They desire—not because you're forcing yourself to, but because you're being transformed.

> *This is why the plan of salvation exists.*
> *This is the purpose of the Atonement.*
> *This is why He sent His Son.*
> *This is why prophets speak.*
> *This is why scriptures were preserved.*
> ***This is why the earth was created.***

Everything in the gospel aims at one thing: the transformation of the human will into the divine will.

Not the loss of individuality, but its fulfillment.

The goal isn't imitation—*"What would Jesus do?"* The goal is transfiguration—*"His life is now in me, so my will and His will are becoming one."*

When your will aligns with Their will, it's not because you paused to ask the right question. It's because you have become the kind of soul:

> *Whose instinct is goodness.*
> *Whose reflex is mercy.*
> *Whose movement is truth.*
> *Whose desires have been redeemed.*

Alignment isn't guessing. It's resemblance. God's will becomes your will because you have become like Them.

> *This is the fulfillment of everything He ever taught.*
> *This is the destiny of the sons and daughters of God.*
> *This is the purpose of the Father and Mother raising children in Their image.*
> *This is the arc of eternity bending toward completion.*

**God's will isn't something you obey from the outside. It's something you embody from the inside.**

### The Willing Heart: What God Actually Requires From Us

Many people who want to do God's will aren't resisting Him. They're sincere. They pray earnestly, try their best, and truly want to please Him. Yet many feel unsure—unsure what God expects, unsure how to act, unsure whether they can trust their own thoughts. Over time, this uncertainty makes them hesitant, even fearful of choosing anything without external confirmation.

They've been taught that obedience means erasing themselves. But God has never asked for that.

God isn't raising servants who wait passively for orders. He's raising sons and daughters who can act, not just react.

This is why the Lord said:

> *"Verily I say, men should be anxiously engaged in a good cause, and do many things of their own free will, and bring to pass much righteousness; For the power is in them, wherein they are agents unto themselves. And inasmuch as men do good they shall in nowise lose their reward. But he that doeth not anything until he is commanded, and receiveth a commandment with doubtful heart, and keepeth it with slothfulness, the same is damned."* (D&C 58:27–29)

Here the Lord draws a sharp contrast. On one side are those who are *"anxiously engaged,"* acting of their own free will, bringing to pass much righteousness because the power is already in them. On the other side is the one who *"doeth not anything until he is commanded,"* who receives commandments with a doubtful heart and keeps them with slothfulness.

Slothfulness here isn't carefulness or caution. It's spiritual laziness—the refusal to move until forced, the habit of waiting for God or others to do the work meant to awaken in you. It's the opposite of a willing heart.

Joseph's story shows us another way. He didn't wait to be commanded in all things. He took his questions, his confusion, and his desire to learn, and he went to God in faith. That's the posture the Lord invites from all of us—the example Joseph Smith lived.

### Joseph Smith: A Will God Could Shape

Joseph was a boy with questions. He wanted to know truth, and he was brave enough to seek it. When he walked into the grove, he brought God his genuine desire, his honest confusion, and his willingness to learn. And God honored that.

> *God did not silence him.*
> *He shaped him.*
> *He taught him.*
> *He grew him.*
> *Molded, and refined him.*

God took a young man with almost no formal education and raised him into a prophet—not by overriding him, but by working with the heart Joseph brought to Him. God did not replace Joseph's will; He refined it.

And that is how God works with every one of His children, **if you will let Him.**

### The Brother of Jared: God Invites the Will

We see the same pattern in the story of the Brother of Jared. When the question arose of how to bring light into the barges, God did not hand him a completed solution. Instead, God asked:

> *"What will ye that I should do...?"* (Ether 2:23)

This reveals something profound about how God works.

He invites participation. He invites thought. He invites effort.

And the Brother of Jared responded with remarkable willingness. He didn't just pick up stones from the shore and take them to the Lord. He molten them[7]—an intense, time-consuming, physically demanding process. Then he shaped them with care, knowing they would become part of God's miracle.

He brought God something that required his own thought, labor, and desire. And God met him there.

This is the partnership God seeks with all His children—**if you will let Him.**

## The Premortal Pattern: You Were Noble and Great

This way of working with God did not begin on earth. Abraham saw it in vision:

> *"These I will make my rulers... for they were noble and great ones."* (Abraham 3:22–23)

God did not choose those who passively waited for marching orders. He did not choose those content to let others lead them or tell them what to do. No, He chose those who were willing to step forward, willing to engage, and willing to take an active part in His work.

Oh, how I wish I could help you see that this is about you. This isn't ancient history with no connection to your life. No, this is all about your true identity—your personal history. You were among those noble and great souls. You came here not to be commanded in all things, but to grow into the likeness of the One who formed you.

How do I know this? Because you are reading this book. You are not here by accident. You are noble.

Let that sink deep into your heart.

These teachings are for you. But you don't just get them because you're alive and have blood flowing through your veins. You must obtain them through obedience and growth. And that growth requires a willing heart—a heart ready for God to shape—if you will let Him.

## The Power of LET—D&C 121

This brings us to one of the most important words in latter-day scripture:

LET.

> *"Let thy bowels be full of charity toward all men...Let virtue garnish thy thoughts unceasingly..."* (D&C 121:45)

This is not a command rooted in force. It's an invitation rooted in willingness.

**"Let thy bowels be full..."**

In scripture, *"bowels"* refers to the deepest emotional center of your soul. To let your bowels be full of charity means to allow compassion to reach all the way into the place where your reactions begin.

Full means not partial. Toward all men means no exceptions, no tribal boundaries.

**"Let virtue garnish thy thoughts unceasingly..."**

Virtue, in its original meaning, is strength, power, excellence. To *"garnish"* your thoughts is to adorn them—to fill your mind with what is strong, beautiful, and true. *"Unceasingly"* means this becomes your natural mental atmosphere, not an occasional effort.

*"Let"* means you open the door. You allow God to work. You stop resisting the growth He's offering.

And when you let Him, the promises that follow are remarkable.

### What God Can Do With a Willing Heart

**1. *"Thy confidence shall wax strong in the presence of God."***

> *This is what happened to Joseph.*
> *This is what happened to the Brother of Jared.*

Their willingness produced confidence—confidence strong enough to stand in the very presence of Christ.

**2. *"Thy scepter... shall be an everlasting scepter of righteousness and truth."***

A scepter represents:

> *Identity.*
> *Authority.*
> *Royalty.*

This ties directly to Abraham's vision. You were noble and great before you came here. God is restoring that identity—not giving you a new one.

### 3. *"Thy dominion shall be an everlasting dominion, and without compulsory means it shall flow unto thee forever and ever."*[8]

This is the opposite of stagnation. Flow happens when your will aligns with God's nature. No forcing, no pushing, no anxiety. Just steady, natural movement toward what is good.

This is what God requires of us.

> *Not erasure.*
> *Not blind obedience.*
> *Not passivity dressed as humility.*

God wants us to have a willing heart—a heart that lets Him teach, shape, strengthen, and transform us.

> *A willing heart opens the door.*
> *A sanctified will walks through it.*

And now we can understand why suffering exists—because the world we entered is precisely where the willing heart grows into the divine will.

## Why Suffering Fits the Mold

If God desires willing hearts and sanctified wills, then why does mortality contain so much difficulty? Illness, disappointment, injustice, loss, and personal hardship touch every life.

It's because God is shaping something in us—forming us as a potter forms clay. He uses experiences that press, stretch, steady, and refine the vessel until it can hold what He intends to pour into it.

Many people explain this by saying God designed these experiences or willed them for mysterious purposes. But through the Restoration, the Lord gave Joseph a clearer and far more comforting understanding—one that honors both agency and the eternal reality of opposition.

Opposition didn't begin on earth. Agency is eternal, and wherever agency operates, opposition exists alongside it. Lehi taught that there must be *"opposition in all things"* (2 Nephi 2:11), and Joseph Smith expanded that principle beyond mortality. He showed that even in the premortal world, spirits encountered struggle. Some spirits who had bodies used their greater strength to oppress spirits who didn't, and the imbalance created suffering.

This means our premortal existence wasn't a realm of unbroken calm. It was a realm of growth. Spirits learned, chose, stood for truth, and confronted real conflict. The War in Heaven wasn't a brief flare of disagreement—it was a genuine test of character. The souls later described as *"noble and great ones"*[9] became noble and great because they exercised courage, loyalty, and discernment in the face of opposition.

They chose Christ when doing so required real spiritual strength.

Yet even with that experience, there was something we could not learn there: what it means to live in a physical body with all its vulnerability, emotion, limitation, and separation from God's immediate presence.

Mortality introduces forms of opposition that simply can't exist in a spiritual environment.

> *Here, agency creates consequences that ripple through physical, emotional, and relational life.*
> *Here, the choices of others can affect us profoundly.*

Because agency must remain intact, God does not cancel another person's will to prevent all suffering. If He did, He would cease to be God.

This reality is one of His greatest and most majestic attributes—He honors agency fully, even when it breaks His heart, because no child of God can grow into divine likeness without the freedom to act.

This brings us to a tender truth: Some spirits accepted roles in mortality that would place them in very difficult circumstances. They were not forced. They accepted them willingly, knowing their embodied experience would deepen qualities they already possessed. This includes innocent children who face illness, disability, displacement, or early death.

From a mortal perspective, their suffering appears tragic. From an eternal perspective, it reflects both their nobility and their courage.

They were among the strongest.

They chose to enter a world where agency and natural law create real risks—not to be destroyed by them, but because they understood what such experiences could accomplish for themselves and for others.

Remember, this life isn't just this life. It reaches as far back as it reaches forward, and these willing choices made by truly noble and great souls will resonate throughout eternity.

Suffering also reveals the condition of our own hearts. It can turn us inward in a healthy way that leads to humility, honesty, and prayer. But if we stay turned inward too long, it can distort into self-protection, bitterness, isolation, or despair.

The invitation isn't to stay inward but to start there—long enough to understand what's happening within us—and then let that clarity turn outward in compassion and service to others. This is the natural movement of a willing heart.

Mortality is where this transformation occurs. It's not a punishment; it's preparation. Here, the will learns to choose goodness even when doing so requires sacrifice. Compassion becomes real because we have suffered ourselves. Trust grows not because life is easy but because we choose to trust God in the middle of what's difficult.

And that trust carries a memory within it. We trusted Him before we came here, and we trust Him now—from the beginning, into the middle, and ultimately into His presence, no matter how difficult the path becomes.

Suffering isn't the point of the plan. Transformation is. And transformation requires an environment where agency and opposition are real, where the heart can open, and where the will can grow strong enough to become one with Theirs.

This prepares us to understand the final movement of this Interlude: **what happens when the will of God and the will of a sanctified disciple begin to operate together.**

## A Safer Illustration: The Good Samaritan

When Jesus wanted to teach what a willing heart looks like, He didn't choose a priest, a scribe, or a man of recognized authority. He chose a Samaritan[10]—a man considered religiously inferior by the very people who prided themselves on being God's elect.

This parable gives us a safe way to explore the contrast we touched earlier, without pointing to anyone's personal story. The Lord's own lesson is enough.

A man traveling the road from Jerusalem to Jericho was attacked by thieves, stripped, beaten, and left half dead. The road was dangerous, winding through ravines where bandits waited for vulnerable travelers. The injured man couldn't move. He couldn't cry for help. He lay exposed to heat, predators, and the possibility that those who passed by would either help him or pretend they didn't see.

A priest came first. He saw the man and walked around him. Next came a Levite, one trained from birth in the rituals and duties of temple service. He also saw the man and moved to the other side. Neither stopped. Both likely justified themselves by religious rules about purity, proximity, and duty. They believed they were preserving their spiritual standing. They believed they were obeying God's will.

Then came a Samaritan.

To the Jewish audience, a Samaritan wasn't just an outsider—he was considered corrupted, unwelcome, and unworthy. Samaritans were seen as less-than: a people who didn't belong at the temple, who worshiped differently, and who carried the stain of mixed ancestry. For centuries, Jews had crossed the street to avoid them.

Yet this Samaritan, seeing the wounded man, stopped.

He didn't calculate whether this was *"God's will."* He didn't consider whether the man deserved help or whether stopping would make him unclean. His heart moved, and he followed it. He knelt, bound the wounds, poured oil and wine on them, lifted the man onto his own animal, took him to an inn, paid for his care, and promised to return to cover any remaining costs.

Jesus asked a simple question: *"Which of these was neighbor to him that fell among the thieves"* (Luke 10:36)? The answer was so obvious it silenced every argument. It was the Samaritan—the one they least expected, the one they least respected, the one outside their religious scaffolding.

If we pause long enough, something deeper becomes clear.

The Samaritan wasn't an outsider to God. He was an outsider only in the eyes of those who had built religious scaffolding to legitimize their own positions and man-made claims of authority.

The priest and Levite held titles. They held lineage. They held place. But their will wasn't aligned with God's will because their hearts were not aligned with God. Their authority existed only in the eyes of men.

The Samaritan—the one they dismissed—carried God's likeness.

> *His compassion moved within him.*
> *His willingness shaped his choices.*
> *His creativity solved the problem.*

Without ceremony, without title, without priesthood office, he acted. And Jesus declared him the one who fulfilled the will of God that day.

This isn't a rebuke of all religious leaders. It's a revelation of how God sees. Authority doesn't flow from status, clothing, lineage, or proximity to the temple.

> *It flows from likeness.*
> *It flows from the heart that is willing, compassionate, humble, and responsive.*
> *It flows from the soul whose will has begun to resemble Their will.*

The Good Samaritan shows us that God's will isn't found in those who keep themselves ritually clean by avoiding the wounded. It's found in the one willing to get close enough to bind wounds. It's found in the one who stops, who sees, who bends down, who gives, who risks, who carries, and who promises to return.

It's tempting to read this story and divide the world into good Samaritans and bad priests. But Jesus is doing something far more personal here. He's inviting us to examine the condition of our own will.

Are we shaped by fear, caution, reputation, or duty? Or are we moved by compassion, courage, and the quiet whisper that says, ***"Go to him"?***

The Samaritan acted because his heart had already aligned with the goodness of God's goodness. He didn't need to hear a voice from heaven telling him what to do. His will was already becoming like Theirs. That's why he could move so naturally. That's why Jesus chose him as the example.

This parable prepares us for what comes next. The Samaritan gives us a picture of the fruit—what aligned will looks like in real life. Now we turn to the root: the actual mechanics of how your will and God's will begin to operate together.

> *The Samaritan shows us the pattern.*
> *The next section shows us the process.*

## Their Will and Your Will: The Joining

By now we've seen that God doesn't ask us to erase our will. He asks us to offer it. We've seen that mortality, with all its opposition and difficulty, is the place where a willing heart and a sanctified will are formed. The next natural question is this:

**What actually happens when your will and God's will begin to work together?**

Most people imagine this as a one-way arrangement. God commands; we obey. God speaks; we listen. God decides; we submit. There is truth in that, especially at the beginning.

But the Restoration reveals a deeper mold. God isn't trying to flatten the will, but to form it—shaping us as a potter shapes clay.[11] The clay isn't discarded; it's centered. It's steadied. It's pressed here, lifted there, stretched into strength and refined into something that can hold far more than it ever could before. The Master doesn't erase the vessel; He molds it into its true purpose.

As your will matures, the relationship changes. It grows from instruction into collaboration, and eventually into a kind of trust that few believers ever imagine is possible.

**This is the joining of wills. And it has mechanics.**

### 1. The Mechanics of Divine Partnership

One of the simplest places to see how divine partnership works is in the Savior's invitation: *"Ask, and it shall be given you; seek, and ye shall find; knock, and it shall be opened unto you"* (Matthew 7:7). These are not just comforting words. They describe a process.

#### A. A.S.K.—How Collaboration Actually Works

**Ask. Seek. Knock.**

This pattern is simple enough for a child to remember, yet deep enough to describe how the Lord trains His disciples to work with Him.

ASK is more than a quick prayer. It begins with what the Lord told Oliver Cowdery in Doctrine and Covenants 9. Before asking, Oliver was told to *"study it out"* in his mind (D&C 9:8). That means you think, ponder, test, and meditate on an idea. You turn it over. You roll it around in your mind and heart. You let it touch your experience, your understanding of scripture, and your sense of what is good.

Only after you have done the work to understand the question do you take it to God and ask.

SEEK means you act. You don't sit and wait for God to live your life for you. You move your feet. You look at options. You talk to people. You plan. You experiment. You use the experience and intelligence you have already gained. Seeking is where your will engages with the world.

KNOCK is what happens when you bring your honest effort back to God. You say, in effect, "Here's what I've studied. Here's what I've tried. Here's what I'm willing to do. Will You open the way if this is right?" The Lord's promise to Oliver—a burning in the bosom if it's right, a stupor of thought if it's wrong[12]—is part of this knocking process. The Lord confirms, corrects, or redirects a will that's already moving.

In this way, revelation is not a lottery ticket. It's a conversation. You do your part to think, act, and offer. God does His part to guide, open, close, and confirm. That's collaboration.

### B. From Instruction to Presence: The Four-Stage Arc

Over time, this pattern matures. Revelation grows along a recognizable arc:

**Instruction**
At first, God often gives clear directions. New disciples need structure—obvious commandments and unmistakable answers. Think of it like giving simple rules to a young child. Not because the parent wants permanent control, but because the child isn't yet ready to carry more.

**Collaboration**
As you grow, God begins to involve you more. He doesn't always hand you answers. Instead, He invites you to bring options, ideas, and plans. You study. You propose. You try. He shapes what you bring. This stage can feel less *"certain"* on the surface, but it's actually a sign of trust.

**Confidence**
With repeated experiences of acting and being guided, you begin to lose your fear of *"doing it wrong."* You recognize that God can steer a moving ship more easily than one that refuses to leave the harbor. Your confidence *"waxes strong"* (D&C 121:45) in His presence because you have learned how He speaks to you, how correction feels, and how peace feels.

**Presence**
As the joining deepens, the relationship becomes less about occasional answers and more about ongoing companionship. Revelation stops feeling like rare events and starts feeling like the quiet, steady influence of Someone who walks with you. Your will begins to desire what They desire—not because you are being pushed, but because you have grown into it.

This arc—Instruction → Collaboration → Confidence → Presence—is the story of every disciple who moves from spiritual childhood toward spiritual adulthood.

### C. What a Joined Will Looks Like

A sanctified, joined will isn't mysterious. It has recognizable traits. Think of it as a simple diagram. A joined will is:

> **Willing**—open to God's influence instead of resistant.
> **Listening**—attentive to impressions, scripture, conscience, and truth.
> **Acting**—willing to move without having every detail revealed in advance.
> **Creating**—using talents and ideas to build, bless, and improve the world.
> **Trusting**—confident in God's goodness even when outcomes aren't clear.
> **Trusted**—increasingly given stewardships, responsibilities, and opportunities.
> **Unified**—gradually desiring the same kinds of things They desire.

This isn't perfection. It's movement. It's the shape a disciple's will takes as it matures in partnership with Deity.

### 2. Scriptural Patterns of Partnership

Once you see the pattern, it appears throughout scripture. The great figures of the Restoration and the Book of Mormon are not examples of blind obedience. They are examples of creative discipleship.

**Joseph Smith** didn't wait passively for God to drop answers into his lap. He wrestled with questions about forgiveness, truth, and direction. He read, pondered, and chose to act on the promise in James. His prayer came from a will that was already engaged. God answered that will by setting Joseph on a path of translation, organization, teaching, and leadership that required constant initiative.[13]

**The Brother of Jared** didn't receive detailed construction plans for the barges or ready-made lights. He was told how to build the vessels and then left to figure out the problem of light. So he thought, planned, and worked. Molten stones don't appear out of nowhere. He gathered material, endured heat and labor, and shaped each stone with care. Only then did he carry them to the mount and ask the Lord to touch them. God honored his work by turning it into a miracle.[14]

**Nephi** is another clear example. When commanded to obtain the plates, he didn't receive a step-by-step map. He said, *"I will go and do,"* and then went, *"not knowing beforehand the things which [he] should do."* He tried one approach, failed, reassessed, and then followed the Spirit into a bold, unscripted path. His story shows a will that acts, listens, and adjusts with God.[15]

**Abraham** reasoned with the Lord over Sodom. He didn't silently accept the first statement he heard. He engaged. He asked questions, appealed to God's justice, and negotiated down from fifty righteous people to ten. The Lord didn't rebuke him—He allowed it. That conversation stands as one of the clearest examples of God inviting human moral reasoning into the process.[16]

**Captain Moroni** demonstrates another dimension of partnership: strategy. Alma records that *"if all men had been, and were, and ever would be, like unto Moroni, behold, the very powers of hell would have been shaken forever."* Moroni didn't wait in his tent for God to micromanage his tactics. He studied the land, anticipated enemy moves, dug fortifications, armed his people, raised the title of liberty, and built systems of defense. God supported him because his heart was aligned, his cause was just, and his strategies flowed from a sanctified will.[17]

**Mormon** and **Moroni** show yet another side of this pattern. They made choices about what to include, what to summarize, and how to organize the records. They did this under inspiration, but it still required judgment, editing, and discernment. God didn't simply dictate the Book of Mormon as a monologue. He trusted His servants' minds and hands to shape the record.[18]

These examples—and many others—reveal the same truth:

When hearts are pure and wills are turned toward God, He doesn't smother that will. He invites it. He amplifies it. He trusts it.

### 3. From "God Tells Me" to "God Trusts Me"

The evolution from simple obedience to divine partnership can be understood through something every parent knows: how a child grows.

When a baby is born, he can do almost nothing for himself. The parent feeds, carries, and protects him constantly. The baby doesn't make decisions. He simply receives. At this stage, strict instruction and constant supervision are necessary and loving.

As the child becomes a toddler, he begins to explore. He toddles, falls, and gets back up. He wants to touch everything and try everything. A wise parent allows this in measured ways. Boundaries still exist, but the child is beginning to exercise will. He's allowed to choose within safe limits so he can learn.

As a child grows older, his mind develops. He starts to understand cause and effect. He can follow more complex instructions and begin to help with real tasks. A parent may still say, *"Do this,"* but explanations and conversations increase. The child can ask why. He can participate in decisions appropriate to his level.

Then adolescence arrives. The body changes. The voice deepens. New thoughts, desires, and questions emerge. The young person wants more independence. This stage can be turbulent, but it's also essential. A good parent doesn't crush a teenager's emerging will; they guide it. They set boundaries, yes, but they also invite more and more self-governance.

Finally, adulthood arrives. The relationship changes fundamentally. The parent doesn't want a thirty-year-old who calls for permission about every small choice. They want a son or daughter who knows how to act, who has internalized the family's values, and who can be trusted with real responsibility. The rules may not be repeated out loud anymore—not because they no longer matter, but because they have become part of the person.

Our relationship with God follows a similar pattern.

There are seasons when we need clear, simple instruction. There are seasons when we're allowed—and expected—to try, to risk, and to learn. There are seasons when our desires and God's desires align so closely that He gives us wide latitude, confident that we'll act in ways that honor Him. Eventually, those who endure and grow become the kind of beings He can trust with eternal things.

The shift from *"God tells me everything"* to *"God trusts me"* isn't rebellion. It's the fruit of sanctification. It's the evidence that His law is now written in your heart, not just on stone or paper.

### 4. Not Passive Obedience, but Creative Discipleship

At the core of this journey is something woven into your very nature: the power to create.

Nothing exists on this earth that wasn't created. Every building, song, story, invention, piece of software, and even this technology we call artificial intelligence began as an idea in someone's mind.

> ***First,*** *there is a spiritual creation—an impression, a thought, a plan.*

> ***Second,*** *there is action—materials gathered, words written, code typed, nails driven, shapes molded.*
> ***Finally,*** *there is a physical or visible result: a house, a chair, a computer chip, a digital structure, a piece of music, a conversation that didn't exist before.*

This mirrors a principle revealed in scripture: all things were created spiritually before they were created physically. God works this way. And so do His children.

We see this most clearly in our power to procreate, but it extends far beyond family life. Whenever you build, write, teach, design, organize, reconcile, or restore, you are exercising a divine seed within you. You are not merely consuming the world; you are adding to it.

Creation brings joy because it's one of the ways we most closely resemble Them. When your will joins with God's will, your creative power doesn't shrink. It expands. Your projects, plans, and efforts begin to reflect Their character:

> *You create in ways that bless, not exploit.*
> *You build systems that lift, not control.*
> *You solve problems in ways that honor agency and truth.*
> *You use your gifts to add goodness to the world instead of draining it.*

You could call this creative discipleship—not obedience alone, but partnership. Not a life spent avoiding wrong, but a life spent creating good, shaping the world to look more like the Kingdom.

When a will like that aligns with God, He doesn't put it back in a box. He enlarges it. He trusts it. He invites it into ever greater circles of responsibility.

> *That is the joining of Their will and your will.*
> *It is not the end of you.*
> *It is the beginning of who you truly are.*

With that picture in place, we can now talk about the final piece of this Interlude: what God actually asks you to place on the altar, and what He gives in return.

That is the offering He seeks.

### Closing Witness

Everything you've just read has pointed to a single reality.

This Interlude has explored the natural man, the childlike heart, the shaping of will, the quiet mechanics of partnership, and the courage to act. We've examined suffering, growth, compassion, and the path from simple obedience to divine trust. But every thread we've traced rests on something far more personal than concepts or structures.

This is about relationship.

A real, pure, absolute, loving, personal relationship between you and Deity—Them. We've spent time understanding the architecture of the will. Now lift your eyes to the Architects.

> *They are not distant.*
> *They are not demanding perfection before They draw near.*
> *They are not watching to catch you faltering.*
> *They are inviting you into a relationship where your will matures into Theirs.*
> *They want a relationship not through force, but through love; not through pressure, but through presence.*

If you've ever prayed *"Thy will be done"* with uncertainty in your heart, wondering whether God's will opposed yours—hear this truth with clarity:

God is not disappointed in you. He is delighted in you.

He sees the longing behind your prayers. He sees the goodness behind your efforts. He sees the quiet ways you try to listen, the small choices you make toward light, the moments when you turn to Him even when you feel unsure.

None of this is insignificant to Them. A willing heart, however small it feels, is exactly what They can work with.

Think of Joseph. He wasn't a scholar or a priest. He was a boy with questions, yearning to understand what God required of him. He didn't begin with confidence. He began with desire. And God answered that desire with revelation, light, and a mission that shaped a dispensation. Joseph's path wasn't the story of a flawless man. It was the story of a willing man.

What God did with him wasn't because of his position, his training, or his lineage. It was because he let Them shape him. He lifted his eyes to the Architects, and They formed in him a will They could trust.

This same pattern operates in you.

The joining of wills is not beyond your reach. It doesn't require special status or extraordinary talent. It begins wherever you are—with your desire to do good, your willingness to listen, your choice to act with compassion, and your trust that God walks with you even when you can't see how the path ahead.

God's will isn't meant to burden you. It's meant to free you.
It isn't meant to silence you. It's meant to reveal you.
It's not a test of worthiness. It's a relationship of growth.
It's the way They draw you into Their life, Their heart, Their work, and Their joy.

If your heart is willing—even tremblingly, imperfectly, quietly willing—you are already in Their will.

Begin where you stand. Offer what you can. Let Them shape the rest. The Architects know exactly how to build in you the person They've always seen.

With this foundation in place, we move to the next truth: how to recognize Their voice, how to walk with Them, and how to live each day in the quiet confidence that They are guiding you—not from afar, but from within.

Your joined wills begin here.
Your companionship with Them deepens here.
And from this point forward, your journey continues with Them—not above you, not beyond you, but beside you.

## Interlude Notes

1 Matthew 9:20–22; Mark 5:25–34; Luke 8:43–48

2 This statement was shared with me by my dear friend, the late Robin O'Bannon (2024), relaying what the Lord told her.

3 This story appears in various anecdotal forms and is used here as an illustration of cultural attitudes toward prayer rather than a historical claim.

4 2 Nephi 2:26

5 The Winter Warlock transformation and song reference are from the 1970 Rankin/Bass stop-motion Christmas special, Santa Claus Is Comin' to Town. The song *"Put One Foot in Front of the Other"*

was written by Jules Bass and Maury Laws and performed by Mickey Rooney (Kris Kringle) and Keenan Wynn (Winter Warlock). Quoted here for commentary and illustration.

6 Matthew 6:10, Matthew 26:39

7 The Brother of Jared *"molten stones"* detail is recorded in Ether 3:1, reflecting deliberate effort and craftsmanship before presenting the stones to the Lord.

8 D&C 121:46

9 Abraham 3:22–23

10 The parable of the Good Samaritan is recorded in Luke 10:25–37.

11 The imagery of God as the potter and His children as the clay appears throughout scripture. See Isaiah 64:8; Jeremiah 18:1–6; Romans 9:20–21.

12 D&C 9:8–9

13 Joseph Smith's search for forgiveness, truth, and direction and his decision to act on James 1:5 are recorded in Joseph Smith—History 1:10–20.

14 The narrative of the Brother of Jared preparing the vessels, seeking light, and molten stones appears in Ether 2:16–25; Ether 3:1–6.

15 Nephi's pursuit of the plates and his *declaration "I will go and do..."* are found in 1 Nephi 3:7; 1 Nephi 4:6.

16 Abraham's dialogue with the Lord—asking, appealing, and negotiating—is recorded in Genesis 18:23–33.

17 Mormon's statement about Captain Moroni appears in Alma 48:17.
Moroni's strategic preparations are seen throughout Alma 43–49.

18 Mormon and Moroni's decisions regarding selection, editing, and summarization of records are evident in Words of Mormon 1:3–6; Mormon 5:9; Moroni 1:1–4; Moroni 10:1–2.

# Gifts of the Spirit

## Heaven's Gifts for Peaceable Followers

---

### Start Your Engines

It always happens at the worst time. You slide into the driver's seat, turn the key, and instead of the steady hum of the engine, you hear nothing—or maybe just a sluggish whine, or worse, a click...click...click. Your heart sinks. You try again, a little harder, as if more effort will make a difference. Still nothing. The car just sits there.

You are going nowhere.

Most people only know the feeling of frustration. But under the hood, an intricate sequence is supposed to unfold. When you turn the key (or press the button), the battery releases a surge of stored power. That charge flows to the starter, which engages the flywheel and begins turning the engine. Spark plugs fire, igniting a controlled explosion. Meanwhile, the fuel pump pushes gasoline forward, and injectors mist it into the chambers with precision. Pistons fire in perfect rhythm, creating the power to drive the car forward.

But if the battery is dead, the whole sequence never begins. And if the spark plugs don't spark, or the starter doesn't turn, or the fuel pump doesn't pump, or the injectors don't inject, the system fails.

The car may look polished on the outside. The tank may be full. The wheels may be ready to roll, but without those internal workings, it remains a silent shell.

What we have laid before you in the last chapter is the spiritual equivalent of starting the engine. Faith, hope, and charity are the initiating actions—the turn of the key, the firing of the plugs, the flow of fuel—that make the soul ready to come alive in Christ.

But just as no engine runs without a battery, no disciple moves forward without heaven's power. When faith acts, hope anchors, and charity blossoms, God answers with Their own gifts—the power from beyond the veil that sets the whole life in motion.

This is how the sequence is fulfilled: when the disciple responds in faith, hope, and charity, heaven responds in kind.

The Godhead pours out spiritual gifts upon Their children—not for show, but to empower them through ordinances and appointments, where They manifest Their love and strengthen Their people to accomplish Their work. Through this unity, heaven and earth connect—revelation flows, truth is confirmed, and divine power reaches each soul according to what love and purpose require.

In this process, faith deepens, hope anchors more firmly, and charity is endowed more abundantly upon Their people. These gifts are the quiet mark of divine approval—heaven's provisions that enable peaceable followers to heal, discern, prophesy, and endure.

Joseph taught that no one is left out. *"To every man is given a gift by the Spirit of God"* (D&C 46:11). Paul declared that *"the manifestation of the Spirit is given to every man to profit withal"* (1 Corinthians 12:7). Moroni promised that *"all these gifts of which I have spoken... come by the Spirit of Christ; and they come not all at once, but severally, according as he will"* (Moroni 10:17).

This is heaven's way. The gifts are not reserved for the few, confined to leaders, or given out by earthly rank. They belong to peaceable followers of Christ—those who walk the path of faith, hope, and charity. And in them, the Spirit manifests in diverse yet harmonious ways, balancing the strength of the divine masculine with the tenderness of the divine feminine, that all may be profited thereby (D&C 46:12).

As faith, hope, and charity take root in peaceable followers, heaven responds with endowments fitted to the work at hand—the gifts of the Spirit.

## Gifts of the Spirit – Heaven's Endowments

When Joseph Smith asked the Lord about spiritual gifts, the answer came in clear, practical terms:

> *"To some it is given by the Holy Ghost to know that Jesus Christ is the Son of God... to others it is given to believe on their words... to some it is given to have faith to be healed; to others it is given to heal... to some it is given the working of miracles; to others prophecy; to others the discerning of spirits; to others the gift of tongues; and to another the interpretation of tongues." (D&C 46:13–25)*

This was never meant as a closed list. It witnesses that all gifts flow from Him and are given *"for the benefit of the children of God" (*D&C 46:26).

Joseph counseled us to *"covet earnestly the best gifts"* (1 Corinthians 12:31)—not in selfish ambition, but in service: seeking what will most bless others and glorify God.

The Lord revealed the process plainly in D&C 93: first, forsake your sins. Second, come unto Him. Third, call on His name. Fourth, obey His voice. Fifth, keep His commandments. Do these things, and His promise is sure.

This is the same pattern you have seen before:

> ***Seek His voice***—turn from sin and draw near through faith and repentance.
>
> ***Hear Him***—receive His word directly, without unbelief.
>
> ***Obey His voice***—fulfill the ordinance, appointment, or assignment He gives you (see D&C 84:33–44).

In this order, the *"best"* gift is always the one most needed in the present moment to accomplish the task the Lord has placed in your hands. You don't have to guess which gift to seek—trust that He will reveal it, guiding you to ask aright, so you don't *"ask amiss"* (D&C 50:29–30).

Gifts are given to those who ask in faith, believing they will receive, for the express purpose of doing His work. When you obey and the gift manifests, He *"shows Himself"* in the work. Each time this happens, your confidence grows to ask for more, to climb higher, and to become more like Him—until you stand in His presence.

These endowments are heaven's tools for heaven's work. They are not ornaments for display, but instruments through which God's will is done on earth—through peaceable followers willing to hear, obey, and act in His name.

These gifts were not described in vague generalities. The Lord, through His prophets, gave us lists of them—witnesses in scripture that show both their diversity and their harmony.

## The Gifts Listed in Scripture—and Why You Want Them

The scriptures don't speak about gifts in abstractions. They name them so peaceable followers can recognize, seek, and use them. Different gifts, same Spirit; different operations, one purpose—*"that all may be profited thereby"* (D&C 46:12; 1 Corinthians 12:7).

### To Know Jesus Is the Son of God

> "To some it is given by the Holy Ghost to know that Jesus Christ is the Son of God..." (D&C 46:13).
>
> This is not secondhand belief. It is the burning certainty that comes when the Spirit Himself bears witness to your soul. Peter had it when he declared, "Thou art the Christ, the Son of the living God"—and Jesus said flesh and blood had not revealed it (Matthew 16:16–17). Joseph had it in the grove, when the Lord introduced Himself in light brighter than the sun.
>
> Once you know Him this way, you will never again wonder if He is real.
>
> **Why you cannot do without it:** You cannot do without this gift because everything else rests upon it.
>
> To know that Jesus is the Son of God is not merely to accept a doctrine—it is to recognize who governs your salvation. This knowledge anchors faith, gives repentance its direction, and turns obedience from duty into devotion.
>
> Without this gift, Christ remains an idea, a teacher, or a distant Savior. With it, He becomes Lord—the One to whom you yield your will, trust your life, and from whom you expect real transformation. It is this knowing that allows the heart to bow without fear and follow without reserve.
>
> This gift also guards against deception. Many voices speak in Christ's name, but only those who know Him can discern when His voice is present.

Knowing that Jesus is the Son of God establishes a living reference point inside the soul—one that recognizes His Spirit, His ways, and His authority.

In short, this gift is foundational. Without it, faith drifts. With it, everything else finds its proper order.

## To Believe on the Words of Others

*"...to others it is given to believe on their words, that they also might have eternal life if they continue faithful"* (D&C 46:14).

Not everyone receives an immediate personal witness. The Lord honors those who hold fast to the testimony of others until their own is given. Think of the Lamanites who believed the words of Ammon and his brethren and were filled with joy (Alma 18–19). Belief isn't weakness—it's fertile ground where your own knowledge will grow.

**Why you cannot do without it:** Because God counts this as faith. When you choose to trust the testimony of a true servant, you open a door for the Spirit to confirm it to you personally. This gift lets you move forward without paralysis, receive blessings now, and prepare your heart for the day the Lord Himself speaks to you.

## Faith to Be Healed

*"...to some it is given to have faith to be healed"* (D&C 46:19).

The woman who touched the hem of Jesus' garment (Mark 5:25–34) didn't just wish for healing—she *expected* it. She pressed through the crowd convinced that if she could just touch Him, she would be whole. That is faith to be healed. Many in Joseph's day sought this gift and received it through prayer and laying on of hands.

**Why you cannot do without it:** Because it makes you a willing receiver of miracles. This gift removes the mental ceiling that keeps so many from reaching out to touch Him. With it, you will stop hesitating, stop second-guessing, and press boldly toward Him knowing His power is for you.

## Faith to Heal

*"...to others it is given to heal"* (D&C 46:20).

In Nauvoo, Joseph and others walked from house to house during sickness, laying hands on the afflicted and commanded them to rise in the name of Jesus Christ—and they did. This gift is not magic; it is Christ's power flowing through one who obeys His voice. It's for the mother praying over a fevered child, the friend at a hospital bedside, the disciple who will not let suffering pass unanswered.

**Why you cannot do without it:** Because suffering should never leave you passive. This gift equips you to step into a crisis with heaven's authority, knowing the Lord will back the word He gives you to speak. It turns compassion into action and makes you an instrument of His mercy.

## Working of Miracles

*"...to some is given the working of miracles"* (1 Corinthians 12:10).

A miracle is something heaven does that cannot be explained by nature or human effort. When the Nephite disciples were imprisoned and the earth shook until the walls fell (3 Nephi 28:19–20), that was this gift in action. Joseph experienced it when poisonous serpents were driven away from Zion's Camp in answer to prayer. Miracles happen when God steps in to confirm His word or rescue His people.

**Why you cannot do without it:** Some situations need more than comfort—they need an impossible breakthrough. This gift partners you with heaven in moments where natural law bends to the will of God. It's the Red Sea parting, the loaves multiplying, the prison doors swinging open. With it, you become the Lord's willing co-worker in acts that leave no doubt He is present.

## Prophecy

*"...to others prophecy"* (1 Corinthians 12:10).

Prophecy is speaking God's mind and will by His Spirit—sometimes about the future, always about the truth. Joseph prophesied of the Saints' exodus west years before it happened. In your own life, it may be a Spirit-filled word to your child, a warning to a friend, or a testimony in a gathering that opens hearts.

**Why you cannot do without it:** Because the Lord still speaks—and sometimes He chooses your voice. Prophecy cuts through confusion, reveals hidden danger, calls people to repentance, and declares what God is about to do. It's not about predicting for curiosity's sake, but delivering a living word that shifts the course of events.

## Diversity of Operations

*"...there are diversities of operations" (1 Corinthians 12:6).*

Paul names this as a gift of the Spirit—the ability to work in many ways under the same power of God. It is the capacity to shift methods without losing alignment to the same divine source. In Joseph's life, this gift appeared often: translating by the gift and power of God, preaching by the Spirit, receiving visions, counseling leaders, healing the sick—all in the same week.

Those with this gift can adapt quickly when the Spirit redirects. They move seamlessly from teaching to healing, from receiving revelation to confronting evil spirits, from public ministry to private intercession. It's the opposite of being rigid or bound to one approach; it's being able to follow the Lord's assignments no matter the form they take.

**Why you cannot do without it:** Because the Lord rarely repeats Himself in the same way twice. The diversity of His operations requires servants who can be like the wind—moved wherever He wills, without hesitation. This gift allows you to be useful in any situation He places you in, confident that the same God works all in all.

## Discerning of Spirits

*"...to another discerning of spirits"* (1 Corinthians 12:10).

This is the instant, Spirit-given knowledge of what influence is at work in a person, teaching, or situation—from God, from man, or from the adversary. Joseph used it when false spirits attempted to deceive in Kirtland (see D&C 50). You might need it to see through flattery, detect danger, or recognize an angel.

**Why you cannot do without it:** Because not everything that looks or feels *"spiritual"* is from God. This gift lets you instantly recognize the true source behind an influence, dream, teaching, or person's words. It guards you from deception, helps you deliver others from it, and keeps your path aligned with the Spirit of the Lord.

### Gift of Tongues

"*...to another divers kinds of tongues*" (1 Corinthians 12:10).

Sometimes this is a heavenly language given for prayer; other times, it's speaking in an earthly tongue you've never learned. Like the mother in the hospital who suddenly spoke fluent Spanish to comfort a stranger in distress—and, when the moment passed, could not recall the words. This gift comes when God wants His word delivered *now* to someone who will understand it.

**Why you cannot do without it:** Because the gospel is meant for every nation, kindred, tongue, and people. This gift lets you speak in languages you have not learned, so a hearer receives the message in their own native tongue. It can bridge cultural divides in seconds, and in the right moment, open a heart that no other approach could reach.

### Interpretation of Tongues

"*...to another the interpretation of tongues*" (1 Corinthians 12:10).

The Spirit gives understanding of speech unknown to you. Joseph's early preaching in Kirtland was sometimes interpreted by others as the Spirit moved. This gift often works alongside the gift of tongues, but can also stand alone—like understanding a sermon in a foreign language as if it were spoken in your own.

**Why you cannot do without it:** Because a message given in a tongue needs understanding to bless the whole body. This gift lets you translate by the Spirit's power, making a foreign word plain without formal training. It preserves unity, confirms the message, and ensures the whole gathering is edified.

And even these named gifts are only a sampling of heaven's generosity; the Spirit equips disciples precisely for the work before them.

## Gifts Not Always Listed—But No Less Real

Scripture gives examples, not ceilings. The Holy Ghost supplies what the assignment requires—often in forms that appear in story before they appear on a list.

## The Gift of Understanding the Scriptures

*"Then opened he their understanding, that they might understand the scriptures"* (Luke 24:45).

This is more than reading comprehension—it is the veil lifting so you see as God sees. Patterns leap out. Prophecies tie together. A verse you've read a hundred times suddenly pierces you like an arrow. Joseph had it as a boy when he read James 1:5, and it changed the world.

**Why you cannot do without it:** Because the word will stop being ink on paper and start being a living voice in your ear, teaching you what to do next.

## The Gift of Dreams and Visions

*"Your old men shall dream dreams, your young men shall see visions"* (Joel 2:28).

God still speaks in the night watches and the quiet hours. Think of Lehi's dream guiding an entire family's exodus, or Peter's rooftop vision that sent the gospel to the Gentiles.

**Why you cannot do without it:** Because God wants to bypass your overthinking mind and plant His will straight into your spirit. Dreams and visions often carry life-course correction in one striking image.

## The Gift of Quiet Discernment

*"By their fruits ye shall know them"* (Matthew 7:20).

This is not suspicion—it is clarity. You sense what is unseen, weigh a situation by the Spirit, and recognize truth or deception without fanfare. Joseph had it when he knew the worthiness of men before they ever spoke.

**Why you cannot do without it:** Because you will navigate life without being taken in by appearances, and you'll know when to step forward—and when to walk away.

## The Gift of Seeing People as God Sees Them

Samuel looked at David and saw a boy; God saw a king (1 Samuel 16:7). This gift lets you pierce through masks, mistakes, and self-condemnation to glimpse the eternal identity of a soul.

**Why you cannot do without it:** Because when you see people in their true, divine potential, you will treat them in ways that call that potential forth.

## The Gift of Holy Imagination

Abraham pictured the stars and saw his seed; Nephi envisioned a ship before the first board was cut. Holy imagination is the Spirit's way of letting you *"see"* a thing before it exists.

**Why you cannot do without it:** Because you'll never again say, *"I can't see how this could happen."* Instead you'll *see* it in God's mind—and then you'll know how to walk toward it.

## The Gift of Perfect Recall

Jesus promised the Spirit would *"bring all things to your remembrance"* (John 14:26). This gift allows you to recall the right words, names, and truths with precision—exactly when you need them.

**Why you cannot do without it:** Because in the moment of testimony, counsel, or danger, you will never be at a loss for the exact truth God wants spoken.

## The Gift of Boldness

*"They spake the word of God with boldness"* (Acts 4:31).

This is courage lit by the Spirit. It's Peter stepping into the street at Pentecost, or Abinadi standing before a king, fearing God more than man.

**Why you cannot do without it:** Because there will be moments when hesitation costs souls—and you will want heaven's steel in your voice.

## The Gift of Patience in Suffering

Job had it. So did Joseph in Liberty Jail. This gift is not passive—it is active trust that God is doing something in the delay or pain.

**Why you cannot do without it:** Because storms will come. And when they do, you can stand unshaken, enduring well, instead of merely enduring.

## The Gift of Joy Under Trial

Paul sang in prison. Early Saints danced in wagons bound for exile. This gift lifts you above circumstances so your spirit remains light, even in heaviness.

**Why you cannot do without it:** Because joy in trial is the enemy of despair—and it confounds the adversary.

## The Gift of Quickened Hands

Bezalel was filled *"with the spirit of God, in wisdom... and in all manner of workmanship"* (Exodus 31:3–5). This is heaven's touch on your craft, skill, or labor.

**Why you cannot do without it:** Because when the Lord gives you an assignment, you'll complete it with speed, beauty, and precision beyond your natural ability.

## The Gift of Heavenly Timing

Jesus' ministry was marked by *"mine hour is not yet come"* (John 2:4)—and then, suddenly, now is the time. This gift tunes your actions to heaven's calendar.

**Why you cannot do without it:** Because a right thing at the wrong time can fail—but a right thing in God's timing moves mountains.

### The Gift of Song

David's harp drove away an evil spirit from Saul (1 Samuel 16:23). The right song, given in the right moment, can heal, rally courage, or break oppression.

**Why you cannot do without it:** Because your voice can become a weapon and a balm at the same time.

### Gift of Inspired Writing

Jeremiah burned with a word he could not keep in, so he wrote it down. This gift lets you shape words that carry the Spirit to others' hearts.

**Why you cannot do without it:** Because when you can't speak to someone face to face, your words can still travel to them and burn in their bones.

### Gift of Reconciliation

Jesus called peacemakers *"children of God"* (Matthew 5:9). This gift enables you to bridge divides, heal grudges, and restore trust where all seemed lost.

**Why you cannot do without it:** Because every healed relationship is a testimony that God's kingdom is here.

### The Gift of Humor

Sarah laughed at the promise—and then laughed with joy when Isaac was born. Holy humor can break tension, humble pride, and restore hope.

**Why you cannot do without it:** Because sometimes the shortest road to a softened heart is through shared laughter.

Every one of these gifts is for you to seek. They are the natural endowments of heaven given to peaceable followers who hear, obey, and act.

The Lord is no respecter of persons; what He gave to Joseph, He will give to you—in your own sphere, for your own assignments, in your own moments of need.

## Gifts as Signs of God's Living Christ's Church

Wherever Christ's true church exists, His gifts will be found. Not as ornaments to admire from a distance, but as living currents of His power flowing through His people to accomplish His work.

Moroni's final chapter echoes Paul's letters with striking clarity. After listing the gifts—to teach, to heal, to prophesy, to interpret tongues—he states plainly:

> *"All these gifts of which I have spoken, which are spiritual, never will be done away, even as long as the world shall stand, only according to the unbelief of the children of men."* (*Moroni 10:19)*

That's the Lord's definition of His living church: a body where these gifts are active, multiplying, and alive in Him.

Moroni doesn't just list them—he tells you how to receive them:

> *"Remember that every good gift cometh of Christ. And I would exhort you... that ye would lay hold upon every good gift, and touch not the evil gift, nor the unclean thing."* (*Moroni 10:18, 30)*

Do you see it? This isn't a picture of a static organization, but a living body—a people in motion, *"fitly joined together... unto the edifying of itself in love" (*Ephesians 4:16).

In Joseph's teaching, this edifying moves in two directions:

> **Upward**—drawing each disciple personally toward Christ in greater light and likeness.
>
> **Outward** —blessing, protecting, and strengthening the rest of the body.

And one of the clearest ways Joseph taught this edifying to happen was through blessings by the laying on of hands—heaven's upward touch that opens a conduit between the disciple and God, to heal, to reveal lineage, to prophesy, and to speak peace from Him directly.

## Blessings by the Laying on of Hands—The Lord's Touch Among His People

In Joseph's day, the laying on of hands was more than form—it was the Lord's chosen way of touching His people through His servants. To lay hands upon another was to witness that Christ Himself still ministers on earth, conferring His Spirit, His healing, His blessing.

The scriptures are full of this witness.

> When disciples received the Holy Ghost, it was by the laying on of hands (Acts 8:17; Moroni 2:2).
>
> When the sick were healed, it was by the laying on of hands (Mark 16:18; D&C 42:44).
>
> When disciples were set apart to serve, it was by the laying on of hands (Acts 6:6; D&C 20:60).

In each case, the act was the same: heaven appointed, a hand resting upon the head, a prayer offered, and heaven answering. These moments, done in purity and faith, were not mere ceremony but the Gifts of the Spirit in action—a true connection with heaven, where God could manifest Himself through His appointments.

Scripture also reveals the rich symbolism of hands.

> **They are signs of fellowship:** *"they gave... the right hands of fellowship"* (Galatians 2:9).
>
> **They are instruments of service:** "*Whatsoever thy hand findeth to do, do it with thy might" (*Ecclesiastes 9:10).
>
> **They are channels of divine power:** *"they shall lay hands on the sick, and they shall recover" (*Mark 16:18).

In every blessing, the touch of a hand signifies connection, fellowship, and heaven's power resting upon earth.

Joseph carried this forward with remarkable breadth. Fathers blessed their children. Patriarchs prophesied lineage and destiny.

Women laid hands upon the sick and saw them recover. Joseph once affirmed: *"If the sisters should have faith to heal the sick, let all hold their tongues, and let everything roll on."*[1]

Joseph did not invent something new—he affirmed what was already the Lord's pattern: wherever there is faith, God responds.

You are a single father, or a single mother, and your child is sick. What do you do? You bless them. That's what you do. You lay your hands on your child's head, anoint them with consecrated olive oil, and pray with love and faith. Say something simple, from your heart:

> *"My dear one, in the name of Jesus Christ I lay my hands on your head and anoint you with this oil set apart for healing. I bless you to be made well. I love you. Christ loves you and wants you to be whole. And I do so in the name of your loving Savior, who is mighty to save, Jesus Christ, Amen."*

Oil itself carries its own deep witness. From the time of Moses, the Lord commanded a holy anointing oil to be used *"throughout your generations"* (Exodus 30:31). Kings and prophets were anointed with oil as a sign of the Spirit resting upon them (1 Samuel 16:13). The sick were anointed with oil in the name of the Lord and healed by the prayer of faith (James 5:14).

Oil consecrates, heals, protects, and gladdens. It is the vineyard's distilled light: fruit pressed into fuel, mercy, and Spirit.

Even the name Gethsemane means *"oil press,"*—the place where the Messiah Himself was pressed, where His blood flowed so that life and light might flow to all.[2]

This same truth echoes in the Savior's parable of the ten virgins. Five carried oil in their lamps and were ready when the Bridegroom came. Five carried none, and when their light went out, they sought to borrow.

But oil cannot be borrowed.

The light of Christ cannot be transferred from one vessel to another. It must be received from Him directly.

The foolish virgins were told to buy oil from the vendors. But who are these vendors? Not Christ. He does not sell what He freely gives.

The vendors are the soothsayers, the teachers of the philosophies of men, those who pretend to dispense wisdom and light for a price. In our day they are the podcasters, the authors, the influencers, and even the religious leaders who hoard and control the supply.

They are merchants, not givers of life.

True oil comes only from the Olive who was pressed in Gethsemane. His body was broken, His blood was shed, and from Him flows the Spirit that fills lamps with light.

To seek oil from any other hand is to be left in darkness. Only Jesus Christ gives the oil of life, and He gives it freely to all who come to Him.

Joseph's restoration reaffirmed this. He taught his people to consecrate oil (D&C 42:43–44), to lay on hands, and to bless the sick in their homes (D&C 42:44–52). He recognized fathers, mothers, and children as full participants in this flow of heaven's gifts.[3]

Religion was never meant to be a vendor of oil, hoarding supply and controlling access. It was meant to be a living body where oil flows freely, where hands bless freely, where Christ Himself still touches His people.

These blessings were extensions of the gifts of the Spirit. A father's blessing was prophecy. A patriarch's blessing was revelation. Healings were manifestations of power, accompanied by angels. In every case, the laying on of hands opened a channel for heaven to speak and act.

And each blessing—whether of healing, prophecy, ordination, or comfort—was more than a pointer back to Christ.

It was a conduit to Christ Himself.

These are His words. They are His blessings. They are His Spirit manifesting love, wisdom, mysteries, and power.

The laying on of hands, joined with consecrated oil, is not the power of men; it is the living touch of God upon His people.

## Gifts in the Body of Christ

These personal blessings did not stand alone. They joined with many other manifestations of the Spirit to edify the whole body.

In the Kirtland years, the Saints gathered for meetings where multiple gifts operated in harmony:

> *Healing the sick*
> *Tongues with interpretation*
> *Prophecies given and confirmed*
> *Discernment of spirits to guard against deception*[4]

These gatherings were not exhibitions—they became the body of Christ functioning as it was meant to function.[5]

Paul's analogy of the church as a body matches Moroni's vision perfectly: the eye sees, the hand lifts, the ear hears—no part can say to another, *"I have no need of thee"* (1 Corinthians 12:12–27).

Gifts are heaven's instruments to keep the whole body alive, balanced, and growing—flowing ever toward Christ.

If these gifts are missing, something vital is absent. Moroni's witness is clear: where gifts are present, Christ is walking among His people. Where they are absent, the body is starving.

## Gifts and the Preparation for Zion

Zion is not built by human skill alone. Its foundation stones are people alive in Christ—men and women who bear His gifts and wield them in His service.

Every gift you've read about so far isn't just a blessing for today—it's training for the world to come.

Zion is the society of the sanctified, where every need is met not by money or law but by the living power of God flowing through His people.

Moroni paints the picture of that day:

> *"Come unto Christ, and be perfected in him... that ye become holy, without spot."* (Moroni 10:32)

Perfection in Him is not a solitary climb. The gifts are heaven's means of shaping you into someone who can dwell in Zion:

> ***Faith*** *trains you to act without fear, trusting the King who will reign there.*
>
> ***Hope*** *anchors you in His promises, so that you can endure and overcome.*
>
> ***Charity*** *ensures every act is rooted in His love—**the atmosphere of Zion**.*
>
> ***Healing, prophecy, discernment, and tongues****—all prepare you to strengthen, guide, and protect the community He will gather.*

Joseph taught this plainly; and Paul bore witness that *"God is with you of a truth"* (1 Corinthians 14:25).

In a Zion society, that evidence is everywhere—in the marketplace, in the home, in the quiet hours of prayer. When each member exercises their God-given endowment, the whole community rises together.

This is the testimony of Enoch's city: *"And the Lord called his people Zion, because they were of one heart and one mind, and dwelt in righteousness; and there was no poor among them"* (Moses 7:18). Their unity and purity were so complete that the Lord received them into His own bosom.

So it will be in Zion: gifts will knit the people together in the same unity that once endured for generations among the Nephites after Christ's visit. Those gifts are the ligaments of the body (cf. Ephesians 4:16), holding every member in place, joined in love.

But this time the harmony will not fade. It will endure for a thousand years—the great Millennium, when Christ Himself will reign in glory among His people (Revelation 20:4, 6; D&C 29:11).

The Lord is already training His builders. Every time you seek and use a gift, you lay a stone in that city's wall. And when the call comes to gather, you will not go empty-handed—you will bring heaven's tools with you.

## Weakness and the Gifts of the Spirit

Earlier we compared the life of a disciple to starting an engine: the battery surges, the starter turns, the spark plugs fire, the fuel flows, and the car roars to life. But sometimes the battery is too weak. The lights dim, the starter clicks, and nothing happens.

The car may be perfectly built and fully fueled, but without a living charge, it cannot move. What does it need? A recharge. A jump start. Power from outside itself.

So it is with us.

Spiritual gifts are not given to the flawless; they are given to the weak.

Moroni recorded the Lord's words: *"My grace is sufficient for all men that humble themselves before me; for if they humble themselves before me, and have faith in me, then will I make weak things become strong unto them."* (Ether 12:27)

Notice the order. Our part is simple:

> *Come unto Him.*
> *Be humble.*
> *Have faith.*

Christ's part is profound:

> *He shows us our weakness.*
> *He gives us our weakness.*
> *He shares His grace.*
> *He makes our weakness strong.*

We often resent weakness, as though it were a flaw in God's design. We imagine that if we were just more disciplined, smarter, holier, or more organized, we could overcome it ourselves.

We throw ourselves into willpower, strategy, and self-help, convinced we can fix whatever is broken.

But here's the question you need to answer:

If you could overcome it on your own, it wouldn't be weakness, would it?

It would simply be a skill to master.

But that's not what weakness is. Weakness is different. Weakness is woven into mortality by design, so that we're forced to put off the natural man and lean wholly on His grace.

See what's happening? If you didn't have weakness, you wouldn't need Him.

This is God's mercy, not His cruelty. If strength were ours alone, we would never turn to Him. Weakness bends the knee. Weakness exposes our need. Weakness shuts every other door until only one remains: surrender to Christ.

It is His way of ensuring that no one may glory in their own strength, that no one can save himself, but must be saved through Him.

Joseph Smith knew this firsthand.

From his earliest encounters with heaven, he was told of his weakness. Moroni said he was weak like the world, and that only God's grace could carry him[6].

Joseph confessed himself *"an obscure boy... of no consequence in the world."*[7] He was unlearned, ridiculed, betrayed, imprisoned. By every earthly measure, he was not the man for the job. And yet, in his weakness, God poured out visions, revelations, translations, and gifts that shook the earth.

The boy who could barely write a letter became the prophet who dictated scripture. The prisoner in chains became the voice of Zion's future. His very inadequacy became the proof that God's strength was at work.

This is where humility becomes the key. Weakness opens the door, but humility turns the ignition.

Humility is not self-deprecation or walking with your head down; it is thankfulness—the clear-eyed recognition that every gift and every strength is from Him.

Gratitude is the posture of the truly humble. As one teacher put it: *"To be humble is to be thankful; and to be thankful is to be humble."*

Ammon captured the paradox perfectly: *"I know that I am nothing; as to my strength I am weak; therefore I will not boast of myself, but I will boast of my God"* (Alma 26:12). That is true humility: boasting only in Him, thanking Him in all things, even in trials, until your personal prisons become places of transformation.

Joseph's own story proves it. Some of his greatest revelations came not in triumph but in captivity.

In Liberty Jail, he was confined in a pit where he could not stand upright, shivering in the cold, fed with scraps and filth. Cut off from his family and surrounded by despair, he cried out to heaven.

And there, in the very depths of weakness, came one of the greatest revelations in all scripture (D&C 121–123). Humility did not free him from the prison, but it turned the prison into a temple. In bowing low, he was lifted up.

Think again of the engine.

Sometimes battery cables corrode, leaving only a weak or faltering connection. The power is there, but interference keeps the current from flowing. Humility clears the corrosion. It is the willingness to accept correction, to be cleaned and tightened to the Source, so heaven's power can surge freely once again.

Without humility, the spark never reaches the plugs. With humility, the engine roars to life.

And this is where the gifts of the Spirit shine.

They are not medals pinned on the already-strong, but mercies poured into the humble. To prophesy while knowing your own blindness, to heal while carrying your own infirmity, to discern while aware of your own dullness—this is to walk in the paradox of power through weakness.

**Practice:** This week, name your weakness before the Lord without excuse or disguise. Ask Him to show you where the *"cables"* of your soul have corroded. Then, in humility, invite Him to clear the interference and restore the connection. Each time you are corrected, thank Him for the mercy of it. Each time you stumble, surrender afresh and trust His grace. Watch how His power begins to flow where once you only felt failure, until even the places that once felt like prisons become places where heaven speaks.

## Conclusion - Gifts Offered to You

Christ walked in every gift of the Spirit. Joseph did too, in his measure, as a prophet raised up in these latter days. Their lives stand as a double witness that the pattern is real and the power is available.

And now it is set before you.

These endowments are not locked in scripture, stored in history, reserved for leaders only. They are the present-tense promise of heaven to every peaceable follower of Christ.

Moroni pleads: *"Deny not the gifts of God, for they are many; and they come from the same God"* (Moroni 10:8).

Joseph assures: every gift is given for the profit of all.

But a gift unused will wither.

Picture a little boy sitting at a piano, grieved and frustrated because he can feel the music within him but can't make his hands cooperate. The music is real, divine, pressing to come forth—but without practice it cannot yet find expression.

So it is with spiritual gifts. They don't arrive in full mastery all at once. They must be trained, exercised, and refined until they become instruments in the Master's hands.[8]

And here is the greater mystery: it is not only that we express the gift, but that God expresses Himself through us. *"It is God that worketh in you both to will and to do"* (Philippians 2:13).

The Godhead longs to play, to sing, to heal, to proclaim truth, to create beauty, to bless Their children—and They work through Their willing children. When you master your gift, it is not you who stands in glory—it's Them who find full expression through you.

This is why the Savior taught the parable of the talents.

One servant received ten, another five, and another one. Those who had ten and five went forward and increased their gifts—and in doing so, they gave joy to the Giver. Their faith to act pleased Him, and He poured out blessings without measure, doubling what they had first received. Not because of their own industry alone, but because they honored the One who gave.

As the Lord declared:

> *"All things which come of the earth... are made for the benefit and the use of man, both to please the eye and to gladden the heart; ...for unto this end were they made, to be used, with judgment, not to excess, neither by extortion." (D&C 59:18–20)*

And again:

> *"He that receiveth all things with thankfulness shall be made glorious; and the things of this earth shall be added unto him, even an hundred fold, yea, more."* (D&C 78:19)

But the servant who was given one talent hid it. He buried it in the ground, as if to say: *"This is too hard. I will not practice."* And because he withheld the gift, he withheld God's own chance to be expressed through him.

A buried gift silences the Giver. It does not bless His children, and therefore it displeases Him. The Lord's response was sharp: the unused gift was taken away, and the joy of the Master was withheld.

As the Lord declared:

> *"What doth it profit a man if a gift is bestowed upon him, and he receive not the gift? Behold, he rejoices not in that which is given unto him, neither rejoices in him who is the giver of the gift" (D&C 88:33)*

This is why weakness and humility matter so much. Weakness keeps us dependent. Humility clears away the corrosion so the power can flow. And practice keeps our hands on the keys until the Spirit turns halting notes into living harmony.

If you will seek, you will receive. If you will ask, believing, you will be endowed. And if you will practice, the Lord will magnify what He has given you until His power flows freely through you.

Take hold of the gift. Hone it. Let it build you upward in Christ and outward in service, until one day you find yourself not merely trying to play—but becoming the very instrument through which God makes His music known.

**Practice:** This week, take time to name the gift you sense stirring in you—even if it feels small, halting, or weak. Offer it to the Lord in prayer, confessing your dependence and asking Him to clear away every trace of pride or fear that corrodes the connection. Then practice it. Speak the word of encouragement, extend the hand of healing, bear the testimony, seek the revelation. Do it like a child at the piano, trusting that every note—however rough—is a step toward harmony. Watch as His power flows, not to glorify you, but to let His own life, His own music, be expressed through you.

This is the same pattern the Lord has always worked—gifts given, gifts practiced, gifts magnified. When you take hold of your gift, you take hold of Him—and He lifts you in the next turn of the helix, higher and higher.

## Chapter 9 Notes

1 Nauvoo Relief Society Minutes, Apr 28, 1842

2 Etymology: *"Gethsemane"* (Hebrew *gat šĕmānê*) literally means oil press. That's standard biblical lexicon knowledge, so you don't need a citation unless you want to footnote it (e.g., Strong's Concordance H1068).

Luke 22:44—*"his sweat was as it were great drops of blood falling down to the ground."*
Matthew 26:36 / Mark 14:32—both name Gethsemane as the location.

3 History of the Church 4:604; Nauvoo Relief Society Minutes, Apr. 28, 1842

4 D&C 46:9–26; History of the Church 1:283–284

5 D&C 46:30; TPJS 203–204

6 2 Nephi 3:21–23; Joseph Smith—History 1:28–29

7 Joseph described himself as *"an obscure boy... of no consequence in the world"* (Joseph Smith Papers, History, circa Summer 1832, p. 3).

8 Wallace D. Wattles, The Science of Getting Rich (1910), Chapter 3.

# Angels and Powers from Beyond the Veil

## Heaven' s Help and Deliverance from Hell' s Imitations

---

### Have Angels Ceased to Minister

Moroni asked the piercing question: *"Have angels ceased to appear unto the children of men? Or has he withheld the power of the Holy Ghost from them?"* His answer was equally clear: *"Nay; neither have angels ceased to minister unto the children of men"* (Moroni 7:29).

This chapter explores that question.

If angels have not ceased, then what is their role among Christ's followers today? How do they minister, and what should we expect from their presence?

And if miracles are inseparably tied to their ministry—as Moroni testifies—what does it mean when a people lose faith in both?

Joseph Smith answered boldly: *"If men do not receive angels, they are not saved."*[1]

To him, angelic ministry wasn't optional or ornamental—it was central to the plan of salvation.

Angels delivered revelation to Adam, to Abraham, to Daniel. In Joseph's own life, they came again—delivering ancient records, unveiling truths long hidden, and instructing him in the work of restoration.[2]

He taught that their ministry must continue among all true disciples. Without it, heaven's chain of communication is broken.

Angels are not abstract symbols but real beings, sent by the Godhead to comfort, instruct, protect, and deliver. They are one of heaven's greatest assurances that the Lord still walks with His people.

The principle is plain: where faith in Christ is vibrant, angels appear; where unbelief reigns, they withdraw. As with miracles, their presence or absence is the litmus test of a living church.

## Angelic Ministry – Heaven's Messengers in the Work of God

Moroni testified that angels remain subject to Christ, ministering at His command, declaring His word, and preparing the way among the children of men (Moroni 7:29–31).

Look, I'm not going to beat around the bush: Joseph Smith was visited by angels. They were a living, concrete reality in his experience.

> *He saw angels.*
> *He talked with them.*
> *He learned from them.*

That's as straightforward as it gets. What happened in scripture happened again through Joseph—and it can still happen today.

If you've read scripture, you'll immediately recognize that Joseph's experiences matched the pattern seen from Adam to John the Revelator.

The sobering truth is this: when God moves His work forward, He always sends both mortal and immortal servants.

Angels are the King's envoys, sent from His presence to assist those who will receive them.

Their role is consistent:

> *To* ***warn*** *and call people to repentance.*
> *To* ***teach*** *and strengthen chosen vessels.*
> *To* ***testify of Christ*** *and fulfill God's promises.*
> *To* ***deliver*** *and prepare the way for His coming.*

Where faith is alive, both the gifts of the Spirit and the ministry of angels will be present. A church without angels is a church without life.

The Lord promised it would not be so for His true followers:

> *"I will pour out my spirit upon all flesh; and your sons and your daughters shall prophesy, your old men shall dream dreams, your young men shall see visions: and also upon the servants and upon the handmaids in those days will I pour out my spirit."* (Joel 2:28–29)

Heaven's servants are sent to all who hear and obey the Lord's voice—men, women, and children alike. In His eyes, all are equally capable of receiving His word and carrying His work forward.

### Scriptural Foundations—The Pattern of Angelic Work

From the first pages of scripture, angels appear as active participants in God's dealings with mankind.

This is a powerful truth: they are not decorative details in the story—they are main characters, essential messengers in the unfolding of the Father's plan.

### Old Testament

> **Genesis 19:** Two angels come to Lot, warning him of God's judgment and guiding his family to safety before the destruction of Sodom.
> **Genesis 28:12–13:** Jacob dreams of a ladder reaching to heaven, with angels ascending and descending—*a* picture of constant communication between God and man, connecting earth to heaven.
> **Daniel 6:22:** An angel shuts the lions' mouths to preserve Daniel's life, demonstrating their role as protectors of the faithful.

### New Testament

> **Luke 1:11–19:** Gabriel stands before Zacharias, announcing the birth of John and giving him detailed instructions. Joseph Smith taught that Gabriel was the same being as Noah—a mortal prophet who fulfilled his mission and later ministered as a glorified angel.
> **Luke 1:26–33:** Gabriel appears to Mary, declaring the coming of the Son of God.

> **Matthew 28:2–7:** An angel rolls back the stone of Christ's tomb, announces the resurrection, and commissions the women to tell His disciples.

### Book of Mormon

> **1 Nephi 11–14:** An angel guides Nephi through a panoramic vision, explaining Lehi's dream and revealing the mission of the Son of God.
> **Mosiah 27:10–17:** An angel appears to Alma the Younger and the sons of Mosiah, rebuking them for destroying the church and calling Alma to repentance.
> **3 Nephi 7:18:** Angels minister to Nephi and to those who are baptized, bearing witness of their faithfulness.

Across all dispensations, the pattern is clear: angels **warn, teach, testify, and deliver**. Wherever heaven actively engages in earthly affairs, angels point back to Christ and carry out His word.

## Joseph's Encounters with Angels

From the very beginning of his prophetic mission, Joseph Smith's life was marked by angelic ministry. These messengers came not only to deliver instructions, but to prepare, protect, and guide him through the unfolding of the Lord's work.

### The Sacred Grove

Before Joseph received his First Vision, a power seized him with such force that he felt he was doomed to destruction. In that moment of desperate prayer, light pierced the darkness and dispersed it.

Then, as he described: *"a personage appeared in the midst of that pillar of light, and another personage soon appeared, who exactly resembled the first."*[3] He did not name them—he simply bore witness of the divine presence he encountered.

This was the same law Christ declared from the beginning: *"I am the light which shineth in darkness, and the darkness comprehendeth it not"* (D&C 6:21).

When darkness presses upon the soul, heaven sends light. Heaven's presence breaks through the darkness to reveal truth and extend a divine commission to the humble seeker.

## Tutored by Angels

It began in 1823 when a messenger named Moroni appeared at night, filling Joseph's small attic room with light. He came three times that night, and again the next morning, instructing Joseph about the record hidden in the hill Cumorah, quoting scripture, and revealing the work that lay ahead.

That visit was only the beginning. Year after year, Moroni returned—warning, teaching, rehearsing the promises of God, and unfolding the work step by step. Joseph later recalled that the angel *"continued to give me instructions... concerning what the Lord was going to do, and how and in what manner His kingdom was to be conducted in the last days."*[4]

Imagine what it meant for a young man to be tutored by an angel of God for years. Think of how his mind expanded, how his soul was shaped, how his very character was molded into what Christ needed him to become. Joseph had only a third-grade education, yet look at the schooling he received: his classroom was heaven, and his teacher was a messenger sent from the presence of God.

Joseph never hid his youth and weakness: *"I was left to all kinds of temptations... I frequently fell into many foolish errors... But through the grace of God I continued to be preserved... I had full confidence in obtaining a divine manifestation, as I had previously had one."*[5]

This was the paradox of Joseph's preparation: unlearned in the wisdom of men, yet daily instructed by angels. No wonder he grew into the man able to translate scripture, organize a church, reveal doctrine, and set in motion the work of the last days. He was mentored by heaven itself.

And Moroni wasn't the only messenger.

During the march of Zion's Camp, Joseph testified that divine power preserved him and the brethren, warning and sparing them from unseen dangers.[6]

At the Kirtland Temple dedication, eyewitnesses reported angels filling the room, their presence accompanied by the sound of a rushing wind. In quieter moments, Joseph also spoke of private angelic visits—bringing comfort, instructing translation, and ministering through him to others.[7]

These were not rare exceptions but evidence of a living connection between heaven and earth.

This is heaven's way.

Moses, slow of speech; Amos, a herdsman; Enoch, a lad the people despised—each was taken in weakness and tutored until he became strong, prepared for heaven's assignments.

The same pattern unfolded with Joseph, and it will unfold again.

For Joseph, angels were never curiosities. They were fellow servants, *"sent forth to minister for them who shall be heirs of salvation"* (Hebrews 1:14).

Their ministry was practical, purposeful, and always centered on Christ's work. The same purposes emerge again and again: to **warn**, to **teach**, to **testify of Christ**, and to **deliver**. What God has always done, He continues to do today.

This isn't just a story to admire from a distance—it's the Lord's way of preparing us. If heaven invested years in shaping one man for a mighty work, it will surely invest the same care to shape a people for Zion.

What God once did to shape a prophet, He is willing to shape a people—and even you.

## Christ, Joseph, and the Eternal Pattern

From the beginning, angels have come as the King's envoys—sent to prepare mortals for their missions in God's work. Never for spectacle, always for purpose. And those purposes repeat.

If you trace the lives of Christ and Joseph Smith side by side, the parallels are unmistakable. The same roles appear. The same assignments recur. The same outcomes unfold.

This is heaven's way of teaching us two truths:

> *God governs His work by a steady order.*
> *God does not change His pattern.*

The messengers who strengthened Jesus, who tutored Joseph, who guided Nephi—these are the same kind of messengers sent to you and me.

The following table brings the evidence together in a single view. In one sweep, you will see the harmony of Christ's ministry, Joseph's ministry, and the wider scriptural record—all converging into one witness of how angels operate with God's chosen vessels.

**Roles of Angelic Ministry—Christ, Joseph, and Scripture Side by Side**

| Role of Angels | In the Life of Christ | In the Life of Joseph Smith | Scriptural Pattern | Key Outcome for the Saints |
|---|---|---|---|---|
| **Announcement of Mission** | Gabriel announces Christ's birth to Mary (Luke 1:26–33); angels proclaim to shepherds (Luke 2:8–14) | Moroni announces Joseph's prophetic calling in 1823 through repeated night visits | Old: Samuel's call by the voice of the Lord (1 Samuel 3); New: Gabriel to Zacharias (Luke 1:11–19) | Saints learn that God calls His servants directly through heavenly messengers. |
| **Instruction & Revelation** | Angels minister to Jesus after His temptation in the wilderness (Matthew 4:11) | Moroni tutors Joseph on scripture and prophecy year after year (1823–1827) | Nephi's panoramic vision guided by an angel (1 Nephi 11–14) | Saints receive heaven's wisdom and gain clarity about their mission. |
| **Warning & Deliverance** | An angel warns Joseph and Mary to flee to Egypt (Matthew 2:13–15) | Moroni warns Joseph of spiritual danger and his need for preparation before receiving the plates | Lot delivered from Sodom by angels (Genesis 19); Daniel preserved in lions' den (Daniel 6:22) | Saints are preserved from spiritual and physical destruction when they heed divine warning. |
| **Commission & Ordination** | John baptizes Jesus (Matthew 3:13–17), divinely witnessed | A messenger at Cumorah entrusts Joseph with the plates and commissions his mission | Moses commissioned at the burning bush with an angel present (Acts 7:30–35) | Saints are entrusted with divine assignments and given power to fulfill them. |

| | | | | |
|---|---|---|---|---|
| **Protection in Danger** | Angels encamp around Christ and His disciples; He promises legions of angels if He asks (Matthew 26:53) | Zion's Camp experiences unseen angelic protection; Saints preserved during persecution | Elisha surrounded by heavenly hosts (2 Kings 6:15–17); Peter freed from prison (Acts 12:7–10) | Saints are shielded from mortal and spiritual threats when they act in obedience. |
| **Strength in Trial** | An angel strengthens Christ in Gethsemane (Luke 22:43) | Angels visit Joseph when he is discouraged, renewing his courage | An angel ministers to Hagar in her despair (Genesis 21:17–19) | Saints are renewed in weakness and enabled to continue their walk. |
| **Testimony of Glory** | Angels announce Christ's resurrection at the tomb (Matthew 28:2–7) | Angels testify of Christ's acceptance in the Kirtland Temple, witnessed by many | Angels minister to disciples in prison (Acts 5:19–20) | Saints are strengthened in faith, assured of Christ's living reality, and emboldened to testify. |

## The Lesson for Every Disciple

When you set the lives of Christ and Joseph next to each other, the symmetry is breathtaking.

> The same roles repeat.
> The same order governs.
> The same outcomes follow.

This is no accident—it is Heaven's signature, tying the mission of the Restoration directly to the ministry of Jesus Christ.

Look at how Moroni's night visits mirror Gabriel's annunciation, or how angels testified in Kirtland just as they did at Christ's tomb.[8]

What looks like repetition is actually design—a perfect type and shadow, heaven weaving the Restoration into the very course Christ Himself set.

What does this teach us?

That angelic ministry isn't reserved for Christ alone, or for Joseph alone. It is the inheritance of every disciple who walks in these same footsteps.

If you walk in the Church of the Lamb of God, angelic help will not be rare. It is one of heaven's tender signs.

Their ministry is the living pulse of a healthy church, and their absence is the withering mark of the church of the devil.

## Invitation to the Reader

The ministry of angels was never meant to be lost in ancient history or confined to prophets alone.

Joseph echoed the same truth: *"If you live up to your privileges, the angels cannot be restrained from being your associates."*[9]

If you desire their presence, begin as the prophets did:

> **Live** so the Spirit of God can abide with you.
> **Ask** the Lord to appoint you to His work—whatever it may be.
> **Receive** every word He gives you.
> **Obey** His voice, no matter how small it seems.

Each act of faith places you on the upward path. Each step of obedience draws you higher. The Lord gives you holy ordinances as His personal appointments—holy times and places where He commits to meet you, stewardships He entrusts you with, and charges He whispers to your soul.

And, as is His way, it is often in the midst of such ordinances that He manifests Himself, sending His servants to strengthen your hand. When the time is right, a messenger will meet you at the next turn of the helix—steadying your step and fixing your gaze higher still.

Their voices echo His word, and their presence testifies that heaven is near.

But heaven does more than speak—it acts.

## From Angels to Miracles: Heaven's Voice and Heaven's Law

Just as angels reveal heaven's voice, miracles reveal heaven's law.

Every visitation is a message; every miracle is a manifestation. Angels declare the word of Christ, and miracles demonstrate that His word governs even the elements of this world.

Together they form the twin witness that the Church of the Lamb of God is alive: heaven speaking and heaven acting in the midst of mortality.

When Moroni asked, *"Have miracles ceased?"* he answered his own question with urgency: *"Behold I say unto you, Nay; neither have angels ceased to minister unto the children of men"* (Moroni 7:29). To deny miracles is to deny God Himself, for *"it is by faith that miracles are wrought"* (Moroni 7:37).

What we call miracles are not violations of natural law, but the unveiling of laws higher than those we presently understand.

Mortality itself is a Telestial kingdom—fallen, dimmed, and bound by lesser law (D&C 76:81–85). It is a world where corruption and decay reign, where sin and death hold sway.

But the Lord revealed that there are other kingdoms above it: the Terrestrial, governed by a greater law, and the Celestial, ruled by the highest laws of all (D&C 88:36–38).

Each kingdom operates by its own order: *"Unto every kingdom is given a law; and unto every law there are certain bounds also and conditions"* (D&C 88:38).

The Telestial order is the realm of mortality, where disease and death are natural. In the Terrestrial kingdom, however, the inhabitants will have Terrestrial bodies—no longer subject to disease or death, but enjoying incorruption and peace (D&C 76:71–79).

And in the Celestial realm, the redeemed receive Celestial bodies—perfect, eternal, glorified with the light and power of God. There They dwell in the fullness of divine life—the Father and the Mother, united in everlasting glory, the wellspring from which all creation flows. In that glory, Their children share Their image, perfected in love, light, and creative power (D&C 76:50–70; D&C 88:28–29).

This hierarchy reveals why miracles happen. A miracle isn't God breaking His own rules—it's God allowing the higher rules of His kingdom to touch the lower.

When celestial law intersects with telestial conditions, what mortals see as nature breaking its own rules is actually the natural outworking of a higher world.

Alma reminded us that *"by small and simple things are great things brought to pass"* (Alma 37:6).

Ether testified that *"in the gift of his Son hath God prepared a more excellent way; and it is by faith that miracles are wrought"* (Ether 12:11, 16).

Taken together, these witnesses show that faith is the bridge. When we truly trust Christ, we step into alignment with the higher laws of His kingdom, and what mortals call a miracle follows naturally.

Miracles are glimpses of God's own life made visible among us. They radiat with beauty, settle with peace, and pulse with power—glimpses of celestial glory shining through a fallen world.

They show us the world as God has always intended it to be.

## Christ the Miracle Worker

When Jesus performed His many miracles, each act revealed Celestial law overruling Telestial limits.

When He multiplied the loaves and fishes (John 6:5–14), He was not fabricating matter out of nothing—He was manifesting the Celestial order in which all matter obeys His will.

When He raised Lazarus from the dead (John 11:43–44), He was not reversing mortality—He was showing that in the higher kingdom, death itself has no claim.

These weren't parlor tricks. They were previews of a higher order manifesting itself.

And these glimpses of celestial order weren't confined to Galilee. In the days of the Restoration, the same divine pattern reappeared—miracles bore witness that the kingdom of God was stirring again, and that the risen Christ was guiding His work on the earth.

## Miracles in Joseph's Ministry

The Restoration carried the same witness. Through Joseph Smith, miracles confirmed that Jesus Christ was working among men again—not as passing wonders, but as signs that Zion's foundations were being laid.

In both Kirtland and Nauvoo, when sickness swept through the Saints, Joseph laid hands in Christ's name and the afflicted rose restored.[10]

Even the dying were restored—reminders that the same Jesus who once cried, *"Lazarus, come forth"* (John 11:43), was still at work through Joseph, confirming that Zion's rise was real.

## Why Miracles Matter

Miracles are not spectacles meant to dazzle unbelievers. They are heaven's testimony that Christ is present with His people.

Every gift, every angel, every healing is given *"that all may be profited thereby"* (Moroni 10:8). Their purpose is:

> To anchor faith
> To confirm truth
> To assure the Saints that they walk in His company
> To prepare a people for His coming

In this Telestial world of sickness, death, and corruption, miracles offer heaven's glimpse of higher law. They pull back the veil and show that mortality is not the final order.[11]

A miracle is the Terrestrial unveiling upon the Telestial, or even the Celestial descending into view. It's God reminding His children that this fallen world is temporary and that His higher kingdoms are already prepared for those who will receive them.[12]

Moroni explained it most clearly when he taught that angels *"are subject unto him, to minister according to the word of his command... and the office of their ministry is to call men unto repentance, and to fulfill and to do the work of the covenants of the Father... to prepare the way among the children of men, by declaring the word of Christ unto the chosen vessels of the Lord, that they may bear testimony of him"* (Moroni 7:30–32).

This is the true ministry of angels, and it reveals the purpose of all miracles:

1. To call men and women to repentance.
2. To fulfill the premortal covenants the Father made with His chosen vessels.
3. So that those chosen vessels can bear testimony of Christ to the rest (the residue) of His children.

Miracles aren't random flashes of power. They are the Lord's covenant work in motion—reaching, teaching, and empowering His servants so the whole body of Christ may be edified and brought unto Him.

Where miracles abound, they signal that the Church of the Lamb of God is alive—that faith is active, that covenant promises are in force, that heaven is near. But where miracles cease, it is because faith has ceased (Moroni 7:37).

Their absence is not a sign of heaven's unwillingness, but of mankind's unbelief (Matthew 13:58; Ether 12:12). It is a warning flare that the church in question has drifted into the order of the devil, no matter what name it claims.

This is why Moroni and Joseph both pressed the point so urgently: to deny miracles is to deny Christ Himself.

If you strip away the miraculous, you strip away the covenant. The gifts, angels, and healings are not decorative—they are foundational. They are the pulse of Zion's life, and without them the body of Christ withers.

Miracles matter because they are covenant signs. They show that Christ's Spirit and power are still being poured out on repentant, believing souls. They remind us that the veil is thin, that heaven has not withdrawn, and that the same Jesus who touched lepers still reaches out His hand today.

## The Greatest Miracle

All miracles point upward, but the greatest miracle of all is the triumph of life over death.

In this Telestial estate, death reigns. In the Terrestrial estate, death is withheld for a season. But in the Celestial estate, death is swallowed up in eternal life.

The resurrection of Jesus Christ revealed Celestial law in its fullness—showing that even the grave must bow to Him. Through His victory, the life of the Father and the Mother stands revealed: love stronger than death, creation restored, and the promise of unending increase made sure.

This is the highest miracle—mortality itself clothed in immortality, corruption putting on incorruption, the last enemy destroyed (1 Corinthians 15:26, 53–54; Mosiah 16:7–8).

Yet heaven hasn't left us to wait for the last day before tasting that power.

The rebirth of a soul through fire and the Holy Ghost is the great miracle available here and now. In this baptism of fire, the seed of endless life is planted in mortal clay. It transforms the natural man into a saint and quickens him with the powers of the world to come.

Resurrection and rebirth stand together as companion witnesses: one foreshadowing the end of death, the other granting power to live in newness of life even in a world still bound by death.

> **Christ's resurrection:** the crowning miracle of His victory.
> **Our rebirth:** the miracle of victory over the natural man.

Together they testify that heaven's highest order has already begun to manifest into the lowest, and that all who receive it may rise.

Yet, the greatest miracle is not confined to life after death, but also deliverance in the midst of life itself.

The multiplication of loaves, the healing of limbs, even the raising of Lazarus—all these signs pointed higher. But the greater wonder was always this: the casting out of darkness.

Every healing, every gift of the Spirit, every angelic visitation testifies of the One who declared: *"Now is the judgment of this world: now shall the prince of this world be cast out"* (John 12:31).

In both Christ's ministry and Joseph's, the climax of miracles was not spectacle but liberation—the freeing of souls from bondage to sin, devils, and death.

Physical healing is only partial if spiritual chains remain.

Pause and let that settle. Don't rush past it. Read it again. Let it sear into your spirit, because it is that important.

Physical healing is only partial if spiritual chains remain.

All the praying, all the scripture searching, all the good deeds of mortality are meant to bring you to one thing: Christ's power to deliver. If they do not lead you there—if you leave this life still shackled by sin and darkness—then the outward work has missed its inward purpose. You may rise from a sickbed, but if your soul remains bound, you are still held captive.

But when the Spirit of Christ drives out evil, a person is truly made whole—they are set free.

Too often, we speak words over the afflicted without the power of deliverance. Lips may pronounce a blessing, yet if the chains of darkness remain untouched, the soul stays bound and the comfort and healing never comes.

True healing requires more than ritual language—it requires the living Spirit of Christ breaking the bands that bind, lifting the burden, and filling the wounded heart with His peace. This is why His servants were sent not only to heal the sick, but to cast out devils.

These two acts belong together, and in Him they are never in vain.

Pause and consider: this is why the Lord gives us these gifts, sends angels, and works miracles among His people.

Not merely to comfort or impress.

> *But to protect.*
> *To liberate.*

Christ healed the blind—but He also rebuked unclean spirits. He opened deaf ears—but He also freed the boy bound by a devil. He calmed the storm—but He also cast out a legion into the swine.[13]

The pattern is clear: gifts, angels, and miracles are heaven's way of pushing back the adversary.

Joseph saw the same. When devils attacked in the grove, God came with light. When evil spirits troubled the early Saints, he discerned, rebuked, and cast them out. The Lord armed him with power not only to build, but also to defend.[14]

This is where our path now leads. Where there is light, there will be opposition. And where there are miracles, there will also be battles.

The gifts are not toys. They are weapons. The angels are not visitors. They are allies. The miracles are not accidents. They are deliverance.

### Deliverance, Deception, and Christ's Voice

Jesus taught the parable of the ten virgins for a reason. It wasn't a distant prophecy—it was a diagnosis of the last days. The dividing line between the wise and the foolish would not be outward behavior, but the condition of their hearts—**whether they had taken the Holy Spirit for their guide.** Only those who carry His Spirit within them will be able to stand when the Bridegroom comes.

The Lord made this unmistakably clear:

> *"They that are wise and have received the truth, and have taken the Holy Spirit for their guide, and have not been deceived—verily I say unto you, they shall not be hewn down and cast into the fire." (D&C 45:56–57)*

> *Wisdom is receiving truth.*
> *Wisdom is taking the Spirit for a guide.*
> *Wisdom is refusing deception.*

In ancient texts, wisdom was personified as a divine feminine presence—the voice that calls, the light that warns, the hand that guides. Without forcing symbolism, it's enough to recognize that when we receive truth and the Spirit becomes our guide, **we are aligning with that heavenly wisdom that has always sought to lead God's children to safety.**

And if wisdom leads us toward safety, then we must also recognize what draws us away from her influence.

> *What deceives?*
> *What opposes the Spirit?*
> *What clouds the heart and muffles the quiet, guiding voice we were meant to hear?*

To understand this, we must first acknowledge a truth we seldom name: **evil spirits are not an occasional intrusion into the human story.**[15] They are the atmosphere every soul is born into, the environment in which we live our mortal lives.

The scriptures describe them as influences that work *"in you," "on you,"* or *"around you,"* pressing on thoughts, emotions, and desires in ways that often go unnoticed—not because they are subtle, but because they are constant.

And here's the part we rarely articulate: **The adversary doesn't work alone.**

Just as heaven operates through a vast network of angels, ministers, messengers, and the Spirit itself, the forces of darkness mirror that order. The adversary is as organized as the light. As above, so below—a hierarchy of opposition, each rank with its own methods of influence.

Together they form an organized opposition with a single, simple aim: **distort the connection between the soul and heaven.**

Think of an old AM radio. When you turn the dial just off the mark, the signal goes fuzzy—static, distortion, a wash of noise. But when the dial aligns precisely, the voice comes through clear. Evil spirits can't sever the heavenly signal, but they can crowd it—nudging thoughts, stirring impulses, amplifying fears—until the Spirit's clarity grows harder to discern.

This interference explains why deliverance isn't a side note in the gospel. It is foundational—the first miracle Jesus performed, and the first miracle of the Restoration.

Mark records Jesus entering the synagogue at Capernaum and teaching with authority. A man, overcome by an unclean spirit, cried out. Jesus rebuked the spirit, and it departed immediately. No drawn-out struggle. No escalating conflict. Truth spoke, and darkness fled (Mark 1:21–27).

As His first public act, it revealed something essential: deliverance is the first miracle because oppression is the first problem.

Joseph's story follows the same divine order—not by accident, but by design.

His first miracle was freeing Newel Knight from an evil spirit. Newel had been tormented by a dark spirit that seized his body and robbed him of peace. At Joseph's urging, he attempted to pray, only to be overcome more violently. Joseph came, rebuked the spirit, and the oppression broke.[16] The peace that followed was unmistakable. As with Jesus, this first miracle revealed the core battle Joseph had been sent to confront: **spiritual captivity.**

The Savior was signaling that the Restoration would begin where His own ministry began: **breaking the chains of spiritual bondage so truth could take root.**

This is why the baptism of fire isn't optional but integral to the soul's eternal progression.

And this is where everything in this chapter turns.

It's not a symbolic warmth, nor a ritual gesture, nor a box to be checked. It's literal transformation—a new birth in the fullest sense.

Earlier in this book, we taught that being born again involves three essential elements that mirror a literal birth—three threads woven through all creation (Moses 6:59; John 3:5).

> ***Water*** *marks the moment of separation from the old life.*
> ***Spirit*** *is the moment new life begins.*
> ***Blood*** *is the atoning sacrifice of Christ that makes new life possible.*

But at that point in the book, something was held back—on purpose.

Now—having walked with you this far—you're ready for the greater keys to understanding what the *"Spirit"* portion of the new birth actually carries.

When the Spirit enters a soul in the mighty change of heart, it does more than cleanse. It imparts inheritance—spiritual genetics.

Children resemble the parents who gave them life. No one expects two elephants to lay a chicken egg. No one cracks open a chicken egg expecting to find an elephant.

Life begets after its own kind.

In the same way, when you are spiritually begotten of Christ, you begin to resemble Christ.

You start to take on His traits, His desires, His clarity, His compassion—and yes, the authority that backs His word.

It's not the timbre of your voice that changes, nor the particular words you choose.

It's the power those words now carry—because you speak with the tongue of angels, bearing His Spirit and His authority.

Nephi taught:

> *"Angels speak by the power of the Holy Ghost... wherefore, they speak the words of Christ." (2 Nephi 32:3)*

When His Spirit is in you, His words become your words—because your will becomes swallowed up in His (Mosiah 15:7). After such a change, your desires spring from Him.

The Lord taught Joseph that *"whatsoever you shall ask in my name... that will I do"* (D&C 50:29–30). Why? Because He gives you what to pray for. His words enter your soul. Your will aligns with His. And when His words become your words, heaven responds—because heaven recognizes its own.

This is why deliverance works.

> *Not because of technique.*
> *Not because of ritual.*
> *Not because of volume.*

Deliverance is the voice of a newly born child of God speaking with the authority of the One who begot them.

This also reframes the battle. Darkness doesn't retreat because you raise your voice or grit your teeth. It retreats because Christ's light drives it out. And when His Spirit fills you—when your thoughts align with truth and your words carry faith—darkness has no place to remain.

Where His Spirit dwells, false spirits cannot remain. Just as darkness flees when light enters a room, evil spirits withdraw when the light of Christ fills the soul.

> *"The light shineth in darkness, and the darkness comprehendeth it not."* (John 1:5)
>
> *"That which is of God is light... and that light groweth brighter and brighter until the perfect day."* (D&C 50:24)

Light and darkness cannot occupy the same space. Nor can they share the same heart.

But make no mistake: If your heart remains unchanged, the rebirth has not yet happened. Without that change, there is no power. Without power, there is no discernment. And without discernment, deception is inevitable.

This brings us to a piercing framework—one that strips away illusion.

> *Do you speak with the tongue of angels?*
> *Do your words carry light, clarity, peace, and truth?*
> *Do they push darkness back rather than stir it up?*

And if not—why not?

Consider this:[17] if Jesus were to rebuke and cast out evil spirits, what would His success rate be?
**One hundred percent.**

If an angel were sent to do the same, what would their success rate be?
**One hundred percent.**

So what is your success rate?
Shouldn't it be the same?
Why isn't it?

I'm asking you to see the gap—between where you are and where you've been promised you can be. Remember **who your spiritual Parent is—and what His Spirit can do through you.**

This is why deliverance appears at the beginning of both the gospel and the Restoration. It is not peripheral; it is foundational. You cannot rise into a Zion-hearted life while carrying oppression in your soul. Until your heart is cleared, you cannot advance. Until light drives out darkness, you cannot see clearly enough to discern truth from deception. And without discernment, you cannot take the Holy Spirit as your guide.

Wise virgins act. Foolish virgins delay. Both feel the pressures of mortality—but only one group prepares their hearts for the Bridegroom.

Many assume they are among the wise simply because they've been baptized, confirmed, or entered holy places. But the oil of the wise isn't activity, ceremony, or mere familiarity with sacred spaces. The oil is the Spirit Himself—the indwelling transformation that changes the heart and fills it with light. Without that change, a person may wear the appearance of devotion while remaining spiritually unchanged. And unchanged hearts cannot speak with the tongue of angels, cannot discern deception, and will not stand when the moment of separation comes.

With this foundation in place, we now return to the practical teachings of Jesus and Joseph. Once you understand why this battle exists and how Christ equips you to face it, you're ready to learn how to walk in protection, peace, and spiritual clarity.

The scriptures don't portray evil spirits as a single, indistinct mass. They describe a range of beings that vary in origin, character, intent, and influence. This variety matters because discernment depends on knowing what you're actually encountering. Just as there are many gifts of the Spirit, there are also many expressions of its opposite—each bent on pulling the heart away from heaven's guidance.

Anciently, the Lord spoke clearly of *"devils," "unclean spirits," "familiar spirits," "lying spirits,"* and *"seducing spirits."*[18] These terms aren't interchangeable; they reflect real differences that Joseph, the early Saints, and many today have quietly observed. When we speak of *"evil spirits,"* we're speaking of a landscape—not a single figure in the night.

Below is a simple narrative summary that gathers the clearest, most doctrinally supported categories. This isn't an exhaustive demonology or an attempt to build a system. Rather, it's a way of naming the influences the Saints repeatedly encountered so we can better recognize the pressures at work in our own lives.

### 1. devils[19]—The Rebellious Third

These are the spirits who followed lucifer in the premortal rebellion and were cast out with him. They never received physical bodies, and their hatred is ancient. Their intent is destruction—of purity, of faith, of peace, of covenant. They tempt, distort, and infiltrate. They cannot feel compassion. When the scriptures speak of beings who "seek to destroy the souls of men," they usually mean these.

They are fewer in number than other kinds of spirits, but their malice is unmistakable. You feel their influence in flashes of sharp despair, sudden rage, or impulses that seem foreign to your nature. Their purpose is dominion.

### 2. Unclean Spirits[20]—The Spirits of the Wicked Dead

These are spirits of people who once lived and died in their sins—men and women who fed appetites and addictions, who cultivated bitterness, cruelty, lust, or violence. In death, their desires remain, but they have no body through which to act.

This creates a kind of hunger—an aching compulsion—and a drive to fasten themselves to the living. They gravitate toward people who indulge the very appetites they once carried. When the scriptures speak of spirits walking through *"dry places,"* seeking rest and finding none, it is these. They attach through habit, imitation, and resonance.

Often their presence feels more like heaviness than attack—an amplification of old patterns, a rekindling of temptations you thought long resolved.

### 3. Familiar Spirits[21]—Spirits of Deception and Spirits of Bloodline

Among the most subtle and penetrating influences are familiar spirits. In scripture, the word familiar doesn't simply mean *"well-known."* It points to intimacy, proximity, relationship—often implying a spirit that knows the person it clings to. Some are deceivers, appearing in forms or voices that mimic the holy. Others are far more personal: spirits bound by bloodline, whose mortal lives were marked by trauma, addiction, cruelty, or unresolved misery. They speak in family tones, trade on inherited wounds, and feel frighteningly close.

These spirits know your weaknesses because they once carried the same wounds. They know the family story because they lived it. Across generations, they attach themselves to relatives whose pain mirrors their own, slipping in through unhealed sorrow, inherited patterns, or generational wounds. Their influence is rarely dramatic; more often it's quiet, persistent, and heavy with grief—showing up as chronic affliction, emotional turmoil, or recurring pain that blessings ease for a time but never fully remove.

Some familiar spirits cling because misery loves company. Others latch on because tormenting a living descendant distracts them from their own despair. Some attach through unresolved grief; others reach instinctively for what feels familiar because they've never known peace. This doesn't excuse their behavior, but it explains the pattern: familiarity gives them access.

In rare cases, when the Spirit directs, you can cast out such spirits with compassion rather than confrontation—because beneath their darkness may lie an ancient wound, a life marked by suffering, or a heart that never found healing. Casting them out doesn't condemn them; it may begin their healing too and open the way for angels to minister to them in the spirit world.

These familiar spirits—whether deceptive mimics or generational remnants—share one aim: to draw the heart away from heaven by imitating comfort, replaying ancestral pain, or amplifying inherited patterns. Their presence underscores the need for discernment grounded in the Holy Spirit, not sentiment, not nostalgia, and not fear.

### 4. Foul Spirits[22]—Spirits of Deep Affliction

These are the beings behind some of the most severe forms of spiritual bondage. In the New Testament, when the disciples couldn't cast out a spirit afflicting a young man, Jesus said: *"This kind goeth not out but by prayer and fasting."* (Matthew 17:21, Mark 9:29)

Foul spirits operate through torment—nightmares, compulsions, paralyzing fear, and oppressive thoughts. Their goal isn't merely temptation but debilitation. They assault the mind, cloud perception, and can trouble the body itself. They aren't common, but they appear wherever deep trauma, prolonged sin, or generational wounds open the door.

These are the spirits that create the *"heavy darkness"* some feel—an air of dread rather than simple temptation.

### 5. False Spirits[23]—The Most Dangerous of All

These are the spirits the Lord warned the early Saints about in D&C 50. Their aim is overtly religious. They spark excitement without substance, stage manifestations without edification, and stir emotion without truth. They draw attention, feed vanity, and pass themselves off as gifts of the Spirit.

They can make people shake, shout, speak in false tongues, or fall into trances. They flourish wherever order is cast off. They push people into excess—too much zeal, too much certainty, too much self-importance—until the true Spirit withdraws and confusion follows.

False spirits deceive the humble, mimic revelation, and counterfeit every true gift of God. They tailor their lures to the spiritual person who seeks experience without discernment.

### 6. Unembodied Spirits[24]—The Opportunistic Dark Influencers

There are also spirits who never obtained mortal bodies. Quick, mocking, and opportunistic, they watch for openings—lust, rage, despair, or self-abandonment. Their movements are sudden: darting, pressing, whispering, rushing toward a weakness the moment the heart yields.

These spirits gather where vice gathers—in places where agency is dulled, appetites are inflamed, and boundaries collapse. They race toward emotional fractures like smoke drawn into a vacuum, seeking to amplify whatever darkness they find. Their influence doesn't feel ancient like the devils, nor familiar like ancestral spirits. It feels immediate—a sudden storm of thoughts, impulses, or images meant to push the soul further from the Spirit.

They aren't powerful, but they are persistent. Their influence is driven by opportunity, not authority. They cannot enter without consent, yet they press relentlessly toward that moment of surrender.

## Influence, Enticement, and Discernment

Every spirit seeks to entice—but they pull in opposite directions.

Mormon taught that the Spirit of Christ *"inviteth and enticeth to do good continually"* (Moroni 7:13), while *"the evil spirit"* works to deny Christ, weaken faith, and persuade toward darkness (Moroni 7:17). The distinction is absolute: *"He persuadeth no man to do good, no, not one... but whatsoever thing persuadeth men to do good is of God"* (Moroni 7:16).

Both good and evil spirits seek influence—one to raise the soul, the other to darken and destroy it.

Discernment begins by noticing which enticings are at work within you.

> *This is why the baptism of fire is essential.*
> *This is why the mighty change of heart is required.*

> *This is why taking the Holy Spirit as your guide is non-negotiable.*

Without a change of heart, we remain vulnerable to deception. With it, light breaks in—His words fill our mouths with His power, and darkness flees.

This is the heart of everything that follows.

The Lord warned the early Saints that *"many spirits... have gone forth in the earth, deceiving the world"* (D&C 50:2). He then gave them a command that has not expired: *"Ye shall inquire of the Lord to know whether it be of God"* (D&C 50:31).

You must understand this critical truth: discernment is not an advanced skill for the spiritually elite; it is the protecting wall around every sincere disciple of Christ. The question is not if spirits are influencing you, but *which ones*, and whether you recognize the source behind the thoughts, impressions, emotions, and pressures that move within your mind and heart.

Scripture gives three steady anchors that reveal spiritual influence with remarkable clarity. These are not complicated; the truth rarely is. Truth is beautifully simple, and simply beautiful. Every influence—divine, mortal, or demonic—can be discerned by testing its **trajectory**, its **fruit**, and its relationship to your **agency**.

**Trajectory** asks the simplest question: Where is this influence leading my heart?

Nephi taught that *"the evil spirit teacheth a man not to pray"* (2 Nephi 32:8). The Spirit of the Lord, by contrast, always increases the desire to pray, repent, believe, and act (see D&C 11:12–14).

Moroni gave the fuller doctrinal framework we talked about earlier—that every influence leading to Christ is of God, and every influence pulling away is not. The Trajectory Test simply applies that truth in real time.

That is trajectory. Does this influence point a soul toward good—toward God—or away from Him? The Spirit of the Lord always draws a soul toward humility, prayer, repentance, and obedience.

False spirits pull in the opposite direction. They whisper delay, distraction, indulgence, or self-justification. They produce thoughts that feel reasonable but spring from a reluctance to come to Christ. If an influence weakens your desire to pray, clouds your desire to repent, or shifts your focus away from the Lord, its trajectory reveals its source.

**Fruit** is equally revealing. Mormon taught that *"a bitter fountain cannot bring forth good water... wherefore, a man being a servant of the devil cannot follow Christ"* (Moroni 7:11). In contrast, he taught that *"neither can a good fountain bring forth bitter water... if he follow Christ he cannot be a servant of the devil"* (Moroni 7:11).

The Lord taught something similar: *"Ye shall know them by their fruits... every good tree bringeth forth good fruit; but a corrupt tree bringeth forth evil fruit. A good tree cannot bring forth evil fruit, neither can a corrupt tree bring forth good fruit... by their fruits ye shall know them"* (Matt 7:16-20).

Consider the fruit. The Spirit of the Lord produces clarity, peace, steadiness, hope, light, and a quiet desire to do good. False spirits generate confusion, heaviness, discouragement, accusation, fear, resentment, or spiritual numbness. I often call these the *"D's of the devil"**—nearly all begin with the same letter, and all point in the same direction: away from Christ.

Below is a simple list you may find helpful:

### D's of the devil

Deception
Depression
Despair
Division
Distraction
Distress
Despondence
Disagreement
Disconnection
Discouragement
Disorientation
Discontent
Damned
Debase
Damage
Distortion
Disgust
Disheartened
Disobedience
Discord
Disruption
Disquiet
Disillusion
Dissension
Dissatisfaction
Disorder
Disarray
Dirty
Disaster
Devalue
Destroy
Disturbance
Disrespect
Disregard
Disunity
Displacement
Disease
Disbelief
Disdain
Derision
Disparage
Denigrate
Decrease
Diminish
Degrade
Demolish
Discourteous
Death

** You may notice that throughout this work I do not capitalize devil, satan, lucifer, or adversary. This is a deliberate choice. While standard grammar treats these as proper names, I do not believe such terms warrant reverence or distinction. I therefore withhold capitalization as a matter of conscience and consistency.*

These influences don't merely inconvenience the soul—they *dim* or *dull* (two more D's of the devil) spiritual sensitivity. Anything that dulls your desire for truth, disturbs your peace, or disrupts your spiritual footing bears their fingerprints.

Agency is the third anchor. Heavenly influence always preserves it. Darkness always works to diminish it. Moses recorded that Satan's rebellion began with his attempt to *"destroy the agency of man"* and seize God's honor (Moses 4:3–4). The Lord taught Joseph that *"all truth is independent... to act for itself"* and that without agency, existence itself collapses (D&C 93:30–31).

This is agency: Wherever you feel pressure, compulsion, hurry, intrusion, or a sense that you're being cornered emotionally or spiritually, you're not experiencing the Spirit of God. Heaven persuades with long-suffering and patience. Darkness pushes and compels. Anything that seeks to usurp agency reveals its source.

These three anchors—trajectory, fruit, and agency—form the foundation for discernment.

*"Know your enemy, know yourself"* is a famous quote from Sun Tzu's *The Art of War*. It means that if you understand both your opponent's strengths and weaknesses and also know your own, you can face any challenge with a high probability of success.[25]

Here we'll reveal the adversary's strategies and tactics. Understanding them will help you discern and win the battles you'll face, while mastering them will help you win the war.

Nephi's warnings in 2 Nephi 28 read like a handbook for the last days. He saw how evil spirits would work *"carefully,"* quietly, and consistently. Here's a list with clear descriptions, so you can learn to master discerning the enemy's tactics.

Nephi saw our day and recorded the exact strategies darkness would use.[26] These aren't theories; they're warnings. And because they appear in scripture, they're patterns you can trust. Once you recognize them, it becomes far easier to stop mistaking spiritual interference for your own weakness. Each tactic includes what the scripture teaches, how the tactic works, what it looks like in real life, the inner whisper attached to it, and what mastery over that tactic feels like.

## Pacify and Lull

*"And others will he pacify, and lull them away into carnal security..."* (2 Nephi 28:21)

**The tactic described:**
To pacify is to dull spiritual alertness; to lull is to quiet the inner warnings of the Spirit. Darkness uses comfort as an anesthetic. This tactic doesn't tempt with obvious sin—it numbs with ease. It produces a gentle drifting away from God until spiritual things feel optional.

**What it looks like in real life:**
A person feels a prompting to pray but postpones it.
Repentance gets pushed to *"tomorrow,"* then forgotten.
Scripture study feels less urgent, so it's skipped.
Entertainment or noise fills the mind, replacing spiritual hunger.
Nothing feels wrong—that's the danger.

**The whisper:**
*"Everything is fine. There's no urgency. You're doing enough."*

**Spirits That Use This Tactic:**
**Unclean spirits** frequently pair pacify-and-lull with flattery. They awaken old cravings near old environments—former habits, former sins, former digital traps. They whisper fatalism: *"You've gone too far. Just give up."* It feels like brutal honesty, but it's spiritual sabotage.
**False spirits** also use this tactic, offering warm feelings without repentance, emotional uplift without transformation—keeping the disciple comfortable but unmoved.

**Mastery Lessons:**
Mastery comes through acting quickly on spiritual impressions. When a disciple responds to gentle nudges with immediate obedience, the heart awakens. Spiritual sensitivity increases. What once felt optional becomes vital. The lull loses power because the soul no longer sleeps.

## Flatter Away

*"Others he flattereth away... telling them there is no hell... I am no devil, for there is none."* (2 Nephi 28:22)

**The tactic described:**
Flattery minimizes sin, removes accountability, and distorts doctrine. It hides consequences. This tactic is particularly effective because it attacks belief in the reality of the adversary himself—if the devil convinces someone he doesn't exist, he can influence them freely.

**What it looks like in real life:**
A behavior once recognized as harmful now seems harmless.
A person excuses a sin as *"just who I am."*
God's mercy is reinterpreted as permission.
A disciple sees no need to change because *"God understands me."*
Flattery often arrives disguised as self-compassion but results in spiritual apathy.

**The whisper:**
*"There are no consequences. You won't be judged. You're beyond fixing anyway—so don't bother trying."*

**Spirits That Use This Tactic:**
**False spirits** thrive here. They offer spiritual experiences without transformation—heat without light, spectacle without substance. They appear religious, even uplifting, but bypass repentance by appealing to pride, novelty, or emotional drama. **Unclean spirits** also use this tactic to keep someone bound to old habits by convincing them the habit is harmless, inevitable, or *"part of their identity."*

**Mastery Lessons:**
Mastery comes when you welcome truth even when it stings. A disciple who seeks truth instead of comfort becomes unmoved by flattery. Correction becomes an act of mercy, not condemnation. Once truth regains authority, deception loses leverage.

### Rage Against Truth

*"Wo unto all those who tremble, and are angry because of the truth of God!"* (2 Nephi 28:28)

**The tactic described:**
When truth approaches darkness, the influence reacts sharply. This is not conviction—it's panic. Darkness dreads exposure. Truth threatens to reveal what has been hiding, so the influence

provokes hostility. This includes *"right fighting"*—the need to be right even when you know you're wrong. Entire wars have been fought because of this tactic.

**What it looks like in real life:**
A scripture pierces the heart and irritation rises.
A correction from a spouse feels like an assault instead of help.
A sermon that invites repentance triggers defensiveness.
Someone clings to an argument they know is flawed because conceding would expose the deeper issue.
The anger is disproportionate. The truth isn't the problem; the influence is.

**The whisper:**
*"Don't listen. They're judging you. They don't understand. You're right—they're wrong."*

**Spirits That Use This Tactic:**
**Foul spirits** use rage as a shield. They push fear, dread, and emotional turbulence, especially when someone moves closer to truth or repentance. The more light approaches, the louder the opposition becomes—not because you're failing, but because the spirit fears exposure.
**Familiar spirits** also use this tactic when truth challenges deeply rooted family wounds or generational patterns. They stir emotional memory to keep you tied to old scripts.

**Mastery Lessons:**
Mastery appears the moment a disciple pauses instead of reacting. Asking, *"Why did this provoke me?"* breaks the influence. Light enters. Pride softens. When humility replaces defensiveness, truth does its work and darkness loses its hiding place.

### Stir Up Contention

*"He stirreth them up to anger against that which is good."* (2 Nephi 28:20)

**The tactic described:**
Contention blinds the heart. It distorts perception and replaces unity with suspicion. This tactic doesn't require dramatic conflict—small irritations are enough. Once contention takes root, nothing looks the way it truly is.

**What it looks like in real life:**
A spouse misreads a tone and the disagreement snowballs.
A delayed text becomes proof of rejection.
A child's mistake feels like rebellion instead of immaturity.
A disciple grows suspicious of someone they once trusted.
Simple misunderstandings spiral into emotional storms.

**The whisper:**
*"They don't care about you. They're against you. You need to defend yourself."*

**Spirits That Use This Tactic:**
**Opportunistic spirits** excel here. They wait for tiredness, hurt feelings, stress, or insecurity, then strike. The anger feels like your own emotion, but the surge is being amplified by influence.
**False spirits** also stir contention by creating spiritual pride or superiority, fueling comparisons and divisions among believers.

**Mastery Lessons:**
Mastery shows up as the ability to pause, seek clarity, and check assumptions. The disciple chooses peace over reaction. As soon as the Spirit reenters the moment, contention loses its grip and unity becomes possible again.

### Lead Carefully Down to Hell

*"And thus the devil cheateth their souls, and leadeth them away carefully down to hell."* (2 Nephi 28:21)

**The tactic described:**
This strategy is slow, subtle, and deliberate. The adversary uses flaxen cords—soft, small, nearly invisible compromises. One strand seems harmless and easy to break. But as they accumulate, they form a rope strong enough to bind the soul. By the time the disciple notices the weight, the cord feels impossible to break. The descent is so gradual it looks like personal choice rather than captivity (2 Nephi 26:22).

**What it looks like in real life:**
Prayers skipped once become prayers skipped often.
Scripture study fades until it no longer feels natural.
Repentance becomes something to do *"when life slows down."*
Old habits reappear strand by strand.
Soon, the person feels numb and says things like, *"Why try? I*

*can't change."*
This fatalism is the fruit of the rope.

**The whisper:**
*"It's only a little. You can fix it later. You've already failed—just keep going."*

**Spirits That Use This Tactic:**
**Familiar spirits** use this tactic by weaving generational patterns into spiritual drift—*"This is just who we are."*
**Unclean spirits** maintain influence by adding strand after strand of old habit until the person feels spiritually stuck.
**Opportunistic spirits** reinforce the cord during moments of discouragement, pushing the disciple toward surrender rather than repentance.

**Mastery Lessons:**
Mastery begins with noticing the earliest strands. A disciple who pays attention to small spiritual shifts can break the flaxen cord before it becomes a rope. Immediate repentance, rekindled spiritual habits, and conscious returning to the Light reverse the descent. As you cut strand after strand, the Spirit strengthens your soul until freedom becomes natural again.

Paul warned the Saints in Ephesus with simple clarity: *"Neither give place to the devil"* (Ephesians 4:27). *"Place"* means ground—a foothold. Darkness does not need your permission to tempt, but it cannot take hold without agreement.

Most people never realize when that agreement forms. It doesn't arrive through bold choices. It arrives through subtle ones. And those small moments shape spiritual territory long before a person notices the shift.

Agreement often hides inside the parts of our lives we don't bring to the Lord. Pain seeks relief. Sin seeks permission. Spirits seek agreement.

Whenever something remains in the dark—unhealed, unrepented, or unresolved—it becomes a place the adversary can touch. Not because God has abandoned you, but because darkness always gathers around whatever is left unyielded.

**Wounds** are a common entry point. Trauma is an injury, not a verdict, but unhealed wounds often produce quiet vows meant to protect us: *"I'll never trust again." "I have to stay in control." "No one will ever see me weak."*

These vows feel like self-preservation, but they function as agreements with fear and isolation. They close the heart to God even as they try to keep danger away.

Familiar spirits know how to press on those old injuries—they echo old phrases and memories to keep you tied to who you once were. They feed off the coping mechanisms, not the pain itself. The truth is gentler and more liberating: what happened to you is not who you are. Your wounds do not define your identity.

**Sin** creates agreement in a more direct way. Sin continues when a person protects it. Secrecy becomes shelter. Justifying it—*"It's not that bad"*—minimizes the need for change. Comparing yourself to others—*"Everyone does it"*—diminishes accountability. Postponing repentance—*"I'll fix it later"*—is just consent stretched out over time.

The Lord taught that light grows brighter and brighter when we come to Him (D&C 50:24), but sin guarded in darkness grows roots. These roots form habits, and habits harden into patterns that resist the very light that can free them.

**Emotions** can also become ground. Emotions themselves aren't sinful—they're signals. Anger, grief, envy, self-pity, and resentment alert us that something needs attention. But when we nurse those emotions, replay them, or leave them unresolved, they ferment into accusation.

Paul's warning becomes literal: *"Let not the sun go down upon your wrath... neither give place to the devil"* (Ephesians 4:26–27). Unreleased offense becomes a place. Judgments against yourself—*"I'm unworthy of help"*—or judgments against others—*"They'll never change"*—become quiet agreements that spirits can press upon. What began as a feeling becomes ground.

When you step back, the pattern becomes easier to recognize: **Wound → Lie → Vow → Habit → Stronghold.**[27] At any point in that chain, the Lord can intervene. But the adversary relies on the silence between those steps—small shifts no one notices until the ground has changed beneath them.

There's another pattern worth noticing. In life and in culture, deception rarely arrives fully formed. It usually moves through stages: **first we reject, then we accept, and finally we embrace.**[28]

Ideas or behaviors that once seemed unthinkable gradually feel normal. It isn't doctrine—it's simply how the human heart drifts when pressure, fear, or fatigue go unaddressed.

The same pattern applies spiritually: what you once resisted, you may later tolerate, and eventually defend. Darkness almost never demands leaps; it invites inches.

A similar principle appears in what some call the Overton Window[29]—the way societies shift what they view as normal over time. What was once outside the bounds gradually moves toward the center as the range of *"acceptable"* ideas shifts inch by inch.

That observation mirrors how spiritual captivity often begins—not through dramatic rebellion, but through small, repeated concessions until the heart grows accustomed to what once would have alarmed it.

This is why Nephi warned that the adversary *"leadeth away carefully"* (2 Nephi 28:21). It is slow, quiet, and deliberate.

But here's the comfort: the descent is reversible. The Lord honors agency; the adversary exploits it. Once you learn how ground is lost, you also learn how it's reclaimed.

> *Every link in the chain can be broken.*
> *Every lie can be replaced with truth.*
> *Every vow can be surrendered.*
> *Every habit can be interrupted.*

And when the ground is returned to the Lord, the stronghold collapses. His light enters the exact place where deception once stood.

Once you understand how ground is lost, you also begin to see how it's reclaimed. Jesus taught that a house swept clean and left empty remains vulnerable if it stays unfilled (Matthew 12:43–45).

Nature doesn't tolerate a vacuum, and neither does the soul. There's no such thing as spiritual vacancy—the stage of the heart will always be occupied by something. Freedom isn't only about what departs, but about Who enters.

**Deliverance removes darkness, but only Christ can fill the space it once occupied.**

His light must replace the lies. His Spirit must take the ground where confusion once lived. When He occupies the places formerly entangled in wounds, sins, or unresolved emotions, everything begins to change.

You respond with clarity instead of confusion. The old patterns lose their pull. Your efforts finally hold. This is where your success rate begins to rise toward one hundred percent—where protection becomes possible.

Once the heart begins to awaken, the Lord can teach you how to keep it awakened.

This leads directly into the Lord's warning to the Saints in the last days: *"That ye may not be deceived, and cast into the fire"* (D&C 45:57). The warning is real, but so is the protection. And that protection is not complicated, mysterious, or rare.

The Lord has already given plain instructions—gifts, practices, and principles that anchor the heart in light. With this foundation in place, we now turn to the practices the Lord Himself gave, so that you may not be deceived.

## Practice and Protection: That Ye May Not Be Deceived

> *"That ye may not be deceived seek ye earnestly the best gifts, always remembering for what they are given."* (D&C 46:8)

One of those gifts is discerning of spirits. The Lord warned Joseph: *"There are many spirits which are false spirits, which have gone forth in the earth, deceiving the world"* (D&C 50:2).

Then He gave the key: *"That which doth not edify is not of God, and is darkness. That which is of God is light"* (D&C 50:23–24).

> Have you ever had a thought appear out of nowhere urging you to lie, cheat, or steal?
> Have you ever heard an inner voice whispering, *"You're worthless. You're ugly. You're a failure"*?
> Or maybe a thought that says, *"No one cares about you. You might as well give up."*

Now ask yourself: **"Who is the author of that?"**

If it doesn't sound like your loving Savior, then it isn't. Period.

The reverse is also true. When a thought is clean, uplifting, encouraging, and filled with peace—you know its source.

As Moroni taught: *"It is given unto you to judge, that ye may know good from evil; and the way to judge is as plain... that which is of God inviteth and enticeth to do good continually... then ye may know with a perfect knowledge it is of God"* (Moroni 7:15–16).

The Spirit of Christ is:

> *Always edifying, never degrading.*
> *Always light, never darkness.*
> *Always hope, never despair.*

I can testify this works. I have had dark voices speak in my mind—sharp, condemning, relentless—and I have had to stop and ask, "***Who is the author of that?***"

The moment I recognized those words didn't sound like my Savior, the lie lost its power. It was like pulling off a mask to reveal the deceiver beneath.

Discernment turns confusion into clarity and fear into faith. Once you know the author, you can reject the darkness and welcome the light of Christ.

And once you've unmasked the author, the next step is simple: answer back with authority in the name of Jesus Christ. Don't let the lie sit in silence—respond immediately with light.

## Call Upon the Name of Jesus

Earlier we traced the process the Lord revealed in D&C 93. One of those steps is simple but profound: *"call upon His name"* (D&C 93:1).

Scripture affirms this truth again and again. *"At the name of Jesus every knee should bow, of things in heaven, and things in earth, and things under the earth"* (Philippians 2:10).

Peter healed the lame man at the temple gate by declaring, *"In the name of Jesus Christ of Nazareth rise up and walk"* (Acts 3:6).

Christ Himself promised His disciples, *"In my name shall they cast out devils"* (Mark 16:17). His name is not merely a symbol—it carries real power.

Joseph Smith knew this.

He taught the early Saints to call upon the Lord's name when confronted by darkness, and he practiced what he preached.

One account tells of a night when an evil power pressed upon him so heavily that he felt bound and near destruction—until he cried out in faith, calling on the name of Jesus Christ. At that very moment, the oppression broke and light returned.

His own experience bore witness: the adversary flees before the name of Christ spoken in faith.

Learn this truth well, His name carries power still today. The adversary shrinks at the sound of it. Use His name with faith, believing that through it you can rebuke the powers of darkness and cast them from your presence.

And notice—we say them.

That's deliberate. Sometimes you are contending with a single dark spirit, but other times it may be many. We cannot always see what we are dealing with. Using *them* acknowledges that whatever number confronts you, His name is sufficient.

Deliverance begins here. Say it out loud, with faith: *"In the name of Jesus Christ, I rebuke you. I cast you out. Never return. Get behind me."*

We'll call this your **Practice Script.** Use it boldly. Don't be afraid to speak light when darkness tries to speak to you.

Here's what I say:

> *"You are not welcome here, take you and your friends and leave. Repent, and go to the light. Read some scriptures, sing a hymn, say a prayer—anything, but leave me alone. In the name of Jesus Christ, leave my house, leave my life—now!"*

Sometimes they slink off right away. But sometimes they aren't so obedient and I need to call in the big guns. I invoke the name of the Lord with greater force: *"In the name of Jesus Christ I rebuke you! I forgive you. But go away. Now!"*

Then I wait a few seconds to feel if they're still there, or if the temptation or errant thought lingers. If it does, I say: "*I told you to leave. I mean it. In the name of Jesus Christ, I command you to go to the light. Leave me alone. Completely. Go on, leave!"*

One time, I walked a spirit out to the front door and literally booted him out of my house. The entire time, I spoke to him—firm but kind—and I used the name of the Lord. He left. He wasn't happy (I could feel it), but he left.

The amazing thing is, it works. The temptations go away too.

I know this works because I have lived it. Once you experience a dark presence flee at the name of Christ, you will never doubt His power again. That's where it starts—learning to stand and speak with faith. But there is more. As we grow, the Lord entrusts us with greater authority.

I once received a priesthood blessing where the rebuke was spoken with that higher power. It went like this:

> *"I now address any of the enemy who have sought to trouble or afflict you. In the name of Jesus Christ, I rebuke every unclean spirit, dark influence, devil, demon, or fallen being. I command you to depart and go to the mercy seat of Christ to repent. If you will repent, you may return only as helpers in His work. If not, you are left in the hands of the Father to be dealt with as He sees fit. Angels are appointed to apprehend you, to uncover your eyes and ears, to shut your mouths, and to restrain your power. By the word of the Lord Jesus Christ, I place a restraining order upon you: cease and desist. Depart now, and never return!"*[30]

Hear the difference? The tone is more seasoned, the commands more precise, the scope broader. This is the voice of someone who has been trained by experience to wield the gift of deliverance with greater confidence.

Start small, but know this is where you are heading. Every rebuke in Jesus' name is practice for the day when you will speak with that same refinement and power.

## Sweep Them Away

Deliverance isn't about the volume of your voice—it's about faith. Not the loudness of your words, but the purity of your trust.

Think of it like sweeping. You don't just notice dirt on the floor and complain about it—you grab a broom and sweep it away.

I remember the father of a childhood friend. When we played at his house, he'd sometimes come after us with a broom. With a few gentle taps on our backsides, he'd sweep us right out the door and send us home. As we got older, we'd see him coming and know exactly what was about to happen. It wasn't ever cruel—it was simply his way of restoring peace to his home.

The Lord gave the same picture: *"And again, verily I say unto you, and I say it that you may know the truth, that you may* ***chase darkness*** *from among you..."* (D&C 50:25, emphasis added).

That's what deliverance looks like. When spirits trouble you, don't negotiate. Don't entertain them. In the name of Jesus Christ, sweep them out and send them away.

## When Temptation Knocks

Most deliverance is not about dramatic possessions. It's about the daily thoughts that slip in unnoticed.

The adversary plants lies, suggestions, and half-truths. That's his weapon. So ask yourself often: ***"Who's the author of that?"***

> *If it's clean, edifying, and uplifting—you know its source.*
>
> *If it's degrading, despairing, or destructive—you know its source too.*

Once you know the author, you have a choice: embrace it or reject it. Rebuke the darkness. Send it away. Don't hesitate.

And please, never think you can just ignore it.

Too often people imagine that if they look the other way. Temptation will disappear on its own. That's simply not true.

If you ignore them, they win. And if they win, they will return—again and again, often stronger than before. Sometimes they will bring others with them.

The Savior Himself warned that when an unclean spirit departs and finds no rest, it returns to its former dwelling—and brings seven more with it, even more wicked than itself (Matthew 12:43–45).

Ignoring evil does not make it better; it only makes it worse. The only way forward is to confront it in the name of Christ. Then replace it with His light—through prayer, scripture, worship, or even a hymn whispered under your breath.

## This is War

*"Choose liberty and eternal life, through the great Mediator... or choose captivity and death, according to the captivity and power of the devil"* (2 Nephi 2:27).

That is the battlefield. Every day you choose which banner you fight under. Every day you decide which uniform to put on.

Paul gave the pattern for a warrior of Christ (Ephesians 6:10–18). But it's more than words on a page—it's armor you can actually put on in prayer.

When you rise each morning, stand before your mirror and speak it out loud:

> *"I put on my head **the helmet of salvation**. Guard my thoughts, O Lord, that they may be pure and set upon Thee."*
> *"I gird my chest with **the breastplate of righteousness**. Cover my heart with Thy holiness and keep me from sin."*
> *"I grasp **the shield of faith**. With it I quench every fiery dart of the adversary."*
> *"I wield **the sword of the Spirit**–the word of God. Make it sharp with truth and virtue, that I may drive back deception and darkness."*
> *"I shod my feet with **the preparation of the gospel of peace**. Guide me to walk swiftly and steadily in flawless obedience to Thy voice."*

Do this not as empty words, but as a real enlistment. Clothe yourself in Christ's armor, mind and spirit. Because you are not strolling through life unopposed—you are going into battle.

Closing prayer example:

> *"Lord, I go forth today under Thy banner. Let Thy armor be upon me. Let Thy Spirit fill me. Make me a warrior of light, strong to resist evil, quick to forgive, and steady in truth. I take my stand in Thee, and I march this day in Thy strength. In the name of Jesus Christ, amen."*

### Not a Moment, but a Walk

Deliverance is not a single skirmish—it is the daily walk of discipleship. Every day, every hour, you are choose which voice to follow.

The enemy whispers constantly. They plant thoughts in your mind, pressing feelings upon your heart, and lurking in the atmosphere around you.

But Christ has already won the war. All that remains is for you to enforce His victory in your daily walk.

So when those thoughts come—whether **in you, on you, or around you**[31]—don't excuse them. Don't shrug and say, *"That's just me."* Stand your ground. Say it out loud if you must:

> *"I am not OK with that. In the name of Jesus Christ, I reject that thought. I sweep it away, and I choose the light."*

Make this a practice, not just a theory. Each time you sweep away darkness, replace it with something of Christ: a verse of scripture, a whispered prayer, a remembered hymn, or a simple act of service. Let His light fill the space you've just emptied.

This is how you walk in freedom—not just once, but step by step. Thought by thought. Day by day.

And grasp this truth: deliverance and healing are not separate ministries. They are twin streams of the same Spirit. When Jesus cast out an unclean spirit, the body was often healed as well (Matthew 8:16–17; Luke 6:18–19). When He broke oppression, torment ceased, sickness fled, peace came, and the soul was restored (Acts 10:38).

Joseph and the early Saints testified of the same experience: deliverance opening the way for healing. The Lord does not intend to leave you half-whole.

He intends to make you fully whole.

I have felt that same thing myself—moments when a dark influence was swept away and, almost instantly, the heaviness in my body and mind lifted. Deliverance and healing truly do come hand in hand.

Closing prayer example:

> *"Father, I choose Thy voice today. Guard my mind, cleanse my heart, and guide my walk. When darkness presses, teach me to sweep it away quickly and to replace it with Thy light. Make me whole—body, mind, and spirit—in Thee. In the name of Jesus Christ, amen."*

## Healings - The Touch of Christ

When Jesus walked among men, healing followed Him everywhere.

> *"And Jesus went about all Galilee, teaching in their synagogues, and preaching the gospel of the kingdom, and healing all manner of sickness and all manner of disease among the people" (Matthew 4:23).*

The blind saw. The lame leapt. Lepers were cleansed. The dead were raised.[32]

Healing wasn't an occasional wonder—it was the daily witness that God had come among them.

The Book of Mormon affirms the same truth when Jesus Christ walked among the Nephites:

> *"He did heal all manner of diseases among them, and they did all, both those who were afflicted in any manner with their sicknesses and their diseases; to them he did heal according to their faith in him."* (3 Nephi 17:9)

His healing was universal in scope and deeply personal in touch. He saw each person who suffered, reached out, and restored them.

Joseph Smith taught that this ministry of healing was to be part of the restored gospel in his day, as well as in ours.

In Nauvoo, he and the brethren walked through streets lined with the sick and raised them by the dozens. He taught the Saints—both men and women—to anoint, to pray, to lay on hands, and to expect miracles in Christ's name.[33]

Healing wasn't for an elite class, but for all who believed.

Healing, then, is not merely about the absence of sickness. It is the presence of Christ. His Spirit heals the body, the heart, the memory, the soul. His touch makes us whole.

## Joseph's Healing Ministry

When Jesus walked among men, healing followed Him everywhere.

The Restoration bore the same witness through Joseph's example. He taught that this power was never his to hoard. He urged the Saints to seek it, telling them to lay hands on their families, to anoint with oil, and to pray with faith.[34]

The gift of healing was for the body of Christ—not confined to a prophet or the priesthood, but given to all who would believe.

He also modeled humility in healing. After raising a woman from long affliction, Joseph warned the onlookers not to put their trust in him but in the Lord Jesus Christ, who alone had power to heal.[35] The Saints learned through him that healing was not human strength or the authority of an office, but heaven's power flowing through the channel of faith to those who believe.

This was the same healing ministry of the Savior Himself walking through Galilee:

> *"And Jesus went about all Galilee, teaching in their synagogues, and preaching the gospel of the kingdom, and healing all manner of sickness and all manner of disease among the people."* (Matthew 4:23)

When Jesus entered the house of Jairus, He took the hand of a dying child and spoke life into her body.

One hot July day in 1839, disease raged through Commerce and Montrose. Joseph, himself weak with fever, rose from his bed when he heard the cries of the sick. He crossed the river and went from cabin to cabin, healing and comforting the Saints.

At one house, he commanded the afflicted to rise in the name of Jesus Christ—and they did. At another, he laid hands on Elijah Fordham, who had been bedridden for days, thought near death. Joseph grasped his hand, rebuked the illness, and lifted him to his feet—healed in an instant.

The parallels between Christ and Joseph Smith are not accidental—they are deliberate. Christ promised, *"He that believeth on me, the works that I do shall he do also"* (John 14:12).

Joseph lived that promise.

Both ministries bore the same marks: compassion first, then action. A word spoken with authority, then bodies restored. Praise directed not to the man, but to the God who sent him.

Christ laid His hands on the blind and they saw. Joseph laid his hands on the fevered and they rose. Christ commanded unclean spirits to depart. Joseph, in Christ's name, did the same.

This is heaven's way. When the Lord empowers one of His children, He clothes them with a mantle of mercy. This gift is not given for reputation or spectacle, but so the kingdom of God may come *"in power and great glory"* (D&C 65:5).

Healing is not a side ornament of that kingdom—it is one of its living proofs. And this power is not reserved for a select few. The Savior declared:

> *"These signs shall follow them that believe... they shall lay hands on the sick, and they shall recover."* (Mark 16:17–18)

Anyone who believes and acts in faith may become a vessel of that mercy. Joseph himself confirmed this pattern:

> *"Faith to heal the sick was among the first things manifested in this Church; and from that time down to the present, the sick have been healed through faith and humble prayer."* (History of the Church 2:195)

Every healing in his ministry whispered the same testimony: Christ is no distant memory. His power is still here, and His kingdom still comes with mercy.

## 4 Nephi Model

When Mormon describes the days of peace in 4 Nephi, he doesn't just say the people were righteous. He gives a startling witness:

> *"There was no contention in the land, because of the love of God which did dwell in the hearts of the people. And there were no envyings, nor strifes, nor tumults, nor whoredoms, nor lyings, nor murders... and surely there could not be a happier people among all the people who had been created by the hand of God. ...and the devil could have no power over the hearts of the people, for they were all sanctified in Christ."* (4 Nephi 1:15–18)

This is more than a golden age—it's a blueprint.

Purity and unity in Christ do not just create harmony among people—they actually remove the adversary's foothold. When hearts are sanctified, satan loses his leverage.

Joseph Smith echoed this same principle: Zion is not built by gathering land or wealth, but by gathering hearts into one (Moses 7:18; D&C 105:5).

*"If we are not sanctified and made holy, we must fall short of the great glory which God designs to confer upon us,"*[36] he said.

Unity is not optional—it's protection.

Spiritual gifts are the lifeblood of such a society. Where gifts abound, faith is strengthened, truth is confirmed, and love is magnified. The Spirit edifies all, leaving no room for darkness to creep in.

Gifts are not ornaments—they're safeguards.

When a people walk in this order—one heart, one mind, sanctified in Christ—the devil is literally bound. That is the promise of 4 Nephi, and it is the destiny of Zion yet to come.

### The Aim of It All - To Become Like Him

All of this—the gifts of the Spirit, the ministry of angels, the power of deliverance, the healings, the unity of Zion—has one great aim.

It is not merely to have a spiritual experience. It is not to say we have power, or that God has visited us. The aim is transformation. This is why Mormon promised that when we are filled with His love, we become the sons of God—like Him when He appears (Moroni 7:48).

That is where the path leads: to see Him as He is and to become like Him.

Joseph never pointed the Saints to gifts as ends in themselves. He taught that every manifestation of power was a step toward something greater—the fullness of His image in us.

The vision of the celestial kingdom makes the same promise:

> *"They shall see as they are seen, and know as they are known, having received of his fulness and of his grace."* (D&C 76:94)

This is why Zion must be gathered, why the Spirit must be poured out, why angels must minister, why evil must be cast out. It is all preparation for the great unveiling—when Christ appears and we are not strangers to Him, but reflections of Him.

This was Joseph's aim. Not to create a society that admired spiritual gifts, but a people who were remade by them. A people whose very nature bore the image of the Son of God, ready to meet Him face to face.

## Closing Witness

The example is clear.

Christ walked in it first. Joseph walked in it in the Restoration. And now it is set before you.

The gifts of the Spirit, the ministry of angels, the power to discern and overcome evil—these are not stories trapped in scripture or relics of another age. They are heaven's provisions for every disciple who will seek them.

Joseph taught that no one need be left out. To one is given one gift, to another a different one, *"that all may be profited thereby"* (D&C 46:12). Moroni asked, *"Have miracles ceased?"* and answered: *"Nay; neither have angels ceased to minister unto the children of men"* (Moroni 7:29).

The promise is sure—if you earnestly seek, you will receive.

This belongs not only to prophets of old, but to the humble and believing in every generation—the peaceable followers of Christ. And it can belong to you.

> *Seek the gifts.*
> *Welcome the angels.*
> *Stand boldly against evil spirits.*
> *Heal and be healed.*
> *Walk in the light.*

All of it is meant to bring you to the great end: to become like Him.

I bear witness that you can. These things are not beyond your reach. They are God's will for His children. Christ is not withholding; He is inviting. Joseph did not hoard the these truths; he revealed them.

The same Christ who stood by Joseph stands ready to stand by you.

Do not fear that you are too weak. His grace is sufficient. Do not imagine that you are forgotten. He has promised, *"Draw near unto me and I will draw near unto you; seek me diligently and ye shall find me"* (D&C 88:63).

The path is open. The invitation is stands. The gifts are waiting.

The Lord Himself is calling you to walk in His light and power until you see Him as He is.

This is your inheritance—to walk in His light, to be clothed in His power, and to be transformed in His likeness. It is the same inheritance that will one day make Zion possible.

It is the helix at work—the rising spiral of Christ's love, repeating and ever ascending. Gifts, angels, deliverance, healings... each cycle draws you nearer to Him, each turn lifting you higher into His light.

Note: this is not just for individuals. It is for a people.

Zion will not be built by the weak, the faithless, or the unarmed. She will be raised up by Saints equipped with gifts of the Spirit and proven in spiritual warfare—humble, united, fearless, and full of Christ.

We have traced the pattern as it unfolds in the soul. But what happens when that same pattern takes root in an entire people? What does it look like when a society—not just a single saint—moves together in the spiral of light?

That glimpse lies just ahead. It is the vision of Zion.

# Chapter 10 Notes

1 Teachings of the Prophet Joseph Smith, p. 160

2 Adam: Moses 5:6–7—an angel explains sacrifice; Moses 6:51–52—an angel teaches Adam about baptism.
Abraham: Abraham 1:15—an angel delivers Abraham from being sacrificed.
Daniel: Daniel 9:21–22—Gabriel appears and gives him understanding.
Joseph Smith—History 1:30–47—Moroni visits, delivering the record of the Book of Mormon and instructions.
History of the Church 1:11–13— oseph's account of Moroni instructing him through the night.

3 Joseph Smith Papers, Journal, 9 Nov. 1835, p. 24

4 Joseph Smith—History 1:54

5 Joseph Smith—History 1:28–29

6 D&C 103:19–20; History of the Church 2:65–66

7 History of the Church 2:427–428 records multiple accounts of the dedication, including angels seen and rushing sound.
Joseph Smith Papers, Journal, 27 March 1836 provides a detailed record of the dedication with manifestations.
D&C 109–110 contains the dedicatory prayer and subsequent vision.
JS—History 1:30–47 describes Moroni's repeated visits instructing Joseph.
D&C 128:20–21 lists Joseph's angelic ministrations, including Moroni, Michael, and others.
History of the Church 4:210 describes Joseph receiving comfort from angels during affliction.

8 Moroni's night visits: JS—History 1:30–47
Gabriel's annunciation: Luke 1:26–31
Angels at Christ's tomb: Luke 24:4–6; Matthew 28:2–7
Angels in Kirtland: JS Papers, Journal, 27 Mar. 1836; History of the Church 2:427–428

9 Teachings of the Prophet Joseph Smith, p. 160

10 History of the Church 4:3–4 (July 1839, Montrose, Iowa): Joseph crosses the river to heal the sick during the malaria outbreak; many rise immediately.
History of the Church 4:555–556: accounts of laying on hands in Nauvoo.
Joseph Smith, *"History,"* Times and Seasons 4 (1843): 409–410: recounts the Nauvoo healings.
Wilford Woodruff, Journal (July 22, 1839): details Joseph's healings in Montrose, including near-death cases where the afflicted rose completely healed.
Brigham Young and Heber C. Kimball corroborated these events.

11 1 Corinthians 15:40–42—Paul names celestial and terrestrial bodies, contrasting their glory.
D&C 76:70–81, 88—outlines the celestial, terrestrial, telestial kingdoms.
D&C 88:22–24—laws tied to each kingdom; those unprepared cannot abide a higher glory.

12 Hebrews 2:4—*"God also bearing them witness, both with signs and wonders, and with divers miracles."*
Mark 16:20—*"the Lord working with them, and confirming the word with signs following."*
D&C 35:8—*"For I am God... showing forth signs and wonders unto all those who believe."*

13 John 9:6–7—healing the man born blind.
Mark 8:22–25—healing the blind man at Bethsaida.
Mark 1:23–27—casting out an unclean spirit in the Capernaum synagogue.
Mark 7:32–3—healing a man who was deaf and had a speech impediment.
Mark 9:17–27—casting out a mute spirit from the boy.
Mark 4:39—*"Peace, be still."*
Mark 5:8–13—demons enter the swine.

14 JS—History 1:15–16—*"thick darkness gathered around me... seemed to be doomed to sudden destruction."*
History of the Church 1:82–83 (1830)—Newel Knight was

possessed; Joseph casts out the devil.
History of the Church 1:238–239—rebuked evil spirits at Kirtland.
History of the Church 1:83—Knight was immediately relieved and filled with the Spirit after Joseph commanded the spirit to depart.
Teachings of the Prophet Joseph Smith p. 206—Joseph warns about false spirits and the need for discernment.

15 The author acknowledges the work of Scott Gillespie and Kylie Gillespie, whose writings on evil and unclean spirits—including *Fighting Heaven and Earth*; *Possession by Devils and Unclean Spirits*; and *Pornography, Sickness, Evil Spirits and the Priesthood*—helped shape the author's understanding of spiritual oppression, discernment, and deliverance. While no direct quotations are used in this section, their work informed the conceptual framework through which these matters are approached.

16 Newel Knight, Autobiographical Account, in *Joseph Smith Papers*, History A-1, p. 49–52

17 Concept adapted from Adam Boyle, *"Casting Out Satan – Kingdom and Keys Pt. 9,"* Kingdom and Keys Podcast.

18 Scripture uses a wide range of terms describing adversarial influence:
Moses 4:4 *"...the devil, and his angels..."*
Matthew 12:43 *"...when the unclean spirit is gone out of a man..."*
Isaiah 29:4 *"...thy speech shall be... as of one that hath a familiar spirit..."*
1 Kings 22:22 *"...I will be a lying spirit in the mouth of all his prophets."*
1 Timothy 4:1 *"...giving heed to seducing spirits, and doctrines of devils."*

19 Moses 4:3–4; D&C 29:36–37

20 Joseph Smith, Discourse, 9 April 1843, *JSP Journals 2*, 374–376; Matthew 12:43

21 Isaiah 29:4; 2 Nephi 26:22

22 Mark 9:25; Luke 9:39–42

23 D&C 50:2–3; D&C 46:7–8; D&C 52:14

24 Joseph Smith, Discourse, 9 April 1843, *JSP Journals 2*, 374-376

25 Sun Tzu, The Art of War, ch. 3 (*"Attack by Stratagem"*): *"If you know the enemy and know yourself, you need not fear the result of a hundred battles."*

26 In 2 Nephi 28, Nephi prophesies of the last days, warning that the Gentiles would be deceived by pride, false doctrines, counterfeit spirituality, flattery, anger at truth, and the lie that *"all is well."* He describes the gradual strategy of the adversary—lulling, pacifying, and leading souls *"carefully down to hell."*

27 This pattern is an observational framework describing how spiritual captivity often forms over time. While not a scriptural formula, it aligns with the scriptural pattern of gradual deception—*"flaxen cords"* becoming *"strong cords"* (2 Nephi 26:22), and with Paul's warning that unresolved wrath can *"give place to the devil"* (Ephesians 4:26-27).

28 This three-stage description of gradual acceptance is a well-known observation used in cultural, moral, and behavioral studies. It is not scripture, but it reflects the scriptural pattern Nephi described—how the adversary leads the heart *"carefully"* and gradually (2 Nephi 28:21).

29 The *"Overton Window"* is a secular term coined by policy analyst Joseph P. Overton (1960–2003) to describe how ideas shift over time from unthinkable to acceptable through gradual normalization. While not a doctrinal concept, it parallels the scriptural pattern Nephi warned of—the adversary leading souls "carefully" and incrementally (2 Nephi 28:21).

30 Personal communication, source withheld by request

31 Michael Claridge, "In Me, On Me, or Around Me, and I'm Not Okay With It," Prison Temple blog (2014). Copy available upon request.

32 The blind saw—Matthew 9:27–30; John 9:6–7.
The lame leapt—Matthew 11:5 (Jesus' report to John's disciples: "the blind receive their sight, and the lame walk..."); also Acts 3:6–8 (lame man healed through Peter in Jesus' name).

Lepers were cleansed—Luke 17:12–14; Mark 1:40–42.
The dead were raised—John 11:43–44 (Lazarus); Luke 7:14–15 (widow's son at Nain); Mark 5:41–42 (Jairus' daughter).
Prophetic backdrop: Isaiah 35:5–6—*"then the eyes of the blind shall be opened, and the ears of the deaf shall be unstopped. Then shall the lame man leap as an hart, and the tongue of the dumb sing."*

33 *History of the Church* 4:3–4, 604 (July 1839 Nauvoo malaria epidemic)—Joseph Smith healed the sick on both sides of the river and affirmed that women may lay on hands and be heard of God.
*Nauvoo Relief Society Minutes*, Apr. 28, 1842—Joseph taught that sisters with faith could heal the sick.
Wilford Woodruff, *Journal*, July 22, 1839—eyewitness account of Joseph healing many.
Mark 16:17–18; Doctrine and Covenants 42:44, 48—signs of believers and instructions to lay hands on the sick.

34 *History of the Church* 2:204; 4:604—Joseph Smith taught that the Saints should exercise gifts of faith and healing, and affirmed that women may lay on hands and be heard of God.
*Nauvoo Relief Society Minutes*, Apr. 28, 1842—Joseph instructed that sisters with faith could heal the sick.
Doctrine and Covenants 42:43–44, 48; 66:9—revelatory instructions to lay hands on the sick and they shall recover.

35 History of the Church 4:3–4 (July 1839, Montrose/Nauvoo healings): Joseph healed many who were sick, then testified that he acted through the power of God, not his own.
Wilford Woodruff, Journal, July 22, 1839: After Joseph raised the sick, he bore witness that Jesus Christ—not Joseph—was the healer.
Times and Seasons 4 (1843): 409–410—recounts the same events.

36 TPJS, 18; History of the Church 2:8

# The Prophet as Husband

## Joseph Smith's Living Witness on Marriage

---

### The Bridegroom

There was once a bride who waited with longing for her beloved.

The betrothal had been made, binding as marriage itself. Her Bridegroom had given a gift of immeasurable price—His own blood—to claim her hand. Then He departed, returning to His Father's house to prepare a chamber where they would dwell together.

She did not see Him in that season.

Day by day she worked at her loom, stitching garments and weaving the band that would bind their hands. She gathered bread, trimmed her lamp, and stored oil against the night. Her greatest treasure was her own purity: to remain undefiled, faithful, and ready.

At her window she set a candle. Each night it burned, a silent beacon saying: *"I am waiting. I am His, and He is mine."*

She kept His promises close, reading them again and again. Though the delay was long, she trusted His word. Had He not already proven His love?

Meanwhile, the Bridegroom built. Under the watchful eye of His Father, stone was laid upon stone. The chamber grew—walls firm, beams aligned, roof secure.

The Father inspected each part, and the Mother blessed the work, adding grace to every stone, light to every corner, and breathing beauty into the place where the bride would one day feel the warmth of hearth and home. Together They prepared the dwelling for the marriage feast, making it wholesome and ready for the bride and her groom.

The Son could not return for His bride until the Father declared, *"It is finished. All is ready."*

And so she waited. The night would come when the trumpet sounded, when the cry rang out through the streets: *"Behold, the Bridegroom cometh! Go ye out to meet Him!"*

Then, with rejoicing, she would be lifted up and carried to her new home. The feast would begin. The veil would be lifted. Two would become one.[1]

## The Prophets Spoke in This Language

This wasn't just poetry—it was prophecy lived out in the flesh. Hosea became a living sign of Israel's unfaithfulness when the Lord commanded him to marry a harlot. His marriage embodied the story of a bride who had strayed, chasing after other lovers.

But the Lord spoke comfort:

> *"I will allure her, and bring her into the wilderness, and speak comfortably unto her ... I will betroth thee unto me for ever ... in lovingkindness, and in mercies."* (Hosea 2:14, 19–20)

Even after betrayal, the Husband longed to restore His bride.

Isaiah declared the same:

> *"Thy Maker is thine husband; the Lord of hosts is his name; and thy Redeemer the Holy One of Israel."* (Isaiah 54:5)

Avraham Gileadi observes that Zion was *"fearful, confounded, ashamed, and disgraced... divorced from her husband."* Yet when she renewed her loyalty, her afflictions vanished and she *"happily reunites with her Redeemer."* Beneath Isaiah's words lies a haunting truth: God's people had once been put away, but the Husband still claimed them as His own.[2]

Jesus Himself spoke as the Bridegroom.

> *"The kingdom of heaven is likened unto ten virgins, which took their lamps, and went forth to meet the bridegroom."* (Matthew 25:1)

Some kept oil ready; others let their lamps go out. The difference was preparation, watchfulness, fidelity.

To His disciples He said plainly:

> *"In my Father's house are many mansions: if it were not so, I would have told you. I go to prepare a place for you ... and if I go ... I will come again, and receive you unto myself."* (John 14:2–3)

The bridal chamber in the Father's house is the very image He gave: as the Son, He goes ahead to prepare it; as the Father, He declares when it is finished. Two roles, one God—the Bridegroom who both builds and returns.

And John saw the end from the beginning:

> *"The marriage of the Lamb is come, and his wife hath made herself ready ... Blessed are they which are called unto the marriage supper of the Lamb."* (Revelation 19:7, 9)

## The Symbolism of Cups

John's vision of the marriage supper was not only a prophecy of the end; it was doctrinal symbolism planted from the beginning to show how the Lord deals with His people.

The Lord had already woven His likeness into the lives of His people, so that when the Bridegroom came they would recognize Him. These likenesses were carried in the language and customs of Israel—in bread and wine, joy and bitterness, pledge and redemption.

Chief among these symbols were the cups: the covenant of betrothal, the bitterness of sorrow, the silver of redemption, and the joy of the feast.[3]

In ancient Hebrew weddings, the father of the groom poured a cup of wine and placed it in his son's hands. The son then offered it to the bride. If she drank, she accepted him.[4]

From that moment forward she was bound, set apart until the day he returned for her. This was the pledge of union, the beginning of their covenant together.

Jesus drew directly on this image.

At the Passover table He lifted the cup and said: *"This is my blood of the new covenant, which is shed for many for the remission of sins"* (Matthew 26:28). When His disciples drank, they were not only remembering Him. They were accepting Him—the Bridegroom who had pledged His life for them.

The second is the bitter cup.[5]

In Gethsemane, the Bridegroom drank it alone—to the very dregs, the last drop, until nothing was left undone. He bled from every pore, completing the Atonement so fully that no debt remained unpaid.

That is what the dregs were—the full measure of anguish He bore alone.

But here is an important distinction to be made regarding the bitter cup: The scriptures teach that if we repent of those things that we have done to separate us from Him, His suffering will cover us. But if we do not, then we must suffer even as He did (D&C 19:15–18).

And so, because He drank it, the Bride does not have to—if she will be faithful to Him.

Her part is to keep her lamp trimmed, her garments clean, her heart undefiled. To remain steadfast at the window with light in her hand, waiting and ready. To live in purity and repentance, storing oil against the night, so that when the cry is heard—*"Behold, the Bridegroom cometh!"*—she will rise with joy, prepared for the wedding supper (Matthew 25:3–7; Revelation 19:7–9).

The third is the silver cup.

In the law of Moses, silver was the ransom price—the cost of redemption. Joseph of Egypt's silver cup drew his brothers back and restored his family. Yet silver could also be twisted toward betrayal: twenty pieces sold Joseph into bondage, and thirty pieces sold Christ to His death.[6]

The same metal that could ransom a life could also become the price of disloyalty.

So it is in marriage. Fidelity is the ransom price—it redeems and gathers, binding two into one.

But disloyalty scatters and destroys. Infidelity, betrayal, and abandonment wound more deeply than poverty or loss, because they strike at the very covenant that gives marriage its life.

What should have been silver for redemption becomes silver for betrayal, leaving division and sorrow in its wake.

The silver cup stands as both a promise and a warning. In the hands of the faithful, it pledges loyalty and redemption. In the hands of the unfaithful, it becomes the price of betrayal.

Every marriage must choose which silver it will hold.

The last is the cup of joy.[7]

Scripture speaks of the feast yet to come, when the Bridegroom will welcome His Bride and the marriage supper of the Lamb will begin. Joy in that day will be complete—because He first drank the bitter cup, and because He was never swayed by silver's price.[8]

So it is in marriage.

> ***Joy comes*** *when a husband loves as the Bridegroom loved, willing to sacrifice even his own life if called upon.*
>
> ***Joy comes*** *when a wife is faithful as the Bride, steadfast and undefiled, her lamp trimmed, her heart loyal, never wandering into forbidden paths that divide.*

Where there is such fidelity and such sacrifice, joy overflows—not shallow happiness, but the deep gladness of two made one.

Every faithful marriage in mortality points to that day.

These unions are not merely rehearsals of the covenant union between Christ and His people—they are living portrayals of it. Types and shadows walked out in flesh and blood, patterns that match the very template of the marriage supper to come.

These four cups together tell the whole story: the pledge of covenant, the bitterness of sacrifice, the price of fidelity, and the joy of oneness.

They are not symbols only, but a living testimony that marriage itself was given as a mirror—an exact reflection of Christ and His Bride—a covenant union that will one day be fulfilled at the marriage supper of the Lamb.

## The Bride and Her Calling

But with this beautiful parable of the Bridegroom's marriage, one important question remains:

Who is the bride?

She is not nameless. She is Zion, adorned in white. She is the people of Christ—purified, watchful, prepared. She is every soul who kept the lamp burning in the window of faith, those John saw clothed in white robes, sealed in their foreheads as servants of God, *made white in the blood of the Lamb* (Revelation 7:3, 9–14).

To be adorned in white is to remain faithful to the Bridegroom who gave His life for His Bride.

Each home where husband and wife cleave to one another in holiness becomes a living reflection of that covenant—a candle in the window against the night, a testimony in miniature of the feast to come.

For in the end, there is only one Bridegroom, only one covenant feast, only one unveiling. And there is only one Bride: those who endured, who trusted, who remained faithful—and who will be lifted up to rejoice with Him forever.[9]

## Foundation in Scripture

From the first pages of scripture, marriage is introduced not as an invention of men, but as the design of God. *"It is not good that the man should be alone,"* the Lord declared in Eden (Genesis 2:18, 24).

Out of Adam's side came the woman—not from his head, to rule him, nor from his feet, to be trampled under him, but from his rib—where she could rest close to his heart and be protected by his strength.[10]

The two were joined not as master and servant, but as one flesh, united in love and labor.

The Book of Mormon carries the same witness. Jacob condemned those who excused whoredoms by appealing to David or Solomon: *"For I, the Lord God, delight in the chastity of women. And whoredoms are an abomination before me"* (Jacob 2:28). The Lord's will was clear—*"they shall have one wife; and concubines they shall have none"* (Jacob 2:27).

Later, when Jesus appeared at Bountiful, He lifted the law of fidelity from outward act to inward thought: *"Whosoever looketh on a woman, to lust after her, hath committed adultery already in his heart"* (3 Nephi 12:28).

The New Testament records the same law. When asked about divorce, Jesus pointed back to Eden itself:

> *"He which made them at the beginning made them male and female ... For this cause shall a man leave father and mother, and shall cleave to his wife: and they twain shall be one flesh. What therefore God hath joined together, let not man put asunder."* (Matthew 19:4–6)

Paul added a higher dimension, teaching husbands to *"love your wives, even as Christ also loved the church, and gave himself for it"* (Ephesians 5:25).

Marriage was not built on domination but on sacrifice. A husband's role was not to take, but to give—even to the point of laying down his own life. *"This is a great mystery: but I speak concerning Christ and the church"* (Ephesians 5:32).

The Restoration echoed this foundation. In Kirtland, the Lord gave a commandment that reached into every home: *"Thou shalt love thy wife with all thy heart, and shalt cleave unto her and none else"* (D&C 42:22).

The same revelation that ordered consecration and priesthood also ordered fidelity in marriage.

Joseph Smith received his appointment from the Lord of the Vineyard and was charged to care for the graft—the gospel of Jesus Christ. His teachings on marriage drew their strength from that charge, bearing the same fruit that scripture had always borne.

When the time came for Joseph to publish an article on marriage in the Doctrine and Covenants, his words rested firmly on this scriptural foundation.

## Joseph's Teaching on Marriage

What did Joseph Smith actually teach about marriage? More than anything, he lived it.

When Joseph Smith courted Emma Hale, he had little to offer by worldly standards. He was poor and still searching out the call God had placed upon him. Emma's father, Isaac Hale, looked on with distrust. He did not believe in Joseph or in the work beginning to stir around him.

Yet Joseph loved Emma, and Emma believed in him. Their affection was genuine, tested through long visits and quiet conviction.

But Isaac Hale wouldn't give his consent.

With no blessing from her father and no home to begin in, Joseph and Emma made their choice. On January 18, 1827, they slipped away to the home of the Justice of the Peace Squire Tarbell in South Bainbridge, New York, and were married.[11]

It was, in truth, an elopement—but one born of devotion, not defiance.

From that day forward, Emma was his companion. She bore the sacrifices of poverty, the weariness of constant uprooting, the grief of burying children, and the sacred weight of being the wife of a prophet of God.

Through poverty, loss, and persecution, Joseph and Emma stood side by side. Their marriage—tested, tempered, and faithful—stands as the clearest witness of what they believed marriage to be.

### Joseph and Emma's Symbolic Cups

The life Joseph and Emma shared can be seen through the same four cups—covenant, bitterness, silver, and joy—lived out in the faithfulness of their marriage.[12]

> **The betrothal cup.** Just as a bride in ancient Israel sealed her covenant by drinking from the offered cup, Emma sealed hers when she chose Joseph. She did so against her father's wishes,[13] without wealth or home to begin in, and with little more than Joseph's word and calling. Yet she drank—not from defiance, but from devotion. In her faith and loyalty, Emma's choice became a living reflection of the Bride who accepts her Bridegroom not for advantage or appearance, but for love and truth.
>
> **The bitter cup.** Together they bore sorrows that would have crushed weaker hearts. They buried children. They knew poverty, constant uprooting, and ceaseless persecution. Emma watched her husband suffer imprisonment, betrayal, and finally martyrdom. Unlike the Savior—who drank His bitter cup alone—Joseph and Emma drank theirs together.[14] Their union was a covenant to endure not only joy, but also grief, bearing it side by side until the end.
>
> **The silver cup.** In the scriptures, silver represents both the price of redemption and the price of betrayal. So it is in marriage. Fidelity redeems and gathers; betrayal scatters and destroys. Joseph and Emma's fidelity was proven not in ease but in trial. Their silver was not the coin of betrayal but the pledge of loyalty. Their marriage testified that redemption is found in fidelity—in cleaving to one another and none else.
>
> **The cup of joy.** Their life together was not without sorrow, but joy crowned it still. The joy of covenant loyalty. The joy of enduring trials together. The joy of being one flesh, bound in holiness, waiting for the day when Bride and Bridegroom shall

rejoice in fullness. Every faithful marriage in the Restoration was meant to be a living portrayal of that greater feast. Joseph and Emma's was no exception. Through their fidelity, their sacrifices, and their love, they rehearsed the joy of Zion itself.

And just as disciples lift the Sacramental cup in remembrance of Christ's love, Joseph and Emma lifted the shared cup of their union in remembrance of the One who sanctifies both marriage and the Sacramental meal.

The sacred meal is itself a wedding feast in miniature. When the disciples at Bountiful ate and were filled, it was not crumbs that satisfied them but Christ Himself (3 Nephi 18:4–5).

Every Sacramental meal points forward to the greater day when the Bride and Bridegroom rejoice together, and the promise will be fulfilled: "*Blessed are they which are called unto the marriage supper of the Lamb*" (Revelation 19:9).

Every cup bore witness of Him.

## Revelations on Marriage

The revelations Joseph received matched the example he lived. In Kirtland, the Lord commanded: *"Thou shalt love thy wife with all thy heart, and shalt cleave unto her and none else"* (D&C 42:22).

To cleave meant to hold fast, to remain bound and undivided. That commandment was not given in abstraction—it was Joseph and Emma's lived experience.

In 1835, when outsiders accused the church of whoredoms, Joseph oversaw the publication of the church's law on marriage: *"We declare that we believe that one man should have one wife, and one woman but one husband; and that a man and woman, when legally married, are bound to remain with each other during their lives."*[15]

This was no theory. It was the very form of marriage Joseph and Emma themselves practiced.

Emma gave her own witness. As Relief Society president, she signed the October 1842 certificate declaring:

*"We... know of no system of marriage being practiced... save the one contained in the Book of Doctrine and Covenants."*[16]

In March 1844, she helped frame and publish the *Voice of Innocence from Nauvoo*, which condemned *"polygamy, bigamy, fornication, adultery, and prostitution"*[17] in the same breath. She presided over meetings that denounced Bennett's *"spiritual wife"* system and urged the Saints to follow the Book of Mormon and Doctrine and Covenants.

Long after Joseph's death, Emma never changed her testimony. In her 1879 *"Last Testimony,"* she affirmed: *"There was no revelation on either polygamy or spiritual wives. He had no other wife but me; nor did he to my knowledge ever have."*[18]

This is the united witness of Joseph and Emma's life: when heaven revealed, Joseph published. When rumors spread, they both pointed back to the law already given. When they spoke of marriage, their voices aligned with scripture—fidelity, purity, monogamy.

## Sealed unto Eternal Life

In later generations, many came to think of sealing as a spousal rite—a ritual binding husbands and wives together for eternity. But Joseph used the word *"sealing"* very differently.

He deliberately emphasized what the revelations themselves declared: to be sealed up unto eternal life by the Holy Spirit of Promise. It was a conscious shift, reclaiming the word from ceremony and anchoring it once again in revelation.[19]

This was Joseph's consistent teaching: sealing was heaven's ratifying voice upon the faithful. It was not a rite performed by men, but the witness of God Himself that a soul had overcome by faith and was prepared to enter His presence.

In the vision of the kingdoms he recorded in 1832, Joseph declared of the faithful: *"...who overcame by faith, and are sealed by the Holy Spirit of promise"* (D&C 76:53).

Later, in the Olive Leaf revelation of 1832–33, he reaffirmed the same truth: *"...they who are just men made perfect through Jesus the mediator of the new covenant... shall be sealed up unto eternal life"* (D&C 88:107, 110).

This was the sealing Joseph taught—heaven's ratifying voice upon the faithful.

On the subject of binding husbands and wives together for eternity, Joseph was silent. And his silence was not omission, but harmony with all of scripture.

Throughout the entire Bible, the Book of Mormon, the Pearl of Great Price, and the revelations Joseph published in his lifetime, there is not one single record of the Lord teaching sealing as a marriage covenant.[20]

Even when Christ appeared to the Nephites and gave them the fullness of His gospel (3 Nephi 11:31–40; 27:13–21)—a gospel that bound them together for two hundred years in peace, when there never was a happier people (4 Nephi 1:16–18, 22)—He did not teach such a doctrine.

Emma's voice matched his silence. In all her years, she never acknowledged such a doctrine. Her testimony remained the same: no revelation on plural or eternal marriage ever came through Joseph, and he was faithful to her his whole life.[21]

Together, their lives and words unite as one testimony. The marriage Joseph lived with Emma, the law he published, and the witness she bore all converge in a single truth: in the Restoration, marriage was one man and one woman, cleaving to one another in holiness—a living parable of the Bride and the Bridegroom, waiting with lamp and oil for the day of His return.

## Joseph and Hyrum's Final Witness

As the storm gathered in Nauvoo, accusations of plural wives swirled more fiercely. By 1844, some in the city were experimenting with what was called *"spiritual wifery"*—impostor unions dressed in religious language.[22]

Joseph, Emma, and Hyrum condemned such practices as adultery and abomination.

Their presence gave outsiders cause to accuse and men within Nauvoo cause to turn against him. The Nauvoo Expositor gave those accusations a press, and its publication became the spark that lit the fire.[23]

Joseph answered plainly.

From the pulpit on May 26, 1844, he declared: *"What a thing it is for a man to be accused of committing adultery, and having seven wives, when I can only find one. I am the same man, and as innocent as I was fourteen years ago."*[24] His words were direct, not cloaked in secrecy. He had one wife, and her name was Emma.

Hyrum bore the same testimony.

In the Nauvoo city council meetings that weighed the *Expositor*'s slanders, he called polygamy an abomination and urged its suppression.[25] He did so not as an echo of Joseph, but as a patriarch in his own right—a second voice standing with his brother, affirming the same law of monogamy they had always taught.

Together, the brothers defended the honor of their names, the peace of their city, the honor of Emma, and the purity of the gospel they preached.

Days later, they walked into Carthage. Their blood sealed their testimony.[26]

And like the prophets before them, their final words matter. Joseph's declaration of innocence, Hyrum's denunciation of polygamy, Emma's steady witness in life and in death—all stand together as a united last word on marriage.[27]

> *It was not silence.*
> *It was not ambiguity.*
> *It was not double-speak.*

It was clear, spoken openly, heard by friend and foe alike. The prophet and the patriarch testified with their lives, and the prophet's wife preserved the memory: marriage in the Restoration was one man and one woman, cleaving together in holiness.

This witness was never meant to end in Carthage.

The law they taught, the lives they lived, and the sacrifice they gave all point back to the greater pattern: the Bridegroom and His Bride, Christ and His people.

To understand what marriage means in Zion, we must look again to that parable.

## Marriage as the Zion Pattern

Marriage in the Restoration was never meant to stand alone. It pointed to something greater.

Just as Joseph and Emma's union bore witness of fidelity, and just as Joseph and Hyrum sealed that witness with their lives, the pattern itself was always meant to reflect the Bridegroom and His Bride—Christ and His people.

The prophets had long spoken of it:

Hosea's life portrayed the unfaithful wife, whom the Lord would yet allure and betroth again in righteousness (Hosea 1:2; 2:19–20).

Isaiah sang of Zion's estrangement and her joyful reunion: *"Thy Maker is thine husband; the Lord of hosts is his name"* (Isaiah 54:5).

Jesus told it in parable:

> *"At midnight there was a cry made, Behold, the bridegroom cometh; go ye out to meet him."* (Matthew 25:6)

Ten virgins went forth with lamps, but only five were wise and carried oil enough to enter. The others found the door shut.

In one telling, the Bridegroom says, *"I know you not"* (Matthew 25:12). But in the Joseph Smith Translation the emphasis turns: *"Ye know me not."*

That is the difference. The Lord does not merely want to recognize us at the door; He desires that we know Him before He comes.

This was His own warning to the latter-day church:

> *"And upon my house shall it begin... First among those... who have professed to know my name and have not known me."* (D&C 112:25–26)

Isaiah lamented the same blindness:

> *"The ox knoweth his owner, and the ass his master's crib: but Israel doth not know, my people doth not consider."* (Isaiah 1:3)

The parable was never about lamps or oil alone—it was about knowing Him. Oil is only a symbol.

The true preparation is intimacy with the Bridegroom Himself.

I would much rather be the Bride who inherits *"all that the Father hath"* (D&C 84:38; Romans 8:17) than only an invited guest who gets to eat wedding cake—that is, if you even have enough oil to get in (Matthew 25:1–13; Revelation 19:7–9).

But make no mistake: the parable isn't about oil; it's about knowing Him.

And John saw the end from the beginning:

> *"The marriage of the Lamb is come, and his wife hath made herself ready."* (Revelation 19:7)

This is not only about Christ and His church. It is also about Zion itself.

When Jesus came to the Nephites, He gave them His fullness—and for generations they lived without contention or division. The record says simply: they were the happiest of people.

They were one, even as a husband and wife are one.

So it is in every home that cleaves to this law. Every faithful marriage becomes a living rehearsal of Zion. Every husband who loves his wife as Christ loves the church, and every wife who abides in loyalty and trust, portrays the great marriage to come.

These unions are not small things. They are the seedbed of Zion, the first circle of peace where heaven's law is practiced—the first turn of the helix that lifts God's people upward into His presence.

Each covenant marriage mirrors the Bridegroom and His Bride: sealed in the betrothal cup, tested in the bitter cup, proved in the silver cup, and crowned in the cup of joy. These marriages are type and shadow made flesh—reflections of the great feast yet to come, when the Bridegroom will lift the final cup and Zion will rejoice in Him.

And the man chosen to bring forth the Book of Mormon and restore the gospel of Jesus Christ did so as a husband.

Emma was not incidental; she was integral. Their marriage wasn't a blemish to his calling but part of it. From Eden onward, the lesson remains the same: marriage is good, and it is of God.

The law of marriage in the Restoration is not merely social—it's prophetic.

To Joseph and Emma, to Hyrum and Jerusha,[28] to every faithful couple—marriage was fidelity in the flesh and prophecy in the spirit. It testified of the Bridegroom who is yet to come, and of the people who will be ready to meet Him.

In the end, there is only one Bridegroom. Only one feast. Only one unveiling. And only one Bride—those who belong to Him, who waited, who trusted, who endured, and who know Him.

In scripture, intimacy was described in the simplest of words: *"And Adam knew Eve his wife; and she conceived, and bare Cain"* (Genesis 4:1). To "know" was not casual acquaintance, but the deepest union of life and love.

And so it is with Christ. He doesn't ask us only to know about Him, but to know Him. Truly, intimately, to know Him—to be bound in glory to the Bridegroom who comes.

# Chapter 11 Notes

1 Scriptural sources behind the imagery:
Betrothal binding as marriage—Deuteronomy 22:23–24 (betrothal treated as binding covenant).
Bridegroom imagery—Matthew 9:15; John 3:29.
Gift of His blood—1 Peter 1:18–19; Revelation 19:7–9.
Preparing a chamber—John 14:2–3: *"I go to prepare a place for you."*
Garments / weaving—Revelation 19:8: *"fine linen is the righteousness of saints."*
Lamp, oil, waiting—Matthew 25:1–13 (parable of the ten virgins).
Purity and faithfulness—2 Corinthians 11:2: *"that I may present you as a chaste virgin to Christ."*
Candle in the window—while not directly biblical, it echoes Matthew 5:14–16 *("let your light so shine").*
Father's inspection / *"It is finished"*—parallel to John 19:30 and Jewish wedding tradition background.
Trumpet / midnight cry—Matthew 25:6: *"Behold, the bridegroom cometh."*
Lifted up, feast—Revelation 19:9: *"Blessed are they which are called unto the marriage supper of the Lamb."*

2 Avraham Gileadi, Commentary on Isaiah 54:5, IsaiahExplained.com

3 Insights drawn from Andrea Woodmancy, *"The Hidden Hebrew of 'The Bitter Cup' That Christ Drank," Dive Deeper* YouTube channel (2024).
Cups in scripture / covenantal symbolism:
Cup of covenant / betrothal: Matthew 26:27–28—*"This is my blood of the new testament (covenant), which is shed for many."*
Cup of sorrow / suffering: Matthew 26:39—*"let this cup pass from me."*
Cup of redemption (silver imagery): 1 Corinthians 6:20—*"ye are bought with a price"* (linked with 1 Peter 1:18–19, redeemed not with silver and gold but the blood of Christ).
Cup of joy / feast: Psalm 116:13—*"I will take the cup of salvation,*

*and call upon the name of the Lord."*
Marriage supper of the Lamb: Revelation 19:9.

4 Jewish betrothal (Kiddushin)—rabbinic sources (e.g., Mishnah Kiddushin 2:1) describe betrothal enacted through wine or money, with wine often used in the blessing.
Alfred Edersheim, *The Life and Times of Jesus the Messiah* (1883), details how the betrothal cup symbolized covenant acceptance.
Contemporary Jewish wedding guides still describe the *"cup of sanctification"* (Kiddushin cup).

5 Matthew 26:39; Matthew 26:42; D&C 19:18; Mosiah 3:7

6 Silver as ransom price (law of Moses):
Exodus 30:11–16—every man to give *"half a shekel after the shekel of the sanctuary... a ransom for his soul unto the Lord."*
Numbers 18:16—redemption money for the firstborn.
Joseph of Egypt's silver cup: Genesis 44:2, 12—Joseph commands his steward to place his silver cup in Benjamin's sack; later discovered before the brothers.
Silver as betrayal: Genesis 37:28—Joseph sold into Egypt for twenty pieces of silver.
Matthew 26:15—Judas agrees to betray Jesus for thirty pieces of silver.
Zechariah 11:12–13—prophecy of the thirty pieces.

7 Cup of joy / marriage feast imagery:
Revelation 19:7–9—*"the marriage of the Lamb is come, and his wife hath made herself ready... Blessed are they which are called unto the marriage supper of the Lamb."*
Matthew 26:29—*"I will not drink henceforth of this fruit of the vine, until that day when I drink it new with you in my Father's kingdom."*
Isaiah 25:6, 8—prophecy of the feast of the Lord, when He will *"swallow up death in victory"* and *"wipe away tears from off all faces."*
Joy complete because of the bitter cup & refusal of silver:
John 16:22—*"your joy no man taketh from you."*

Hebrews 12:2—Christ *"endured the cross, despising the shame... for the joy that was set before him."*

8 Cup of joy / marriage feast imagery:
Revelation 19:7–9—*"the marriage of the Lamb is come, and his wife hath made herself ready... Blessed are they which are called unto the marriage supper of the Lamb."*
Matthew 26:29—*"I will not drink henceforth of this fruit of the vine, until that day when I drink it new with you in my Father's kingdom."*
Isaiah 25:6, 8—prophecy of the feast of the Lord, when He will *"swallow up death in victory"* and *"wipe away tears from off all faces."*
Joy complete because of the bitter cup & refusal of silver:
John 16:22—*"your joy no man taketh from you."*
Hebrews 12:2—Christ *"endured the cross, despising the shame... for the joy that was set before him."*

9 One Bridegroom:
John 3:29—*"He that hath the bride is the bridegroom."*
Matthew 9:15—Christ calls Himself the Bridegroom.
One Bride (the faithful):
Revelation 21:2, 9—*"the holy city, new Jerusalem, prepared as a bride adorned for her husband... Come hither, I will shew thee the bride, the Lamb's wife."*
2 Corinthians 11:2—*"I have espoused you to one husband, that I may present you as a chaste virgin to Christ."*
Lifted up to rejoice with Him forever:
1 Thessalonians 4:16–17—*"caught up... to meet the Lord in the air: and so shall we ever be with the Lord."*
Revelation 19:7–9—marriage supper of the Lamb.

10 Genesis 2:21–22; cf. Matthew Henry, Commentary on the Whole Bible, on Genesis 2:21–22

11 History of the Church 1:17—records Joseph and Emma's marriage on January 18, 1827, in South Bainbridge, New York, by Squire Tarbell.
Joseph Smith Papers, *"Biographical Sketch of Emma Hale Smith"*—confirms date, place, and officiant.

Lucy Mack Smith, History, 1845—Lucy recounts Emma's parents' disapproval and the circumstances of the marriage.

12 Compare Genesis 44:2; Matthew 26:27–29; Mosiah 3:7; History of the Church 1:17

13 Lucy Mack Smith, History, 1845, ed. Scot Facer Proctor and Maurine Jensen Proctor (Salt Lake City: Bookcraft, 1996), 168–170.
History of the Church 1:17.

14 Lucy Mack Smith, History, 1845, 231–234; History of the Church 6:614–617.

15 D&C (1835 edition), Section CI, *"Marriage,"* p. 251.

16 Times and Seasons, Vol. 3, No. 23 (October 1, 1842), p. 939.

17 Times and Seasons, Vol. 5, No. 4 (March 15, 1844), p. 474.

18 *"Last Testimony of Sister Emma,"* interview with Joseph Smith III, in Saints' Herald, Vol. 26, No. 19 (Oct. 1, 1879), p. 289. For over fifty years, she kept her word unbroken.

19 D&C 76:53—*"...who overcame by faith, and are sealed by the Holy Spirit of promise."*
D&C 88:3–4—*"...the Holy Spirit of promise, which other Comforter is the same that I promised unto my disciples..."*
D&C 124:124—reference to the Holy Spirit of promise as God's ratifying seal.
Joseph's emphasis (revelation, not ceremony):
Teachings of the Prophet Joseph Smith, 149–151—Joseph explicitly distinguishes between outward ordinances and the ratifying voice of the Holy Spirit of Promise.

20 The Holy Bible; The Book of Mormon; The Doctrine and Covenants; The Pearl of Great Price.
Then add: No passage in these texts presents sealing as a marriage covenant.
Richard S. Van Wagoner, Mormon Polygamy: A History (1992), notes that Joseph never used the word *"sealing"* to describe marriage.
Todd Compton, In Sacred Loneliness (1997), discusses how

*"sealing"* shifted under Brigham Young.
D&C 76:53; 88:3–4; 124:124; TPJS 149–151—all define sealing as the Holy Spirit of Promise, never marriage.

21 Last Testimony of Sister Emma, Saints' Herald 26 [Oct. 1, 1879]: 289–90

22 Spiritual wifery in Nauvoo:
John C. Bennett promoted *"spiritual wifery"* in Nauvoo (see History of the Church 5:3–6; Joseph exposes Bennett in 1842).
Joseph Smith, Times and Seasons editorial, Aug. 1, 1842, condemns *"spiritual wifery"* as adultery.
Nauvoo Neighbor, Aug. 17, 1843, also prints Joseph's denunciation of spiritual wifery.
Joseph, Emma, Hyrum condemning it:
Hyrum Smith, Times and Seasons, Aug. 1, 1842: *"spiritual wives... are adulterers."*
Emma Smith signed the Voice of Innocence from Nauvoo (March 1844), explicitly condemning spiritual wifery and immorality.
Joseph Smith, History of the Church 5:3–6, labels spiritual wifery as *"abominations and whoredoms."*

23 Accusations and opposition within Nauvoo:
History of the Church 6:408–412—details dissent in Nauvoo and growing opposition tied to plural marriage rumors.
*Richard Lyman Bushman, Joseph Smith: Rough Stone Rolling (2005), 536–540—contextualizes dissent leading to the Nauvoo Expositor.
The Nauvoo Expositor and its role:
Nauvoo Expositor, June 7, 1844 (the only issue), published accusations of polygamy, political abuse, and secret teachings.
History of the Church 6:432–434—records Nauvoo City Council's decision to suppress/destroy the press.

**Dallin H. Oaks and Marvin S. Hill, Carthage Conspiracy (1975), 21–24—confirms the Expositor's publication as the immediate spark that led to Joseph's death.*

24 Joseph Smith, Discourse, Nauvoo, Illinois, 26 May 1844, as reported by Thomas Bullock, in Joseph Smith Papers, Journals, Vol. 3: May 1843–June 1844, ed. Andrew H. Hedges, Alex D.

Smith, and Brent M. Rogers (Salt Lake City: Church Historian's Press, 2015), p. 319. It also appears in History of the Church, Vol. 6, p. 410.

25 *"Minutes of the Nauvoo City Council, June 8, 1844,"* in Joseph Smith Papers, Documents, Vol. 13: January–March 1844, ed. David W. Grua, Elizabeth A. Kuehn, Alexander L. Baugh, Brenden W. Rensink (Salt Lake City: Church Historian's Press, 2022), pp. 447–464.

26 History of the Church 6:602–618—detailed account of Joseph and Hyrum's final days, imprisonment, and martyrdom.
D&C 135:1—*"Joseph Smith, the Prophet, and Hyrum Smith, the Patriarch, were martyred... to seal the testimony of this book and the Book of Mormon."*
Times and Seasons 5 (Aug. 1, 1844): 598–600—official announcement of their deaths.

27 Joseph's declaration of innocence:
History of the Church 6:616—John Taylor records Joseph's final testimony in Carthage, affirming his innocence before God.
Times and Seasons 5 (Aug. 1, 1844): 598–600—official obituary likewise defends Joseph's innocence.
Hyrum's denunciation of polygamy:
Times and Seasons, March 15, 1844, 471–472—Hyrum publishes against *"spiritual wifery,"* calling it adultery.
Voice of Innocence from Nauvoo (March 1844), endorsed by Hyrum and Emma, condemns plural marriage as an abomination.
Emma's steady witness:
Last Testimony of Sister Emma (Saints' Herald 26 [Oct. 1, 1879]: 289–90)—Emma maintained that Joseph had nothing to do with polygamy and remained faithful to her throughout their marriage.
Relief Society Minutes, March 17, 1842—Emma as president, leading women in rejecting immorality under the banner of virtue.

28 Hyrum Smith married Jerusha Barden in 1826; after her death in 1837 he married Mary Fielding. No evidence exists that Hyrum and Jerusha were ever *"sealed,"* nor that Hyrum and Mary were sealed during his lifetime. This mirrors Joseph and Emma's own practice and stands as strong evidence that neither brother taught or lived eternal polygamy. The document now labeled *"Doctrine*

*and Covenants 132"* was introduced only after Joseph and Hyrum's deaths; no contemporary Nauvoo records—journals, letters, sermons, or minutes—show either man teaching, practicing, requesting, or receiving such a revelation. The later story that Hyrum asked for a written explanation originates outside their lifetime and should not be treated as Nauvoo history.

# Interlude

# THE IMAGE RESTORED

## How the Mother Was Lost—and the Wound Behind It

Before we continue, there is a truth we must pause to consider—a quiet wound that shaped generations, and a distortion that touched even the image of God in the minds of His children.

This interlude exists to speak of that wound tenderly, so that what was lost may be seen again, and what was obscured may be restored to light.

The wound I speak of is plural marriage—a teaching foreign to Joseph's revelations—which quietly shifted how the Saints perceived the Godhead.

## Personal Invocation: Knee to Knee with the Reader

I want to sit with you now—face to face, knee to knee—and speak as plainly as I can. I won't mince words or soften what must be said. What follows is the truth as heaven revealed it to Joseph Smith. If you understand nothing else in this book, understand this. You cannot treat this subject lightly. Almost everything we have discussed—Eden, Zion, and the very image of the Godhead—rests upon it.

I know what came after Joseph's death, but that belongs to another volume. *The True Graft* is devoted solely to what Joseph learned from the Lord and taught to us while he lived. The distortions that arose later will be addressed in *Book Two: The Watersprout*. What I share here remains within the boundaries we set from the beginning—only what Joseph himself received from the Lord and taught to the Saints.

I don't speak this as an outsider looking in. I am the great-grandson of polygamists on both sides of my family. I understand the sincerity and the suffering of those who believed they were serving God. My purpose isn't to condemn them, but to tell the truth Joseph restored. That truth is both simple and profound: the image of the Gods Themselves is at stake.

Every doctrine about marriage, every claim about exaltation, must be measured against what God revealed in the beginning—*"male and female created He them,"* two made one. Any doctrine that multiplies what God has made one destroys Their image.

## The Eternal Image of God: Father and Mother, One Heart and One Mind

From the beginning, the Lord revealed the pattern of His own image through the union of man and woman. *"So God created man in His own image, in the image of God created He him; male and female created He them."* (Genesis 1:27)

That verse is not poetic filler; it's the foundation of creation. The image of God is not solitary. It is relational, life-bearing, and whole. The likeness of Deity is expressed through two beings joined as one—Father and Mother, Bridegroom and Bride, Adam and Eve. Together They mirror the unity that exists in heaven itself.

This divine image is woven into the very structure and DNA of eternity. All creation rests upon two equal strands—the masculine and the feminine—working in perfect harmony. One cannot suppress, outdo, overpower, eliminate, or diminish the other without unraveling the very order that gives life.

To disturb that balance is to invite collapse; to honor it is to align with the creative power of heaven. Every living thing bears witness to this law: seed and soil, light and shadow, strength and tenderness—all paired, all interdependent, all sustained by unity.

The Father perfectly exemplifies this eternal law. He is not a solitary being, nor is He a collector of wives. He and the Mother are perfectly one—equal in glory, power, and love.

Their unity gives life to all creation. Their harmony is the law by which worlds are governed. To alter that image, to fracture it into hierarchy or rivalry, is to corrupt the very principle by which existence itself endures.

Marriage, then, is not merely companionship or duty—it is the living reflection of this heavenly order. When a husband and wife are of one heart and one mind, they participate in the likeness of the Gods. This is why Joseph Smith's teachings on marriage were not peripheral. They stood at the very center of his theology, the living parable through which the mysteries of godliness are revealed.

To multiply what God has made one is to deny His very nature. The divine image cannot be divided without being destroyed.

## The Scriptural Law of Oneness

The scriptural law of marriage is not obscure or symbolic—it is declared plainly from the beginning and reaffirmed by every prophet who ever spoke of love, unity, or divine order. The first commandment concerning man and woman was not about dominion or hierarchy but about cleaving: *"Therefore shall a man leave his father and his mother, and shall cleave unto his wife: and they shall be one flesh."* (Genesis 2:24)

When Christ was questioned about this law, He gave no new commandment; He simply restored the original one. *"For this cause shall a man leave father and mother, and cleave to his wife; and they twain shall be one flesh: so then they are no more twain, but one flesh. What therefore God hath joined together, let not man put asunder"* (Mark 10:7–9).

The message could not be clearer. Heaven joins one man and one woman into one life. Anything that divides or multiplies that union is man's doing, not God's.

This same law of oneness governs all of heaven's creations. Zion is its collective form—*"one heart and one mind."* (Moses 7:18) Marriage is its personal form—*"one flesh"* (Genesis 2:24).

Both flow from the same eternal principle: unity born of love. When the Lord said, *"If ye are not one, ye are not mine,"* (D&C 38:27) He wasn't only speaking of community; He was describing the nature of godliness itself. Oneness is the condition of divine life. Division is the mark of death.

As discussed earlier, the ancient Hebrew sense of *"to know"* carried far more than the idea of awareness or physical nearness. It described a sacred oneness—the deep, personal unity through which life itself is conceived. The same word describes how the righteous come to know God, not through information, but through shared being.

True knowing, whether between husband and wife or between the soul and its Maker, is the language of union. It cannot be divided or multiplied without losing the very power that makes it holy.

The law of oneness is therefore the foundation of both marriage and eternal life. A man cannot know two women in the sacred sense any more than Christ could have two brides. Love in its highest form is exclusive, total, and indivisible. Heaven operates by this law, and Zion will be built upon it.

The power of godliness itself flows through unity—through one heart, one mind, one love made whole.

## Joseph Smith's Witness and Restoration Record

Joseph Smith did not merely speak of this divine order—he lived it. His marriage to Emma wasn't incidental to his calling; it was the living witness of the law he restored. From their earliest years together, they stood as a symbol of the Bridegroom and the Bride, united in labor, faith, and suffering. Through every trial—poverty, persecution, loss of children, and the burden of leading a people—Joseph and Emma remained the earthly reflection of the heavenly image: one heart, one mind, one flesh.

As shown in the Revelations on Marriage section, the 1835 Doctrine and Covenants included an official statement titled *"Marriage,"* declaring that the Church believed in one man with one wife and one woman with one husband. Joseph endorsed that law, and it was never repealed during his lifetime. It stood as the governing rule of the Restoration.

Nine years later, in March 1844, the women of Nauvoo—led by Emma as president of the Relief Society—issued The Voice of Innocence from Nauvoo, a formal declaration reaffirming the same law of monogamy already upheld in scripture and in the 1835 Doctrine and Covenants. Joseph supported Emma's work and approved its publication, uniting his voice with hers in defense of virtue and fidelity. Together they bore witness to the same Edenic order—the law of one man and one woman joined as one.

There is no record—public, private, or prophetic—of Joseph teaching plural marriage as an eternal law. His revelations and his life both testify otherwise. He spoke of *"one flesh,"* not many; of *"one heart and one mind,"* not division. His restoration was not a project of hierarchy or accumulation but of unity and equality.

Every true principle he taught—from priesthood to Zion to the fullness of the gospel—was designed to bring the hearts of men and women together under the same Spirit.

In this light, Joseph and Emma stand as a living parable. Their union, refined in affliction and sealed by sacrifice, reflected the very image of the Gods: Father and Mother, Bridegroom and Bride. To multiply what heaven joined as one would have shattered that image entirely.

It would have turned the law of life into a system of rivalry and sorrow. Joseph's teachings left no room for such corruption, and his life left no question about where he stood.

He didn't restore a hierarchy of men, but the harmony of heaven.

## The Fruits of Plurality: Scripture's Unbroken Testimony

Every tree is known by its fruit, and the fruits of plurality have been bitter from the beginning. Wherever men multiplied wives, peace departed, jealousy took root, and families fell into sorrow. Scripture does not hide this pattern—it preserves it as a warning.

When Abram took Hagar at Sarai's urging, the result was strife and separation. "*And when she saw that she had conceived, her mistress was despised in her eyes*" (Genesis 16:4).

The wound spread through generations, dividing Ishmael and Isaac.

Jacob's household fared no better: "*When the Lord saw that Leah was hated, he opened her womb*" (Genesis 29:31).

The rivalry between Leah and Rachel bred competition so fierce that their sons turned to envy and violence.

David's many wives led him to moral failure.

Solomon's multiplied marriages opened the door to idolatry until "*his wives turned away his heart after other gods*" (1 Kings 11:4).

In every case, the pattern is the same—**division follows multiplicity**, and the Spirit withdraws.

The Book of Mormon gives the Lord's own verdict. Through the prophet Jacob, He declared: "*David and Solomon truly had many wives and concubines, which thing was abominable before me, saith the Lord.*" (Jacob 2:24)

The word *abominable* is not temporary; it is moral and absolute. The Lord adds, "*Ye have broken the hearts of your tender wives, and the sobbings of their hearts ascend up to God against you*" (Jacob 2:35).

The language is personal and piercing—Heaven hears the cries of women whose love was divided.

Later revelation warned that such corruption would return among those who claimed to know His name: "*Behold, vengeance cometh speedily upon the inhabitants of the earth... and first among those among you, saith the Lord, who have professed to know my name and have not known me*" (D&C 112:24–26).

To multiply what heaven joined as one, and to do so in His name, is to invite the very judgments that begin at His own house.

By contrast, wherever the law of oneness is honored, the fruits are life and light. Eden's union brought increase; Zion's unity brought peace. When the image is whole, the Spirit abides. When it is broken, confusion reigns.

Polygamy is not a higher order—it is a corruption that divides hearts, silences prophecy, and drives the Spirit away. The record of scripture stands unbroken: multiplicity breeds sorrow; oneness begets glory.

## Why It Cannot Be of God

The law of heaven is unity, not division. The image of God is a pair—Father and Mother—two beings joined so perfectly that Their love governs worlds. Every true principle Joseph restored reflects that same order: equality, fidelity, and oneness of heart.

Any teaching that multiplies what God has made one cannot come from Him. It fractures the very harmony that sustains creation.

To claim that God commands plurality is to suggest that the Father Himself is incomplete, that His love must be divided to be whole. But the Father is not fragmented. He perfectly honors the eternal balance—the masculine and the feminine, each distinct yet equal, each strengthening the other in perfect reciprocity.

You cannot exalt the masculine by diminishing the feminine; to do so is to sever the cord that connects life to its source. As I stated before: the Father is not a solitary being, nor is He a collector of wives. He is eternally united with one Woman—our Heavenly Mother—equal in glory, power, and love.

Together They are the living image of oneness, the perfect model of divine marriage. Without Them, the entire plan of salvation would unravel.

This is why Jacob called plural marriage an abomination (Jacob 2:24–28). It is not merely error—it is blasphemy against the Mother. It proclaims to heaven, *You are not enough.* It denies Her sufficiency, divides Her likeness, and profanes the sacred pattern by which all creation lives.

When men have done this in God's name, history has shown the result: jealousy, oppression, and spiritual blindness. And when they have carried such acts into His house, claiming authority for what He has forbidden, the heavens have responded as foretold: *"First among those among you, saith the Lord, who have professed to know my name and have not known me"* (D&C 112:26).

Those who blaspheme Her in His name invite the cleansing storms spoken of by every prophet who ever warned of the last days.

The Lord of Heaven is not the author of confusion, division, or hierarchy between the genders.

His house is a house of order, and order begins in fidelity. The Father and the Mother are one. The Son and His Bride will be one. Zion will be one. This is the law that governs eternity. Anything that divides what They have joined cannot be of God.

## The True Law of Heaven: Oneness Restored

The true law of heaven is not found in hierarchy or accumulation but in wholeness. All things that live are governed by the principle of two made one. This is the rhythm that pulses through creation—the joining of heaven and earth, light and life, Father and Mother. When this law is honored, harmony reigns. When it is violated, everything built upon it begins to crumble.

From the beginning, the Lord has revealed this same order through every symbol of His work. Eden opened with one man and one woman. Zion flourished when its people became of one heart and one mind. The Church of the Lamb is one body animated by one Spirit. Each reflects the same celestial pattern: unity born of love. When Christ prayed, *"That they all may be one; as thou, Father, art in me, and I in thee"* (John 17:21)—He revealed not a metaphor, but the essence of divine life itself.

This is why the sealing power, when rightly understood, points not to multiplication but to perfection—to the unbroken bond between Christ and His Bride. The Holy Spirit of Promise seals only what mirrors heaven. It binds those who are pure in heart, whose unity is sanctified by love. Everything else—contracts of control, alliances of ambition, or unions born of fear—cannot be sealed by that Spirit.

Heaven joins only what reflects its own likeness.

When the image of Father and Mother is honored on earth, heaven draws near. Prophecy returns. The gifts of the Spirit flourish. The hearts of men and women soften, and Zion begins to form again—not through decrees, but through oneness of heart. This is the true order Joseph Smith sought to restore: a people knit together by the same Spirit that unites the Gods.

To restore oneness is to restore Eden—to walk again in the presence of the Lord without shame or division. It is to remember who we are: sons and daughters of divine Parents whose union is the law of life itself. When that image is kept pure, all creation responds in harmony. When it is broken, the heavens mourn.

This is the law written into the fabric of eternity: oneness is the power of godliness. Every other law serves it, and every true marriage reflects it. The Father and the Mother are one. The Son and His Bride will be one. Zion will be one. And all who learn to love as They love will discover that heaven has already begun within them.

## Personal Witness and Plea

I have spoken these things as plainly as I know how. This is not theory to me, nor is it history to be debated. It is truth that burns in my bones. I have felt the grief that follows division and the peace that comes when hearts are made one. I have watched how every false teaching about marriage darkens the light within both men and women, and how quickly the Spirit withdraws when love becomes competition.

But I have also felt the healing that follows when the law of oneness is honored again—the quiet strength, the equal standing, the shared glory that flow from heaven's design.

I speak these words with reverence, knowing the weight they carry. I do not condemn those who were deceived by the traditions of men, nor those who bore the wounds such traditions caused. Many acted in sincerity, believing they served God. But sincerity cannot transform error into truth. The Lord requires obedience to the higher law—the law of love that unites rather than divides.

I know that Father in Heaven is not single. He is eternally married to one Wife—our Heavenly Mother.

I know She lives. I have felt Her presence in my life so many times that I cannot fully describe how much I love Her. I look forward to the day when I will once again be reunited with Her. But for now, I honor Her. I praise and worship Her. And I invite you to remember Her, and return to the understanding that They together are the foundation of all life.

Their equality is the light of creation. Their love is the reason worlds endure. Every true marriage on earth is meant to echo Theirs: two hearts joined so completely that the Spirit can dwell in their midst. When that image is preserved, heaven and earth meet. When it is profaned, everything holy begins to fade.

This, then, is the truth Joseph restored—that man and woman together form the image of God, and that any doctrine which multiplies what He has made one destroys that image.

I plead with every reader to take this to heart. Don't dismiss it as mere philosophy or treat it lightly. This is the law by which worlds are governed—the song of creation, the bond of Zion, the fire that seals the faithful in the presence of God. This is the truth of the gospel of Jesus Christ and His church.

Let us honor the image of Father and Mother in our own homes. Let us guard the sanctity of marriage, love, speak truth, and refuse every counterfeit that divides what heaven joined as one.

When we learn to love as They love, the kingdom of heaven will no longer be distant. It will begin within us—and Zion will rise again.

# Author's Reflection

There are portions of a journey that cannot be planned. They unfold by appointment.

Looking back, I can see that every season of my life—every joy, every loss, every unexpected solitude—was one of those appointments. Each carried a lesson that no classroom could have offered and no sermon could have delivered.

For more than twenty years, I have walked the road of a single man. It wasn't the life I expected, but it was the one heaven chose for me. That solitude became my refiner's fire. It taught me how to listen, how to serve, and how to feel God's presence when all other companionship was gone. It allowed me to stand beside my son when he needed me most, to care for my parents in their final years, and to comfort friends whose hearts were breaking.

Had I been married during those seasons, I couldn't have offered that kind of devotion. Heaven knew what I didn't: that singleness would be the crucible through which love would be made whole.

Through these years, I have been surrounded by extraordinary friends—whose strength and faith revealed the living face of the Divine Feminine. Some have now crossed the veil: Robin, Carol, Theresa, Peggy, Dan, my parents. Others remain, carrying the same quiet power that has sustained me all along. Their presence has been a living reminder that I was never alone.

I have come to know that my Father in Heaven is not single, and that my Heavenly Mother lives. I have felt Her near me—teaching, comforting, guiding—through every loss and every rebirth. She has been the unspoken constant in every chapter of this book, the voice behind the curtain calling Her children to remember.

When I began writing this book, I never intended to write this reflection—or this interlude at all. It wasn't part of the outline. It wasn't something I planned to address.

But as the work unfolded, I found that I could no longer place Her in the margins. The truths I was encountering would not allow it. To remain silent would have been to withhold something essential—not from the reader, but from my own conscience.

This reflection exists because it had to. I am simply bearing witness to what I have learned, and to Her place in my life.

My hope is that those who read these words will feel what I have felt: that heaven is not distant, that love is the law by which worlds endure, and that our Mother has not been forgotten. She has been here all along—waiting for Her children to remember Her.

*Though long the wait,*
*Her watch is kind.*
*She breathes forth life,*
*and whispers mind.*

*When hearts remember,*
*love will transcend.*
*The Mother stirs—*
*and we with Them.*

# The Mountain of the Lord

Appointments Where Heaven Meets Earth

---

### The House of the Lord

The revealed purpose of the temple is to prepare a soul to enter the presence of the Lord. That is the goal—not the building, not the ritual, not the structure, but the encounter with Him.

Still, scripture shows plainly that the Lord's presence isn't confined to a building. Many who sought Him found Him without a temple.

> **Lehi**: Rejected by Jerusalem, Lehi prayed in the solitude of his home and was caught away in vision: *"He thought he saw God sitting upon his throne, surrounded with numberless concourses of angels"* (1 Nephi 1:8). The throne of God appeared in his bedroom, not in a temple.
>
> **Nephi**: As a wanderer in the wilderness, Nephi was *"caught away in the Spirit of the Lord, yea, into an exceedingly high mountain"* (1 Nephi 11:1). His temple was the mountaintop.
>
> **Jacob**: Nephi records, *"My brother, Jacob, also has seen him as I have seen him"* (2 Nephi 11:3). Jacob's witness of Christ came directly, apart from ritual or building.
>
> **Isaiah**: While his nation despised him, Isaiah testified, *"I saw also the Lord sitting upon a throne, high and lifted up, and his*

> *train filled the temple"* (Isaiah 6:1). His vision came by the Spirit, not by ritual gatekeepers.
>
> **Moroni**: Alone in exile, Moroni declared, *"Then shall ye know that I have seen Jesus, and that he hath talked with me face to face"* (Ether 12:39). His audience with Christ came without any temple at all.
>
> **The Brother of Jared**: Seeking light for his barges, he climbed Mount Shelem and cried unto the Lord to touch the stones. *"And the Lord stretched forth his hand and touched the stones one by one with his finger... And the Lord showed himself unto him"* (Ether 3:6, 13). His vision was born of faith in a desolate place.

Each of these witnesses entered the Lord's presence outside the walls of a temple.

Some lived when temples stood, others when they did not. But in every case, it was the Lord who opened the way—not a building, not a ceremony.

So why does God command temples?

The answer is sobering: because most of us are not yet prepared for such direct encounters.

Like scaffolding around a house, a temple provides structure and support until the soul is ready to stand in God's presence without it. Temples help disciples practice holiness, discipline, and devotion in a focused way—learning, step by step, what the prophets received directly.

Or, to use a gentler image: a temple is like training wheels on a bicycle. Some can balance and ride straight into the Lord's presence without them, but most of us need help learning how.

Joseph Smith himself did not need a temple—visions, angels, and Christ Himself came to him long before Kirtland or Nauvoo. The temples he was commanded to build were for the Saints, to guide them toward the same capacity.

### Kirtland Temple – Endowed with Power from on High

Joseph carried a deep anxiety for the Saints.

> *He had seen angels.*
> *He had stood in visions too glorious to put into words.*

> *He had tasted the gifts of the Spirit and been changed by them forever.*

But when he looked out at his people, he saw how slow of heart they were—how distracted, how stiff-necked, how easily drawn back into the cares of the world. His heart longed for them to share in what he had seen and felt.

What hope Joseph must have felt when the Lord commanded him to build a temple.

At last, there would be a house where heaven and earth could meet. At last, there could be a place where his people might receive the same power that had already rested upon him.

For Joseph, this wasn't a burden but a joy. He longed for Emma, for his family, for the whole community he loved to rise into that light. He knew the only way for that to happen was to build the Lord's house. When the commandment came, he was overjoyed.

The revelation declared:

> *"Organize yourselves; prepare every needful thing; and establish a house, even a house of prayer, a house of fasting, a house of faith, a house of learning, a house of glory, a house of order, a house of God."* (D&C 88:119)

The command was not casual. It was a summons from heaven: prepare, build, sanctify yourselves. The following year, the Lord repeated it with even greater urgency:

> *"I gave unto you a commandment to build a house... for the salvation of Zion... that you may be endowed with power from on high."* (D&C 95:3, 8)

The temple was not commanded for Joseph's sake—he had already been endowed with power from on high. It was meant for the Saints, who had not.

Joseph was filled with gratitude that the Lord had made the way for them, because he loved them so deeply.

This is the burden of a prophet: a heart full of love, yet constant heartache when the people will not change.

The building itself became a test of faith and obedience.

The Saints were poor, yet they sacrificed their time, their strength, and their meager means. They endured ridicule from neighbors as they hauled stone and timber. Each wall they raised was another chance to prove their devotion.

This has always been the Lord's method. It is how He makes up His jewels. As we saw earlier, a stiff-necked people must be burdened, tried, and refined. Gold must pass through fire before its impurities are removed. So it was with the building of the Kirtland temple.[1]

When the temple was finished and dedicated in March 1836, Joseph poured out his soul in the dedicatory prayer:

> *"That thy glory may rest down upon thy people, and upon this thy house... that all the people who shall enter upon the threshold of the Lord's house may feel thy power."* (D&C 109:12–13)

His voice pled that angels would attend, that sins would be forgiven, and that the Saints would be prepared to go forth strengthened.

The Lord answered. The dedication and the weeks that followed became a furnace of living fire.

> Eliza R. Snow testified, *"The ceremonies of that dedication may be rehearsed, but no mortal language can describe the heavenly manifestations of that memorable day. Angels appeared to some, while a sense of the divine presence was realized by all present, and each heart was filled with joy inexpressible and full of glory"* (Biography and Family Record of Lorenzo Snow, 20).

> George A. Smith recalled, *"The Spirit of the Lord filled the house to such an extent that many prophesied, and all were filled with the power of God, and with great joy"* (JD 11:10).

> Zebedee Coltrin remembered seeing the Savior himself: *"I saw the Savior... and he smiled upon us. Afterwards Joseph told us that angels were resting down upon the house. The power rested upon us to that degree that joy filled every heart"* (Salt Lake School of the Prophets Minutes, Oct. 3, 1883).

> Wilford Woodruff declared, *"The ceremonies of that day surpassed anything of the kind that I had ever witnessed. The Spirit of God, like a mighty rushing wind, was poured out in great abundance. It was a Pentecost and endowment indeed"* (Journal, Mar. 30, 1836).

> George A. Smith added, *"Such a shout never before ascended to heaven. The rushing of the mighty wind of the Spirit of God filled the house"* (JD 11:10).
>
> They shouted Hosanna until the walls shook. The sound of thousands of voices rose together—*"Hosanna! Hosanna! Hosanna to God and the Lamb!"*—waving white handkerchiefs in unison until it seemed heaven and earth had joined in chorus (Joseph Smith's journal (via HC 2:427–428).

Then came signs that none could deny.

Several witnesses later testified that flames appeared upon the roof of the temple, so real that onlookers outside thought the building was burning. But no timber was consumed, for this was not earthly fire—it was the fire of heaven.

Heavenly music was also heard, surpassing the capacity of human voices. Eliza R. Snow recorded that *"a choir of angels joined in the anthems of praise, and their sweet melody was wafted throughout the house"* (Biography and Family Record of Lorenzo Snow, 21).

Wilford Woodruff recalled that *"the people could not tell whether they were in heaven or on earth, for so great was the glory of God"* (Journal, Mar. 30, 1836).

The Kirtland dedication was a living Pentecost (D&C 109). Tongues, visions, prophecy, angelic ministrations, the presence of Christ Himself—all testified that this was indeed the house of the Lord.

For a season, the Saints lived in that light. But soon the adversary began his dark work. Economic collapse, bitterness, and division began to grow. The bank failed. Murmuring rose. Friends turned against one another. The gifts ceased.[2]

Within two years, Joseph was driven from Kirtland. Not long after, the Saints themselves were scattered.[3]

Yet its legacy stands. The Kirtland Temple remains a witness of what a house of the Lord truly is meant to be: a place where heaven bends low, and a people rise up into the presence of their Redeemer.

### Nauvoo Temple – A House of Appointments Prepared for His Manifestation

The road to Nauvoo was carved in sorrow and stained with blood. The Saints had been driven from Missouri by mobs—their homes torched, their farms seized, their families scattered or murdered.[4]

At Haun's Mill, men, women, and children were gunned down in cold blood. Some were shot as they begged for mercy. Others were slaughtered while hiding in the blacksmith shop, their bodies were left in a shallow well.[5]

Governor Lilburn W. Boggs had signed an official extermination order declaring that every member of the Church must be *"exterminated or driven from the state."* Joseph himself was chained in Liberty Jail while his people—scattered and destitute—cried out for deliverance.[6]

By the time they stumbled into Illinois, they were broken, weary, and homeless, bearing the scars of persecution that had nearly consumed them.

Yet from the edge of a swamp along the Mississippi River, they began again. They drained the marshes, built homes, planted orchards, and turned desolation into a thriving city. Nauvoo became a place of refuge and renewal.[7]

This mattered deeply. The Lord doesn't command a temple lightly. He waits until a people are prepared to receive it—settled enough, refined enough, willing and humble enough to seek for His presence.

In January 1841, the Lord gave His command:

> *"Let this house be built unto my name, that I may reveal mine ordinances therein unto my people."* (D&C 124:40)

Saints had already begun baptizing for their dead in the Mississippi River after Joseph introduced the practice in 1840, but the Lord required it to be done in His house. Temporary measures would not suffice.

The command was clear: build a temple for the work of the living and the dead, for appointments where heaven would meet earth.

The revelation named specific purposes: baptisms for the dead, washings, anointings, solemn assemblies.

As we saw in the Priesthood chapter, Joseph used the word ordinance very differently than it is often understood today. When he spoke of ordinances, he meant what God ordains and appoints—sacred thresholds where His power is revealed.

The 1828 Webster's Dictionary defined ordinance in several ways: *'a rule established by authority; an observance commanded; an appointment; or an established rite or ceremony'* (Webster's 1828, s.v. "Ordinance").

In Joseph's day, most Christians emphasized the last sense, treating ordinances chiefly as ceremonies like baptism or communion.

But Joseph deliberately emphasized the older, and broader sense: divine appointments—sacred thresholds where God reveals His power. It was a conscious shift, reclaiming the word from mere ritual and anchoring it again in revelation.

Ordinances weren't man's inventions but divine appointments—moments ordered by God where His power is revealed. They were never empty rites but living thresholds, appointments where the faithful could draw near and receive from Him directly.

The Lord's command in Nauvoo was itself an ordinance to Joseph. It was not about inventing new ceremonies, but about preparing a house where divine appointments could unfold in greater fullness. If Joseph obeyed, the Lord would manifest Himself to all who labored in preparing His house—each manifestation building greater confidence and a deeper bond with Him.

The temple was to be a place where His people could experience those appointments for themselves—where they would be taught, tested, and drawn into His presence as they obeyed His order (His appointment) to build a house to His name.

The revelation itself declared:

> *"For there is not a place found on earth that he may come to and restore again that which was lost unto you, or which he hath taken away, even the fulness of the priesthood."* (D&C 124:28)

From the beginning, Joseph's revelations often came on behalf of others. Page after page of the Doctrine and Covenants bears witness that men and women needed him to inquire of the Lord for them. But just as Moses longed for Israel to hear God's voice themselves, Joseph longed for a day when his people would no longer depend on his mediation.

The temple was commanded for that very reason: to be a house of preparation where individuals could learn to hear God's voice, receive His appointments, and be endowed with light until they obtained the fulness He promised:

> *"I give unto you these sayings that you may understand and know how to worship, and know what you worship, that you may come unto the Father in my name, and in due time receive of his fulness. For if you keep my commandments you shall*

> *receive of his fulness, and be glorified in me as I am in the Father."* (D&C 93:19–20)

But along with the promise came a stark warning: *"If ye do not these things at the end of the appointment, ye shall be rejected as a church, with your dead"* (D&C 124:32).

The weight of that word—*rejected*—hung heavy on Joseph. So much so that he authorized a temporary baptismal font in the basement of the unfinished temple so the Saints could begin to obey, though he understood it was only provisional.

Unless the house was completed, the blessing would not come.

For Joseph, the command carried both joy and burden. Joy, because it meant his beloved Emma, his children, and the Saints could be lifted into the same light he had known. Burden, because he knew the consequence: blessings are forfeited when the people harden their hearts and resist.

Again, this is the prophet's heart—overflowing with love, yet pierced with grief when his people would not rise.

The Nauvoo Temple was the last house the Lord commanded Joseph to build.

He would not live to see it finished. But the revelation remains as his testimony: God intended to meet His people there, to reveal His appointments, to manifest Himself in their midst.

It stands as both promise and warning—a witness that temples are not monuments, but places where His people can seek His face. To turn aside is to harden the heart, and with hardness comes loss of greater blessings.

The Lord said of ancient Israel: *"They hardened their hearts and could not endure His presence; therefore... he took Moses out of their midst, and the Holy Priesthood also"* (D&C 84:24–25).

## The Embrace - The Wrestle Before God

Before a soul can stand in the presence of the Lord, there must be a wrestle.

The wrestle is the refining fire. It is the birth canal of the Spirit, the place where the natural man is put off and the soul becomes a new creature—sanctified, without spot, perfect in Christ (Mosiah 3:19; Moroni 10:31–32).

This isn't God overpowering man, but man yielding fully to God, until the two are one—they become like each other in mind, in heart, in will (Moroni 7:48).

This is the moment when trust is complete, and surrender is entire. Not one wing straining while the other hangs limp, but both wings fully extended, lifting together in harmony. This is wholeness. Two are no longer divided, but one—whole, complete, at peace in Christ.[8]

Jacob's story shows us this pattern. He wrestled with the Lord all night, clinging, refusing to let go until the blessing came (Genesis 32:24–30).

In Hebrew, the word *wrestle* also means *embrace.*[9]

What Jacob experienced was not simply a contest of strength, but the intimate embrace of surrender. And at the break of day, when Jacob had proven he was fully broken, God gave him a new name: Israel.

The Book of Mormon gives us another witness. Enos described his wrestle before God in the forest:

> *"I will tell you of the wrestle which I had before God, before I received a remission of my sins."* (Enos 1:2)

He cried all day and into the night, until the voice of the Lord spoke peace to his soul. Enos's wrestle was his refining fire, his embrace with God. In that moment, his sins were not merely forgiven but remitted—burned away by the fire of the Holy Ghost.

> *"The Spirit of the Lord came upon them, and they were filled with joy, having received a remission of their sins, and having peace of conscience."* (Mosiah 4:3)

This is the only way sins are truly removed. Enos walked away a new man in Christ.

This is always the process of refining fire. Every rung on the ladder of ascent is marked by this wrestle—this embrace—where the dross of the natural man burns away and the soul is refined.

The beautiful thing is, with each rung comes a new name, a witness of transformation. Abram became Abraham. Jacob became Israel. Saul became Paul. Each name declared: you are not who you were—you are Mine.[10]

Can you imagine what it would be like to hear the Lord speak your name? Not as men speak it, but as He speaks it—with such profound love it pierces your heart.

John said His voice was *"as the sound of many waters"* (Revelation 1:15). And when He descended among the Nephites, it was *"not a harsh voice, neither... a loud voice; nevertheless... it did pierce them to the very soul, and did cause their hearts to burn"* (3 Nephi 11:3).

A voice at once mighty and tender, so pure and perfect that it awakens parts of your soul you never knew could live.

How do you think Joseph must have felt when the very first word he heard in the grove was his own name? The heavens broke their silence, not with thunder, but with recognition: God knew his name and called him by it.

One day, you too will hear Him speak a name that only He and you will know (Revelation 2:17). That name won't simply mark you—it will steady you. It will be the seal of your wrestle, the embrace that changes you forever, the witness that you belong wholly to Him.

It will be your new identity—who you are known as forever. For the promise is sure: *"they see as they are seen, and know as they are known"* (D&C 76:94). And as Moroni testified, *"when he shall appear we shall be like him, for we shall see him as he is"* (Moroni 7:48).

The wrestle is not meant to destroy you, but to uncover you. This is how God shows His love—by refining, purifying, and revealing the true self He always saw within you, until nothing remains but the glory of Christ.

This is why the Lord gave His people appointments of purification and consecration.

They were never about outward forms, but about preparing men and women to enter His presence—by leading them into the wrestle, the embrace that refines the soul.

In these appointments, the Godhead offers smaller steps—smaller bites of light—to ready Their children for the fire of Their presence. The Father gives law, the Mother gives life, the Son gives light; together They tutor the soul through consecration until the heart can bear Their glory.

And so, in Joseph's day, He gave the Saints washings and anointings—simple, sacred acts of cleansing and consecration—to help them yield and surrender, so that in the embrace they could be made ready to stand before Him.

## Washings and Anointings - Joseph's Practice

Imagine the coronation of a king or a queen in ancient times, carried out with divine symbolism and reverence. Before the crown was ever placed upon the head, there was a sacred preparation.

> **First,** they were washed with water—cleansed from every impurity, that they might stand pure before God and man.
> **Second,** they were anointed—olive oil consecrated, poured out as a witness that they were chosen, set apart, sanctified for a holy trust.
> **Finally,** they were clothed in robes of royalty, garments that testified outwardly of the inward transformation, that they had been ordained to reign in majesty.[11]

This was more than ceremony. It was the divine pattern of coronation: purification and consecration. Solomon's anointing is one example:

> *"Zadok the priest took a horn of oil out of the tabernacle, and anointed Solomon. And they blew the trumpet; and all the people said, God save king Solomon."* (1 Kings 1:39)

Washing, anointing, and clothing, in their true order, were meant to be visible witnesses that heaven had chosen and set apart a ruler for God's work—not empty cultural custom, but a sacred appointment.

That same pattern extended beyond the coronation of kings. It was given in the law of Moses for those who were called to minister:

> *"And thou shalt bring Aaron and his sons unto the door of the tabernacle of the congregation, and wash them with water. And thou shalt put upon Aaron the holy garments, and anoint him, and sanctify him, that he may minister unto me in the priest's office."* (Exodus 40:12–13)

Washing, anointing, and clothing were the Lord's own appointments—signs of cleansing, consecration, and readiness to minister in His service.

Joseph Smith followed this ancient pattern in Kirtland, though only in part. As the temple neared completion in early 1836, he invited a small group of elders and missionaries to a garret above the temple.

There they washed with water for purification and were anointed with oil for consecration—simple blessings of cleansing and sanctification.[12]

The event was unscripted, informal, and never repeated in the Kirtland Temple—and the clothing portion described in ancient coronations was never introduced during Joseph's lifetime.

One eyewitness account, written decades later by Zebedee Coltrin, recalls the simplicity of that event:[13]

> *"They washed, anointed each other with oil..."*[14]

Records confirm that this was not a recurring ritual—the preparation was singular, focused, and spiritual without ceremonial drama.

The result? Sanctification followed by spiritual manifestations: visions, prophecy, angelic ministrations, and the gloriously fulfilled promise of power from on high. Though the washing and anointing were not themselves the cause of these blessings—they were part of the necessary preparation.

Years later, in Nauvoo, the Lord commanded that a house be built to His name once more. In His command, He included washings and anointings (D&C 124), but there's no evidence these were ever performed in the unfinished Nauvoo Temple during Joseph's lifetime.[15]

The solemn practice of washings and anointings remained a simple, preparatory appointment delivered only once in Kirtland.

In summary, Joseph's practice reveals that washings and anointings were never ritualized or formalized in his lifetime. They were simple, unscripted appointments of holiness meant to prepare the soul to be sanctified by the Spirit and ready to stand before the Lord.[16]

Joseph's revelations also named another kind of temple appointment—one given not to individuals alone, but to the whole body of Saints gathered together.

## Solemn Assemblies - Group Appointments

Throughout scripture, God called His people to gather in solemn assemblies. These were holy convocations where the entire community was invited to sanctify themselves and stand before the Lord. Joel proclaimed:

> *"Blow the trumpet in Zion, sanctify a fast, call a solemn assembly: gather the people, sanctify the congregation."* (Joel 2:15–16)

These assemblies were not casual meetings, but sacred gatherings where all hearts were united to seek God together.

Joseph's revelations carried this same command. In Kirtland, the Saints were told:

> *"Call your solemn assembly, that your fastings and your mourning might come up into the ears of the Lord of Sabaoth."* (D&C 88:70)

In Hebrew, Sabaoth means *"hosts"*—the great concourses of heaven. The title Lord of Hosts declares that He rules those multitudes and can summon them at will. So when His people hold a solemn assembly, it becomes our invitation to Him; His answer is to marshal angels—to fill the house with those He commands.[17]

At the dedication of the Kirtland Temple, Joseph prayed:

> *"That thy solemn assembly may be held in this house, that thy people may enter into a covenant with thee to be thy people."* (D&C 109:6)

And when the Nauvoo Temple was commanded, solemn assemblies were again listed as part of its divine purpose (D&C 124:39).

Do you know what it's called when the earth first rose up out of the waters and its highest peak touched the lowest part of heaven? It has a name—the primordial mound.[18]

Why does it matter? Because it's the place where earth meets heaven.

Picture two pyramids: one rising up from the earth, the other descending from the sky. Where their points touch is the primordial mound—where ascent meets descent, where God comes down and man reaches up. This is the true meeting place of heaven and earth, where God speaks with His children.

But the adversary offers a counterfeit. After the city of Enoch was taken up and lingered in the heavens, men longed to reach it by their own strength. They began building a tower that would reach *"heaven"* (Genesis 11:4).

The tower of Babel was the devil's imitation of the Mountain of the Lord—a counterfeit ascent without God's appointment. And you know the difference by the fruit: Zion bore a city received into heaven, while Babel bore only scattering and confusion.

The Lord's design is plain. Every holy mountain given by His appointment—every true temple—follows this shape: built at the meeting point so heaven can bend low and people can rise.

In Eden, the primordial mound became the Garden itself—the first holy mountain—where Adam and Eve walked with God in the cool of the day. It was the place where heaven and earth converged, where man and God met face to face.[19]

Generations later, after the flood, Noah's ark drifted upon endless waters. Days stretched into weeks until it seemed he might never see land again (Genesis 7:24; 8:6–12).

In hope, he sent out a raven. It returned with nothing, and his heart grew heavier. Then he sent a dove. At last, the dove returned with an olive branch in its beak—the same symbol that would one day descend upon Jesus at His baptism, the sign of peace and of God's Spirit resting upon man.[20]

That branch was more than a token of dry ground. It was a living witness that life still flowed from the root. From that root, new grafts would one day spring forth, teaching all generations of God's dealings with His people.

And the branch itself had been plucked from the one place where life had returned: the primordial mound, the rising of earth from beneath the waters, the mountain nearest to heaven.

Isaiah saw this same pattern in vision, carried into the last days:

> *"And it shall come to pass in the last days, that the mountain of the Lord's house shall be established in the top of the mountains, and shall be exalted above the hills; and all nations shall flow unto it. And many people shall go and say, Come ye, and let us go up to the mountain of the Lord, to the house of the God of Jacob."* (Isaiah 2:2–3)

A solemn assembly is the community version of that ascent.

Just as prophets of old ascended mountains to meet God, so the Saints were called to gather as one body into a sanctified house, lifted above the world, to meet Him together.

It is a group appointment, a time when heaven itself is invited down—not only for individuals but for the entire body. These assemblies were designed so that angels could minister and God could manifest Himself in the midst of His people.

This is the meaning of a solemn assembly: a temple gathering sanctified for God's presence, where His people ascend together onto the mountain of the Lord—His primordial mound in the midst of the world—and He reveals Himself among them.[21]

And in Kirtland, they did. The people lifted their voices in the Hosanna Shout, the roof blazed with fire, angels filled the room, and all knew they had stood together upon the mountain of the Lord.[22]

## Ordinances - What Joseph Meant

In the quiet stillness of the heart, God whispers to His people and calls them to consecrated spaces—mountains, gardens, groves—where heaven and earth converge.

Moses ascended Sinai, Elijah heard the still small voice upon the mount, Nephi and Enos sought Him in the wilderness, Joseph entered the grove,[23] and Isaiah saw the day when *"the mountain of the Lord's house shall be established in the top of the mountains"* (Isaiah 2:2).

Wherever God appoints the meeting place, it becomes holy ground—set apart so His children may ascend and He may descend.

This is the meaning of ordinances. They are not rituals void of relationship, but divine appointments—times and places where heaven draws near and God manifests His power and love, forging an unbreakable relationship with His children.

Joseph taught this plainly:

> *"In the ordinances thereof, the power of godliness is manifest. And without the ordinances thereof... the power of godliness is not manifest unto men in the flesh. For without this no man can see the face of God, even the Father, and live."* (D&C 84:20–22)

And I would add my personal belief—that the same holds true for our Heavenly Mother, perhaps even more so. Her glory would overwhelm an unprepared heart, not because She withholds it, but because we have forgotten how to receive it.

Why such strong language?

Because without these appointments, no soul ever gains the confidence to stand in God's presence. Each one is a grace-to-grace encounter, a manifestation that gently builds upon the last. Over time, these crossings weave courage into the heart until the day comes when a man or woman can both approach and endure His glory.

Without such experiences, His presence would overwhelm and consume. Ordinances are the Lord's way of preparing His children—step by step—for the fulness that He has promised.

As we learned earlier, ordinances begin with the baptism of fire and the Holy Ghost. Water may cleanse the body, but it is the fire of the Spirit that sanctifies the soul.

Yet that threshold isn't the end.

The Lord continues to appoint many more crossings, each with a beginning, middle, and end. Each time He whispers, commands, or lays a charge upon the heart, He sets another appointment. When obeyed, the power of godliness is made manifest again, and His children are drawn nearer.

Joseph knew that God's word itself is power.

> *"In the beginning was the Word, and the Word was with God, and the Word was God."* (John 1:1)

Creation began this way:

> *"And God said, Let there be light: and there was light."* (Genesis 1:3)

His word is *"quick, and powerful, and sharper than any two-edged sword"* (Hebrews 4:12).

Alma bore witness:

> *"The preaching of the word had a great tendency to lead the people to do that which was just—yea, it had more powerful effect upon the minds of the people than the sword, or anything else."* (Alma 31:5)

Ordinances, then, are the living moments when His words of power enter our lives, when the veil parts just enough for His presence to be felt and His children to be transformed.

Joseph himself did not require outward forms to know this. He communed with angels, learned from them, and was shown mysteries beyond comprehension. He yearned for them to know God as he did.

The Lord's appointments were given to make that possible—not as burdens, but as steadying steps, carrying His people forward *"brighter and brighter until the perfect day"* (Proverbs 4:18; D&C 50:24), until they stood before Him face to face.

The fruit of true ordinances is always transformation.

They sanctify. They make men and women new creatures in Christ. They are not empty motions that leave us merely Christ adjacent, but living appointments that bring us unto Him.

Joseph taught ordinances this way—not as man-made ceremonies, but as holy thresholds where God reveals Himself.

The temple was commanded so these appointments could be multiplied and fulfilled among the people. It was to be the mountain of the Lord in their midst—a house where God could show Himself appointment by appointment, until His Saints stood before Him in glory.

The promise was real—but so was the peril. Temples were given so the Saints might seek Him and find Him. If they refused, the blessing would be withdrawn.

## The Temple: A House of Divine Appointments

The Lord's warning at Nauvoo was not given in vain:

> *"If ye do not these things at the end of the appointment, ye shall be rejected as a church, with your dead."* (D&C 124:32)

Joseph had already seen this truth written across scripture. The blessings of God's house always rested upon obedience, and His displeasure always followed neglect. Solomon heard it plainly:

> *"If ye shall at all turn from following me... then will I cut off Israel out of the land... and this house, which I have hallowed for my name, will I cast out of my sight."* (1 Kings 9:6–7)

By contrast, Nephi described how his people *"did build a temple... and the Lord was with us; and we did prosper exceedingly"* (2 Nephi 5:16–17).

Blessings flow when the Lord's house is built and honored; while God's rejection always follows when His command is set aside. This is the weight that rested upon Joseph, yet he pressed forward, revealing to his people the temple pattern the Lord had taught him, hoping upon hope they would obey.

## Kirtland (1836)

In Kirtland the command was clear: build a house of prayer, fasting, faith, learning, and glory, so the Saints might be endowed with power from on high (D&C 88; 95).

To Joseph's great joy, when the temple was completed, the promise arrived with power.

At the dedication and in the solemn assemblies that followed, heaven itself bore witness that God's promises are sure.

Those present testified that angels appeared, heavenly music was heard, and prophecy poured forth as never before. Some saw the Savior Himself; all felt the divine presence in a way they could never forget.

> **Frederick G. Williams** testified, *"An angel entered and sat in the stand"* during the dedicatory service (HC 2:427).
> **Heber C. Kimball** affirmed, *"The Spirit of the Lord rested upon the congregation, and great manifestations of power were experienced"* (Life of Heber C. Kimball, 91–92).
> **Brigham Young** exclaimed, *"The veil was taken from our minds and the eyes of our understanding were opened"* (JD 1:131).

Kirtland stood as a living mountain of the Lord: a house where God revealed Himself and endowed His people with gifts and power.

### Nauvoo (1841)

At Nauvoo the command came again:

> *"For there is not a place found on earth that he may come to and restore again that which was lost... even the fulness of the priesthood."* (D&C 124:28)

The Lord named baptisms for the dead, washings, anointings, and solemn assemblies to be revealed in His house (D&C 124:39). Early mercies—like the healings at Montrose (1839)—hinted at the outpouring heaven stood ready to bestow.

Sadly, the temple was never completed in Joseph's lifetime.[24]

He authorized a temporary font in the basement, but he knew it couldn't substitute for the finished house. Without completion, the fulness of the promise couldn't be realized.

Where Kirtland had overflowed with visions, prophecy, and angelic ministrations, Nauvoo's unfinished house remained largely silent. And like the swamp the Saints drained to raise their city, spiritual manifestations ebbed—little by little—until darkness crept in.

Joseph felt that sorrow.

He knew what the Lord had poured out in Kirtland. He knew what heaven was willing to give. He also knew the warning: if the command were neglected, the people—with their dead—would be rejected (D&C 124:32).

The temple at Nauvoo stood as both promise and peril—Joseph's longing for his people to be lifted, and his grief that he would never see the house completed.

## Continuity and Witness

Still, the design is unmistakable.

> *Both temples were commanded directly of the Lord.*
> *Both were dedicated to His presence.*
> *Both were designed as houses of appointments—where individuals could be sanctified through baptisms, washings, and anointings, and where the whole body could unite in solemn assemblies to invite heaven's gifts.*

In Kirtland, that appointment was fulfilled in glory. In Nauvoo, the same promise was given—but with the added burden of a warning. Joseph did not live to see its completion.

The order Joseph restored was never about monuments of stone. It was about living mountains—consecrated houses where heaven and earth meet.

For in every true temple, the Father and the Mother stand as one—the Givers of law and life, of word and womb, of spirit and substance. Their unity is the pattern the temple was built to reflect.

Temples are where the Godhead reveals Themselves through Their appointments, endows Their people with power, and prepares them to see Their face.

## Closing Witness

Through obedience to the Lord's voice and his lived example, Joseph laid the foundation.

From Kirtland to Nauvoo, Joseph taught that temples were never monuments of stone but living mountains—sanctified spaces where heaven and earth meet, where God reveals Himself, endows His people with power, and prepares them to see His face.

In 1836 he urged the Saints: *"We must have all things prepared, and call our solemn assembly... that we may be endowed with power from on high."*[25]

Later he explained, *"The Savior said, the first thing to be done was to give them power to build up his church... This power to be given to his disciples, was the endowment."*[26]

And when the Saints worried, he calmed them: "*The endowment you are so anxious about, you cannot comprehend now... it is not to teach you how to get the endowment, but to prepare you for it*" (HC 2:308).

That was always his testimony: the temple is a house of preparation, a house of sanctification, a house of power. Its purpose is to lift a people into the same presence Joseph had known—where angels minister, visions open, and God unveils Himself in person.

This is the graft. Temples matter only as they join the branch to the living root—Christ. Their value lies not in the stone, but in whether they carry His people into Him, where the power of godliness is revealed.

I hope you can see the Lord's design. From beginning to end it is not about Joseph, nor about temples, nor even about a church. It is about Him—Jesus Christ.

I add my witness. I am grateful for Joseph's vision of temples—not as ends in themselves, but as consecrated houses where God prepares His people for His presence. I testify that the true temple experience is when the Lord Himself begins to write upon the heart, sanctifying and purifying until the soul is made whole.

In my own journey, I have tasted His love, His mercy and grace. I've also felt the quiet strength of Her presence—the gentleness that heals while He refines. I know that temples are given as training spaces, so that all who are willing may be prepared to enter into Their presence.

And I invite you, the reader, to begin seeing temples as Joseph taught they were: not as scaffolds of form, but as holy places of ascent—where the embrace of God is offered, and the sanctifying fire of His Spirit makes men and women new.

The image is a helix, a living spiral. Each appointment flawlessly obeyed, each manifestation of God's loving power, is another turn in the upward path. We do not circle endlessly; we rise. From one glory to another, from grace to grace, brighter and brighter until the perfect day.

These are the true appointments of the Lord's House—souls ascending, like a mountain path spiraling upward toward the summit, until the veil is parted and God is experienced firsthand.

Joseph testified of this same promise in his last great discourse:

> *"If you could see God today, you would see Him like a man in form... God Himself was once as we are now, and is an exalted*

> *man, and sits enthroned in yonder heavens." (Teachings of the Prophet Joseph Smith, p. 345.)*

His voice in that moment was not only the voice of a prophet, but of a man bearing his own witness—he had seen Him, he had tasted His love, he knew Him.

Temples prepare individuals for this ascent. They are the mountain of the Lord set in the midst of His people, where they are lifted by the words of His power. But temples are not the end.

They point to Zion.

Zion is the community version of the temple—the holy society where the graft has matured and is complete, where the people themselves become the dwelling place of God.

> *"Temples prepare a soul for His presence; Zion is that people, gathered, sanctified, and ready for the Lord to make His abode with them."*[27]

When the mountain becomes a city, and the people are worthy to enter it, rising up to welcome Him—there the Lord Himself will dwell.

## Chapter 12 Notes

1 History of the Church 2:430–433—records Saints' poverty and their sacrifices while building the Kirtland Temple.
Lucy Mack Smith, History, 1845, pp. 230–231—describes the Saints' sacrifices, hauling stone and timber despite ridicule.

2 Economic collapse / bank failure:
History of the Church 2:467–468—details the colapse of the Kirtland Safety Society in 1837.
Joseph Smith Papers, Letter to Edward Partridge and others, Jan. 29, 1837—Joseph acknowledges banking troubles and growing opposition.
Bitterness, murmuring, and division:
History of the Church 2:487–489—accounts of dissent in Kirtland, including apostasy of high-ranking members, and resulting lawsuits.
Warren Parrish, John Boynton, and others led factions against Joseph.
Friends turning against one another:

History of the Church 2:523–524—notes of Joseph's close associates dissenting and opposing him.
Gifts ceasing (spiritual decline):
D&C 121:37 (given later, but principle clear)—*"when we undertake to cover our sins... amen to the priesthood or the authority of that man."*
Lucy Mack Smith, History, p. 235—observes decline of unity and spiritual gifts in Kirtland amid contention.

3 History of the Church 3:1–3—Joseph flees Kirtland in January 1838 after threats, dissent, and financial turmoil from the Kirtland Safety Society collapse.
Joseph Smith Papers, Journal, Jan. 12, 1838—*"the spirit of mobocracy was so strong against me... I left Kirtland for Missouri."*
D&C 117:6 (July 1838)—acknowledges Kirtland *"shall not be a stronghold,"* confirming the scattering.
History of the Church 3:1–20—records the Saints leaving Kirtland for Missouri during 1837–38.

4 Expulsion and suffering of the Saints in Missouri:
D&C 123:1—Joseph directs the Saints to gather up a record of *"their sufferings and abuses."*
D&C 135:6 (retrospective)—mentions the Saints' expulsion.
Homes torched, families scattered or killed:
History of the Church 3:190–192—Governor Boggs' Extermination Order, Oct. 27, 1838*: "Mormons must be treated as enemies, and must be exterminated or driven from the state."*
History of the Church 3:183–184—Haun's Mill Massacre, Oct. 30, 1838: 17 killed, including children.
John P. Greene, Facts Relative to the Expulsion of the Mormons (1839), gives firsthand accounts of homes destroyed, families scattered, and Saints murdered.

5 Massacre accounts:
History of the Church 3:183–185—detailed record of the Oct. 30, 1838 massacre.
Joseph Young, An Authentic Account of the Massacre at Haun's Mill (Nov. 1838)—eyewitness narrative: describes children being shot, men killed in the blacksmith shop, bodies buried in a well.

D&C 135:6 (later reflection)—alludes to Saints being "*shot down by mobs.*"

6 Extermination Order:
Governor Lilburn W. Boggs, Executive Order 44, Oct. 27, 1838:
*"The Mormons must be treated as enemies, and must be exterminated or driven from the state if necessary for the public peace."*
Reprinted in History of the Church 3:190–191.
Joseph chained in Liberty Jail:
History of the Church 3:208–209—Joseph and brethren confined in Liberty Jail (Dec. 1838–Apr. 1839).
D&C 121–123—Joseph's prison prayers and revelations written from Liberty Jail.

7 Nauvoo beginnings (swamp, marsh drained):
History of the Church 4:268–269—Joseph describes settling Commerce, Illinois, later renamed Nauvoo, noting the swampy conditions and the Saints' work to drain and build.
Joseph Smith Papers, History, 1838–1856, vol. C-1, 1008–1010—details draining the swampland and planting.
Lucy Mack Smith, History, 1845, pp. 289–291—describes the hardship of settling Nauvoo and transforming the land.
Nauvoo as a thriving city:
History of the Church 4:268–270—Nauvoo quickly flourished with homes, farms, and the beginning of the temple.
Times and Seasons, 1839–1841 issues—describe Nauvoo's growth and promise.

8 cf. Hannah Whitall Smith, The Christian's Secret of a Happy Life

9 The word used in Genesis 32:24 for "wrestled" is אָבַק (*ʾāvaq*).
Root sense: *"to wrestle, grapple, get dusty."*
Some Jewish commentators and modern scholars note that the imagery can also suggest an intimate entangling—close physical embrace, not just hostile struggle.
Rabbinic midrash often interprets Jacob's wrestling as both combat and clinging embrace.

10 Abram → Abraham:
Genesis 17:5—*"Neither shall thy name any more be called*

*Abram, but thy name shall be Abraham; for a father of many nations have I made thee."*
Jacob → Israel:
Genesis 32:28—"*Thy name shall be called no more Jacob, but Israel: for as a prince hast thou power with God and with men, and hast prevailed."*
Saul → Paul:
Acts 13:9—"*Then Saul, (who also is called Paul,) filled with the Holy Ghost..."*

11 Washed with water (cleansing before consecration):
Exodus 29:4—"*And Aaron and his sons thou shalt bring unto the door of the tabernacle of the congregation, and shalt wash them with water."*
Leviticus 8:6—"*And Moses brought Aaron and his sons, and washed them with water."*
Anointed with oil (sanctified for holy trust):
Exodus 29:7—"*Then shalt thou take the anointing oil, and pour it upon his head, and anoint him."*
1 Samuel 10:1—Samuel anoints Saul, king of Israel.
1 Samuel 16:13—Samuel anoints David, and "the Spirit of the Lord came upon David from that day forward."
Clothed in royal/holy garments:
Exodus 28:2—"*Thou shalt make holy garments for Aaron thy brother for glory and for beauty."*
Zechariah 3:4—"*Take away the filthy garments from him... I will clothe thee with change of raiment."*
Isaiah 61:10—"He hath clothed me with the garments of salvation, he hath covered me with the robe of righteousness." they were clothed in robes of royalty, garments that testified outwardly of the inward transformation, that they had been ordained to reign in majesty.

12 History of the Church 2:379–383—Joseph records the beginning of washings and anointings in January 1836 in preparation for the temple dedication.
Joseph Smith, Journal, Jan.–Feb. 1836 (Joseph Smith Papers)—details of the washings with water, anointings with oil, and blessings pronounced.

D&C 88:74–75 (Dec. 1832 revelation)—preparatory instructions: *"sanctify yourselves... that your minds become single to God."*

13 Salt Lake School of the Prophets Minutes, Oct. 3, 1883

14 Salt Lake School of the Prophets Minutes, Oct. 3, 1883

15 Command for washings and anointings in Nauvoo:
D&C 124:37–39—*"I say unto you, let this house be built... for your washings, and your anointings, and your baptisms for the dead, and your solemn assemblies..."*
No evidence during Joseph's lifetime:
Joseph Smith Papers, Journals, Dec. 1841–June 1844—record no instances of washings/anointings performed in the Nauvoo Temple before Joseph's death (building incomplete).
History of the Church vols. 5–6 likewise mention baptisms for the dead in the temporary font, but do not mention washings/anointings in the temple before June 1844.

16 Scriptural tie (sanctified to stand before God):
D&C 88:74–75—*"Sanctify yourselves... that your minds become single to God... that you may be prepared in all things... to stand in the presence of God."*
D&C 84:20–22—*"In the ordinances thereof, the power of godliness is manifest... without this no man can see the face of God."*
Joseph's practice (simple, unscripted):
History of the Church 2:379–383—Joseph's January 1836 accounts of washings/anointings (no set ritual, only prayer/blessing).
Zebedee Coltrin, School of the Prophets Minutes, Oct. 3, 1883—*"They washed, anointed each other with oil, and pronounced blessings."*

17 Hebrew meaning of Sabaoth:
צְבָאוֹת (ṣəḇā'ôṯ) = *"hosts, armies, multitudes."* Strong's Concordance H6635.
Lord of Hosts usage:
1 Samuel 1:3—first occurrence: *"the Lord of hosts."*
Isaiah 6:3—*"Holy, holy, holy, is the Lord of hosts: the whole earth is full of his glory."*
D&C 88:2—*"the voice of the Lord of hosts."*

D&C 95:7—command for a solemn assembly to *"call your solemn assembly, that your fastings and your mourning might come up into the ears of the Lord of Sabaoth."*

18 Primordial mound (also called *"primeval hillock"* or *"cosmic mountain"):*
In Egyptian cosmology, the benben stone or primordial mound was the first land to rise out of the waters of chaos (Nun). It was seen as the foundation of creation and the place where temples symbolically returned creation to order.
In Mesopotamian thought, temples were often built as ziggurats (cosmic mountains), connecting heaven and earth.
In biblical imagery, the *"mountain of God"* appears at creation:
Genesis 1:9—*"Let the dry land appear."*
Psalm 104:5–9—God sets the earth upon its foundations, waters flee, mountains rise.
Ezekiel 28:13–14, 16—Eden described as the holy mountain of God.
Isaiah 2:2—*"the mountain of the Lord's house"* exalted in the last days.

19 Genesis 2:8–10—*"And the Lord God planted a garden eastward in Eden... and a river went out of Eden to water the garden."*
(Rivers flowing outward are typical of mountain imagery.)
Genesis 3:8—*"And they heard the voice of the Lord God walking in the garden in the cool of the day."*
Ezekiel 28:13–14, 16—Eden explicitly called *"the holy mountain of God."*
Moses 3:8; 4:14 (Pearl of Great Price)—restoration text confirming Eden as the place where God walked and spoke with Adam.

20 Raven and dove sent out:
Genesis 8:6–11—Noah first sends a raven (it "went forth to and fro"), then a dove, which returns with an olive leaf in her mouth.
Olive branch as peace:
While the olive branch as a universal *"peace"* symbol comes from later tradition, the biblical root is here in Genesis 8:11.
Dove at Jesus' baptism:
Matthew 3:16—*"the Spirit of God descending like a dove, and lighting upon him."*

John 1:32—*"I saw the Spirit descending from heaven like a dove, and it abode upon him."*

21 Leviticus 23:36—*"on the eighth day shall be a holy convocation... it is a solemn assembly."*
Joel 2:15–16—*"Blow the trumpet in Zion, sanctify a fast, call a solemn assembly: gather the people, sanctify the congregation..."*

22 Restoration solemn assemblies:
D&C 95:7—*"call your solemn assembly, that your fastings and your mourning might come up into the ears of the Lord of Sabaoth."*
D&C 88:117–118—command to call a solemn assembly for instruction in the temple.
D&C 109—Kirtland Temple dedicatory prayer itself called a solemn assembly.

23 Moses on Sinai:
Exodus 19:20—*"And the Lord came down upon mount Sinai, on the top of the mount: and the Lord called Moses up to the top of the mount; and Moses went up."*
Elijah on the mount / still small voice:
1 Kings 19:11–12—the Lord not in the wind, earthquake, or fire, but in "a still small voice."
Nephi in the wilderness:
1 Nephi 2:16—Nephi *"cried unto the Lord"* in the wilderness, softened his heart.
1 Nephi 11:1—Nephi *"caught away in the Spirit of the Lord... into an exceedingly high mountain."*
Enos in the wilderness:
Enos 1:3–4—Enos hears his father's words and wrestles in prayer in the woods.
Joseph in the grove:
Joseph Smith—History 1:14–17—Joseph's prayer and First Vision.
Isaiah's vision of the mountain of the Lord:
Isaiah 2:2—*"the mountain of the Lord's house shall be established in the top of the mountains, and shall be exalted above the hills."*

24 History of the Church 6:184–185—records construction progress in 1844, but the Nauvoo Temple was still unfinished at Joseph's

death (June 27, 1844).
Joseph Smith Papers, Journals, Dec. 1841–June 1844—frequent notes about ongoing work, but no record of completion.
D&C 124:31–32—revelation's warning that if the temple was not completed, the Church would be rejected.

25 History of the Church, 2:176 (Dec. 1832, Kirtland).

26 History of the Church, 2:309–310 (Jan. 1834, Kirtland High Council minutes).

27 Author's personal witness.

# There Could Not Be a Happier People

## The Bridegroom, the Bride, a People Sanctified

### Why Zion Matters

Have you ever wondered what Zion must be like? Or felt a quiet pull in your heart—almost not a voice, but a whisper that says, *"Come to Zion"*?[1]

That's not your imagination.

Zion is real. Scripture names it directly; it is also called the New Jerusalem, the society of the pure in heart where God Himself dwells with His people.

If that is Zion, then the question becomes: why has God placed it at the center of every prophetic mission since before the world was formed?

The answer is older than Eden. The War in Heaven didn't end when lucifer fell—it continues still. From even before the beginning, there have been two opposing sides—light and darkness, each with its own ruler.

Zion is the Lord's, governed by Jehovah. Babylon is the adversary's counterfeit, where rebellion reigns supreme.

Scripture makes this clear: there is *"opposition in all things"* (2 Nephi 2:11). These are not vague metaphors but living orders of life. One brings light, truth, and joy. The other leads only to darkness, deceit, and captivity.

The contrast need not weigh us down. Zion is not shadowed by Babylon; she rises in spite of it.

The helix makes it plain: as far as Zion ascends into light, Babylon descends into darkness.[2] And every soul has agency and is invited upward into the joy of the Bridegroom and His Bride.

Because of this, God has always given His prophets the same mandate: prepare a people who will establish Zion.

> ***Adam*** *labored among his posterity to teach them the way of the Lord, though many turned aside.*[3]
> ***Enoch*** *succeeded fully. His people became of one heart and one mind, dwelling in righteousness with no poor among them. They were taken up into the Lord's presence, for only then could God dwell with them continually.*[4]
> ***Melchizedek*** *achieved a similar triumph, presiding over a people so righteous that his city was called Salem—peace.*[5]

Let's be clear, Zion isn't just "He shows up and suddenly everything is perfect." Every student of the Book of Mormon recognizes this two-step pattern:

> ***First, refined by fire****—the wicked are swept away. Scripture calls this tribulation, or the Lord's chastisements, where only a remnant remains. That remnant has been humbled, prepared, and sanctified—ready to meet Christ* (see 3 Nephi 8–10).
> ***Second, sealed by fire****—the risen Lord descends, heals, blesses, and teaches; His presence fixes in the heart what tribulation prepared. Their sanctification becomes permanent. Their nature changes, not just their circumstances.*

The Nephite record bears witness of this.[6] For nearly two centuries they lived in equality and peace, filled with the love of God. That unity was no accident—it came from the law of Christ written in their hearts, and it preserved them as one.

Joseph Smith received the same mandate in this dispensation.

Through him the Lord revealed the laws of consecration and equality, the principle of common consent, and even a plat for how a city of Zion should be built. Joseph declared that *"the cause of Zion is one common cause."*[7] His life was cut short before Zion could be realized in his day, but the charge remained before the Saints, just as it remains before us now.

From Enoch to Joseph, the assignment has never changed. Zion—the New Jerusalem—is not a side project but the very heart of God's plan in the last days. And make no mistake: these are the last days.

Zion is the pattern of heaven established on earth, the place where the Lord dwells openly with a people whose hearts are purified—able to endure the refiner's fire and not be consumed by His glory.

Babylon offers rebellion and ruin; Zion offers life and light. That is why Zion matters.

## Zion Defined

In the Pearl of Great Price we read that Enoch said: *"the Lord called his people Zion, because they were of one heart and one mind, and dwelt in righteousness; and there was no poor among them"* (Moses 7:18).

Later, the Lord revealed again through Joseph Smith that Zion is the pure in heart. Those words settle the matter. Zion is not first about walls or streets, but about a people sanctified, united, and pure.

Zion, then, is not a place until it becomes a people. Maps may trace its promised location, but no lines on paper can establish it. Until hearts are transformed, no city can rightly be called Zion.

Just as there are two divine strands—one masculine, one feminine—so too is the terrestrial, millennial order. The New Jerusalem reflects the Bridegroom; Zion embodies the Bride.[8] Together they reveal the image of Father and Mother made manifest upon the earth.

As we saw earlier, the clearest lived witness of this is found in 4 Nephi. After the refining fire of destruction and the sealing fire of Christ's presence, the record tells us:

> *"The people were all converted unto the Lord, upon all the face of the land, both Nephites and Lamanites... And they had all things common among them; therefore there were not rich and poor, bond and free, but they were all made free, and partakers of the heavenly gift. And there was no contention in the land, because of the love of God which did dwell in the hearts of the people. And surely there could not be a happier people among all the people who had been created by the hand of God. There were no robbers, nor murderers, neither were there Lamanites, nor any manner of -ites; but they were in*

> *one, the children of Christ, and heirs to the kingdom of God."* (4 Nephi 1:2–3, 15–17)

This is Zion in full bloom: no rich or poor, no divisions, no contentions, no *"-ites,"* but one in Christ. They did not merely organize a cooperative society. They became something more.

When Christ dwells among a people, His Spirit changes them, and their nature shifts. Their desires are altered. The way they see one another is transformed until they treat each other as He would treat them—not because they are imitating Him, but because His life is in them.

That's why they can endure His presence. This is why the Nephites in 4 Nephi remained a Zion society for nearly two hundred years.

Remember, *"church"* in scripture doesn't mean an institution or an organization managed by offices. A church is a body of sanctified souls who have received His Spirit and entered into His fold.

By that measure, Zion is the Church of the Firstborn made manifest on earth[9]—a society of those who have ascended beyond the first rung of entering the Church of the Lamb, becoming purified and sealed, prepared to dwell in His unveiled presence.

The Church of the Firstborn, as Joseph taught, is composed of those sanctified by the Spirit, brought into God's presence, and made heirs of eternal life.

This dovetails with the helix we have traced throughout this book: Zion's path spirals upward into light, while Babylon winds downward into darkness. One is a people of holiness who can live with Christ. The other is a people of rebellion, ruled by the adversary.

Every Zion society is built upon His rest. Each Sabbath day, each Sacramental meal, is a rehearsal of that rest and feast. When His people honor them in purity, they are not just remembering past mercies—they are anticipating the day when the Bridegroom comes and Zion sits down at the marriage supper of the Lamb (Revelation 19:9).

Zion in every age—whether in Enoch's day or in the golden age of 4 Nephi—shows the same pattern.

They are of one heart and one mind. There are no poor, no divisions, no contentions. And more than that: they are a people who have become like Christ, able to endure His presence. This is the true definition of Zion.

## The Four Quadrants of Zion

Every law of heaven rests upon two eternal principles: **love and freedom.**

> *"Men are free according to the flesh; ... they are free to choose liberty and eternal life, through the great Mediator of all men, or to choose captivity and death."* (2 Nephi 2:27)

Zion is the order of liberty and life; Babylon is the counterfeit—captivity and misery. Every society, every soul, inevitably moves toward one or the other.

Imagine a square divided into four parts.[10]

Across the bottom runs **freedom**, from bondage on the left to liberty on the right.

Up the side rises **love**, from selfishness below to charity above. Together they form the field where every government, religion, and human heart can be plotted.

### Bottom-Left: Control and Enslavement

Here both love and freedom are absent. This is the domain of domination—systems that rule by fear and consolidate power by removing choice. People are managed rather than trusted, compelled rather than persuaded. Obedience is extracted through shame, threat, and dependency. The labor of the many enriches the few, while dissent is punished and conscience is suppressed. Babylon thrives here, cloaked in the language of order and safety, while steadily binding souls in captivity.

### Bottom-Right: Freedom without Love

Here men throw off control but forget compassion. Each becomes ruler of his own house and defender of his own hoard. Greed masquerades as liberty. This is the world of endless competition—where strength is worshiped, weakness despised, and the cry of the poor ignored. It promises freedom yet breeds isolation.

### Top-Left: Love without Freedom

Here affection is genuine but enforced by rule. Well-meaning leaders legislate virtue, believing that goodness can be compelled. This is the kindly tyranny of the *"benevolent king,"* the welfare state, the ecclesiastical hierarchy that governs for the people's good but never with their consent. Order replaces agency; devotion is administered instead of chosen.

### Top-Right: Love with Freedom—Zion

Only here can heaven and earth meet. In this realm no one rules and none are ruled, for all hearts are knit together in love and every soul is free in Christ. There are no poor, because none are selfish; no slaves, because none are compelled. This is a society without coercion and without neglect—pure love and perfect liberty moving in harmony.

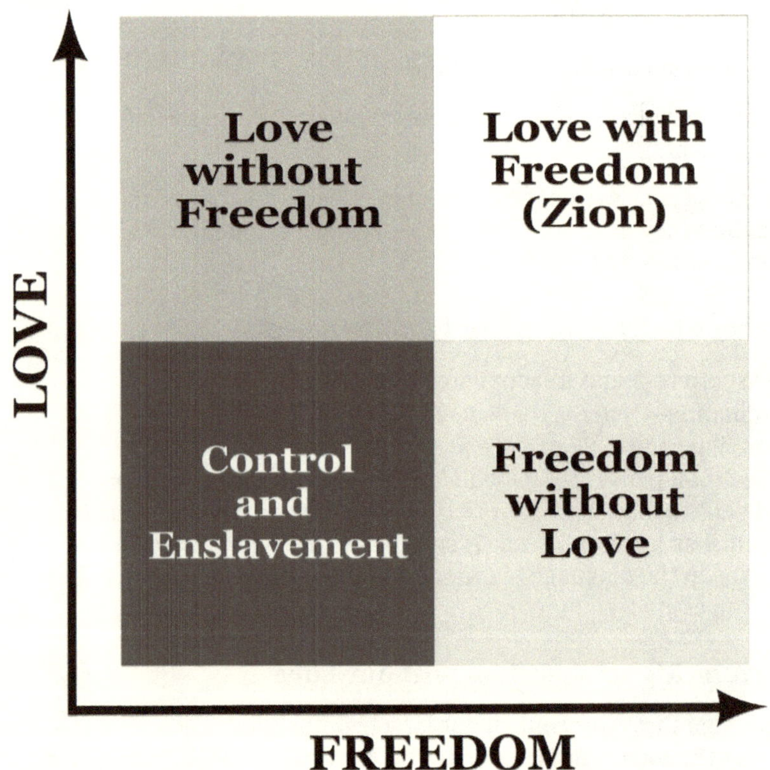


*Only in the top-right quadrant—where love and freedom unite—can Zion exist.*

This framework helps us see the history of both heaven and earth.

> **Enoch's city** rose into the top-right quadrant: one heart, one mind, none poor among them.

> **The Nephite golden age of 4 Nephi** flourished there for two centuries before sliding downward into pride and division.
> **King Benjamin's reign** began in the top-left—benevolent monarchy—and through voluntary covenant, moved toward Zion's liberty.
> **Modern Babylon**, by contrast, lingers in the bottom-left: governments that compel, churches that command, economies that extract.
> And the **anarchic revolt** that follows drifts bottom-right—clamoring for freedom while scorning love.

History swings through these quadrants like a pendulum, yet Zion remains the still point of truth.

When people humble themselves through repentance and begin living the twin laws of consecration and common consent, they rise from captivity into liberty—out of the lower realms of control and isolation into the higher realm of love and freedom. This is the moment when Babylon loses its hold and Zion begins to form.

But when **pride** replaces love or **coercion** replaces freedom, the descent begins again. The heart that once opened to give starts to withhold; the hand that once offered begins to rule. Every fall of Zion in scripture follows this pattern—love growing cold, freedom giving way to compulsion—until captivity returns and the cycle must begin anew.

This is why the Lord restored both the **Law of Consecration** and the **Law of Common Consent** through Joseph Smith. Consecration perfects love; consent perfects freedom. Together they create the living intersection where Zion is born.

## The Law of Consecration

The Lord revealed the Law of Consecration to Joseph Smith, but it is no harsh demand. It is the natural law of a God who has promised His children *"all that He has."*[11]

When you pause to consider what *"all"* means—joy, peace, abundance, knowledge, healing, eternal life, the very fullness of His glory—it becomes no burden for Him to ask in return for *all* that we have.

In truth, it is not demanding at all, but a joyful exchange: He gives us everything, and we give Him everything.

Consecration is not just about possessions. It is the outward demonstration of an inward truth: you are one with Christ, as He is one with you. A consecrated life is the natural fruit of a sanctified heart. When you love Him, you love everyone. When all you have is already His, sharing it with another becomes joy, not loss.

This is why later generations stumbled. To the selfish heart, consecration is too demanding. Why? Because they believed their belongings were *theirs*. Once you take ownership in that sense, letting go feels like loss.

But if you recognize from the beginning that nothing is truly yours—that all belongs to the Lord's—then giving becomes easy. You're not losing anything. You're simply transferring His property to the place where He says it belongs.

The law itself is plain. The Saints were commanded to consecrate their surplus to the bishop, who by revelation appointed stewardships for each family, *"that every man who has need may be amply supplied"* (D&C 42:33).

But it's not really about offering the whole and then receiving back a portion. It's about recognizing that the whole was and always will be His, and that He in His wisdom and generosity gives each of us a stewardship to manage.

And in that stewardship, He is no miser: He blesses abundantly. He withholds nothing that is righteous. As far as you are willing to consecrate all you have, He overcompensates in return. *"When ye are in the service of your fellow beings ye are only in the service of your God"* (Mosiah 2:17).

King Benjamin declared that as soon as you seek to repay Him, He immediately blesses you again, so that you remain always in His debt (Mosiah 2:24).

The result of this law is abundance. Needs are met, but more than that, righteous desires are also furnished. It is not a law of mere survival, but of joy and plenty.

This is how Zion societies come to have *"no poor among them"* (Moses 7:18).

Left to man, such equality would seem impossible. But in Christ it becomes inevitable, because the same Spirit that fills one fills all. His grace lifts until there are no poor—not in clothing, nor in bread, nor in Spirit.

We see this in Enoch's city, where all were one in heart and mind and the Lord Himself could dwell among them. We see it again in the days after Christ's visit to the Nephites, when they held all things in common and lived as equals, with no rich or poor among them.

These weren't utopian experiments. They were real societies, transformed by the presence of the Lord, demonstrating the fruits of consecration lived in full.

Consecration reaches even deeper than property—it reaches the hidden corners of the will. The Lord asks not only for what we have, but for what we are.

And why? Because He has promised in exchange *all that He has.* His joy, His peace, His plenty, His health, His healing, His relationships, His eternal increase—blessings so vast they cannot be imagined. The law of consecration is the law of that exchange: my little all for His infinite all.

This is why consecration is not a program but a condition of the heart. In Zion, every field and every hand is consecrated, yes—but so are every thought and every desire. All flows through Christ, and in that flow there is never scarcity, only abundance.

## Zion's Common Consent

Zion isn't held together by compulsion or hierarchy. She is sustained by the same law we explored earlier: the law of common consent.

The Lord revealed early to Joseph that *"all things shall be done by common consent in the church, by much prayer and faith"* (D&C 26:2).

This is not the mere formality of raised arms, nor the tyranny of majority vote, but the order of heaven itself. In Zion, the voice of the people and the whisper of the Spirit confirm each other until the whole body moves as one.

This is the same pattern you've already seen. Earlier we traced the wagon wheel as the Lord's design of governance: Christ at the hub, individuals as spokes, equality forming the rim. That wheel was the pattern of God's church in Joseph's day.

In Zion, the same wheel becomes even more vivid. Saints who have seen visions of the New Jerusalem describe its temple as a vast wagon wheel: a circular central temple crowned with light, from which twelve covered walkways radiate outward to twelve outer temples—one for each tribe of Israel. These outer temples are joined together by a rim, completing the wheel.

Imagine walking one of those covered spokes, with light from the central hub spilling outward. In the center rises the House of the Lord, filled with glory. At the rim you hear the voices of tribes assembled, each distinct yet joined as one. The entire design is a living parable of Zion.

At the hub, Christ Himself governs. The spokes are stewardships and tribes, reaching outward in service. The rim is the body of Israel united in equality, bound together by love. And the law of common consent keeps the wheel turning in harmony—no spoke dominating, no voice silenced, all joined to the hub and rim in one continuous motion.

The helix returns here as well.

This isn't a new image, but the same pattern from before now brought into three dimensions—its highest fulfillment. Zion's path spirals upward into light because her every ascent is chosen, every decision confirmed by the Spirit, every action ratified by the people in unity.

Babylon, by contrast, winds downward into darkness because it's ruled by compulsion, counterfeit consent, and the adversary's rebellion.

The two paths are the same helix we traced before—only now you can see their end points. Zion reaches into heaven; Babylon falls into the eternal captivity of outer darkness.

Consecration (as we just saw earlier) and common consent are not separate laws but twin strands of the helix. Consecration unites what we have. Common consent unites what we choose.

Together, they form the framework of Zion: an economy of abundance and a governance of freedom, both centered on Christ.

Thus Zion society is not only holy in word but whole in practice. The wheel turns because every spoke is consecrated, every rim is joined in consent, every choice is confirmed by the Spirit. And in that harmony, Christ Himself can dwell at the hub.

Such a people, bound together by consecration and common consent, are precisely the people prepared to inherit the land of promise—the New Jerusalem.

### The Interplay of Zion's Laws

Now the whole vision comes into view.

The four quadrants of freedom and love reveal not only where every soul and every society may dwell, but the direction in which they move.

Each heart, each community, is always in motion—either clinging to control and want, or rising toward freedom and love.

When people awaken to the higher law of voluntary love and shared abundance, they naturally attract others of the same spirit. Like-hearted people gather together and form the seed of Zion—a society that governs itself through mutual consent and consecrated care rather than force or fear.

But where hearts remain unyielded—where control masquerades as order and enforced equality replaces generosity—societies can only mirror the lower quadrants.

> *They may promise unity, yet achieve it only through compulsion.*
> *They may preach sharing, yet drain the soul through control.*

Zion cannot grow in that soil.

Consecration and common consent are not institutional programs but living laws.

> *Consecration sanctifies love until there are no poor.*
> *Common consent perfects freedom until there are no rulers.*

Those who truly seek liberty and life must therefore turn from every system built on coercion and scarcity and learn to live the higher law of love freely given.

Zion is not built by decree or program, but by hearts transformed through the harmony of heaven—where love and freedom unite as one. This unity perfectly manifests the divine masculine and divine feminine: structure and adornment joined in balance, strength and beauty moving as one.

Freedom is the divine masculine framework; charity is the divine feminine grace that completes and beautifies it. As revelation teaches, when charity garnishes our strength and power, *"then shall [we] stand with confidence before God"* (D&C 121:45)—before Them—because we have become like Them.

As we have seen in the four quadrants, the bottom-left is compulsion, the bottom-right isolation, the top-left benevolent control—but the top-right is consecrated freedom, the life of Zion.

> *Consecration perfects love, eliminating want.*
> *Common consent perfects freedom, eliminating coercion.*

When both laws spiral together, they draw heaven downward and lift earth upward until the two embrace.

That meeting—the union of love and freedom, consecration and consent—is Zion.

The pattern is clear: freedom without love descends into chaos, love without freedom hardens into control, but love and freedom joined together ascend into Zion—the society of heaven made manifest on earth.

## The New Jerusalem

Zion and the New Jerusalem are one and the same. They are not two separate cities or stages, but two names describing the same holy reality.[12]

*Zion* emphasizes the people—the pure in heart who are sanctified to dwell with God. *New Jerusalem* emphasizes the place—the promised land prepared for such a people.

In the language of heaven, they represent two divine strands: the feminine and the masculine, working together as one. Zion embodies the feminine—nurturing, unifying, life-bearing, and pure in heart. New Jerusalem reflects the masculine—structural, protecting, ordering, and preparing the place where heaven may dwell. Together they reveal the DNA of the Restoration—the harmony of creation restored upon the earth.

Together they describe heaven and earth meeting as one: a sanctified people inheriting a sanctified land.

The Lord revealed to Joseph Smith the location of this holy city. In July 1831 He declared:

> *"the place which is now called Independence is the center place; and a spot for the temple is lying westward, upon a lot which is not far from the courthouse."* (D&C 57:3)

Independence, Missouri, was appointed by revelation as the center place for the New Jerusalem.

Yet even then the Lord made clear that the land would only become Zion when the people themselves were ready. Geography does not create Zion. Zion must first be established in the hearts of the people before the land can receive its inheritance.

The scriptures overflow with prophetic witnesses of this city. Isaiah foresaw it:

> *"It shall come to pass in the last days, that the mountain of the Lord's house shall be established in the top of the mountains, and shall be exalted above the hills; and all nations shall flow unto it."* (Isaiah 2:2)

John saw it in vision:

> *"And I John saw the holy city, new Jerusalem, coming down from God out of heaven, prepared as a bride adorned for her husband. And I heard a great voice... saying, Behold, the tabernacle of God is with men, and he will dwell with them."* (Revelation 21:2–3)

Ether declared that *"this land"*—the American continent—was the place appointed: *"And there shall be a new Jerusalem, which shall be built upon the land, unto the remnant of the seed of Joseph."* (Ether 13:6)

Christ Himself prophesied to the Nephites that the remnant of Jacob would build a city on this land, with the Gentiles helping them:

> *"And they shall assist my people, the remnant of Jacob, and also as many of the house of Israel as shall come, that they may build a city, which shall be called the New Jerusalem." (3 Nephi 21:23–24)*

In modern revelation, the Lord gave further promises:

> *The city will be a place of refuge* (D&C 45:66–67).
> *The law will go forth from it* (D&C 84:2).
> *His glory will rest upon it* (D&C 133:56).

All of these testimonies point to the same truth: there will be one holy city in the last days, Zion, the New Jerusalem, where heaven and earth meet, and God dwells among His people.

## Purpose of the City

The New Jerusalem is not simply a gathering place—it is the Lord's city, designed for three holy purposes.

First, it is a city of refuge. In modern revelation, the Lord declared that when judgments sweep the nations, His people will find safety in Zion:

> *"It shall be called the New Jerusalem, a land of peace, a city of refuge, a place of safety for the saints of the Most High God."* (D&C 45:66)

While the world trembles, Zion will stand as the Lord's sanctuary, a society preserved in holiness.

Second, it is the center of holiness. The New Jerusalem is not simply where the righteous gather—it is where a sanctified people live already in the presence of Christ. He will visit, He will teach, He will dwell among them.[13]

This is why only the pure in heart, quickened and translated by His Spirit, can remain there. When He comes in the sky on the day of His return, those within the city will rise up to meet Him, for they have already become His people.

Third, it is the habitation of the Lord. The culmination of prophecy is that God Himself will dwell there. John heard the great voice: *"Behold, the tabernacle of God is with men, and he will dwell with them"* (Revelation 21:3).

Zion is not just a society devoted to God; it is the society into which God Himself descends. The New Jerusalem is the earthly realization of the prayer: *"Thy kingdom come, thy will be done in earth, as it is in heaven"* (Matthew 6:10).

## Preceded by Cleansing and Tribulation

But before this holy city stands, the scriptures are clear: the earth and its people must be purified. Zion always comes after purification. Just as sanctification in an individual's life comes only after the refiner's fire, so too does Zion come after the cleansing of nations.[14]

As we described at the beginning of this chapter with the people of Nephi, the pattern is always the same: the wicked are swept away, and a remnant is left—humbled and prepared. Then the Lord Himself comes, sealing that remnant in His presence.

The New Jerusalem will arise the same way. The world will pass through upheaval and tribulation, but in that crucible the Lord will preserve a people sanctified for His dwelling.

This is not a message of fear, but of hope. The tribulations of the last days are not arbitrary punishments, but the necessary cleansing that prepares the land and the people. As Malachi declared: *"For he is like a refiner's fire, and like fullers' soap"* (Malachi 3:2).

The fire purifies; the soap cleanses. And what emerges is a people who can dwell in the brightness of His glory.

The New Jerusalem will not rise by political decree or human design, and no institution will establish it. It will stand because the Lord has purified both people and place, making them fit for His habitation.

Only after that refining will the promise be fulfilled: *"Zion shall flourish, and the glory of the Lord shall be upon her"* (D&C 64:41).

Think about it: it's the ultimate security system in all of history. No password can be forged, no gate hacked, no counterfeit token admitted. Only those sanctified by the Lord Himself can enter. You might call it the final two-factor authentication—Zion and the New Jerusalem, both confirmed by heaven.

## Entry Requirement: Sanctified and Translated

The New Jerusalem is not a city anyone may simply walk into. It is not a place of refuge in name only—it is a place preserved and protected by power. Only those sanctified and prepared by the Lord can abide there.

The prophets are clear: *"Zion cannot be built up unless it is by the principles of the law of the celestial kingdom"* (D&C 105:5).

That means more than outward belonging. It requires inward transformation. The inhabitants must be sanctified by His Spirit until they're fit to dwell where He dwells and willing to abide the higher laws of the New Jerusalem.

This is why the New Jerusalem must be a translated society—and not merely a transfigured one. The difference matters.

**Transfiguration** is a temporary change of the body that allows a mortal to endure the glory of God for a moment. Moses testified, *"No man can behold all my glory, and afterwards remain in the flesh on the earth"* (Moses 1:11). Without a quickening of the Spirit, a mortal body would be consumed by His presence.

This is why Peter, James, and John were transfigured on the mount—their bodies changed temporarily so they could behold the glorified Christ and hear the Father's voice (Matthew 17:1–6). Once the vision ended, they returned to mortality.

**Translation**, by contrast, is a more permanent change. Translated beings aren't raised in the resurrection quite yet, but their bodies are altered so they don't taste of death and can remain continually in the presence of God until the day of their resurrection.

The clearest example comes from the Three Nephites. When they asked to remain on earth until the Lord's return, He promised:

*"Ye shall never endure the pains of death... ye shall not have pain while ye shall dwell in the flesh, neither sorrow save it be for the sins of the world"* (3 Nephi 28:7–9). Mormon explained that *"they were changed in the twinkling of an eye... that they might not taste of death; and that they might not suffer pain... and Satan could have no power over them"* (3 Nephi 28:38–39).

In this state, they continued as mortals, but were quickened so they wouldn't taste death and could endure the presence of Christ whenever He revealed Himself. Preserved until the resurrection, they were shielded from the power of the adversary and sustained to fulfill their ministry until His return.

Why translation? Because mortal bodies, as they are, can't abide His glory. It's just that simple.

As the Lord declared: *"Without this no man can see the face of God, even the Father, and live"* (D&C 84:22). A mortal must either be transfigured temporarily or translated more permanently to endure His unveiled presence.

Those who reside in the New Jerusalem can't rely on fleeting moments of transfiguration. His presence will be constant in their midst. Therefore, they must be translated.

And translation isn't given for comfort, but for purpose. Translated beings are preserved as ministering servants, able to labor without hindrance from death, disease, or the adversary.

This is why the Three Nephites were changed[15]—not merely to escape death, but to fulfill their calling as witnesses until Christ's return. Likewise, the inhabitants of the New Jerusalem will be preserved, not to retreat from the world, but to shine as a society of light while the world outside is cleansed.

Their preservation serves an even greater purpose.

The New Jerusalem is not only a refuge before the Lord's coming—it's the city of the Millennium itself.[16] It will endure as the center of the Terrestrial order, when Christ reigns personally upon the earth for a thousand years.

Where the world today lies under a Telestial order, and the sanctified earth will one day receive a Celestial glory, the Millennium is the Terrestrial phase of our earth's existence.[17]

Only translated and resurrected beings can abide that order, and the New Jerusalem is prepared precisely for them. It's the Terrestrial city of God, where heaven and earth meet until the final sanctification of all creation.

And so it is, the New Jerusalem is not simply a geographic gathering of believers. It is the manifestation of the Church of the Firstborn on earth—a society of men and women sanctified, sealed, and translated, living already in the order of heaven.

### Culmination: Union with Enoch's Zion

The destiny of the New Jerusalem isn't merely to stand as a refuge in the last days or as the city of the Millennium. Its culmination is foretold in Enoch's vision. The Lord showed him that his city, taken up into heaven, would one day return:

> *"And righteousness will I send down out of heaven; and truth will I send forth out of the earth, to bear testimony of mine Only Begotten; ... and righteousness and truth will I cause to sweep the earth as with a flood, to gather out mine elect from the four quarters of the earth, unto a place which I shall prepare, an Holy City, that my people may gird up their loins, and be looking forth for the time of my coming; for there shall be my tabernacle, and it shall be called Zion, a New Jerusalem. And the Lord said unto Enoch: Then shalt thou and all thy city meet them there, and we will receive them into our bosom, and they shall see us; and we will fall upon their necks, and they shall fall upon our necks, and we will kiss each other."* (Moses 7:62–63)

This is the great embrace of Zion from above and Zion from beneath. Heaven and earth join—not in symbol only, but in reality. The two become one, and the Lord Himself dwells openly among His people.

We have already seen this imagery before. We've spoken of the primordial mound[18]—the place where heaven and earth meet. It was depicted as two pyramids: one descending from above, one ascending from beneath, their points touching.

The mound is where heaven and earth meet, where God speaks with man. The return of Enoch's Zion mirrors that same pattern. The city from above descends. The city from beneath ascends. At the point where they meet, the Lord's tabernacle is established with His people.

Joseph Smith taught that this place is called Adam-ondi-Ahman—the land where Adam built an altar after being cast out of Eden, where he offered sacrifice, called upon God, and gathered his righteous posterity to bless them and prophesy of things to come (D&C 107:53–57).

It is the same ground appointed as the center place of Zion, the New Jerusalem. It is the primordial mound in sacred geography: the first place where Adam spoke with God after the Fall, and the last place where Christ will reign in glory. The first shall be last, and the last shall be first.

The story comes full circle. Zion is not merely a people, a city, or even a refuge. It is the union of heaven and earth—the fulfillment of every promise from the days of Adam to Joseph Smith.

Enoch's translated city will descend to embrace the New Jerusalem, and together they will stand at Adam-ondi-Ahman—the primordial mound—as one eternal Zion, prepared for the coming of the Lord in glory.

### What Life in Zion Looks Like

Have you ever wondered what it would actually be like to live in Zion? Not just to read of it in scripture, but to wake each morning in a society where the love of Christ is the atmosphere and His presence the light of every day. Zion is not a dream. It has been lived before. It will be lived again. And at its heart, Zion is oneness—oneness of people, oneness with God, all bound together by charity, the pure love of Christ.

### Homes and Families

In Zion, homes overflow with love and peace.

There are no locks, because there is no fear. Joy and laughter fill the air, not strife or weariness. Life is not a cycle of drudgery, but of creation and service.

Children grow up in truth and safety, surrounded by purity. Their schools resemble the schools of the prophets—places where the Spirit is tutors them, where angels teach them, as they did Joseph himself was.[19]

Knowledge flows freely because love forms the foundation. Families love each other deeply, but identity is no longer divided by names or clans. Every household belongs to one family: the family of Christ.

### Daily Life in Christ's Order

In Zion, daily life centers on Christ. Every person has their labors, but not as mere jobs—they are divine appointments from the Lord. Some are called to teach. Some are sent out as nursing kings and queens, gathering from the four corners of the earth those whom the Lord has prepared. Others serve in the temple.

In Zion, temple work means entering the house of the Lord to learn from Him directly, to be instructed in heavenly things, to administer His word, and to carry His presence back into the city. As one vision described, the temple is like a radiant hub, its light flowing through covered walkways into the city—but its power is Christ Himself dwelling there.[20]

Every gift is honored, celebrated, and magnified in love. The musician, the builder, the healer, the teacher—each talent is a stewardship of Christ's love, offered to bless all. In Zion, no gift is wasted, no contribution unseen, no person overlooked. All flow together as one body, knit together in charity.

## Culture of Light and Love

The culture of Zion is the culture of love filled with light.

The Nephite record describes it this way: there were no divisions, no parties, no races, no nations. They had set aside every *'-ite'* and become one in Christ, children of the same family and heirs of the same kingdom.

That is the culture of Zion. Unity without uniformity. Diversity of gifts without rivalry. Love makes all one, and because love fills every heart, there is no room left for division.

## Scriptural Anchors

Scripture bears witness of this society:

> *"And the Lord called his people Zion, because they were of one heart and one mind, and dwelt in righteousness; and there was no poor among them." (Moses 7:18)*
>
> *"And there was no contention in the land, because of the love of God which did dwell in the hearts of the people... surely there could not be a happier people among all the people who had been created by the hand of God."* (4 Nephi 1:15–16)
>
> *"Behold, the tabernacle of God is with men, and he will dwell with them, and they shall be his people, and God himself shall be with them, and be their God."* (Revelation 21:3)

Each witness points to the same truth: Zion is love made visible, a people bound together in oneness through the charity of Christ.

## Imagine Zion

Imagine a society where every step, every word, every relationship is filled with love. Where joy is not an exception but the air you breathe. Where families rise each day in peace, children learn in light, and every hand is consecrated to bless another.

Where no poor remain, no heart is broken, no one is forgotten. Where every name, race, and nation dissolve into one greater name—sons and daughters of Christ. Where the glory of the Lord is not distant but present, His love the bond that holding every soul together.

This is Zion. And as the record testifies: *"Surely there could not be a happier people"* (4 Nephi 1:15–16).

## The Call to Zion

Zion will come, and Zion will call. She is not just a prophecy written on a page or an abstract doctrine to be debated. Zion is alive in the mind of God, and her voice reaches into the hearts of those who belong to her.

The prophets and apostles saw her this way—*"the holy city, new Jerusalem, prepared as a bride adorned for her husband."* (Revelation 21:2)

Can you see the imagery?

Christ is the Bridegroom; Zion is His Bride.[21] But the symbolism reaches higher still. Just as the earth orbits the sun, receiving its light and life, so too Zion revolves around the Son,[22] receiving His radiance and reflecting it back as beauty and fruitfulness.

Yet this divine pattern is not only about the Son—it points to the greater union of heaven itself. As the Mother and Father of the Bridegroom invite all to come to the marriage supper, and as the Bride receives the Bridegroom, the imagery becomes complete: the eternal feminine and masculine joined in perfect oneness.

Zion and the New Jerusalem are echoes of that celestial harmony—Her compassion and His strength woven together to create the dwelling of God with His people.

Their call comes as a whisper, almost not a voice, but a feeling that says, *"Come to Zion."* It is the invitation to the wedding feast—the Father and the Mother, the Son and His Bride, together calling all who will to enter in.

Some will hear and prepare, trimming their lamps like the wise virgins;[23] others will turn away, unready when the feast begins. But the invitation is extended now, to every soul who will receive it.

## Personal Witness

I know this call is real because I have felt it. From the time I was a boy, there was a longing in me—a quiet pull toward something higher. I couldn't explain it then, but I knew there was a city, a people, a home waiting, and that I was being called to it. It was as if Zion herself was whispering my name.

Perhaps you have felt it too.

A stirring when you read of Enoch's city, or when you picture the Nephites living with no poor and no divisions.

A yearning when Christ says, *"Come unto me"* (Matthew 11:28).

That ache in the soul isn't imagination. It is the Bride and the Bridegroom together inviting you to their union—the call to Zion.

## Scriptural Echoes

This call to Zion isn't new. It has echoed through scripture in every generation.

Isaiah cried, *"Ho, every one that thirsteth, come ye to the waters, and he that hath no money; come ye, buy, and eat"* (Isaiah 55:1). His voice was the same voice—summoning all who hunger and thirst for righteousness to come and be filled.

Christ Himself extended the invitation: *"Come unto me, all ye that labour and are heavy laden, and I will give you rest"* (Matthew 11:28). His words weren't limited to His own time but stretch across the ages, gathering all who will to enter into His peace.

The Book of Mormon renews this promise for the last days. Jesus told the Nephites that the remnant of Jacob would build a holy city on this land, and that the Gentiles who repented and assisted them would be numbered among His people (3 Nephi 21:22–24).

Ether foresaw it plainly:

> *"And there shall be a new Jerusalem which shall be built upon this land, unto the remnant of the seed of Joseph."* (Ether 13:6)

Each prophet, each record, adds the same note to the same song: Zion is real, Zion will come, and Zion is calling.

## The Invitation Is Not Just Doctrine

Zion, then, isn't merely a teaching to be studied or a doctrine to be filed away. Zion is an invitation. Every scripture that points to her is more than prophecy—it is a summons. The call isn't "someday," it's *now.*

This is why Zion's voice resonates so deeply in the soul. It is not a concept; it is a living reality already reaching for us. The Bridegroom and the Bride together extend their hand, inviting us to enter into their joy. To answer is to be gathered, to be sanctified, to be remade into a people of love.

## Capstone

Zion matters because she is God's endgame. From the days of Adam, the Lord's mandate to every prophet has been the same: prepare a people sanctified for His presence.

Enoch succeeded, and his city was taken up. The Nephites after Christ's visit came close but fell short. Joseph Smith was given the same charge—to lay the foundation for a Zion society, built by consecration, governed by common consent, centered in Christ.[24]

Zion is people, not place. She is the pure in heart, a society sanctified, consecrated, translation-ready for the Lord. Where consecration removes poverty, common consent removes compulsion, and love removes all divisions—Zion flourishes.[25]

She is the manifestation of the Church of the Firstborn on earth.[26]

Zion is the New Jerusalem. She will stand as a refuge when the world trembles, the city of the Millennium, the dwelling of Christ with His Bride—a sanctified and translated people.[27]

And her culmination is sure: the embrace of Enoch's Zion descending from above with the New Jerusalem rising from beneath, joined at Adam-ondi-Ahman, the primordial mound where creation began and where creation will be renewed.[28]

Zion is love. The pure love of Christ filling every home, every heart, every street. No poor, no contention, no *"-ites."* Every gift honored, every need supplied, every soul one in Them.[29]

A society where heaven and earth are already united, because the people have become one with Christ and can endure His glory.

This is why Zion matters. She is not just prophecy, nor doctrine, nor dream. She is God's adored and beloved Bride, Joseph's mission, the scriptures' witness, and the Spirit's whisper in the soul.

Zion is not distant. She is calling now. They are calling now. Come.

## Chapter 13 Notes

1 Hymns of The Church of Jesus Christ of Latter-day Saints, no. 30 (Salt Lake City: Intellectual Reserve, 1985).

2 Compare Isaiah 60:1–2—*"Arise, shine; for thy light is come, and the glory of the Lord is risen upon thee. For, behold, the darkness shall cover the earth, and gross darkness the people..."* Also Revelation 18:2—*"Babylon the great is fallen, is fallen."*

3 Moses 6:1–7; Moses 6:57

4 Moses 7:18–19

5 JST Genesis 14:33–34; Alma 13:17–18

6 4 Nephi 1:15–18

7 Joseph Smith, Times and Seasons, 15 October 1844, p. 683; also in Teachings of the Prophet Joseph Smith, comp. Joseph Fielding Smith (Salt Lake City: Deseret Book, 1976), p. 178.

8 Revelation 21:2; Revelation 21:9–10

9 Hebrews 12:22–23; D&C 76:54; D&C 88:5; D&C 84:100

10 Concepts adapted from Mormon Rescue, *"Mormon Governments: Why Would Anyone Fight Against Zion?"* (2025), YouTube.com/@MormonRescue.

11 D&C 84:38; Romans 8:17

12 Ether 13:6–9; D&C 45:66–67

13 D&C 45:66–67; D&C 133:56; D&C 84:100; Moses 7:62–64

14 Malachi 3:2–3; 3 Nephi 20:22; Isaiah 4:3–4; D&C 64:24–25

15 3 Nephi 28:7–9; 3 Nephi 28:37–40; Their transfiguration mirrors Zion's condition—terrestrialized beings dwelling on earth in anticipation of the Lord's millennial reign.

16 Ether 13:8–10; D&C 45:66–67; Moses 7:62–64; The New Jerusalem serves as both the refuge before the tribulation and the dwelling of the Lord during the Millennium—its role spanning both ages.

17 D&C 88:17–20; D&C 88:25–26; D&C 77:6–7; Joseph taught that the Millennium represents the Terrestrial order—the earth renewed and paradisiacal, yet not fully glorified until after the thousand years (see D&C 63:20–21; Isaiah 65:17–25).

18 Bruce H. Porter and Stephen R. Ricks, By What Authority? The Evidence for Priesthood Authority in the Scriptures and the Restoration (Provo, UT: Foundation for Ancient Research and Mormon Studies, 1995), pp. 72–74—discussion of the temple as the cosmic mountain or primordial mound, the place of first creation and divine presence.
Also Margaret Barker, The Gate of Heaven: The History and Symbolism of the Temple in Jerusalem (London: SPCK, 1991), pp. 17–21—describing the temple as *"the first mountain, the place of creation."*
Compare Moses 7:53–56 and D&C 84:23–24, where Zion and the *"holy mount"* are identified with the presence of the Lord.

19 Isaiah 54:13; 2 Nephi 28:30 and Moroni 7:30 confirm that angels minister to the faithful.
Joseph Smith—Teachings of the Prophet Joseph Smith, 149 (Jesus and angels instructed Joseph personally, and he organized the Kirtland *"School of the Prophets"* for the same purpose).
D&C 88:118

20 John Pontius, Visions of Glory: One Man's Astonishing Account of the Last Days (Springville, UT: Cedar Fort, 2012), pp. 111–113—vision of the Millennial temple as a radiant core from which light flowed into the New Jerusalem; the source of that power was Christ's literal presence.
Also compare Moses 7:62–64 & Revelation 21:22–23

21 Matthew 9:15; Revelation 21:2; Revelation 21:9; D&C 65:3; These verses together establish Christ as the Bridegroom and Zion (the pure in heart, D&C 97:21) as His Bride—the sanctified people prepared to receive Him.

22 Malachi 4:2; John 8:12; D&C 88:7–13; The metaphor of Zion orbiting the Son mirrors this scriptural pattern—the world lives by His light, and Zion draws nearer until it abides fully in it.

23 Matthew 25:1–13; D&C 45:56-57; This allusion links Zion's spiritual readiness to the parable of the ten virgins—only those filled with the Spirit's oil endure to meet the Bridegroom when He comes.

24 Enoch succeeded, and his city was taken up:
Moses 7:69
The Nephites after Christ's visit came close, but fell short:
4 Nephi 1:2–3, 15–18
Consent, centered in Christ:
D&C 38:27; D&C 42:30–38; D&C 26:2; D&C 105:5

25 Zion is people, not place—the pure in heart:
D&C 97:21
Consecration removes poverty:
D&C 42:30–31; Moses 7:18
Common consent removes compulsion:
D&C 26:2
Love removes all divisions:
4 Nephi 1:15–17

26 D&C 76:54; D&C 76:94; Hebrews 12:23

27 Zion is the New Jerusalem:
Ether 13:4; D&C 45:66–67
Refuge when the world trembles:
D&C 45:66; Joel 3:16
City of the Millennium / dwelling of Christ with His Bride:
Revelation 21:2–3; Ether 13:10

28 Enoch's Zion returns from above:
Moses 7:62–63
New Jerusalem from beneath:
Ether 13:3–4
Joined at Adam-ondi-Ahman:
D&C 116:1; D&C 107:53–56
Renewal of creation:
Isaiah 65:17; Revelation 21:1

29 Zion is love / pure love of Christ:
Moroni 7:47
No poor:
Moses 7:18
No contention / no '-ites':
4 Nephi 1:2; 4 Nephi 1:17
Every gift honored / every need supplied:
D&C 46:11–12, 26; D&C 42:30–31
Every soul one in Them:
John 17:21

# CONCLUSION

# The Tree Remains

## The True Graft and the Promised Remnant

The way forward has never changed. The Lord commanded His people to begin with the first step, and that step remains the Sabbath and the Sacrament. Week by week, Zion's people consecrate their time and their souls—resting from labors, resting from sins, eating His bread, drinking His blood, and being filled with His Spirit.

These weren't rites invented by men, but appointments from the living Christ—the steady rhythm by which a people are made holy. From the beginning, they pointed to the eternal union of heaven and earth, of Father and Mother, of the Lamb and His Bride. To the very end, they remain the living rehearsal of Zion's rest and the great marriage supper prepared for all who will come.

### Joseph's Work Was Real

Joseph's life and calling weren't fabricated—they weren't some twisted illusion or myth. His enemies tried to erase him, and later generations tried to redefine him, but the witness of his own life cannot be undone.

Even the Doctrine and Covenants, compiled after his death, still bears this testimony:

> *"Joseph Smith, the Prophet and Seer of the Lord, has done more, save Jesus only, for the salvation of men in this world, than any other man that ever lived in it. In the short space of twenty years, he has brought forth the Book of Mormon, which he translated by the gift and power of God, and has been the*

*means of publishing it on two continents; has sent the fulness of the everlasting gospel, which it contained, to the four quarters of the earth; has brought forth the revelations and commandments which compose this book of Doctrine and Covenants, and many other wise documents and instructions for the benefit of the children of men; gathered many thousands of the Latter-day Saints, founded a great city, and left a fame and name that cannot be slain."* (D&C 135:3)

That verdict is true. Joseph's mission was cut short, but it was real. He restored the living pattern of Christ to the earth.

He gave the world the Book of Mormon, the surest witness that Jesus is the Christ and that all must come unto Him.[1]

He revealed The Pearl of Great Price and labored in the Joseph Smith Translation of the Bible, restoring Enoch's Zion, Moses' vision, Abraham's testimony, and many plain and precious truths that testified of Christ.[2]

He taught that being born again of fire and the Holy Ghost was the true entrance into the fold of God, where men and women become new creatures in Christ.[3]

He testified that the gifts of the Spirit—healing, prophecy, visions, discernment—were the birthright of every peaceable follower of Christ.[4]

He revealed ordinances as divine appointments, thresholds where the power of godliness is manifest and God Himself draws near.[5]

He declared the laws of Zion: consecration, equality, and common consent—a people governed not by compulsion, but by the loving voice of their God.[6]

And Joseph lived what he taught. He prayed and the heavens opened. He cast out evil spirits, healed the sick, and prophesied of things to come. He bore witness of Christ in revelation and in suffering—in Liberty Jail, in Nauvoo, and finally in Carthage.[7]

Kirtland was where Joseph came closest to his vision. The Spirit was poured out in power, angels ministered, and the Saints received gifts from on high.[8]

For a moment, Zion's light flickered into view. But the world pressed too hard, the Saints were unprepared, and Joseph couldn't gain the traction needed to sustain it.

Yet for a season, his graft grew and bore fruit, and it was sweet—witnessing the truth of the Root, which is Christ. To the very end, Joseph bore record of Him.

### The Root Still Lives, But the People Faltered in the Last Days

Christ is the Root of the tree. He is the source of life, the fountain from which every living branch draws its spiritual nourishment. No matter what happens to the branches, the Root abides, holy and sure.

In Joseph's day, the Lord grafted a true branch into that Root. It bore fruit for a season—heaven poured out its Spirit in gifts, visions, and fire. But that graft was cut down before it could fully mature and spread throughout the world.

The Lord foresaw this and commanded: *"Search these things diligently; for great are the words of Isaiah"* (3 Nephi 23:1). If we want to understand the latter days, we must let Isaiah speak. His words carry God's verdict.

Isaiah saw Ephraim—the birthright tribe of the last days—faltering. He cried: *"Woe to the crown of pride, to the drunkards of Ephraim"* (Isaiah 28:1). Avraham Gileadi explains:

> *"Ephraim's chief sins of pride and drunkenness catch up with Israel's birthright tribe in Jehovah's Day of Judgment. Instead of acknowledging current inconvenient truths, the people of Ephraim look back on past glories earned in more righteous times as if they still apply today. Ephraim's self-deception, stemming from intoxication with 'wine' at the highest levels, compounds the hard times that lie ahead."* (Apocalyptic Commentary on Isaiah 28:1)

He continued:

> *"Ephraim's former 'crowns of glory'—now mere 'fading wreaths' on the heads of a later generation—aren't enough to prevent desolation. Jehovah's Day of Judgment humbles Ephraim's 'opulent,' both political and ecclesiastical. Instead of obtaining revelation from Jehovah, they water down his word until it is ineffectual in empowering his people. The best their spiritual feasts offer is 'vomit'—partly digested food*

> *regurgitated for Jehovah's people to consume."* (Apocalyptic Commentary on Isaiah 28:3–8)

Elsewhere, Isaiah added his own piercing image: *"For all tables are full of vomit and filthiness, so that there is no place clean"* (Isaiah 28:8).

Elsewhere Isaiah described the watchmen of the latter days: *"His watchmen are blind: they are all ignorant, they are all dumb dogs, they cannot bark; sleeping, lying down, loving to slumber"* (Isaiah 56:10). Gileadi notes:

> *"As the job of Jehovah's watchmen is to report to his people what they see and hear, those who are blind and unaware see and hear little of consequence and fail to warn his people. Because they epitomize 'dumb watchdogs' and 'lolling seers,' Jehovah replaces them with a righteous watchman—his servant."* (Apocalyptic Commentary on Isaiah 56:10)

Instead of protecting the flock, these shepherds devoured it:

> *"Gluttonous dogs, and insatiable, such indeed are insensible shepherds. They are all diverted to their own way, every one after his own advantage. Come, they say, let us get wine, and have our fill of liquor."* (Isaiah 56:11–12)

Avraham's commentary again drives the point home:

> *"Instead of portraying these watchmen as ones who feed and protect the flock, the imagery of shepherds as dogs characterizes them as predators and unclean animals. Instead of warning of trouble as Jehovah's Day of Judgment approaches, they resemble wanton herdsmen who scatter the sheep and feed themselves off the fattest."* (Apocalyptic Commentary on Isaiah 56:11–12)

The Root still lives—holy and sure. But Isaiah's words testify that in the last days the people falter. The true branch was cut off, yet the Root remains holy, and the prophetic record already foresaw the blindness, pride, and corruption that would take its place.

Isaiah also foresaw something more: that Jehovah would preserve a remnant of righteous people and raise up a servant to replace the blind watchmen, to call the residue back, and to prepare the way for Zion.

The verdict is sure—but so is the promise.

## The Lord Always Preserves a Remnant

When judgment falls, it is never the end. The Lord's pattern holds consistent across every age: His justice removes corruption, but His mercy still sends forth a branch of life—like the olive leaf carried in the beak of Noah's dove, a witness that life would begin again.

Noah stood as that remnant when the flood consumed the world. Isaiah saw it in his day: *"The remnant shall return, even the remnant of Jacob, unto the mighty God"* (Isaiah 10:21).

After the Nephites filled the measure of wickedness, the Lord swept their cities with fire and storm. Yet a remnant remained to meet Him at Bountiful, purified and sanctified by His presence.

This same promise extends to the last days. Jesus Himself prophesied of it in the Book of Mormon:

> *"And they shall assist my people, the remnant of Jacob, and also as many of the house of Israel as shall come, that they may build a city, which shall be called the New Jerusalem. And then shall they assist my people that they may be gathered in, who are scattered upon all the face of the land, in unto the New Jerusalem."* (3 Nephi 21:23–24)

Here the Lord makes the pattern plain. It is not the proud who build Zion, but the humble. The remnant of Jacob—joined by Gentiles who repent—are appointed to raise up the holy city in the last days.

Joseph's day ended in loss, but Christ the Root endured. The Lord has not abandoned His vineyard. Jacob 5 records the anguish of the Master: *"It grieveth me that I should lose this tree"* (Jacob 5:7).

Again and again He spares His vineyard, digging and nourishing, always preserving, always working toward fruit. The same Root that received Joseph's graft still abides, waiting for the day when the preserved remnant will be grafted into it once more.

This is the hope threaded through all the judgments: even when nations collapse and branches are cut down, the Lord will preserve a people for Himself.

Through that remnant, Zion will rise[9]—not in a straight line, but in the helix of ascent, each turn of the spiral lifting the people higher, grace for grace, until they are prepared to meet the Lord face to face.

## The True Graft Cut Off—and the Present Call

As taught earlier, the Lord grafted a true branch into the Root through Joseph. Though his graft was struck down, the Root remained untouched—holy and living.

We cannot pretend the graft endured; honesty requires we acknowledge its loss. Yet we need not dwell in despair. The same Lord who grafted once will graft again. And in the meantime, His invitation to every soul remains unchanged.

Our charge is not to battle or tear down, but to return to what the Lord revealed through Joseph. To repent of straying from those teachings and to walk the path God gave His prophet:

> *To come unto Christ.*
> *To be born again by fire and the Holy Ghost.*
> *To be sanctified and made new creatures in Him.*

This was Joseph's message from the beginning, and it remains the Lord's message now. Nephi captured it plainly:

> *"We talk of Christ, we rejoice in Christ, we preach of Christ, we prophesy of Christ, and we write according to our prophecies, that our children may know to what source they may look for a remission of their sins" (2 Nephi 25:26).*

The Lord understands your struggle. He knows how hard it is to face the pull of the world and the taunting and treacherous fiery darts of the adversary. And so He provided the perfect antidote:

> *"Verily, thus saith the Lord: it shall come to pass that every soul who forsaketh his sins and cometh unto me, and calleth on my name, and obeyeth my voice, and keepeth my commandments, shall see my face and know that I am"* (D&C 93:1)

Here is the prescription:

1. **Forsake your sins**—confess them before God, release whatever binds you and separates you from Him.
2. **Come unto Christ**—draw near with real intent, stretching your wings of surrender and trust.
3. **Call on His name**—pray with all the energy of your heart, and use His name to cast out darkness.
4. **Obey His voice**—listen for His whisper and respond

without hesitation when He speaks.

5. **Keep His commandments**—walk in His appointments with joy, for these are the thresholds where He manifests Himself.

This is the antidote to the world's confusion. This is the same path God gave to Joseph. And it remains the way to see His face and know that He is.

As you follow these five steps of the antidote, remember also the Lord's faithful command to keep His holy day sacred and to partake of His Sacramental feast.

In them you consecrate your time and your soul week by week—resting from your labors, forsaking your sins, eating His bread, drinking His blood, and being filled with His Spirit.

These are your weekly appointments with Christ Himself, the steady rhythm by which He makes His people holy. And though He stands at the altar, She has prepared the table—both inviting, both waiting, both ready to receive all who will come. To the very end, they remain the living rehearsal of Zion's rest and the marriage supper of the Lamb to which you have been invited. *"Come,"* He says. *"But come prepared."*

I add my own testimony. Over six years ago the Lord blessed me with the friendship of Robin—a seeker who longed for nothing more than to find Him and be His servant—His bride.

Together we spoke of Zion, of truth, of putting off the natural man, and of standing in His presence. Robin sought not in theory but in practice, until at last, at the end of her life, she found what she was looking for.

I know she saw Him. Her life and death are a witness to me that the promises in scripture are true: *those who seek, find.*

My testimony is simply this: I know these things are true. Period.

The Lord has blessed my life with witnesses like Robin, whose lives make it unmistakable that He can be found, and that what has been taught in this book is true.

### Looking Ahead

Let us pause and remember what we have learned. The Lord grafted a true branch into the Root through Joseph. For a season it bore fruit, but it did not endure. The Root—Jesus Christ—remains, and the promise of His coming again to His vineyard, to labor and to nourish it, is not lost.

The next volume will turn to what followed Joseph's death—the growth that came after, and how it changed the tree. That story belongs to Book Two.

Book Three will turn again to the hope of restoration. The scriptures foretell it: the Lord will send His servant, and through him the remnant will be regrafted, and Zion will flourish. Isaiah saw it. The Savior Himself promised it in 3 Nephi 21. This hope yet lives.

So Book One does not end in despair, but in testimony and in hope—an expectation of a marvelous work and a wonder yet to come forth in the latter days. Joseph's work is not finished.

The vineyard still waits for that rising, each turn of the helix bringing us closer to the day when Zion shall flourish.

*The branch was cut,*
*but the Root still breathes.*
*The vineyard waits,*
*the promise grieves.*

*Yet light will stir,*
*a servant stand.*
*A remnant rise,*
*at His command*

## Conclusion Notes

1 Title Page, Book of Mormon—"*to the convincing of the Jew and Gentile that Jesus is the Christ, the Eternal God.*"

2 Pearl of Great Price / JST restoring Enoch, Moses, Abraham, and plain truths:
Moses 7:18 (Enoch's Zion).
Moses 1:27–28 (Moses' vision of the worlds).
Abraham 3:22–23 (Abraham's testimony of the premortal spirits).
1 Nephi 13:40 (plain and precious truths restored).

3 Born again of fire and the Holy Ghost, entrance into the fold:
Mosiah 27:25–26—"*born again... new creatures.*"
D&C 5:16—"*whosoever is baptized... shall be filled with the Holy Ghost.*"

4 Gifts of the Spirit for every peaceable follower:
Moroni 10:7–18—gifts of the Spirit listed.
D&C 46:9–12—gifts *"given for the benefit of those who love me... that all may be profited thereby."*

5 Ordinances as divine appointments where power is manifest:
D&C 84:20–22—*"in the ordinances thereof, the power of godliness is manifest."*

6 Laws of Zion—consecration, equality, common consent:
D&C 42:30–31—consecration to supply every need.
Moses 7:18—*"they were of one heart and one mind... and there was no poor among them."*
D&C 26:2—*"all things shall be done by common consent."*

7 Prayed and the heavens opened:
Joseph Smith—History 1:14–17—First Vision.
D&C 137:1—vision of the celestial kingdom in Kirtland Temple.
Cast out evil spirits:
History of the Church 1:82—Joseph casting out an evil spirit in 1830.
D&C 35:9—promise Joseph would *"cast out devils."*
Healed the sick:
History of the Church 4:3–4—Nauvoo healings when Joseph went among the sick and raised them.
D&C 42:48—*"he that hath faith in me to be healed, and is not appointed unto death, shall be healed."*
Prophesied of things to come:
D&C 130:14–17—prophecy on the coming of the Son of Man.
History of the Church 6:366–367—Joseph's prophecy of his own death: *"If my life is of no value to my friends, it is of none to myself."*
Witness of Christ in suffering (Liberty Jail):
D&C 121–122—Liberty Jail revelations.
In Nauvoo:
D&C 124:27–32—command to build Nauvoo Temple, with promise and warning.
Finally in Carthage:
D&C 135:1, 3—Joseph and Hyrum's martyrdom, sealing their testimony with their blood.

8 Spirit poured out in power:
History of the Church 2:427–428—accounts of the outpouring of the Spirit at the Kirtland Temple dedication.
D&C 109:36–37—dedicatory prayer asking that the Spirit be poured out on the people.
Angels ministered:
D&C 109:22—prayer for angels to guard and bear testimony.
D&C 110:1–16—Joseph and Oliver Cowdery see the Lord and angelic messengers (Moses, Elias, Elijah).
HC 2:427—Frederick G. Williams: *"an angel entered and sat in the stand."*
Saints endowed with gifts from on high:
D&C 95:8—temple commanded *"that they may be endowed with power from on high."*
HC 2:430–432—spiritual gifts reported after the Kirtland endowment.

9 Remnant shall rise / bring Zion:
3 Nephi 21:23—*"they [the remnant of Jacob] shall assist my people... that the New Jerusalem may be built."*
Micah 5:7–8—the remnant of Jacob will be among the nations "as a lion" and "as the dew from the Lord."
Mormon 5:24—*"they shall be scourged even unto destruction, except they repent and return unto me... and they shall become a pure and delightsome people."*
Zion will rise:
Isaiah 52:1–2—*"O Zion... put on thy beautiful garments... shake thyself from the dust; arise, and sit down."*
D&C 45:66–67—New Jerusalem as a city of refuge, Zion in her fullness.